T0345735

JAN KUKLÍK
RENÉ PETRÁŠ

MINORITIES AND LAW
IN CZECHOSLOVAKIA, 1918-1992

KAROLINUM PRESS
PRAGUE 2017

KAROLINUM PRESS
Karolinum Press is a publishing department of Charles University
www.karolinum.cz

© 2017 by Jan Kuklík and René Petráš
Designed by Jan Šerých
Set and printed in Czech Republic by Karolinum Press

Cataloging-in-Publication data is available from the National Library
of the Czech Republic

ISBN 978-80-246-3583-5
ISBN 978-80-246-3584-2 (pdf)

This book is written under the auspices of institutional support NAKI of the Czech
Ministry of Culture DF12P01OVV013, Problems regarding the legal status of minorities in
praxis and its development in long term perspective

The manuscript was reviewed by Harald Christian Scheu (Prague) and Lukáš Novotný
(Ústí nad Labem)

CONTENTS

FOREWORD

This book provides its readers with an overview of the development of legal status of minorities in Czechoslovakia. Apart from the outline of the law, it is naturally essential to examine basic historical problems in order to make the question understandable for a foreign reader. The greatest interest has been devoted to the interwar period, when the history of Czechoslovakia was distinctly determined by the existence of extraordinarily large minorities, especially German and Hungarian. Large space is also dedicated to the development of World War II and to both historical and legal aspects of the resettlement of the German minority.

Czechoslovakia, which existed between 1918 and 1992, had been through a surprisingly large scope of entirely different historical phases during its development. Czechoslovakia was established after the collapse of the Austria-Hungary. Its foundation was the traditional Czech Kingdom (ergo Bohemia, Moravia and part of Silesia) where aside from Czechs a very numerous German population lived. The second part of Czechoslovakia was Slovakia, which had practically no traditions as a specific entity. Among Slovaks, who are linguistically very close to Czechs, also numerous Hungarians, Germans or Gipsies lived in its territory. During the interwar period Czechoslovakia was the only Central-European state that had a democracy, but numerous minorities, which represented approximately one third of the state population, had often complicated its functioning. Relations with the native states of the Czechoslovak minorities, hence almost all neighbouring countries of the republic, were often tense. The growing tensions between the Czechoslovak state and its national minorities worsened at the beginning of the 1930s due to international crises in Central Europe. As part of its expansive policy, Nazi Germany, headed by Hitler, demanded fundamental changes in the position of the German minority. The need to solve the Czechoslovak minority issues, especially the problem of the Sudeten German minority, served as an excuse for Hitler's threats. The pressure of Nazi Germany enforced secession of areas populated by the minorities, at the Munich Conference in September 1938, which led to rapid disintegration and occupation of the Czech lands by Germany.

During the Nazi occupation the relations between Czechs and Germans worsened and Czechs were regarded second class citizens and persecuted.

The Nazi regime especially brought the existence of the Jewish minority in the Czech lands to a tragic end. After freezing and confiscating virtually all Jewish property, Germans started transporting Jews to the Ghetto in Terezín in 1941, and later to extermination camps.

After the war German and Hungarian minorities in Czechoslovakia were accused of collaboration with Nazi Germany and, as enemy citizens, especially in case of German minority expelled from the country. Their property, along with the property of the German Reich, Nazi organizations and Czech collaborators, was confiscated. However, in 1948 the Communist regime was established and it existed here until 1989 with the exception of temporary liberalization in 1968, suppressed by the soviet invasion. After the displacement of Germans, the minority question did not play such a big role anymore, moreover most of the native states of the Czechoslovak minorities were also incorporated into the Soviet bloc and Moscow was naturally not interested in any interstate minority conflicts. The Communist regime collapsed in November 1989, democracy was quickly re-established in Czechoslovakia, except the relations between Czechs and Slovaks were getting worse. This led to disintegration of Czechoslovakia and creation of the independent Czech and Slovak Republics on 1 January 1993. Unlike in some other East European regions, such as in former Yugoslavia, no striking revival of the minority conflicts took place after the re-establishment of democracy, not even in the case of the most numerous Hungarian minority.

The development of legal regulation of national minorities' status in Czechoslovakia is exceptionally complicated. Major differences in Austrian and Hungarian legal regulation of relations between nations had existed prior to 1918. The new Czechoslovak state set up quite complicated legislation on minority status within several years after its establishment, where the arrangement of the use of languages in contact with the authorities was especially intricate. An important part in the Czechoslovak legislation was played by the international protection of minorities under the supervision of the League of Nations. The legal regulation of relations between nations had gone through substantial changes during Nazi occupation and in the years immediately after the war and the questions of presidential (pejoratively Beneš's) decrees and displacement of Germans provoke discussions up to the present time. Even though quite numerous minorities lived in post-war Czechoslovakia as well (especially about half a million of Hungarians), almost no legal status of minorities existed. Although larger groups had, for instance, schools with education in their mother tongue, bilingual signs or opportunity to use their language with authorities. However these authorizations were not derived from legal regulation but only from secret inner instructions or even documents of the Communist Party. Only during the time of temporary liberalization in 1968, the Constitutional Act on the status of national minorities was enacted, along with the Constitutional Act on the federalization of the state. Overall, the minority question was usually on the edge of interest of both the state bodies and the society. This state indeed remained preserved in the Czech Republic, even after the restoration of democracy in November 1989. The minority rights were newly incorporated into the Charter of Fundamental Rights and Freedoms from 1991, while the implementing law was enacted only in the independent Czech Republic in 2001. The long and short of it is that the development of the legal status of national minorities in Czechoslovakia has been through series of major changes.

The development of the minority question in Czechoslovakia and its legal regulation is remarkable also from the wider European point of view. During the interwar period, Czechoslovakia belonged among the states which had dealt with the status of minorities the most actively and it also had influence on the creation, operation and termination of international protection of minorities. Complicated legal discussions on the topic of German displacement are still in motion. Czechoslovakia was geographically situated right in the centre of the most dangerous minority conflicts after 1918. It collided not only with the demands of the German minority like many other countries in the region but it also posed as the chief enemy to Hungary, which was traditionally the most revisionist state. Legal solution to the minority question in the Czechoslovak territory has aroused interest of foreign researchers.

The authors have studied this issue in depth and this book is a follow-up to an array of previous titles. The works of Prof. Kuklík focus on the Czechoslovak exile during World War II and the problems of presidential decrees as well as overviews of Czechoslovak legal history. Dr. Petráš picked up the threads of his books on the legal status of minorities during the interwar and Communist Czechoslovakia. Both authors work at the Law Faculty of Charles University, but apart from law, they naturally study historical circumstances as well, as it is often impossible to understand the legislation without the historical contexts.

The minority question in Czechoslovakia has been a sharply debated issue up to the present time, especially in connection with the displacement of Germans. The opinions of individual authors are often contrary to each other. Even researchers, or rather publicists, who are often only minimally devoted to this question, do not hesitate to present very categorical statements. It is a typical phenomenon to ignore professional literature of the intellectual opponents, as follows from the annotation. The authors tried to avoid this negative phenomenon and they hope this book will contribute to the objective understanding of this question abroad.

Jan Kuklík, René Petráš

1. THE END OF THE HABSBURG MONARCHY AND THE BEGINNINGS OF CZECHOSLOVAKIA

1.1 THE ISSUE OF NATIONALITIES AT THE END OF THE MONARCHY

Before we look at the situation of minorities at the time of the Czechoslovak Republic, in particular at the origins of legal regulations governing their status, we have to familiarize ourselves with the situation at the end of the Habsburg Monarchy, because there was rather remarkable, although not always remembered nowadays, long-term continuity. Not only will we look at legal rules expressly concerned with the legal status of minorities, i.e. language law in particular, but also at issues of public administration, which was closely connected with the issue of minorities.

A key element having an unremitting impact on the relationship between the Czechs and Germans was a marked predominance of Germans in Central Europe. On the other hand, the Czech nation was, in the 17th and especially in the 18th centuries, in a particularly weak position and had experienced a cultural decline. No sooner than at the end of the 18th and the beginning of the 19th centuries did it start to revive in a significantly different form; according to some historians it actually commenced to come into existence.[1] That was the reason the Czechs were only slowly catching up to the lead of the Germans and their priority position in the Czech lands, where they however had always been only a minority in terms of numbers; the Germans were, on the other hand, rather worried about losing their privileged position as of the beginning of the 19th century. Perhaps the most important element of the so-called National Revival was the Czech language[2] and its assertion in culture, education, and later also in public administration. This situation also manifested itself in the field of law.[3] However, the impact of the Czech national

---

1   See for example Otto Dann, Miroslav Hroch and Johannes Koll, eds., *Patriotismus und Nationsbildung am Ende des Heiligen Römischen Reiches* (Cologne: SH-Verlag, 2003); Otto Urban, "Czech society 1848–1918," in *Bohemia in History*, ed. by Mikuláš Teich (Cambridge: Cambridge University Press, 1998), p. 203ff.

2   See for example Miroslav Hroch, *Na prahu národní existence* (Prague: Mladá fronta, 1999), pp. 26–29, 66–72, 132–140; František Kutnar, *Obrozenské vlastenectví a nacionalismus* (Prague: Karolinum Press, 2003), pp. 167–169, 201–203.

3   Jan Kuklík, *Czech law in historical contexts* (Prague: Karolinum Press, 2015), esp. chap. 8, p. 62ff.

movement should not be overemphasised, particularly its first phases; even as late as the 1840s these efforts were alien to inter alia a great majority of bourgeoisie, who were opportunistically trying to accommodate the establishment even language-wise.[4]

After the consolidation of Austria-Hungary (a specific, and in many aspects peculiar consubstantial Monarchy) at the end of the 1860s, only rare changes occurred regarding the nationalities issue. Minorities in Hungary endeavoured to enforce the practical application of the non-observed Nationalities Law[5], in particular to have non-Hungarian languages recognised in administration. Generally and strictly speaking, it cannot be deemed as changes in minorities law (except for efforts by the revolutionary government in 1918), so this part of the Habsburg Monarchy may be virtually left out. In contrast, in Austria, i.e. so-called Cisleithan regions, at least efforts to make changes were a frequent occurrence. When the struggle over the character of the state was over, and after the accession to the Imperial Council in 1879, conflicts occurred particularly in connection with language and administration issues, which were to a considerable extent interrelated.[6] We can say that there were two principal conceptions for the regulation of the situation in the Czech lands: a separatist one, which advanced administrative demarcation corresponding to, if possible, the language boundaries, and a personal one, which strived to preserve the integrity of lands, namely of Bohemia, and to implement the bilingualism of authorities therein. While the effort to maintain the integrity was particularly supported by Czech parties, German parties rather furthered the division of Bohemia.

The Czech parties often relied on historical arguments, often times in a peculiar manner. Even lawyers made use on many occasions of historic documents, such as the Renewed Constitution of the Czech Province of 1627 (1628 adopted for Moravia), as if they were incontestable arguments. Such methods were however common in vast parts of Europe of the 19th century, namely in national disputes (e.g. Finland, Croatia) and/or in fighting against state centralisation (e.g. Spain), which must be taken into account by a critical contemporary historian. Also, it should not be overlooked that historic arguments could have been and were used against the Czech national movement as well, e.g. by defenders of the independence of Moravia.

---

4   Jana Machačová and Jiří Matějček, *Nástin sociálního vývoje českých zemí 1781–1914* (Opava: Slezské zemské muzeum, 2002), p. 384.
5   For discourse on the nature of hungarianisation see for example Karoly Kocsis and Eszter Kocsis-Hodosi, *Ethnic Geography of the Hungarian Minorities in the Carpathian Basin* (Budapest: Hungarian Academy of Sciences, 1998), pp. 54–57.
6   Karel Kazbunda, *Otázka česko-německá v předvečer velké války* (Prague: Karolinum Press, 1995), p. 48ff.; Karel Malý, "Sprache – Recht und Staat in der tschechischen Vergangenheit," in *Sprache – Recht – Geschichte*, ed. by Joern Eckert and Hans Hattenhauer (Heidelberg: C.F. Müller, 1991), p. 265ff.

The principal issue in these seemingly expert conceptual disputes was the frequent efforts of the German parties to weaken Czech positions and above all to maintain their own privileges from the past.[7] To illustrate, a so-called Pentecost Programme of German parties from 1889 demanded that Bohemia be divided into regions (as well as into districts and municipalities) according to language boundaries. While German regions were to be monolingual, Czech regions were to be bilingual. Moreover, regions should have taken over most of the administration of the lands, which should have been de facto eliminated; however, the Czech parties traditionally insisted on the unity of the historical lands, whose traditions were perceived as a pillar of national efforts (so-called state law). This attempt in 1890 was unsuccessful, though; the only thing that came about was a division of some provincial bodies.[8]

We are getting to issues of public administration and its reform, which combined national, administrative, financial and other reasons, where the most important conception was the one regarding the possibility of replacing too large traditional lands by smaller units – regions ("zhupas"). The idea of constituting regions was not anything entirely new as the regions had had a long tradition in Bohemia, which was however related to the feudal system of administration; regions were abolished in the Czech lands in the 1860s. Generally, the structure of the administration in Cisleithan regions was highly specific, particularly because of the so-called duality of self-government and state administration. The situation in public administration incited, already at the time of the Habsburg Monarchy, both criticism and reformative efforts which, however, had not been successful, mainly for political (particularly national) reasons. The administration in Cisleithania had been criticised for extensive politicization, which also prevented economic development, as well as for utterly inconvenient distribution of responsibilities between the state and self-governing entities. There literally was rivalry between state administration and self-government where the borders of jurisdiction were unclear and the mutual communication cumbersome, which led to wastage of financial resources and to hindrances to activity. The self-government was rather expensive and party line, especially in political and national matters. This situation had many times led to chaos and almost anti-state behaviour of Czech self-governing units in particular;[9] for example, mayors

---

7 Johann Wolfgang Brügel, *Tschechen und Deutsche 1918–1938* (Munich: Nymphenburger Verlagshandlung, 1967), pp. 16–17. He openly speaks about the German fear of democracy, i.e. worries about the loss of their own privileges.

8 Emil Sobota, *Národnostní autonomie v Československu* (Prague: Orbis, 1938), p. 23; Jiří Kořalka, *Češi v habsburské říši a v Evropě 1815–1914* (Prague: Argo, 1996), p. 163ff.

9 There emerged a kind of state within a state, see for example Milan Hlavačka, "Samospráva Království Českého jako předstupeň státní samostatnosti?" in *Vývoj české ústavnosti v letech 1618–1918*, ed. by Karel Malý and Ladislav Soukup (Prague: Karolinum Press, 2006), pp. 600–621.

of municipalities boycotted due co-operation with state bodies, including the military ones, if they did not respect the right to the Czech language.[10] German self-government then considered legal regulations which were disagreeable for them invalid, such as language regulations containing rights to the Czech language.

In efforts for reform, the following issues were considered: joining state administration and self-government, restoring regions, and instituting the system of administrative courts.[11] A critical opinion of possibly the highest quality was contained in the Studies on the reform of administration, the elaboration of which had been set in 1904 by the then Minister of the Interior, Ernest von Koerber, who himself was a well-known expert on Austrian administration. A reform of public administration during the First Czechoslovak Republic, important especially in terms of minorities, also partially followed from his opinions. It was often proposed in reform projects that larger administrative units, i.e. regions ("zhupas"), be established (renewed) as an intermediary between lands and districts. There were some who wanted to make use of the regions to settle conflicts between nationalities in Bohemia. The Czechs were however justifiably worried that any reform would only weaken, or possibly eliminate completely, the land of Bohemia, i.e. the traditional pillar of national requirements (so-called historical state law). Unlike the Czechs, the Germans strived for a so-called closed territory, which they later almost successfully achieved during World War I.[12]

At the time of the Habsburg Monarchy there naturally occurred other efforts, besides the plans for the reform of administration, to settle the issue of nationalities, particularly though the regulation of language law.[13] This publication, however, should not be the elaboration of individual attempted changes, but rather an indication of the society-wide context of legal status of minorities – in conditions of the Habsburg Monarchy, it is better to refer to them as minority nations, especially because of the fact that the complicated situation and mutual animosity remained in existence to a considerable extent also at the time of the First Czechoslovak Republic. The key relationship was the one between the Czechs and Germans (while in the case of the Habsburg Monarchy this relationship was important to a certain extent, it was crucial in the case of the subsequent Czechoslovak Republic). In relationships between the two nations, particularly in Bohemia (the situation was rather different in Moravia) "the mutual separation escalated

---

10   For situation from 1899 see Allgemeines Verwaltungsarchiv Wien, collection Ministerium des Innern, Präsidiale 3–1848–1918, box 73, P.No. 985/M.J. 1899 Priora 3007–99/M.J.

11   See for example Karel Laštovka, *Zákon župní* (Bratislava: Právnická Jednota, 1925), p. 11.

12   Jiří Kovtun, *Slovo má poslanec Masaryk* (Prague: Československý spisovatel, 1991), pp. 244–247.

13   Ibid., pp. 230–250; Harry Klepetař, *Der Sprachenkampf in den Sudetenländern* (Prague: Ed. Strache, 1930), pp. 35–126.

into estrangement, which also led to a notorious nationalities fight which commenced in the 1880s and gradually became one of the typical features of life in the Habsburg Monarchy."[14]

There was an incessant fight for any real or seemingly national position (jobs in civil service, street nameplates, attendance of children at schools with their mother tongue, etc.). Having disputes over any detail, or literally a trifle, it is not surprising that negotiations on the legal regulation of the status of nationalities incited fanatical flares of national tempers. Hatred gradually increased; a strong response had already been provoked by the so-called Stremayr's language regulations in 1880, and in the ensuing year a fight between Czech and German students in Chuchle claimed the first life – the first one in the new history of Czech-German relations; however, not the last one by a long sight.[15]

The Germans were little by little losing their political predominance based chiefly on non-democratic franchise which discriminated in favour of well-off, i.e. primarily German, voters. The steady democratisation of elections thus greatly undermined the positions of the Germans; it also brought about changes in politics, i.e. asserting new political movements, many times influenced by nationalism. The unhurried reinforcement of the Czechs in politics and the economy irritated the Germans a lot, particularly ones from Czech lands, who often considered them as nearly a barbarian nation, and who employed a "racial" issue in their argumentation, where Slavs and Germans were referred to as different races. Compared to the Czechs, the Germans were also losing in demographic development towards the end of the Habsburg Monarchy, and their share in the population of the Czech lands began to decrease.[16]

More and more frequent national unrest contributed to a certain coarsening of public life. It was mainly in Bohemia where the separation of nations occurred, and was connected with the chauvinistically eulogized ignorance of the other language, reduction in private and cultural contacts, boycotts of enterprises and shops, and even split-ups of churches and pubs.[17] The notion of a distinct separation of national communities in the Czech lands is, however, somewhat questioned by some historians. They argue that in spite of the application of the to-each-his-own motto, the utter separation was possible neither in the economy nor in public life, science, or art.

---

14   Jan Křen, *Konfliktní společenství* (Prague: Academia, 1990), p. 226.
15   Ibid., p. 226; Gary B. Cohen, *The Politics of Ethnic Survival: Germans in Prague, 1861–1914*, 2nd ed. (West Lafayette, IN: Purdue University Press, 2006), pp. 107–108.
16   See data in Allgemeines Verwaltungsarchiv Wien, collection Ministerrats-Präsidium, box 354, file Statistische Daten über die sprachliche Zusammensetzung der Zivilbevölkerung des Königreiches Böhmen.
17   Křen, Konfliktní společenství, pp. 258–260; Kovtun, *Slovo má poslanec Masaryk*, p. 124.

In the late 1890s, efforts by the Cisleithanian government to spread the use of the Czech language in authorities were swept aside by the unrest of German nationalists; negotiations on the settlement of the issue continued, however. Czech-German controversies were further escalating, and the situation "sidelined and corrupted all other spheres of state life, and it also absorbed a considerable portion of the energy of the society. This was also reflected in the field of nationalities, where problems were so over-politi-cised (at least in the branches of education and administration) that they could not be resolved rationally."[18] This apt formulation by a well- known historian accurately depicts the problem of the Habsburg Monarchy that was to a considerable extent taken over by the Czechoslovak Republic. Many critics of the First Czechoslovak Republic ignore this crisis situation at the time of the Habsburg Monarchy; after all, there was unrest which claimed lives even there. At the time of the Monarchy, more competent politicians were trying to resolve said problem; some of them did not believe in a parlia-mentary resolution and were contemplating a sort of a small coup, in which the emperor would impose a language law for the whole of Cisleithania, as well as numerous other measures. However, these efforts were unsuccessful and the nationalities issue remained a permanent problem till the end of the Habsburg Monarchy.

An agreement that could have been important for reconcilement between the Czechs and Germans was the so-called Moravian Pact of 1905. That pecu-liar national appeasement was concluded between the Czechs and Germans in Moravia, where the mutual relationships between the two nations were substantially better than in Bohemia; however, it happened only after long negotiations, whereas the common permanent committee was established by the Moravian Provincial Diet already in 1898. When preparing the Mora-vian Pact and subsequent secret agreements, e.g. from 1914, a key part was played by ad hoc created boards which in many cases did not have support in provincial legislation. The key role was assumed by bodies composed of chairpersons of major parties.[19] Actually, the legal and state systems were not able to cope with nationalities issues in a regular, orderly way, which is an exceptionally important aspect.

The basic feature of the Moravian Pact was the division of the provincial Diet into the fractions called "*curiae*" – two national (Czech and German) and one of farmers owning large areas of land; the allocation of mandates

18   Brügel, *Tschechen und Deutsche 1918–1938*, p. 12.

19   Jiří Malíř, "Národnostní klíč z roku 1914 v zemských hospodářských a finančních záležitos-tech – cesta k 'druhému moravskému paktu'?," in *Milý Bore–: profesoru Ctiboru Nečasovi k jeho sedmdesátým narozeninám věnují přátelé, kolegové a žáci*, ed. by Tomáš Dvořák, Radomír Vlček and Libor Vykoupil (Brno: Historický ústav AV ČR; Historický ústav FF MU; Matice moravská, 2003), pp. 139–143.

according to nationality was permanent, which removed a nationalist element from elections. Owing to the Pact the Czechs gained a leading position; however, the Germans had, strictly speaking, the power of veto. A remarkable characteristic of this system was the election based on a so-called nationalities register – a personal element asserted itself to a considerable extent. What was problematic however was sustaining the anachronistic curial system at the time when a universal suffrage was being advanced in the Habsburg Monarchy, and far-reaching strikes and demonstrations for universal suffrage even were one of the main immediate impulses to conclude the Moravian Pact. Apart from this undemocratic character, it is possible to find other questionable aspects (e.g. it did not apply to state administration), therefore, contemporary perspectives on the possibilities of such a settlement of the Czech-German conflict are sometimes sceptical.[20] A sort of a parallel at a local level in Bohemia was the so-called Budweiser Pact, which was debated shortly before the war, and other municipalities were considered (Olomouc).[21]

A peculiar part of the Moravian Pact was the so-called Lex Perek (Perek's Education Act), which may be virtually beyond the comprehension of a person unfamiliar with the minorities issue, but which represented a reaction to problems occurring in many other fields with language controversies. Education in the mother tongue is absolutely crucial for one's identification with a nation, which was well understood by nationalist movements. Therefore, there were frequent efforts to attract to their schools not only all children of their own nations but also children from ambivalent families, and even members of other nations. In circumstances that existed in the Habsburg Monarchy, where German education was of better quality and better ensured (not only) in Moravia, it was the Czechs who suffered from this tug-of-war for children. They thus tried to accomplish the adoption of a legal regulation that would force Czech children to attend Czech schools exclusively.

Despite a long-standing opposition by German deputies,[22] Perek's Act was adopted in 1905 (No. 4/1906 of the Moravian Provincial Code) as a part of the Moravian Pact, and stipulated inter alia that schools providing compulsory education may only admit children who have a command of the language in which the education is provided. There were many disputes over the interpretation of the act, which even allowed for exceptions, whereas the Czechs required that the law be strictly applied. In fact, the law rather brought about

20 Zdeněk Peška, *Kulturní samospráva národních menšin* (Prague: Orbis, 1933), p. 15–17; Křen, *Konfliktní společenství*, pp. 323–325; Kořalka, *Češi v habsburské říši a v Evropě 1815–1914*, pp. 171–173.

21 Kazbunda, *Otázka česko-německá v předvečer velké války*, pp. 336–339, 369–370; Jeremy King, *Budweisers into Czechs and Germans* (Princeton: Princeton University Press, 2002), p. 115ff.

22 Toshiaki Kyogoku, "Národní agitace a obecní školství na Moravě na přelomu 19. a 20. století: Boj o české dítě," in *Místo národních jazyků ve výchově, školství a vědě v habsburské monarchii 1867–1918* (Prague: Výzkumné centrum pro dějiny vědy, 2003), pp. 571–576.

a deepening of nationalist agitation when admitting children to compulsory schooling, as well as numerous complaints about and legal disputes over the language competence of pupils. Moravian Germans feared a decrease in the number of pupils in their own schools and thus challenged the Act on the grounds of it representing unacceptable interference in the responsibilities of parents and schools.[23]

In addition to the Moravian Pact, many other proposals and negotiations occurred towards the end of the Habsburg Monarchy that should have resolved national dissensions, but they usually did not give any real results.[24] It is not possible to deal with the details of those almost permanent appeasement efforts; it is however necessary to point out at least some typical features, particularly for the important reason that personalities jointly forming the status of minorities at the time of the First Czechoslovak Republic, such as T.G. Masaryk or Karel Kramář, participated in talks at the time of the Habsburg Monarchy and were influenced thereby on a long-term basis.

An important attempt to resolve the Czech-German conflict was made, for example, in 1908, and it was the Czech Provincial Diet in Prague that should have occupied the key role; after all, the competence of the Imperial Council (i.e. Austrian Parliament) in language issues was refused by the Czechs as a matter of principle. The Prime Minister at that time, Max W. von Beck, tried hard to manoeuvre because of the German opposition, however he was not successful and the national tensions only increased. The Germans used a hard filibuster in the Diet, and anti-Czech incidents proliferated in the borderlands; for example, attacks on Czech shops and schools occurred, or Czech filings with courts and agencies were rejected, which illustrates that even state machinery was affected by nationalism. A thing which was particularly bad was that the government did not have enough power to prevent provocations, such as aggravating processions. The weakness of the state and the unwillingness to confront nationalism often resembles the situation at the beginning of the First Czechoslovak Republic. A hard filibuster in the Czech Provincial Diet in 1908, which was a total disparagement of parliamentarianism, would have many parallels in the First Czechoslovak Republic as well. This crisis, like many other conflicts between nationalities, finally lead to the fall of the government.

All in all, both Czechs and Germans in the Czech lands constantly tried to stick to their policies, which deadlocked necessary reforms. The Czech-German relationship was not settled despite plentiful negotiations, which significantly complicated life in the Habsburg Monarchy. In Czech-German disputes

---

23   Malíř, "Národnostní klíč z roku 1914," pp. 139–140.
24   For drafts and research papers see Allgemeines Verwaltungsarchiv Wien, collection Ministerrats-Präsidium, box 354.

in Bohemia, the Germans fell back on a long-term stonewalling of the Czech Provincial Diet, which prevented the budget from being approved. "When the ordinary legislative mechanism collapsed after 1908, the Ministerial Council more and more frequently resorted to rule through imperial edicts, and officers by profession were gaining greater influence on the administration in Cisleithania than before."[25] That finally led to cash-flow insolvency of the Czech Commission; then imperial patents (St. Anne's patents) of 26 July 1913 intervened – the Czech Provincial Diet and Czech Commission were dissolved and replaced by a designated Administrative Commission. It should have been a temporary measure that would eliminate a German filibuster disrupting the funding of the land. The regulation from above should have also resolved national issues, and negotiations between Czech and German politicians continued as well. Many Czechs considered St. Anne's Patents to be unlawful and required that constitutionality by renewed.[26] A potentially anti-constitutional, and after 28 October 1918 revolutionary, situation, however, endured in Bohemia under changed circumstances till the end of the operation of the Revolutionary National Assembly in 1920.

Negotiations on the settlement of the Czech-German issue were frequent occurrences, also at the time immediately before World War I. One of the important cases was a secret agreement concluded by chief representatives of Czech and German political parties during the February session of the Moravian Provincial Diet in 1914. The agreement dealt with three main issues: firstly, the allocation of subventions to schools; then, changes in education policy of provincial bodies; and finally, the application of national principle in certain institutions and organisations. Many of these measures actually deepened the separation of the Czechs and Germans in Moravia. It is peculiar that this compromise was agreed upon in Moravia, where the relationships between the nations were less tense, and typical are also some distinctive aspects of this agreement. The agreement was secret, which might be surprising; however, in the context of the time, it was, strictly speaking, a pragmatic approach because many compromises had not succeeded due to loud nationalists on both sides.[27]

Problematic was also one of the reasons for the willingness of Czech politicians to make concessions in relation to the Moravian Germans, namely a fear of a German filibuster which would have led to the collapse of provincial self-government and to the intervention in government like in the case of St. Anne's Patents in Bohemia. Although this compromise agreement was

---

25   See G. B. Cohen, *Politics of Ethnic Survival*, pp. 184–186.
26   Kazbunda, *Otázka česko-německá v předvečer velké války*, pp. 183–243, 387–388; Kořalka, *Češi v habsburské říši a v Evropě 1815–1914*, pp. 179–180.
27   Malíř, "Národnostní klíč z roku 1914," pp. 137–145.

most probably beneficial for the conciliation of tense Czech-German relationships, it is impossible not to see its numerous problematic aspects, like
in the case of the Moravian Pact of 1905. However, contrary to the Moravian
Pact, new laws should not have been adopted; the agreement only contained
the undertaking by signatories thereto to abide by certain rules. The nature
of issues agreed upon did not indeed require embodying in legal regulations;
on the other hand, concluding similar specific agreements represented another unusual element in the regulation of national relations, which itself
was a fairly complicated issue, and often times also unclear distribution of
competences among Austrian parliament, provincial assemblies, and executive bodies. Unfortunately, a minimum legal regulation of the nationalities
issue in Cisleithania, whose basis was a single provision contained in Article 19 of the Fundamental Act of the State No.142/1867 Austrian R.G.B.I., in
which however many elemental issues were not dealt with in detail, led to
such peculiar instruments and in fact to chaos. The true reality in the case
of nationality rights of the Czechs was not bad; however, no system of legal
regulation actually existed, and arbitrariness was frequent and often times
directed not only against the Czechs but also against the Germans or the use
of the German language.

At the time of the Habsburg Monarchy many noteworthy theories of the
resolution of the national issue emerged, and it is possible to say that the local
situation was inspiring for the whole of Europe. Probably the best elaborated
programme of the reform of the nationalities law in Austria was prepared
by Social Democracy. The congress of the (all-Austrian) party in Brno in 1899
put forward a demand for the transformation of Cisleithania into a sort of
a federation of nationally delimited units. Besides this territorial autonomy
there were also ideas for personal autonomy, supported as well by foremen
of Social Democracy, Karl Renner and Otto Bauer.[28] An idea of establishing
national cadastres, i.e. the evidence of persons according to their nationality,
which was produced among others by a Viennese professor Edmund Bernatzik in 1910[29], was also important.

If we look at the Czech-German issue prior to World War I, then the key
element is the successful development of the Czech nation. Around the end of
the 19th century the Czech society reached the level of a modern European nation. What was somewhat in contradiction with the successful economic and
cultural development was the weak position of the Czechs in the Habsburg

---

28 Tove H. Malloy and Francesco Palermo, eds., *Minority Accommodation through Territorial and
Non-Territorial Autonomy* (Oxford: Oxford University Press, 2015), pp. 125–127; see also Brügel,
Tschechen und Deutsche 1918–1938, pp. 13–14.

29 Edmund Bernatzik, *Über nationale Matriken: Inaugurationsrede gehalten von Edmund Bernatzik*
(Vienna: Manz, 1910); see also Sobota, *Národnostní autonomie v Československu?*, pp. 23–25; Peška,
Kulturní samospráva národních menšin, p. 26.

Monarchy. However, despite dissatisfaction with the approach of the Monarchy to, for example, their own legal status, the political establishment of the nation (save for a few exceptions) considered the life of the Czechs in that ancient union of states to be an unalterable, and in essence also favourable, fact. A major part of the political establishment thus pushed for so-called positive politics with the aim of improving the Czech position within the Habsburg Monarchy. These efforts were however met with resistance of, inter alia, a considerable part of the German population, who feared losing their traditional position in both the Czech lands and the Habsburg Monarchy. Thus, prior to World War I, some new streams emerged in the Czech environment[30]; they represented a reaction to the exhaustion of traditional Czech policy. The resistance of the Germans, particularly in the Czech lands, brought about not only the roadblock to further – for Czechs – positive changes, but also a risk or significant disruption of the functioning of established institutions, which was in particular symbolized by St. Anne's Patents. The key relationship between the Czechs and Germans, important to the Czech lands, and to a certain extent also to the Habsburg Monarchy as a whole, remained unresolved.

During World War I, the Czech-German relationships further deteriorated. The Habsburg Monarchy began to regard the Czech national movement as utterly subversive. Spying on, denunciating, interning, imprisoning and even sporadically sentencing Czech national representatives or members of the Sokol movement to death was spreading. Knowing about contemporary totalitarian regimes, the "terror" of that time (more so because it was at the time of a real war) does not seem in any way drastic; however, the situation must have been deeply shocking for people growing up in the liberal 19th century. Czech national positions were being limited when associations and societies were being dissolved, and Czech officials and judges were replaced by Germans, the status of the German language being reinforced.

German nationalists were trying to make use of their supremacy then. Based on the so-called Easter Programme of 1916, which would break up the historical entity of the Czech lands, cutting it along the lines of prevailing language and nation affiliation,[31] they attempted to push through, besides German as the state language, regional system in Bohemia which would virtually eliminate the historical land, i.e. a traditional pillar of Czech politics. In German regions German should have been the sole language (- also the external official language), in Czech regions, the existing situation should have been preserved, i.e. external language bilingualism and internal German. In

---

30 See for example Robert Kvaček, *První světová válka a česká otázka* (Prague: Triton, 2003), pp. 61–62.
31 Zdeněk Beneš and Václav Kural, eds. *Facing History: The Evolution of Czech-German Relations in the Czech Provinces, 1848–1948* (Prague: Gallery, 2002), p. 37.

June 1917 the German National Council for Bohemina issued a resolution on self-determination for Bohemian Germans "in the framework of the united Austrian state and with the enshrinement of German as a state language" and on the speedy establishment of German Bohemia as a province with its own Diet, land committee and other regional authorities.[32] Within the intention of the programme, the Ministry of the Interior issued a regulation in 1918, on the constitution of twelve regional governments in Bohemia according to nationality structure – four regions should have been German, seven "Czech," and Prague should have been subordinate to vice-regency. The regions should have been directly responsible to the government, and the vice-regency should have been in charge of second-rate administration. That would prevent potential federalisation of Cisleithania for good, on the basis of historical lands that had always been disapproved by the Germans. Naturally, this regulation was cancelled by the Czechoslovak Republic when it had been constituted (by regulation of the Minister of the Interior No. 84/1918 Sb.). This anti-Czech attempt by the Austrian government towards the end of the war, when also other administrative measures aimed at the de facto division of Bohemia were taken, was a clear manifestation of the then political situation, in which, at the time of great military successes of Germany, a conciliatory settlement with Czechs was not contemplated.[33] It is necessary to note that this measure, except for its radicalness, did not deviate from traditions in the field where a political situation usually had priority over the need for due administration. Considerations about a radical reform of administration at the beginning of the First Czechoslovak Republic, at a really inconvenient time of a strong economic, and to a considerable degree also political crisis, draw inspiration from the era of the Habsburg Monarchy.

The international situation, i.e. developments on war battlefronts, soon changed to the Habsburg Monarchy's disadvantage, and, as it later similarly happened at the time of the First Czechoslovak Republic, the change of the international situation quickly manifested itself at the domestic level. The emperor tried to change the nationalities order of Cisleithania at the last moment, and promised in the manifesto of 16 October 1918 that national states would be constituted; however, it was too late to preserve the Habsburg Monarchy, i.e. the union of states that had existed for almost four centuries.

---

32   Václav Houžvička, *Czechs and Germans 1848–2004: The Sudeten Question and the Transformation of Central Europe* (Prague: Karolinum Press, 2015), pp. 98–99.

33   Kuklík, *Czech law in historical contexts*, pp. 85–86.

1.2 LEGAL RESOLUTION OF NATIONALITIES ISSUE AT THE END OF THE HABSBURG MONARCHY

There were substantial differences between the legal status of minorities (or rather non-ruling nations) in Cisleithania and in Hungary, which had been caused by a long, distinct legal development. In the Czech lands, it is possible to find the beginnings of nationalities law as early as 16th century during the period of Estates. In fact, it was exclusively language law which started to prefer the Czech language, as the importance of Latin gradually weakened. In the era after the Battle of White Mountain, the parity of the Czech and German languages was asserted, and it was not until the time of the enlightened absolutism when the Czech language was sidelined by centralising measures. It is apparent that it was the issue of the language that played a key, if not exclusive, part, and this situation also persisted to a certain extent later, even at the time of the First Czechoslovak Republic. In the Hungarian state, Latin remained the official language much longer than in the Czech lands; owing to varied nationalities, the Hungarian language had not gained the privileged status until the 18th century, and local languages were used in individual parts of the state. No sooner than at the end of the 18th century and in the first half of the 19th century were legal regulations asserting the Hungarian language adopted.[34]

The most important legal regulations governing the status of minorities in the period of the 50 years preceding the constitution of the Czechoslovak Republic were adopted almost immediately after the establishment of Austria-Hungary in 1867. The basis for the status of minorities was completely different in the two parts of Austria-Hungary. While in Cisleithania the legal regulation of the minorities' status was minimal, and thus opened to various solutions, the national order in Hungary was codified rather minutely in the Act on Nationalities (No. 44/1868), which was not applied in practice, though. It however laid a legal basis for efforts of minorities in Hungary to improve their status when they strove to enforce its application.

It was a brief provision contained in Article 19 of the "Fundamental Law of the State" No. 142/1867 Austrian R.G.Bl., [35] on universal civil rights, a part of the so-called December Constitution, which was the basis of nationalities law (we can hardly say law of minorities, taking the numerical ratio into account) in Cisleithania: *Section 1 read:* "All nations in the state have equal rights and each nation has an inviolable right to keep and cultivate its own nation and language." *Section 2 said:* "An equal right of all languages common in the state to be used in schools, authorities and public life is recognised by the state."

---

34   Emil Sobota, *Národnostní právo československé* (Brno: Barvič a Novotný, 1927), pp. 6–7, 13–14.
35   Edmund Bernatzik, *Die österreichischen Verfassungsgesetze mit Erläuterungen* (Vienna: Manz, 1911), document no. 134, p. 390ff.

Section 3 provided: "In lands where multiple nations reside, schools shall be established in such a way so that each nation has proper means to be instructed in its own language without being forced to acquire another provincial language." In theory, Article 19 may be understood as the reinforcement of the complete equality of nations in the Habsburg Monarchy; however, the actual situation was different.

Implications of this provision had been causing serious disputes up to the end of the Habsburg Monarchy. The main issue was whether said legal rule was a directly applicable provision or just a declaratory one that needed to be implemented by a special act before being applied in practice. Another important issue was a dispute over Section 1 of Article 19, regarding whether it was intended as protection of nations as groups or just as protection of individuals' rights to a nationality. The Court of the Empire (Reichsgericht), which otherwise recognised the direct applicability of said article, did not grant to anyone the right to act in the name of a particular nation. Article 19 was thus interpreted as a guarantee of language and schooling rights of individuals. There were considerable lengthy disputes over the practical application of the provision. As for the Czech lands, there was a cardinal discrepancy between the efforts of the Czechs and Germans, which also extended into the issues of attempted administration reforms.[36]

Nationalities law in Cisleithan regions continued to develop even after 1867, however, mainly in the area of language law only.[37] Considering the rather complicated structure of the state and of the administration of Austria, it was a very difficult problem that was made even more complicated in practice by a miscellany of rules of different legal force, as well as of virtual custom. To illustrate, the official language of the Imperial Council was not regulated in rules of procedure, but a significant predominance of the German language had developed; in certain issues other main languages were equal (e.g. the language of the oath of allegiance). The situation in provincial assemblies was, however, different; at least in some lands the official language was expressly regulated – in Bohemia (in 1899) and Moravia (in 1905) the language equality was adopted. The language of public administration and courts was not legally regulated, save for some exceptions (such as the language of bank notes). It was not even determined whether the issue should be regulated by a law or a decree; neither was it clear whether it would be an imperial act or

---

36   Sobota, *Národnostní autonomie v Československu?*, pp. 17–18; Klepetař, *Der Sprachenkampf in den Sudetenländern*, pp. 35–126.

37   In more details Peter Burian, "The State Language Problem in Old Austria (1848–1918)," *Austrian History Yearbook* 6–7 (1970–1971): pp. 81–103, especially p. 96ff.; see also Zbyněk A.B. Zeman, *The Making and Breaking of Communist Europe* (Oxford: Blackwell, 1991), pp. 32–36; Robert A. Kann, *A History of the Habsburg Empire 1526–1918* (Berkeley: University of California Press, 1974), appendix 1, pp. 603–608.

a provincial one. That was why peculiar disputes often arose when the governments issued decrees but the courts refused to recognise them. Most conflicts were brought about by the issue of so-called external and internal official language – thus the point was chiefly the language law. There were special legal regulations for certain particular fields of public administration, e.g. the army, postal services, customs duty, and railways, issued in the form of orders or just guidelines; however, even there, there often was chaos and arbitrariness when applying them. Besides the regulation of the language in the case of public bodies, which apparently was rather chaotic in essence, there also was a rather important self-government, which differed in various provinces.[38]

Instruction, that is to say the issue of the language in schools, was regulated in Section 3 of Article 19 of the Fundamental Act of the State No. 142/1867 Austrian R.G.Bl.[39], further by Imperial Act No. 62/1869 Austrian R.G.Bl., which however concerned schools providing compulsory schooling (elementary and town schools) and teachers' institutes. There was no legal regulation regarding high schools (Gymnasium) and universities – the issue came under imperial legislation. It is clear that even the distribution of legislative competences in the field of education was not simple. A particular legal regulation left the establishment of schools and the status of nations therein to the discretion of relevant authorities.[40] The question of education had always been of crucial importance in national disputes with respect to both mastering the standard language and increasing collective self-awareness towards other nations, which, in the case of many persons, first manifested itself at school. The key role of education had been well understood as early as the 19th century.

So far, only regulations concerning the issue of the language (i.e. language law and regulation of education) have been presented; however, it was also possible to find isolated legal regulations of other kinds. It was possible to spot unsystematic elements of the so-called national autonomy, created usually by provincial legislation. One of the most important ones was the Czech provincial act No. 17/1873 of Czech Provincial Code ("which concerned local and district supervision of schools"), which prescribed a national division of local (sec. 7) and district (sec. 21) school councils. One of the important special acts of a different kind was the Elections Code of Moravia (No. 2/1906 of Moravian Provincial Code), which introduced electoral curias based on nationalities, and the amendment of the Moravian Provincial Ordinance (No. 1/1906 of Moravian Provincial Code), which established national

---

38   Cyril Horáček, *Jazykové právo československé republiky* (Prague: Knihovna sborníku věd právních a státních, 1928), pp. 39–41; Sobota, *Národnostní právo československé*, pp. 9–12.

39   See for example Hannelore Burger, *Sprachenrecht und Sprachgerechtigkeit im österreichischen Unterrichtswesen 1867–1918* (Vienna: VÖAW, 1995), p. 32ff.

40   Sobota, *Národnostní právo československé*, p. 12.

curias at the Moravian Provincial Diet.[41] Unlike in Moravia, petty elements of national autonomy were not of great importance in Bohemia. What was of significant influence on the national issue in Cisleithania was naturally the complex state structure, where the existence of traditional lands was the pillar of national movements (e.g. the fight for the so-called Czech state law), and the key element was public administration (both legal regulation and its at times peculiar practical operation).

In Hungary, legal regulation was not as chaotic as in Cisleithania. The Hungarian Act on Nationalities was specific and rather extensive with 29 sections. It was just a language law which, unlike Austrian Article 19, did not recognise nations; in the preamble it says that: "as each citizen of the Hungarian homeland is an equal member of one political nation, be he of any nationality whatsoever, special regulations regarding this equal right may only concern the issue of how various provincial languages shall be officially used."[42] The law introduced Hungarian as the state language, i.e. the language used by state bodies – the assembly, government and law. However, the influence of state administration had been weak in Hungary; what had been of great importance was regional self-government, as well as churches and municipalities. The actual status of minorities was thus naturally highly dependent on the state structure, which is after all a common thing at all times and everywhere. In regions it was possible to administrate, besides in Hungarian, also in the language that was required by at least one fifth of the regional assembly. Churches and municipalities chose their languages freely. However, the law was never put into practice; the importance of the Hungarian language had been much more central since the beginning, and the status of minority languages had gradually deteriorated. After all, some provisions of the law were later changed to the detriment of minorities. Minority schooling was not governed by the law and its actual condition was quite bad. Under pressure from the state, even elementary education was being made Hungarian.[43]

1.3 THE ESTABLISHMENT OF CZECHOSLOVAKIA AND MINORITIES

The relation to minorities belonged among the key issues throughout the entire era of the First Czechoslovak Republic, i.e. 1918–1938. Representatives of the newly formed republic had to be concerned with the issue of the approach thereto even prior to the constitution of the republic itself, because

---

41   Peška, *Kulturní samospráva národních menšin*, p. 18.
42   Cited according to Sobota, *Národnostní autonomie v Československu?*, p. 20.
43   Ibid., pp. 20–22.

the existence of this principal issue was, especially due to a numerous German minority in the Czech lands, indisputable. When promoting the Czechoslovak idea with the Allies, the resistance movement abroad also had to deal with this issue during the war. It is necessary to emphasise that T.G. Masaryk, the head of the movement and later the first president, had always been a supporter of the fair settlement of the nationalities issue; that was the reason why minorities policies were moderate and unaffected by the militant nationalism that was so common during the war and afterwards. In the declaration entitled the Declaration of Independence of the Czechoslovak Nation (or the so-called Washington Declaration) adopted by the Czechoslovak Provisional Government in exile on 16 October 1918 it is proclaimed: "We accept the American principles as laid down by President Wilson . . . of the actual equality of nations" and "The rights of the minority shall be safeguarded by proportional representation; national minorities shall enjoy equal rights."[44]

A favourable attitude to extraordinarily numerous minorities was, however, a necessity to a certain extent, also with regards to the dependence on western powers. It was they who were to decide on the preservation of the historic borders of the Czech lands, which was one of the key requirements of the Czechoslovak resistance movement. Masaryk gave countenance to a certain reduction of the area of traditional Czech lands according to ethnic aspects, particularly in the west and south.[45] The Great Powers wished for a stable system in Central Europe, which might have been upset by the repression of new influential minorities.

A domestic resistance movement had also been concerned with the future approach to minorities, particularly the German one, already during the war. On the whole, the Germans were promised that they would be equal citizens of the Czech state, that the denationalisation would not be allowed, and that they would not be treated in a bad way, like they used to treat the Czechs in the past; such declarations were made even by representatives of nationalist groups. It is necessary to remark that in German plans for the organisation after the victorious war, no promises regarding the equality of the Czechs occurred, unlike the ideas of Pangerman Central Europe, which were quite frequent. Apart from general Czech assurances regarding the Germans, no particular solution was made clear, which is not surprising as then, at the time of great changes, almost nothing was clear – the organisation of the state, its borders, or the existence thereof itself. What was a problem was the fact that

44   For its text in English see *Declaration of independence of the Czechoslovak nation by its Provisional Government* (New York: [Printed for the Czechoslovak Arts Club by the Marchbanks Press], 1918); see also George J. Kovtun, *The Czechoslovak Declaration of Independence: A History of the Document* (Washington, DC: Library of Congress, 1985).

45   Jan Galandauer, *Vznik Československé republiky 1918* (Prague: Svoboda, 1988), pp. 42–43; Jiří Kovtun, *Masarykův triumf* (Prague: Odeon, 1991), pp. 454, 468.

there was not even a mere indication of a Czech-German dialogue, because the Germans had long refused to accept the affiliation to the Czech state.

The intentions of Czech experts regarding the status of minorities were favourable; some of them themselves recommended the international protection of the minorities as well. Interesting were the drafts of the Constitution of the Czech state, elaborated by Czech academics at the request of the National Committee. Many of those drafts allowed for the breaking of sovereignty in favour of the protection of national minorities.[46] The Czechs, including nationalist politicians, were aware of the traditional German dominance in Central Europe, as well as of the fact that it was impossible to build the state on the brutal repression of that group.

Now, it is important to mention, at least briefly, the attitude of minorities (particularly the German minority) to the new conditions and the Czech (Czechoslovak) state. An important feature impacting the negative approach of the Sudeten Germans towards Czech efforts to strengthen their positions at the time of the Habsburg Monarchy was the worries about their own existence. "Already back then (at the time of the Habsburg Monarchy) they experienced worries about whether they would compare favourably vis-à-vis the greater Czech vitality and natality, whether they would be able to innovate their stagnating industry; if they had not managed it yet 'at the time of the Austrian Empire', they must have had greater worries 'in the Czech state'."[47] They enthusiastically supported the war efforts of the Habsburg Monarchy, which however resulted in heavy casualties, much heavier than those suffered by the Czechs, as well as in the massive amount of now valueless war bonds. The dispute over their clearance significantly affected the status of the Germans within the Czechoslovak Republic.

The Germans were also afraid of acts of violence by victorious Czechs, though this never happened. There were often riots and unrest, but they were rather social than nationalist. Extreme attitudes and a willingness to fight were on the decline also among the Germans. Considerable worries about their status were felt by the Jewish minority as well, because stable and favourable conditions at the time of the Habsburg Monarchy were to be supplanted by a new, unknown situation, and many people predicted that a new wave of mass anti-Semitism would rise. Although the previous development, when the Jews standing between the Czechs and Germans were often assaulted from either side, might have suggested such a terror, only limited anti-Semite acts of violence occurred despite the general chaos.

The Bohemian and Moravian Germans had long refused their own integration into the emerging Czechoslovak Republic and presumed that they

---

46   Galandauer, *Vznik Československé republiky 1918*, pp. 162–166.
47   Václav Kural, *Konflikt místo společenství?* (Prague: R Press, 1993), p. 27.

would remain a part of Austria or would join Germany.[48] They created four units, the largest of which was the province of Deutschböhmen, whereas they relied on the right to self-determination.[49] Had the borders required by the Germans been implemented, which had been enumerated with virtually comical accuracy in some peculiar act without regard to the Czech stance or practicality of the organisation, the Czechoslovak Republic would not have been viable. As Czech experts emphasised, the German self-determination brought to the utmost limits would have jeopardised the Czech self-determination inasmuch as there are other German states but not another one for the Czechoslovak nation. The Czech representation made an effort to negotiate and offered the Germans, under the condition of voluntary incorporation of the borderlands into the Czechoslovak Republic, the possibility to participate in the government and legislative body; however, the Bohemian and Moravian Germans (later called also Sudeten Germans) were only open to international talks on the basis of equality.[50]

The Bohemian and Moravian Germans tried hard to gain international support – they considered themselves to be a part of Austria, which should have been incorporated into Germany. They hoped for a favourable approach from western politicians, particularly from the American president Woodrow Wilson, to whom they, for example, delivered a protest on 12 November 1918. The Great Powers however approved that the territory be taken over by Czechoslovak forces even before the peace conference was to decide definitively about the borders.[51]

The borderland territories proposed to separate from the Czech lands were not viable, especially in terms of economy, there was a good deal of social unrest, and the willingness of the Germans to engage in another fight, this time with Prague, was minimal after the lost war.[52] German resistance to the taking of the borderlands during November and December 1918 broke down, although the new Czechoslovakia had almost no military forces at its disposal. In some areas of the borderlands the situation got out of the control of German "governments" so much, especially because of social unrest,

---

48 Johann Wolfgang Brügel, "The Germans in pre-war Czechoslovakia," in *A History of the Czechoslovak Republic 1918–1948*, ed. by Victor S. Mamatey and Radomír Luža (Princeton, NJ: Princeton University Press, 1973), pp. 167–186; Elizabeth Wiskemann, *Czechs and Germans: A Study of the Struggle in the Historic Provinces of Bohemia and Moravia* (London: Oxford University Press, 1938), p. 51ff.

49 Harry Klepetař, *Seit 1918: eine Geschichte der Tschechoslowakischen Republik* (M.-Ostrau: Julius Kittls Nachfolger, 1937), p. 36ff.; Leo Epstein, *Studien-Ausgabe der Verfassungsgesetze der Tschechoslowakischen Republik* (Reichenberg: Gebrüder Stiepel, 1923), pp. 55–59.

50 Jaroslav Valenta, "Legenda o 'rebelech, s nimiž se nevyjednává'," *Moderní dějiny* 2 (1994): pp. 197–214.

51 Jan Opočenský, *Vznik národních států v říjnu 1918* (Prague: Orbis, 1927), p. 217.

52 Susanne Maurer-Horn, "Die Landesregierung für Deutschböhmen und das Selbstbestimmungsrecht 1918–1919," *Bohemia* 38, no. 1 (1997): p. 39ff.

that they themselves had to ask for Czech intervention and occupation.[53] The efforts for breaking away did come off, but they hastened the Czech distrust and disqualification of the Germans from the participation in power at the beginning of the Czechoslovak Republic, when key legislation concerning minorities also came into existence.

Markedly more complicated for the new state was the integration of Slovakia, thus inter alia also the Hungarian minority. As a matter of fact, the new government in Budapest refused to cede the territory that had belonged to Hungary for centuries, and was also Hungarianised to a large extent. Fights took place there, and only the pressure exerted by the Allies forced Budapest to abandon the territory. Hungarian bureaucracy, including the railways and telegraph service, left the state, where the situation became problematic afterwards and even anti-Semitic pogroms occurred. In many places there was complete chaos and it was armed groups that ruled, Hungarian ones in some areas, German or Slovak ones in other places.[54]

The Czechoslovak government delegate for Slovakia Vavro Šrobár responded ruthlessly to strikes and unrest against the Czechoslovak Republic organised by Hungarians and Hungarianised Slovaks (Magyarons), namely in Bratislava, where the Slovaks were just a minority in number. "The government made use of the suppressed strike to carry out through purges on personnel of postal and railway enterprises, not only on senior officers but also on ordinary employees: only a few strikers were re-employed again."[55] The status of the Hungarianised Slovaks (Magyarons) was thus, due to the negative attitude to the new Czechoslovak Republic, significantly weakened from the very beginning. A low representation of members of minorities among civil servants (one of the most sensitive issues in Czechoslovakia) thus in this case, which was analogous to the situation in, for example, Transylvania incorporated into Romania, occurred immediately at the time when the power of the new state was being asserted.

Later on, Šrobár declared a state of war in Slovakia, and suspicious persons were placed under surveillance by the police. He also took strong actions against usually pro-Hungarian Jews, whom he considered unreliable, and at the same time he restricted their economic status, e.g. by revoking their licences. According to a regulation issued by him, a cinematographic licence should not have been granted expressly to a Jew or a person with

53   See for example Zdeněk Kárník, *České země v éře první republiky*, vol. 1 (Prague: Libri, 2000), pp. 37–42; Ferdinand Peroutka, *Budování státu*, 3rd ed., vol. 1 (Prague: Academia – NLN, 1991), pp. 102–105, 119–130, 229–237; Dagmar Perman, *The Shaping of the Czechoslovak State: Diplomatic History of the Boundaries of Czechoslovakia, 1914–1920* (Leiden: E.J. Brill, 1962), p. 77ff.

54   See for example Marián Hronský, *The Struggle for Slovakia and the Treaty of Trianon 1918–1920* (Bratislava: Veda, 2001), p. 55ff.

55   Peroutka, *Budování státu*, vol. 1, p. 434.

a "fraudulent past."[56] The frontiers with Hungary as well as position of Hungarians left on the Czechoslovak territory became a pretext for open military conflict, particularly when the Slovak Communist Republic of the Soviets was established in the Eastern Slovak town of Prešov on 16 June 1919 with the assistance of the Hungarian Communist regime of Béla Khun.[57] The Slovak territory was secured by the Czechoslovak armed forces in July 1919. The frontiers with Hungary were finally determined in 1920 by Article 27 of the so-called Trianon Peace Treaty[58] but the attitude of the Hungarians towards the new Czechoslovak Republic remained very negative for a long time.

The attitude of the new Czechoslovak state to numerous minorities was in a way unclear at the beginning. It was because the Czechs did not have any unambiguous offers even for the most important German minority, and the only specific thing debated in the fall of 1918 was the establishment of the office of the Minister-Compatriot for the Germans as well as some aspects of the language law. In the effort to develop the minorities policy, the government decided, in mid December 1918, to set up an expert committee which was to deal with minorities issues (particularly language ones) and to come up with specific suggestions for the organisation of cultural and political rights. However, the committee, which should have been chaired by the Prime Minister Karel Kramář never met, and the conception of the policy was not developed. Although the resolution of minorities issues is among one of the most difficult aspects from the point of view of both the legal system and practice, this rather unmethodical attitude basically remained until the end of the First Czechoslovak Republic.[59] On the other hand, it would be wrong to assume that no talks on the language issues among ministers were held.

The state, i.e. Czechoslovak, nation was gaining certain privileges in the new republic; especially important from a legal point of view was the decision of the Supreme Administrative Court of 19 March 1919 (Decission of the Supreme Administrative Court No. 73/1918, Collection of decisions by dr. Josef Bohuslav, Administrative series, No. V), which emphasised that the national state has the right to exert its character, and minorities may not demand that they be fully emancipated in all aspects. The practice at the constitutional level was different for a long time, though, and many offices unlawfully administrated in the German or Hungarian languages as late as a year after the formation of the republic; in reply to communications in Czech from other

---

56   Peroutka, *Budování státu*, vol. 1, pp. 433–436.
57   Hronský, *The Struggle for Slovakia*, pp. 114–153.
58   Peroutka, *Budování státu*, vol. 1, p. 154ff.
59   Jaroslav Kučera, "Koncepce národního státu Čechů a Slováků a jeho realita v životě první republiky," in *Československo 1918–1938: Osudy demokracie ve střední Evropě*, ed. by Jaroslav Valenta, Emil Voráček and Josef Harna (Prague: Historický ústav AV ČR, 1999), pp. 602–603.

institutions they even said, "unverständlich" (i.e. unintelligible)![60] The parliament also adopted a resolution on the leading status of the Czechoslovak nation then.[61]

Besides those rather prestigious privileges of the state nation, the most important restriction of minorities at the beginning of the Czechoslovak Republic was, from the point of law, their disqualification from the first Czechoslovak parliament. The Provisional or Revolutionary National Assembly, which arose from the Czechoslovak National Committee, was not elected. Its composition was based on the division of seats among Czech political parties according to the results of elections to the Austrian Imperial Council in 1911, and in the case of Slovak members, completely at will. The minorities, with the notable exception of Jews, were not represented at all, although they comprised more than one third of the population!

The duration of the Provisional (Revolutionary) National Assembly was not limited in time because the Provisional Constitution adopted by the National Committee on 13 November 1918 as Act No. 35/1918 Sb did not determine by what time a parliamentary election should take place. That was to be decided solely by political parties of the Czechoslovak state nation: "They made use of this full power to keep the revolutionary assembly in the office much longer than anyone would have dared to assume at the beginning, until such time when parliamentary elections in other European states had long-ago been organised."[62] The reason for this approach, later strongly challenged by the Germans and Hungarians, was the fear of German obstruction in the Parliament and the inability to reach the required majority to adopt laws, namely constitutional ones. The Czechosloval National Committee and the Provisional (Revolutionary) National Assembly adopted a lot of fundamental legal regulations that also governed the status of minorities; they were affected indirectly but significantly by, for example, the land reform.

However, the absence of minorities in the Provisional (Revolutionary) National Assembly was caused more by their negative approach towards the Czechoslovak state than by Czech chauvinism. Actually, the Germans, with whom Czech politicians tried to compromise at the beginning, long refused their incorporation into the republic. Even after the borderlands had been taken and fully cotrolled by Czech forces, the governments of secessional provinces continued to operate – now in exile in Vienna. New Austrian republic considered those areas its territory and even accorded them representation in Vienna parliament. It was on 4 March 1919, when

---

60   Národní archiv v Praze (NA), collection Ministerstvo vnitra, stará registratura (MV), box 502, file 28.

61   Kučera, "Koncepce národního státu Čechů a Slováků," p. 604.

62   Peroutka, *Budování státu*, vol. 1, p. 169; see also for example Ladislav Lipscher, *Verfassung und politische Verwaltung in der Tschechoslowakei 1918–1939* (Vienna: Oldenbourg, 1979), p. 20.

said assembly gathered in Vienna for the first time, when demonstrations and a general strike were organised in the borderlands, which resulted in clashes with Czechoslovak troops and eventually in a tragedy that claimed 54 lives. This event, which was fortunately never repeated again to such an extent during the entire period of the First Czechoslovak Republic, was annually commemorated by the Sudeten Germans and set a really negative tradition for co-existence with the Czechs.[63] The government was overtaken by this event because it wanted to treat minorities in a moderate way, and was afraid of the negative reaction of the Great Powers that were then deciding on the borders of the Czechoslovak Republic. Those powers, however, had no objections to a resolute intervention, as the strong anti-German sentiment from the war time was still wide-spread.[64]

The negative attitude of the Germans to the state did not pay off, because the once appeasing atmosphere among the Czechs was wearing off. The right-winged National Democratic Party, in particular, promoted, as early as the spring of 1919, the idea that the Germans not be granted national citizens' rights and be barred from the army until they submitted to the new state.[65] It was Karel Kramář, the head of the National Democratic Party, who represented (being it a simplification in a way) the nationalist stream in Czech politics; the other stream, more favourable to minorities, was represented by President T.G. Masaryk. While Kramář anticipated a permanent German threat and thus required national unity of the Czechs and Slovaks in the Czechoslovak Republic, as well as a pan-Slavic federation in Europe, Masaryk, on the other hand, advocated attitudes considerably more favourable to the minorities. He himself, however, refused to recognise the Germans as the other state nation, and he even described them as colonists, although he apologised for such declarations later. Kramář advanced the national language and other privileges of the state nation, but he was also rejecting the oppression of the Germans, because, as he said, the Czechs had to rule differently from how the Germans had ruled before. An important discrepancy between Masaryk and Kramář was the issue of the regulation of public administration. Masaryk regarded a truly democratic self-government as a certain substitute for the autonomy required by the Germans, thus an acceptable compromise. The Germans should have had key influence not only in their own municipalities and self-governing districts, which was the tradition from the time of the Habsburg Monarchy, but also in regions ("zhupas") which were required by Masaryk. On the other hand, Kramář was an opponent of large German

---

63 Kárník, *České země v éře první republiky*, vol. 1, p. 43; Karl Braun, "Der 4. März 1919: Zur Herausbildung sudetendeutscher Identität," *Bohemia* 37, no. 2 (1996): pp. 353–380.
64 Peroutka, *Budování státu*, vol. 2, p. 500.
65 Ibid., p. 502; Jaroslav Kučera, *Minderheit im Nationalstaat: Die Sprachenfrage in den tschechisch-deutschen Beziehungen 1918–1938* (Munich: R. Oldenbourg Verlag, 1999), p. 19.

regions ("zhupas") which, according to him, might have become a centre of irredentism.[66]

This brings us to the crucial, although sometimes ignored, issue of the administrative reform and its relation to the question of minorities, which will now be dealt with in more detail. As it has already been said, the issue of the organisation of public administration had traditionally (although somewhat paradoxically) been, along with language law, the key subject of national disputes in the field of law. Public administration represents a vast and complex system penetrating all possible fields, which has been developing for centuries. Attempts to change or influence it are thus met with countless hinderances. One of the rather radical reforms was also the so-called regions' reform ("zhupas' reform") in the 1920s.[67] The most noticeable novelty brought by the regions' reform in the Czech lands represented changes at the middle level of administration, i.e. the elimination of lands and the introduction of new units of a smaller area ("zhupas", which are, according to Czech tradition, called regions). The reform concerned districts as well; however, it did not represent a radical change.

At its inception, the Czechoslovak National Committee issued first Czechoslovak Act on the Establishment of the Independent Czechoslovak State, which was published as Act No. 11 of a new Czechoslovak Collection of Laws. The Act proclaimed, "for the time being," juridical continuity with Austrian imperial laws and provincial laws valid on the territory of the newly established Czechoslovak state. The bodies of state administration remained operative. Juridical continuity also applied to Slovakia, where Hungarian laws remained in force. As a result, a dual legal system within Czechoslovakia was established.[68]

The administrative organisation was substantially different in Cisleithania and in Hungary. During World War I, the state machinery and its representatives were strongly discredited and incited hatred against themselves in the majority of the population[69]. The Minister of the Interior, Alois Švehla, thus tried to give the impression that the upheaval brought about a significant change; in doing so, he wanted to increase the prestige of the state administration. According to him, the establishment of Czechoslovakia meant not only a new form of the state but also an end to the domineering of citizens by public authorities. This, quite a radical reform of administration (so-called

---

66   Kural, *Konflikt místo společenství?*, pp. 19–23; Perman, *The Shaping of the Czechoslovak State*, p. 107.
67   Perman, *The Shaping of the Czechoslovak State*, p. 107; see also Laštovka, *Zákon župní*, p. 11; Kučera, *Minderheit im Nationalstaat*, p. 37; Rudolf Schranil, *Gutachten zur tschechoslowakischen Verwaltungsreform* (Prague: Kommissionsverlag der Prager Juristischen Zeitschrift, 1927), s. 50–52.
68   Kuklík, *Czech law in historical contexts*, pp. 85–86.
69   Jan Janák, *Vývoj správy v českých zemích v epoše kapitalismu*, 2nd ed., vol. 2 (Prague: SPN, 1971), p. 51.

zhupas reform) should have also undoubtedly served as a demonstration of changes in state powers, which manifested itself in the officially acclaimed broadening of self-government, which incited a fear of the possibility of being abused by the German irredentism, although in fact, unlike at the time of the Habsburg Monarchy, the self-government was weakened.

The Ministry of the Interior had represented the most influential portfolio already at the time of the Austria-Hungary. The apt leader of the Agrarian Party, Antonín Švehla, further reinforced the position of the Ministry of the Interior, already strong enough, also through the acquision of significant actual influence on constitutional matters. Within the Ministry, a legislative department was created, which was chaired by a chief clerk – Jiří Hoetzel, an expert on administrative and constitutional law – and in which other brilliant lawyers worked, for example K. Laštovka, V. Joachim, and B. Bobek. It was this department that prepared many of the most important laws, such as the draft of the Czechoslovak constitution of 1920, the draft of the regions' act, later the act on the organisation of political administration, and these key regulations were then, usually without major alterations, adopted by the parliament.[70] On the other hand, experts from the ranks of minorities did not, strictly speaking, participate in the preparation and adoption of the most important laws of the the Czechoslovak state at all. The need for the reform of public administration was considered so topical after October 1918 and the Ministry of the Interior started work on it almost immediately after its establishment. However, pressure for swift changes was rather a political manifestation of radical society-wide sentiment; contrary to that, the economic situation and the condition of the administration at the time of post-war chaos warned against the taking of such crucial and rash steps.[71]

The nationalities issue was extraordinarily influential in the reform of administration where Slovakia and minorities were concerned. The regulation of public administration was used to solve these key problems, which had a goodly, however not really positive, tradition in our territory, particularly efforts for the establishment of regions at the time of the Habsburg Monarchy. The main aim of the reform was considered by many to be the unification of Slovakia and the Czech lands; Slovakia should have been divided into regions and should not have felt as an independent land, so the new system of public administration should have prevented Slovak separatism. After all, many Slovaks themselves feared their own autonomy that had been promised to them by the resistance movement abroad and which might have easily been dominated by so far strong Hungarians and Hungarianised

---

70   Ibid., p. 48.
71   Karel Schelle, *Vývoj správy v předválečném Československu*, vol. 1 (Brno: Masarykova univerzita, 1991), p. 164.

Slovaks (Magyarons). While at the time of the Habsburg Monarchy the Czech lands used to be a pillar for Czech national efforts, it was not so now; many of their former proponents advanced that the lands be eliminated, which also concerned a once strong self-government.[72]

The issue of minorities, namely the Germans, was perhaps even more important. Some of the contemplated administrative units (probably two regions) should have comprised a German majority, which irritated Czech nationalists, and the nationalities issue relating to the regions' reform also had significant international implications. Czechoslovakia was a newly established state without a guaranteed international status, and it was not clear at all whether the Czechoslovak Republic would acquire the areas with the majority of German (or Hungarian) populations.

At the Peace Conference in Paris, the borders of the Czechoslovak Republic were debated and the possibility of handing over certain territories to Germany was pondered, which, however, was prevented, especially by protest of France. This issue has hitherto been controversial for historians, also with regard to the internal organisation of the state that had been promised at the conference by the Czechoslovak delegation, namely by Edvard Beneš. The question is whether the Czechoslovak Republic committed itself at the conference to federalisation or to cantonalisation in the manner of Switzerland, as was written in one of the memoranda by the Czechoslovak delegation: "The intent of the Czechoslovak government is to create a system of the state which embraces as a basis for national rights the principles used in the constitution of the Republic of Switzerland."[73] Both the interpretation and the sense of this commitment is debatable; what is however clear is that it was not internationally binding, as it was a special treaty concluded between Czechoslovakia and the Allied Great Powers, the so-called Minorities Treaty of St. Germain, solely that was legally binding, and it did not contain any such provision. Despite that, federalisation or cantonalisation of Czechoslovakia were discussed in Paris, and it was also exacted by the Bohemian Germans through the Austrian delegation, which propounded to the peace conference, in its proposals in the summer of 1919, an idea for the nationalities cantonal constitutional charter of the Czechoslovak Republic.[74] As for the reform of

---

72   See for example Peroutka, *Budování státu*, vol. 3, pp. 1008–1015.

73   Cited as per Eva Broklová, "Švýcarský vzor pro Československo na Pařížské mírové konferenci," *Český časopis historický* 92, no. 2 (1994), p. 261. For original see Archiv Ministerstva zahraničních věcí (AMZV), collection Pařížský archiv, file 50, 5001.

74   Friedrich Prinz, "Benešův mýtus se rozpadá," *Střední Evropa* 8, no. 24 (1992), p. 43; Hugo Hassinger, *Die Tschechoslowakei: Ein geographisches, politisches und wirtschaftliches Handbuch* (Vienna: Rikola Verlag, 1925), p. 324–327; Jörg K. Hoensch, *Geschichte der Tschechoslowakischen Republik 1918–1965* (Stuttgart: Kohlhammer, 1966), s. 32; Helmut Slapnicka, "Recht und Verfassung der Tschechoslowakei 1918–1938," in *Aktuelle Forschungsprobleme um die Erste Tschechoslowakische Republik*, ed. by Karl Bosl (Munich: Oldenbourg 1969), s. 96.

administration, the delegation promised to the Great Powers a thing whose accomplishment was at that time not by far certain and which eventually did not win out at all.

While the Minorities Treaty of St. Germain did not contain any obligations for the Czechoslova Republic as a whole, regarding the organisation of public administration, the status of Sub-Carpathian Ruthenia was different, and Czechoslovakia bound itself to establish this territory as a self-governing (autonomous) unit.[75] Provisions contained in the Minorities Treaty of St. Germain, along with chaos in the territory, incited considerable uncertainties which later showed also in the so-called Regions Act of 1920, in which it was not made sufficiently clear whether or not it applied to Sub-Carpathian Ruthenia. It was a very underdeveloped area, completely different from the Czech lands, which had not originally been counted in at all when constituting the Czechoslovak Republic, and the government knew only little about it. Provisions of the Minorities Treaty of St. Germain regarding the autonomy were not implemented and the Czechoslovak government also somewhat forgot about its many other earlier promises; however, cultural, and partially also economic, help was commenced. It was assumed that prior to the granting of autonomy, Ruthenians would have had to live for several years under the Czech trusteeship system. Also in this field, like in other issues relating to minorities, the Czechoslovak policy was influenced by both internal and external factors.[76]

The Ministry of the Interior was working on the draft of the administration reform although it had existed for only a few months, and in the then time of chaos it had to solve many other problems than in times of stability. After long talks the government approved the proposed draft of the Regions Act, and at the end of October 1919 it commenced debates with political parties.[77] The ideas of the Ministry of the Interior were not naturally met with a positive response. The radical change of administration got into trouble with interests of political parties, national minorities, local patriots, etc. Besides the Agrarian Party it was chiefly socialistic parties that approved of the carrying out of the reform. Nationalist arguments were in particular expressed by the National Democratic Party, which minded the establishement of two German regions in Bohemia. However, important were also the strong relations of this party to chief officials of state administration in Bohemia who did not want to leave Prague for often provincial regional seats,

75   For its English translation see Beneš and Kural, *Facing History: The Evolution of Czech-German Relations in the Czech Provinces, 1848–1948*, document no. 1, pp. 295–296.
76   Paul Robert Magocsi, "Utváření národní identity: Podkarpatská Rus (1848–1948)," part 2, *Střední Evropa* 15, no. 92/93 (1999): pp. 117–119.
77   Schelle, *Vývoj správy v předválečném Československu*, pp. 164–167.

and therefore were set against the reform.[78] It was also the purely personal interests of influential individuals that probably contributed many times to the virtually ignominious nationalist campaigns of the National Democratic Party. It is important to always bear in mind such a complicated context where the issue of minorities, and especially the issue of the administration reform, are concerned because the uncovering of real motives is usually not easy.

Generally, it has to be said that the interest in the administration reform was expressed most frequently only by persons concerned, such as administration officers and the heads of political parties. A response by the public was not adequate to the key importance of the reform and citizens were at most concerned about whether the two German regions would be established.[79] Besides that, there was one more topic that could rouse at least a part of the public – it was local, often quite trifling interests to become a regional seat. Threats of strikes, non-payment of taxes, and supply of grain cut-offs were made. At such a complicated time crucial laws of the state were being created, including key regulations governing the status of minorities.

We will now move from the topic of administration reform, which was necessary to deal with compactly because of its complexity, back to the issues of the status of minorities at the beginning of the Czechoslovak Republic. The Germans from the Czech lands, as well as other minorities, had long refused their incorporation into Czechoslovakia; however, the conclusions of the Paris Peace conferecne, which resolved the issue of borders, put an unsuccessful end to this policy. The Sudeten Germans had to leave the Austrian parliament and do away with their "governments." Czechoslovakia did not make any problems for short-term emigrants, particularly for the Sudeten German politicians, and T.G. Masaryk announced amnesty for members of the German resistance movement as early as 10 August 1919, i.e. already before the definitive decision by the Paris Peace Conference.[80]

Although German parties had originally strongly rejected the idea of independent Czechoslovakia, they now turned their policy considerably and were trying to compromise with the Czechs. There was practically a race among German parties as they assumed that the party that would come to a favourable agreement with the ruling nation would gain voters. The talks took place before Christmas 1919, namely on 20 and 22 December. The requirements of German parties were far-reaching – such a numerous minority certainly had a right to require a lot; however, taking the recent negative attitude towards

78   Peroutka, *Budování státu*, vol. 3, pp. 1011–1012.
79   Ferdinand Kahánek, *Stát, země a župy* (Prague: Melantrich, 1926), pp. 18–23.
80   Jaroslav César and Bohumil Černý, *Politika německých buržoazních stran v Československu v letech 1918-1938*, vol. 1 (Prague: ČSAV, 1962), pp. 188–190.

the Czechoslovak Republic into account, their requirements sounded almost like a provocation.

The first delegation to visit Prime Minister Vlastimil Tusar (Czech Social Democrat) was the deleglation of the German Social Democratic Party on 20 December, which presented him with a memorandum with requirements necessary, according to it, for agreement. The manners of the delegation were extremely inappropriate; they, for example, threatened violence should their conceptions have been rejected.[81] They demanded that supplies be improved and they rejected restrictions of German schooling, as well as infringements on language rights before authorities. Probably the most important was the requirement that the constituent assembly be convened and that all nations participate in the creation of the Constitutional Charter. Two days later it was the delegation of German non-socialist parties lead by a belligerent German nationalist, Rudolf Lodgman von Auen; they required that the Revolutionary National Assembly be dissolved and that a parliamentary election with the participation of minorities be called.[82]

The response of the Czech side, i.e. of Prime Minister Tusar, to German requirements was unequivocally disapproving, especially in terms of the participation of the Germans in the creation of the constitution. The Revolutionary National Assembly should have first adopted the key laws and only then should the elections with the participation of minorities have taken place: "This democratic and impartial legislative assembly, established by right of revolution, must first accomplish its mission and form a solid basis for our futher state development."[83] The official standpoint relied on the "rights of revolution," which was not then in any way unusual, but emphasis was also put on the fact that the revolutionary government had been recognised by the Allies, and by means of concluding peace also by Austria and Germany. Nevertheless, such an approach, objectively assessed, was problematic to a certain degree from the point of view of democracy. The Germans threatened that they would never recognise laws adopted by the Revolutionary National Assembly and they raised complaints even at the international level. Apart from a fear of German obstructions, the reason for the rejection of German requirements for the participation in the creation of the constitution was also the fact that the basic laws of the state had in fact been ready already before Christmas 1919 and should have shortly been debated in the parliament. The participation of the Germans would have apparently made the issue more complicated.[84] Also, hardly any of the leading Czech politicians was willing

---

81 Peroutka, *Budování státu*, vol. 2, p. 835.
82 César and Černý, *Politika německých buržoazních stran*, pp. 192–193.
83 Cited according to Peroutka, *Budování státu*, vol. 2, p. 837.
84 Kárník, *České země v éře první republiky*, vol. 1, pp. 94–97.

to risk an election in the tense situation in the state prior to consolidating the state system by virtue of adopting the key laws, which was all but a main German requirement.

If we sum up, one of the most significant circumstances influencing the development between 1918 and 1920 was the absence of minorities from the Revolutionary National Assembly, which had adopted the most important laws of the Czechoslovak state. This fact was a consequence of complicated development, where the Czechs originally invited minorities, the Germans in particular, to participate in the preparation of the constitution; they however did not wish it, as well as their incorporation into the Czechoslovak Republic. When they changed their stance at the last moment, they were refused by the Czechs. It was because of this inauspicious development that national unions of political parties remained much longer, which impeded the compromise and participation of minorities in the government. Although ideas of autonomy, or even federation, were rejected, this however did not mean that the responsible officials (including President Masaryk) would have wanted to establish conditions unfavourable to minorities, or that they would have abandoned a compromise with them.[85]

The most important laws of the state were debated and approved by the parliament no sooner than at the end of February 1920. This substantial delay had several causes; besides dissension amongst parties, it was mainly waiting for the end of the Paris Peace Conference. The Peace Conference imposed new obligations on the Czechoslovak Republic (even of a constitutional nature), namely in questions regarding the issue of minorities. It was simultaneous adoption of the Constitutional Charter, language laws, laws on the Constitutional court, on rules of election to the Chamber of Deputies, on the composition and competences of the Senate, and the Regions Act which had critical influence on debating the key laws of the state. Minorites were most affected by the Language Act of 1920 (Act No. 122/1920 Sb.), promulgated on the same date as the Constitutional Charter; strongly influenced by this issue were also the Constitutional Charter itself and the Regions Act of 1920 (Act No. 126/ 1920 Sb.). Other laws also partially pertained to minorities issues, like almost everything at the time of the First Czechoslovak Republic.

The political situation was unfavourable mainly because of the collapse of the Social Democratic Party, and thus, as the elections were coming close, many talks were held in secret in an effort to prevent demagogy. The constutional committee of the Revolutionaty National Assembly had negotiated about the Constitutional Charter and other laws since the autumn of 1919, whereas it used as a basis unofficial talks and secret governmental drafts. "The constitutional committee consulted these drafts, whose basis had been

---

85   Bohumil Černý et al., *Češi, Němci, odsun* (Prague: Academia, 1990), p. 229.

elaborated by Prof. Jiří Hoetzel, in conditions that had been criticised by the participants for a need for 'incredible rush' and for uncertainty, in which all members of the committee were drowning, not knowing whether an order by political leaders would force them to ruin the work that had already been done and start again."[86] Not even debating in a plenary session of the Revolutionary National Assembly was without complication, despite efforts exercised by most parties to adopt the laws. Those laws were a compromise organised namely by the Minister of the Interior, Antonín Švehla, a leader of the Agrarian Party, in agreement with a social democrat and chief author of the Provisional Constitution Alfréd Meissner.

Disputes over basic questions to be dealt with in laws dragged on up until the day of their adoption, and the public were not very well informed of the talks. Let us take the Regions Act, for example, where no sooner than on 2 December 1919, after long political discussions, that basically were kept secret from the public, could Švehla state that a complete agreement among governmental parties had been arrived at. However, many important, if not crucial, elements were questionable even thereafter. The public were informed about the ultimate analysis of the draft regulation and about the final decision on a sensitive question of regional seats as late as on 28 February 1920; the law was then adopted by the parliament in the same wording (in the early hours of 29 February)! The situation was similar with other laws. The Language Act was approved by the government on 2 December 1919 and was referred to the constitutional committee on 10 December. This draft had to be withdrawn, and a new one was put forward at the end of January 1920; it however did not contain thoroughly revised details.[87]

The main political conflict of all these basic laws concerned the critical regulation governing minorities, i.e. the Language Act. It was particularly the case of this law in which it proved that the laws had been debated in a way already at the time of the pre-election campaign. Crowds were addressed from the windows of the parliament building, mass meetings were held, and other events took place in which the National Democratic Party in particular "made its mark." Unlike with other laws, in the case of the Language Act a compromise had not been achieved in the constitutional committee, which furthered wild controversies to considerations of the floor of the Revolutionary National Assembly.[88]

Prior to the debate in the plenary session of the Revolutionary National Assembly, the laws had been debated (in sections and in a random manner) by the constitutional committee. The discussion in the committee had often

---

86   Peroutka, *Budování státu*, vol. 3, p. 923.
87   Kučera, *Minderheit im Nationalstaat*, pp. 44–45.
88   Peroutka, *Budování státu*, vol. 3, pp. 925–926.

been far from an impartial approach, and the strong nationalism of some members manifested itself negatively. Despite that, it is necessary to say in general that the minutes of meetings of the constitutional committee provide us with a more realistic view of the issue of the legal status of minorities than the minutes of plenary sessions of the Revolutionary National Assembly, in which politics and demagoguery showed to a much larger extent, while working in committees, practical problems were being solved.[89]

In analysing talks over laws in the constitutional committee, the seeming paradox, which however does not surprise a scientist familiar with the minorities issue in the Czech lands, is that most impacted by nationalism was probably the preparation of the Act on Administrative (Regional) Reform (Regions Act), perhaps more than the preparation of the Language Act. The influence of the national question was reflected, though to a limited degree, in all those laws. To illustrate, in the case of the rules of election to the Chamber of Deputies, there were variations from the general regulation set forth for ballots in Slovakia (sec. 21), which required, in particular, a significantly higher number of signatures so that the ballots were valid. Such provisions stirred up discussions: "It is clear that this provision is aimed against the candidacies of Hungarianised Slovaks (Magyarons), but a situation may come about that also a Slovak party will be disqualified."[90] A duty had even had been contemplated whereby voters signing ballots would have had to first make a pledge of loyalty to the state. Efforts to settle issues with often unreliable minorities thus lead to the creation of many provisions, peculiar at times.

The minorities issue was directly regulated by the Language Act. Despite the strong nationalism of that time, debate in the constitutional committee was fair-minded and calm, except for some excesses which later found expression when being discussed in the plenary session of the parliament. Crucial was the notorious dispute about whether the Czechoslovak language should be declared the "state" language or "official" language. The governmental draft promoted the official language; however, nationalists, with Kramář in the lead, called for the state language. Without bias, it was a detail insignificant for the practice, but a dispute over this issue cost the constitutional committee, and later the plenary meeting, an incredible amount of time, of which there was none to spare. Some deputies attributed also practical importance to the issue, which however was not too realistic: "If we use the term 'official' in the act, then German judges, who will equivocate, will say

89   For discussions see minutes of the parliament sessions, http://www.psp.cz/eknih/1918ns/ps /stenprot/index.htm.

90   Archiv Poslanecké sněmovny Parlamentu ČR (APS), collection Revoluční národní shromáždění 1918–1920, box 33, 1276/152b, p. 11.

that it is not the language of courts, but only the language for situations when the president accepts envoys."[91]

Also in the case of the dispute over state vs. official language there was a great influence (or rather fear) of abroad, like in all matters of minorities issue. As the necessity of adhering to the Minorities Treaty of St. Germain as accurately as possible was emphasised, there arose a discrepancy regarding the translation of this term of the treaty, whether as official or as state language. There also were worries that victorious powers would even compel the Czechoslovak Republic to change its constitution. It would have been in compliance with the conception of the Minorities Treaty of St. Germain, but, as the later practice proved, it was completely unrealistic; however, such ideas existed in 1920.[92] Generally, the key problem of laws being adopted was that many questions, both international and national, had not yet been straightened out. Edvard Beneš, Minister of Foreign Affairs, recommended that the Minorities Treaty of St. Germain be strictly adhered to, and he informed of efforts to clarify the interpretation of international treaties. On the other hand, Karel Kramář, who also participated in the Paris Peace conference, rejected the kowtowing before foreign countries.

Besides the main, although rather theoretical, dispute over the state or official language, there were other differences. Among them belonged the effort of Karel Kramář for having the Czechoslovak language taught as a mandatory subject at all schools, which the Minorities Treaty allowed after all. Later he was however persuaded that it would not be feasible in practice. Kramář also pushed hard for a duty to be imposed on state servants to have a command of the Czech language, which incited a major dispute in the constitutional committee, and the Minister of Justice František Veselý described such proposals as impractical.[93] Kramář had generally tried to implement legal changes unfavourable to minorities many times, and quickly: "That will be dealt with in one stroke. Otherwise there will be ruckuses in the parliament."[94] All in all, the Revolutionary National Assembly hastily formed the basis for the legal status of minorities for the time of the entire era of the first Czechoslovak Republic; however, it is clear that this still was not enough for some politicians.

The Language Act of 1920 must have of course correlated with other legal regulations, but there was a lot of vagueness in law at that time; difficulties were caused primarily by the upcoming reform of administration. The Regions Act of 1920 was debated in the constitutional committee on 21–23 January,

---

91 Ibid., box 33, 1282/158a, p. 20.

92 Ibid., box 33, 1282/158a, p. 13, 1283/159b, p. 55; differently Kučera, *Minderheit im Nationalstaat*, p. 35.

93 Archiv Poslanecké sněmovny Parlamentu ČR (APS), collection Revoluční národní shromáždění 1918–1920, box 33, 1282/158b, p. 24; ibid., box 34, 1284/160a, p. 14ff.

94 Ibid., box 33, 1282/158b, p. 26.

19–21 February, 24–26 February, and there were numerous experts, such as Minister of Interior Antonín Švehla, taking part therein.[95]

The most discussed issue was the division of regions (i.e. the issue of Schedule A of the Regions Act); at the same time, it was also the key issue from a national point of view. The government had at its disposal possible solutions that had been worked out earlier, but the matter was made complicated by the fact that both the public and deputies started to put forward a lot of demands. The matter thus became uncertain, and naturally it was very difficult to debate on individual provisions of the act, when it was not even clear how large the prepared regions should have been.[96] The area, specific division, and regional seats stirred up discussions till the end, and even things that had just been agreed upon were often changed.

A problem that did not by far concern only regions, but also influenced negotiations on the Constitutional Charter and laws relating thereto, was the effort to "resolve" national issues through administrative measures. The fear of the Pangerman ideas by the young Czechoslovak state, as well as negative experiences from the past, lead to anti-German thinking, sometimes taken to extremes. Regions became a means for assimilation and weakening of minorities; for example, there was a proposal to attach some Czech districts of Českomoravská vrchovina (Bohemian-Moravian Highlands) to the German-dominated town of Jihlava, which should have led to its swift assimilation within the period of 20 years![97]

It is not just comical details but, unfortunately, the clear expression of sentiment and ideas of a part of the then society. Other deputies were also making plans for various manipulations of areas, while they rather used as arguments the German threat and the results of the election from the national point of view than the need for a purposeful division of the state. Such an approach clearly did not correspond with the reform of administration that required a purely rational approach. In general, it is necessary to emphasise that the national issue was not by far the only factor impacting the regions reform; on the contrary, individual interests intertwined intricately with one another. Many deputies advanced their own, personal interests, such as Alfred Meissner, who promoted the regional seat for his hometown of Mladá Boleslav.[98] Worst of all was the pressure exerted by the public, especially in matters of assigning regional seats to particular towns.

Prime Minister Vlastmil Tusar, who also participated in negotiations, stated that considering the pressure used by the deputations, as well as

---

95   Ibid., boxes 32–34.
96   Ibid., box 32, 1244/120, pp. 25, 34.
97   Ibid., box 33, 1277/153a, p. 35.
98   Schelle, *Vývoj správy v předválečném Československu*, pp. 171–173.

threatening unrest, it was necessary to finish the debate on the Regions Act, which was however being adopted along with other key laws of the state, as quickly as possible. "You see in what circumstance we were in session yesterday; should it be protracted by two or three more days, it will be even worse. If the National Assembly hasn't got this out of the way by Sunday, there will be mass protest meetings everywhere on Sunday, and the following week deputations will start coming here by special trains."[99] Luckily, the laws were adopted on the morning of Sunday, 29 February 1920. Protesters usually demanded that a regional seat be located in their town, but they often protested against German regions, too. This all illustrates the climate of the time in which the fundamental laws of the Czechoslovak state originated.

The Regions Act was being debated, along with other key laws, in the constitutional committee until the very last moment. Talks on the utterly crucial conceptual question, which was the size of regions, were stirred up as late as 26 February by Karel Kramář, a supporter of small regions that would not be nationally dangerous which ended up in a quarrel,[100] although the Revolutionary National Assembly was supposed to debate on the law in the morning on 27 February. Actually, the way of debating on the laws in the parliament represented one of the greatest problems. This is the wording of the assessment by MP Viktor Dyk (National Democrat): "A tragic fault of the Revolutionary National Assembly was that drafts had been brought to the parliament unprepared and hurriedly, and any amendment or alteration had been ruled out . . . , when drafts of laws having the strongest impact on the development of the state were being discussed, although nine tenths of the members of the relevant parliamentary assembly were not aware of what was going on."[101] For example, in the plenary session of 25 February, in which it was decided that talks on the fundamental laws would start on 27 February, Dyk objected that some laws had not yet been printed out to be distributed to the deputies; despite this fact, the commencement of debate was approved.

After they had been talked over in the constitutional committee, the laws were referred to a plenary session of the Revolutionary National Assembly. Although the parties tried hard to adopt the fundamental laws, discussions were not easy because not all of the issues had been compromised on beforehand. Most of the problems had already been resolved by the constitutional committee, but in certain cases the controversies were taken over to

99   Archiv Poslanecké sněmovny Parlamentu ČR (APS), collection Revoluční národní shromáždění 1918–1920, box 33, 1283/159a, p. 23.
100 Ibid., box 34, 1284/160a, pp. 2–6.
101 Viktor Dyk, *O národní stát 1925–1928* (Prague: Neubert, 1937), pp. 304–305.

the plenary session; it quite often was the issues that concerned minorities. The conflicts were usually triggered by the (opposition) National Democratic Party, which proposed many amendments, although it had been clear beforehand that the prospects of success were low. During the parliamentary debate on draft laws,[102] many momentous speeches were heard in which a good many flaws thereof were apparent, as well as the official policy in the beginnings of the Czechoslovak state. The first to inform of the laws were the rapporteurs; then there was a debate and finally voting. Speeches were often demagogical, but on the other hand they were of a good formal or theoretical quality and contained vast historical or political explanations. First, the rapporteurs spoke about the constitution; it was particularly the issues of Sub-Carpathian Ruthenia, Slovakia and the Germans that were emphasised, i.e. national issues and issues relating to minorities, which indeed belonged among the most important ones.

At Chapter 6, which regarded minorities, extensive explanations were put forward about the inspiration by the ideas of Havlíček, Palacký, and Masaryk, so officially there was an effort to follow from politicians rejecting chauvinism. In general, the analysis of the constitution was rather temperate and fair from the point of view of minorities. It is worth mentioning that where minorities issues were concerned it was almost exclusively the Germans who were being talked about, and who were reasonably deemed as the most important minority.

The speech of a rapporteur on the Language Act was in a rather nationalist tone. Unlike the other fundamental laws, the talks on the Language Act were quite tense and the chair person often had to call for order and quieten the deputies, who were shouting one another down. The rapporteur determined the elimination of old language controversies, which were, according to him, the cause of the downfall of the Habsburg Monarchy, as the main aim of the act. The era of the Austrian Habsburg Monarchy was not in any way remote then, and it influenced politicians and lawyers even more than they themselves were aware of, which is a fact that is sometimes ignored. The rapporteur also explained why the language law was just a framework regulation; he reasoned that it was because of the fact that many matters in the state, namely in public administration, had not yet been clarified.

The minorities issue was also mentioned in the case of other laws. For example, in the case of the rules of election to the Chamber of Deputies, the system of proportional representation was accented, because the majoritarian system might have allegedly been harmful to minorities. The rapporteur

---

102 Těsnopisecké zprávy o schůzích Narodního shromáždění Československého, vol. 4 (Prague: [Tiskem "Politiky"], 1920), pp. 3663–3877; see also stenographic protocols of 125th and 126th meeting, held on February 27–29, http://www.psp.cz/eknih/1918ns/ps/stenprot/index.htm.

thus underlined the fairness of said system to minorities, although they did not participate in the preparation of the act.[103]

Following the presentations by the rapporteurs, there was a general debate. All laws connected with the Constitutional Charter were debated at the same time; Karel Kramář, being the representative of the opposition National Democratic Party, whose opinions were this way expressed publically, declared against the laws.[104] In his nationalistically-toned speech he advanced the Czech language as the state language; he further required the unity of the Czechoslovak Republic and categorically rejected "parliaments" in regions, because some of them would have been German, etc. He stressed, however, that the Czechs did not wish to oppress minorities; on the other hand they were not to be afraid of the Germans and bow to them. He urged that the Language Act be as wide-ranging and detailed as possible, because the minorities would have been forced to become reconciled to their situation, which was a way in which it differed from the finally adopted governmental conception that wished to regulate many issues in the future through decrees, as needed. Kramář was worried that the Germans would later enforce many concessions dangerous to the Czechoslovak state; however, development in the following years was completely different and the Language regulation of 1926, on the contrary, weakened the chances of minorities.

The person presenting a speech in the debate for the Slovak political group was dr. Ivan Markovič,[105] who expressed the general support of Slovak deputies with the laws being debated. He stressed that the Slovaks were the official nation of the state, not a minority, and that they would not get induced by the Germans and Hungarians to a common fight for minorities rights, which some were in fact attempting. He did not consider autonomy for Slovakia, which had been originally debated during the war, to be convenient, at least for the time being, because powers hostile towards the Czechosloval Republic, particularly Hungarian and pro-Hungarian groups, might have easily got on. This moderate approach of Slovak politicians did not last long, however, and the Slovak question, along with the minorities, became a life issue of the state, menaced, in particular, by nationalism.

Other speakers also mentioned the issue of minorities. A moderate speech was presented by Msgre Jan Šrámek[106], representing the Catholic People's Party. He mentioned and appreciated the difficult work done by the drafters of the new laws; on the other hand, he underlined the undue haste in preparing them. He was one of a few who expressly remarked upon the questionable

---

103 Těsnopisecké zprávy, vol. 4, pp. 3699–3706.
104 Těsnopisecké zprávy, vol. 4, pp. 3706–3718.
105 Těsnopisecké zprávy, vol. 4, pp. 3718–3725.
106 Těsnopisecké zprávy, vol. 4, pp. 3744–3754.

legitimacy of the Revolutionary National Assembly, and in his opinion: "The National Assembly should elaborate the constitution, prepare the election, and leave any other organisation of our state to the elected National Assembly."[107] This speech was rewarded with appreciative shouts from some; however, there also echoed the words "To the Germans?" in reaction thereto, a warning that there would also be disloyal minorities in the new parliament.

Many speeches contained strong, demagogical elements. The general debate was followed by proposals for amendments[108], which often concerned the issues of minorities. It was again Karel Kramář who was particularly active, especially in terms of the question of the official language of the Czechoslovak state. Strong nationalist differences manifested themselves; for example, a threat of the denationalisation of the Czech minority population in the borderlands was being underlined and exaggerated. When voting on the laws,[109] which, unlike in the case of other laws, was very controversial in the case of the Language Act, certain minor changes therein won through. The act was finally passed, along with other regulations, at around 3 a.m. on Sunday, 29 February 1920, which implied not only the completion of the state system of the Czechoslovak Republic, but also until then the most thorough legal regulation of the status of minorities in Czech (Czechosovak) history.

Now, it is necessary to look in general at the issue of minorities in the adoption of the most important laws of the First Czechoslovak Republic. Minorities were dealt with, at least partially, in most of the laws; however, this aspect was of a different intensity. The key law was certainly the already mentioned Language Act of 1920, and besides it also the Constitutional Charter of 1920 and the Regions Act. Another law concerned with minorities was, for example, the Act on the rules of election. The fairness of the rules of election was stressed in discussions in the parliament and it was acknowledged by the minorities themselves; therefore, while many things in the Czechoslovak state incited their criticism, they probably never challenged the rules of election. On the other hand, it is important to emphasise that the largest German minority could have hardly been substantially weakened by changes in the rules of election, such as the introduction of the majoritarian system; also this was a reason why the issue of minorities in election law did not trigger any conflict in the Revolutionary National Assembly.

The key conflict in terms of the minorities issue concerned the Language Act, which in fact reflected the entire attitude to minorities, namely to the Germans and to lesser extend also to the Hungarians. The main maxim underlying

---

107 Těsnopisecké zprávy, vol. 4, p. 3745.
108 Těsnopisecké zprávy, vol. 4, p. 3762ff.
109 Těsnopisecké zprávy, vol. 4, pp. 3873–3876.

the Language Act was officially the principle of purposefulness; everyone should have been granted the right to communicate in his own language. In reality, however, it was principles of prestige which applied; under those principles it was the Czechoslovak nation that was the constituent of the state. It was mainly the National Democratic Party which played a nationalist card against the rulling coalition, and literally made use of the pressure by the public demonstrating and holding mass meetings in front of the parliament building.

Paradoxically, it was, in fact, a declaratory (in practice unimportant) proclamation of the Czechoslovak language as the state or official language which was the key disputed point. "Having been listening to this heated debate, Jiří Hoetzel, an adviser to the government, wrote that the squabbling about the words *state* and *official* gave the impression of medieval wrangling over a sacred word, since everyone meant the same thing: the language of the state."[110] This infamous dispute was not, unfortunately, the only absurd conflict; however, it was probably the most important one and it also cost the parliament the largest amount of time. Reading the minutes of meetings, an unbiased reader sometimes has doubts about the common sense of many deputies, also for the reason that, unlike in the case of the reform of the administration, the practical importance of the dispute over the state and official language was perhaps zero.

Karel Kramář, who also engaged in the dispute over the state language, was not a national extremist who could have then been found in the governments of, for example, Balkan countries. His ideas, which often only accorded the state nation a higher prestige, must have irritated minorities in the Czechoslovak Republic a lot, because most of them had until recently belonged among the ruling nations. Also in relation to the Minorities Agreement of St. Germain, which was otherwise contested by him for being an infringement on sovereignty, Kramář did not question the rights granted to the minorities, and he even stated: "Regarding the Germans, we are bound by such things that I would object if we incorporated them into the law as they are laid down in the St. Germain Agreement, because it would not be enough for the Germans and we have to grant them more."[111] He also rejected, like others, a sort of retaliation for the German attitude at the time of the Austria-Hungary: "I have to object to the first one lest they say I wish that the Czech nation would do what the Germans did in the Habsburg Monarchy. I would not like that. I must say that, granting so many rights the Germans did not want to grant after fights."[112]

---

110   Peroutka, *Budování státu*, vol. 3, p. 998.
111   Archiv Poslanecké sněmovny Parlamentu ČR (APS), collection Revoluční národní shromáždění 1918–1920, box 33, 1282/158a, p. 10.
112   Ibid., box 33, 1282/158b, p. 32.

Such an attitude, which was not in any way unfavourable to minorities, still provoked them in terms of prestigious issues, and did not concern only Kramář but also a significant portion of Czech nationalists in general, because true national extremism was rare in the Czech environment. The Germans might have dreamt, yet at the time of war successes in the spring of 1918, about the complete suppression of the Czech policy, or even about the assimilation of the entire Czech basin; however, every reasonable Czech knew that the Germans would always be of key influence in Central Europe.

All in all, despite a quite favourable attitude to minorities, the laws of 29 February 1920 set a clear trend towards the building of the national state, which also showed in the case of the Language Act. During the debate there occurred a dispute between the government and the opposition (namely Kramář), however, there were no critical differences regarding the rights either the government or the opposition wished to grant to minorities. As for Language Act, the controversy rather concerned the method, where Kramář proposed rigid wording while the government favoured "flexible" wording with the intention not to irritate the minorities at the very beginning. It was those more or less framework regulations that made it possible to put pressure on minorities in further negotiations,[113] which was the task of the executive. On the other hand, Kramář tried, by virtue of rigid formulations, to force the minorities to immediately give up requests for major changes. A peculiar broadening of the powers of the executive was rather extensive; it was supposed to issue in the future, irrespective of the parliament, implementing legislation relating to the framework Language Act, or even decide on the carrying out of the reform of administration, because the date of effect had not been fixed in the Regions Act. There were many similar features, which is not a good advertisement for the Czechoslovak democracy, since they often concerned the status of minorities.

1.4 SYSTEM OF INTERNATIONAL PROTECTION OF MINORITIES SET UP AT PARIS PEACE CONFERENCE

As regards minorities, the situation in the early years of Czechoslovakia was particularly complex, and the matters were further significantly complicated by international politics and law: in 1919–1920 a system of international protection of minorities was set up at Paris Peace Conference. Czechoslovakia participated in the conference, being deeply concerned about minority issues, together with some other central and eastern European

---

113   Kučera, "Koncepce národního státu Čechů a Slováků," p. 605.

countries.[114] Prime Minister Karel Kramář and Minister of Foreign Affiares Edvard Beneš participated on behalf of Czechoslovakia, with a number of collaborators at their side. Their different political and personal attitudes became apparent in respect of minorities; the nationalist Kramář rejected any supposedly humiliating concessions, while the pragmatist Beneš was willing to make a compromise. Beside the Paris delegation, other expert groups were set up in Prague to address the issues relevant for the newly established state – including minorities.[115]

Particularly important for the protection of minorities were the borders ultimately approved at the conference. Several countries, including Czechoslovakia, achieved territorial gains, which eventually backfired (notably on Czechoslovakia and Poland), because such territories were inhabited by large groups of hostile minorities. The concern that minority conflicts could easily cause a new war led, after lengthy negotiations, to the establishment of a system of international minority protection.[116] The treaties were to be drawn up by a special new commission, officially referred to as the "Commission for New States," but unofficially called the Minority Commission, which was to negotiate international obligations for Poland and other new states including Czechoslovakia. Thanks to backstage negotiations and personal contacts, Edvard Beneš managed to significantly influence the minority treaties in favour of Czechoslovakia. The treaty with Czechoslovakia included special provisions concerning Sub-Carpathian Ruthenia which largely corresponded with Beneš's proposals.[117]

---

114 The letters of prominent Czechoslovak politicians often deal with minorities, see Zdeněk Šolle, ed., *Vzájemná neoficiální korespondence T.G.Masaryka s Eduardem Benešem z doby pařížských mírových jednání (říjen 1918 – prosinec 1919)*, vol. 2 (Prague: Archiv Akademie věd ČR, 1994); see also the Archiv Ministerstva zahraničních věcí (AMZV), collection Pařížský archiv, vol. 49 and 50.

115 Archiv Ministerstva zahraničních věcí (AMZV), collection Mírová konference v Paříži a reparace 1918–1938, box 55, file CbIII 1, "Minoritní smlouva s čsl. rep." ["The Minority Treaty with Czechoslovakia"]; "dopis dr. Joachima z Prahy 23.12.1919 [Letter by Dr Joachim from Prague, December 23, 1919]. Prominent lawyers, such as professor Krčmář and professor Kapras also participated in the work of the Paris delegation; see for example the Archiv Národního muzea v Praze (ANM), collection J. Kapras, box 94–96.

116 Manley O. Hudson, "The Protection of Minorities and Natives in Transferred Territories," in *What Really Happened at Paris*, ed. by Edward M. House and Charles Seymour (New York: Charles Scribner's Sons, 1921), p. 210; Christoph Gütermann, *Das Minderheitenschutzverfahren des Völkerbundes* (Berlin: Duncker & Humblot, 1979), pp. 17–19; Harold William Vazeille Temperley, *A History of the Peace Conference of Paris*, vol. 5 (London: Frowde, 1921), p. 123; Zdeněk Peška, "Otázka národnostních menšin na Pařížské mírové konferenci," *Zahraniční politika* 9 (1930): pp. 218–222.

117 David Hunter Miller, *My Diary at the Conference of Peace*, XIII ([New York]: [Printed for the author by the Appeal printing Company], 1924), pp. 74, 89, 90–95, 162–163; Štefan Osuský, "Ochrana menšín," *Prúdy* 4 (1922): pp. 12–17; Jan Rychlík, Thomas D. Marzik and Miroslav Bielik, eds., *R.W. Seton-Watson and His Relations with the Czechs and Slovaks: Documents 1906–1951*, vol. 1 (Prague: Ústav T.G. Masaryka; Martin: Matica slovenská, 1995), p. 299.

After WWI, minority obligations were imposed on many countries constituting a geographically compact bloc from the Baltic states through Central Europe (except Germany) to the Balkans. Formally, the minority obligations of individual states were largely identical, but the actual position of minorities differed in each state. Czechoslovakia entered into the Minority Treaty called "The Treaty between the Principal Allied and Associated Powers and Czechoslovakia, signed in Saint-Germain-en-Laye on 10 September 1919" (published in Czechoslovakia as No. 508/1921 Sb.).[118] Czechoslovakia committed itself to grant to all inhabitants total and complete protection of their life and freedom, the freedom to publicly or privately practise any religion, unless it violates public order rules or good morals (Article 2). Special attention was paid to citizenship in Articles 3-6 providing for its acquisition and loss. In particular, Czechoslovakia was obliged to recognize, without any formalities, the Czechoslovak citizenship of Germans, Austrians and Hungarians who had residence or the right of abode in the territory that was to become a part of Czechoslovakia under the peace treaties (Article 3).[119]

All citizens (not foreigners) were to be equal before the law, enjoying the same civil and political rights irrespective of their race, language or religion. Likewise, no differences in religion, faith or belief of the citizens should be detrimental to their enjoyment of civil or political rights regarding the access to civil service, offices, ranks or professions. Citizens had the right to use any language in private, commercial or religious settings, in the press, public speeches or public assemblies. If Czechoslovakia introduced an official language (Article 7), the citizens speaking a language other than Czech were to be reasonably entitled to use their language before courts both in writing and orally. The citizens belonging to minorities on account of their race, religion or language were entitled to be treated in compliance with the law, and equally as other citizens. In particular, they were to have the same right to establish and manage, at their own cost, charitable, religious or social institutions, as well as schools and other educational institutions, and to use their language in such institutions (Article 8).

Czechoslovakia undertook to recognize Articles 2-8 (not the whole treaty) as "fundamental laws, and no other laws, orders or official acts shall be in contravention of or inconsistent with those provisions, and any law, order or official act shall be without prejudice to those provisions." (Article 1). This commitment was rather problematic in that the most important provisions

---

118   Temperley, *A History of the Peace Conference of Paris*, pp. 144–146; Antonín Hobza, *Úvod do mezinárodního práva mírového*, vol. 1 (Prague: printed by author, 1933), pp. 374–375; Zdeněk Peška, *Československá ústava a zákony s ní souvislé*, vol. 1 (Prague: Československý kompas, 1935), pp. 86–95.
119   Harald Christian Scheu, *Standard ochrany národnostních menšin v rámci Rady Evropy*, Práce posluchačů Právnické fakulty UK 8 (Prague: Charles University, 1997), pp. 8–9.

of the Minorities Treaty were now to prevail over national laws, including the constitutional laws. The interwar Czechoslovak jurists did not know how to deal with such supremacy, and some of them contested this construction as unacceptable. This commitment was implemented in Czechoslovakia by adopting similar legal rules, mostly at the constitutional level: Sections 128–134 of the Constitutional Charter, the (constitutional) Language Act, and the (constitutional) Act on Acquiring Citizenship.

The greatest problem surrounding the protection of minorities within the League of Nations were the procedural aspects, which were regulated rather perfunctorily in the treaties, giving rise to numerous inconsistencies. The proceedings for the protection of minorities were mostly initiated by a petition, and if the members of minorities failed to address a petition (complaint) to the League of Nations, the organization usually could not provide effective protection. The petition was first examined for admissibility; for example, no requests for border changes were allowed, and all requests had to be based on minority obligations. While the petitions were mostly filed by the members of minorities, the actual consideration of the petitions was performed at the state-to-state level; thus, one of the countries had to assume responsibility for the issue, often the "mother" state of the minority. The Secretariat of the Council commenced proceedings against the state in question upon receiving a petition. The Council of the League of Nations and its Minority Committee were entitled to consider the violation of the Treaty and to demand remedy. They could submit the case to the Permanent Court of International Justice or order sanctions. The complaint was usually heard by a panel of three experts of the Minority Committee. However, it became apparent that the League of Nations was reluctant to pursue actions against allegedly violating states.[120] The underlying principle in dealing with petitions was an attempt by the League of Nations to bring peace, to persuade and to seek compromise. Often the only practical sanction available against an unyielding state was to disclose the matter to the global public. Hence, the actual rules of procedure in respect of petitions departed from the relevant legal provisions, and were adapted to the circumstances. The necessary compromises often resulted from the international situation, and less attention was paid to the actual position of minorities.[121]

During the interwar period, many petitions were filed against Czechoslovakia with the League of Nations, usually by the German and to lesser extend also by Hungarian minority. A greater part of them claimed breaches

---

120 See Pablo de Azcárate, *League of Nations and National Minorities: An Experiment*, trans. Eileen E. Brooke (Washington, DC: Carnegie Endowment for International Peace, 1945); for Czechoslovakia p. 35ff.

121 See Martin Scheuermann, *Minderheitenschutz contra Konfliktverhütung?* (Marburg: Verlag Herder-Institute, 2000), p. 38ff.

of the Minorities Treaty in connection with the Czechoslovak Constitution, the language law, the land reform, the proportion of state officials or social security laws. Minority issues were quite burdensome for the Czechoslovak foreign policy. They featured regularly on the agenda of the League of Nations' meetings, and Czechoslovakia had to defend its minority policy; in doing that, Czechoslovakia cooperated notably with other Little Entente states, i.e. Yugoslavia and Romania, which all had similar international minority obligations.[122]

---

122 *Deset let československé zahraniční politiky: činnost Ministerstva zahraničních věcí* (Prague: Nákladem Ministerstva zahraničních věcí, 1928), pp. 89–90.

2. INTER-WAR CZECHOSLOVAKIA AND LEGAL REGULATION OF THE STATUS OF MINORITIES

2.1 CZECHOSLOVAKIA IN THE 1920s

The passage of the most significant acts of the Czechoslovak state on 29 February 1920 was fundamental for the status of minorities in the first Czechoslovak Republic, but further development in the years 1926–1928 was also very important. Generally, minorities could not be particularly critical of their rights laid down in the Constitutional Charter of 1920 and related legislation; however, we should realise that the drafting and consideration of those rights was accompanied by an increase of militant, namely anti-German, nationalism within the Czech society. This resulted in the failure to honour primary Czech promises and such restrictions imposed on minorities which had not been originally planned. The influence of nationalism was also manifested later, and in legal regulation it established itself "mainly in the later freezing of the formation of regions. They were never brought into life in the Czech lands, which meant that possibilities that regional self-government provided to German collectivity as a potential basis of the German status were blocked."[123] The traditional representative of such militant nationalism was Karel Kramář and his National Democracy, while one of the opponents was the president T. G. Masaryk. He strained to use his influence to enforce concessions in favour of minorities and to compromise with them when he, for example, tried to push Germans into the government or raised the possibility of German autonomy.

Very important for the minority issue were the positions of exceptionally powerful political parties, where the effort to achieve a compromise could be found mainly on the left wing. The Czech Social Democracy in particular had been prepared for a nationalities agreement at the time of the Habsburg Monarchy, and when it assumed the leading role in the government of the Czechoslovak Republic it gave the Germans (namely the German Social Democracy) favourable offers should they join the government. The German Social Democracy, on the other hand, brought forward unacceptable requirements, such as the amendment of the Constitution along with the breaking of bonds with the Triple Entente alliance, namely with France. The

---

123 Černý et al., *Češi, Němci, odsun*, p. 230.

Czech Social Democracy, however, did not dare to go too far in order not to strengthen mainly the National Democracy in elections. Yet, probably in the beginning of August 1920, it offered to the Germans three or four ministers in the government, a more favourable educational and language policy, and German regions within an administrative reform, which was more than the Germans got in reality when they finally joined the government in 1926. This great opportunity for a compromise favourable for minorities was not to be repeated, mainly because of the disintegration of the Social Democracy and the creation of the Communist Party of Czechoslovakia (KPC – KSČ), which strongly weakened the state-constituting power of the left wing in Czechoslovakia.[124]

Reconciliation between minorities and the Czechoslovak Republic was very slow; had positive policy been implemented, the time thus spent could have been used for the improvement of the minorities' status. Yet it was at the beginning of the existence of the unstable new state when the Czechs were prepared for many concessions. But minorities almost demonstratively persisted in negative policy, which showed clearly when they entered the parliament after elections in April 1920.[125] German parties refused to recognise the Czechoslovak Republic when they officially declared: "The Czechoslovak Republic is a result of one-sided Czech will; it has unlawfully occupied German territories by use of armed violence.[126] The legal basis of the Czechoslovak Republic created by the legislative activity of the Revolutionary National Assembly was also refused by the Germans. The Hungarians, too, proclaimed that their participation in the parliament did not amount to the recognition of the state.[127]

German parties submitted demonstrative proposals for the review of laws passed by the Revolutionary National Assembly as well as a plebiscite in non-Czech regions. The Czechoslovak parties strictly refused all proposals aimed at the creation of minorities' autonomy – which was the minimum German requirement then – and consequently a possible disintegration of the state. Minorities tried to gain Slovak support for their autonomy requirements. It should be stressed that the Czechoslovak majority did not always treat minorities fairly – namely at the beginning all their proposals were refused and denied debate without any consideration.[128]

---

124 Kural, *Konflikt místo společenství?*, p. 43.
125 Klepetař, *Seit 1918*, p. 123; Kučera, *Minderheit im Nationalstaat*, p. 61ff.
126 Cited according to Peroutka, *Budování státu*, vol. 3, p. 1140.
127 For the Hungarian minority in Czechoslovakia see in more details Štefan Šutaj et al., "Ethnic minorities and their culture in Slovakia in the context of historical development of the twentieth century," in *Slovak contributions to the 19th International Congress of Historical Sciences*, ed. by Dušan Kováč (Bratislava: Veda, 2000), pp. 135–149.
128 Peroutka, *Budování státu*, vol. 3, pp. 1140–1146, 1283.

Unfortunately, nations were engaged in disputes not only over legal issues and in the parliament but also in the streets. In the summer of 1920, there were commotions caused, for example, by German conscripts resisting army service or by removing monuments commemorating the representatives of the Habsburg Monarchy. German parties also attempted to make obstructions in the Czechoslovak parliament – National Assembly. In November 1920, particularly regrettable incidents were incited by Czech nationalists when public German buildings in Prague were captured – editors' offices and mainly Stavovské divadlo (the Estates Theatre). It meant a violation of proprietary rights as well as an endangering of the freedom of the press, and it is distinctive of those unsettled times that neither public bodies nor later courts were able to intervene. The case of the Estates Theatre is typical of nationalist disputes where prestige usually plays the principal role. The theatre was an old building requiring investments and the Germans later obtained substantial compensation for it, so this shameful licence paradoxically caused financial loss to the Czechs.[129] The event resulted in deep deterioration of mutual relations, since the Germans rightfully took it as sheer manifestation of injustice.

In the following years relations between the Czech (Czechoslovak) majority and minorities improved; however, they were far from an acceptable norm, not to mention an ideal. Minorities welcomed the replacement of the care-taker government led by Jan Černý (nominated by President Masaryk after the fall of Vlastimil Tusar) by Cabinet headed by Edvard Beneš in September 1921; Beneš, as Masaryk's man, was deemed to be acceptable. But soon there were incidents during mobilisation which claimed twelve victims, and later there was a scandal in the parliament when the German deputy Alois Baeran used a stink bomb to incite a riot, and German parties were then irritated by the speed with which he was removed from his seat. A big dispute arose over the question of the range and method of the redemption of war bonds, which namely the German investors had subscribed for much more than the Czechs during the war, and further conflicts were caused by other economic issues such as expropriation of some railways belonging to the German owners.[130]

Despite the National Democracy aversion, President Masaryk offered the Germans participation in the government headed by Beneš. But Rudolf Lodgman von Aue, the nationalist leader of German parties, promoted the decline of the proposal, which was actually the last occasion when he successfully forced through his will, as the national unity of German political parties was already a relic. According to the German Legation to Prague it

---

129 Klepetař, *Seit 1918*, p. 149ff.; Kárník, *České země v éře první republiky*, vol. 1, pp. 139–140.
130 Kárník, *České země v éře první republiky*, vol. 1, pp. 222–223.

was a great mistake which gave Czech nationalism a free hand in industry and agriculture, as was shown, for example, during the implemantation of the land reform.[131] Indeed, it was contrary to the economic interests of German industrialists who wanted to influence the policy of the state and win public procurement contracts, so as early as in March 1921 they joined their crucial interest union with the Czech one. The possibility of entering the government was discussed with the German Social Democracy as well, which also declined, but not strictly. Generally, a willingness of the German parties to participate in the executive power began to manifest itself, but the problem could not be successfully solved for several years.[132]

Now we should deal in more detail with minority issues connected with public administration – that is mainly with the administrative (regional) reform under the Regions Act of 29 February 1920. Before bringing the law to life it was necessary to take a number of measures, and one of the more significant obstacles to the reform was the prevailing strong nationalist passions. Most Czechs believed the Czechoslovak Republic was a national state and were afraid that the two planned regions with a German majority would become strongholds of German irredentism. There were even fears that Czech minority populations would be oppressed in those regions. Consequently, an effort was made to create key administrative units of different sizes which would ensure that the Czechs or the Slovaks had a majority in all of them, and it appeared that one of the most convenient options was to retain the existing lands.[133]

Even the most distinguished lawyers were strongly influenced by the issue of nations in expert discussions of the problems of the reform. The strongest response was aroused by the position of Bohumil Baxa, which was adopted by the National Democracy to a degree. Also Otakar Klapka, an important representative of (district) self-government, criticised the alleged vast opportunities given to the Germans by the reform, although he conceded that the position of citizens in administration was weak and the powers of bureaucracy were wide. "Only then, after the members of other ethnic tribes loyally concede to the state, will it be possible to establish regions without fears. Only then will the time come to approximate the regional establishment to democracy."[134] Nationalist arguments against regions were varied and financial questions were raised, too, since surtax would be much higher

---

131   For Czechoslovak land reform see Lucy Elizabeth Textor, *Land Reform in Czechoslovakia* (London: Allen & Unwin, 1923), esp. p. 29ff.; Václav Beneš, "Czechoslovak democracy and its problems, 1918–1920," in Mamatey and Luža, *A History of the Czechoslovak Republic 1918–1948*, pp. 89–92.

132   Kural, *Konflikt místo společenství?*, pp. 47, 50–51.

133   Bohumil Baxa, *Zákon o zřízení župním a jeho nedostatky* (Prague: Státovědecká společnost, 1922), pp. 3–4, 16–17.

134   Otakar Klapka, *Samospráva a zřízení župní* (Prague: Nakladatelství Parlament, 1923), p. 113.

in Czech regions than in the two German ones, which was caused by the different economic power of the regions.[135] The main reason, however, was fear that the reform would lead to the creation of large administrative units with inhabitants hostile to the state because the German minority was not very loyal yet. But we cannot assume that the disapproval of the reform stemmed from national aspects only, as many factual deficiencies, e.g. financial, could be found, and the government was aware of them.[136]

The reform was carried out, after a long hesitation, as of 1 January 1923, but only in Slovakia. After the establishment of the Czechoslovak Republic, the administration in Slovakia was in a pitiable condition, and until 1923 there was only a provisional administration, which sharply contrasted with the situation in the Czech lands. Even before the regional reform was carried out in 1923, strong interventions in the administration of Slovakia had been made. A number of laws tried to transform almost all administration in Slovakia into state administration, as during Hungarian rule there had been a strong self-government, and among other things to restrict the influence of opponents of the Czechoslovak Republic. The Slovaks themselves were afraid of a too extensive self-government or autonomy, as the Hungarians or the Hungarianised Slovaks (Magyaron) could then prevail.[137]

The Hungarians made up a substantial share of the population of Slovakia and their influence was even bigger thanks to the favouritism they had enjoyed under the previous regime. They defied the Czechoslovak Republic and new measures – including administrative ones – aroused strong opposition from them. The Hungarians, as well as the Germans, were unable to forget about their former hegemony and they tried to change the situation. One of the means of doing so was to complain at international forums, where they criticised, among other things, the system of Czechoslovak administration which allegedly did not take into account specific features of Slovakia, tried to make all decisions in the centre, and oppressed them in general. During the implementation of the law on regions in Slovakia many of its deficiencies came to full light. It became evident how weak the self-government was and how many of its powers were only on paper.[138]

One of the problems of the administrative reform consisted of the question of Sub-Carpathian Ruthenia, as it was not clear whether the Regions Law of 1920 applied to it, and another disputable issue was how the reform could

---

135   Ibid., pp. 69–70.
136   Irena Malá, ed., *Z protokolů schůzí 5. československé vlády (Benešovy) 1921–1922* (Prague: Státní ústřední archiv v Praze, 1989), p. 9.
137   Natália Krajčovičová, "Slovakia in Czechoslovakia, 1918–1938," in Teich, Kováč and Brown, *Slovakia in History*, p. 137ff.
138   Jaroslav Houser and Valentin Urfus, "Politická správa na Slovensku za buržoasní předmnichovské republiky," *Historický časopis* 9 no. 2 (1961): pp. 278–282.

comply with the previously uncompleted autonomy which Czechoslovakia had agreed to perform according to the MinorityTreaty of St. Germain. Interest in Sub-Carpathian Ruthenia was manifested at an international level, too. For example in 1921 Dr. Štefan Osuský, the Czechoslovak Envoy to Paris, spoke about the minorities problem in Czechoslovakia during the meeting of the League of Nations "and relying, among other things, on the documents regarding Sub-Carpathian Ruthenia and comparing the administration of that territory under the Hungarian and Czechoslovak regimes, as well as on the Constitutional Charter, he was able to present to the international forum an image of Czechoslovakia in the brightest colours and features."[139] It was a response to the complaint sent to the League of Nations by the Hungarians (and not by the Ruthenians) where they voiced their protest against the deferral of autonomy. The Czechoslovak Republic answered back, referring to the catastrophic backwardness of the region that made it impossible to introduce autonomy, and the League of Nations expressed its provisional consent to that.[140]

It appears that in spite of real problems, autonomy could have been carried out had the Czechoslovak government made an active effort, but it probably preferred political stability in the region to strict compliance with its international obligations. Representative bodies in Sub-Carpathian Ruthenia were first established as late as in 1923. Efforts to introduce a centralised system of public administration like in the rest of Czechoslovakia aroused considerable resistance from the people. In 1927 the competing parties actually got together and petitioned the government, demanding the establishment of a parliament commission for the preparation of elections and a rapid calling of an assembly (Regional Diet), as well as the postponement of the final determination of Slovak-Ruthenian borders after the nationalities plebiscite in Eastern Slovakia would be organised. Despite these protests, Sub-Carpathian Ruthenia finally became one of the lands of the Czechoslovak Republic under the so-called Organisation Act (Act No. 125/1927 Sb.). The fact that authorities were not willing to provide the promised autonomy, to convene the local assembly as well as the influx of Czech officials and their interference with edifying and church activities, caused the animosity of the local people.[141]

Let us now get back to the general issues of minorities in the Czechoslovak Republic – namely to the most important German minority. The important legal regulation which aroused considerable resistance in minorities was the Protection of the Republic Act of 1923 (Act No. 50/1923 Sb.) , adopted

---

139 *Sborník zahraniční politiky*, vol. 2 (Prague: Ministerstvo Zahraničních věcí, 1921), pp. 359 and 416.
140 Peter Švorc, "Zápas o Podkarpatskú Rus v 20. rokoch 20. storočia na pôde Spoločnosti národov," in *Evropa mezi Německem a Ruskem* (Prague: Historický ústav AV ČR, 2000), p. 273ff.
141 Magocsi, "Utváření národní identity," pp. 119–120.

in reaction to some terrorist acts both in Czechoslovakia and abroad. Consequently the government and the President were compelled to make this step, although they had been resisting it for a long time. The Act was considered in February and March 1923 and passed, but it was met by "vigorous protests and demonstrations from those at whom it was aimed: revolutionary left wing, national minorities and actually also members of Hlinka's Slovak People's Party."[142] Minorities' representatives described the law as a threat to democracy, and it should be noted that their criticism was justified to a certain degree, as the penalisation of sedition acts was regulated in a way that was inconceivable in democratic states. It made it possible to abuse the regulation; however, this never occurred.

Antagonism among nations gradually weakened in the following years and in 1924 German participation in the government was seriously discussed again, but many questions remained to be resolved. For example, in September 1924 German deputies protested and finally even boycotted the session where the Act regulating the redemption of war bonds was considered. The question of language used in state bodies and offices was also very sensitive, because the majority of German officials in public administration, self-government, railways, post offices, and in other positions did not have a command of the state, i.e. Czech language. In the years 1923–1924 mass examinations in the Czech language were organised as a requirement for retaining jobs. However, German parties often rightfully protested against the abuse of such exams for the purpose of settling political scores.[143]

Preparedness for principal negotiations among nations was relatively small in those days, as elections were approaching, and such contacts may have been perceived negatively by the electorate. The key problem consisted of the complicated preparations of implementing legislation for the Language Act of 1920, when the Czech nationalist press often wildly attacked the allegedly big concessions made to the Germans, and consequently the government was not willing to tackle such a sensitive issue.[144] Originally, in 1920, it was thought that the Governmental Order would be quickly enacted, but those visions failed. But the Language Act created only a framework and the insufficient legal regulation resulted in many serious inconsistencies in the language practice among districts, which the Germans, among others, criticised and described as a persecution: "Many failures in the resolution of nationalities' issues are to be blamed on frequently insufficient laws and orders, as a result of which it is very difficult for district political administrations to

---

142 Antonín Klimek, *Velké dějiny zemí Koruny české*, vol. 13 (Prague: Paseka, 2000), p. 384.
143 Kárník, *České země v éře první republiky*, vol. 1, pp. 370–371; Kučera, *Minderheit im Nationalstaat*, pp. 246–297.
144 Kučera, *Minderheit im Nationalstaat*, pp. 73–86.

make precise decisions." "The fact that an implementing order for Language Act has not yet been passed causes enormous difficulties and district political administrations often do not know what to do."[145] Hence, the elections of 15 November 1925 were of utmost importance for minorities because the new parliament and government completed the legal status of minorities during the first republic. German negativism as well as the Czech nationalist National Democracy totally lost in the election, which enabled the minorities – mainly the Germans – to join the Czechoslovak government, where they remained almost until the end of the First Czechoslovak Republic in 1938.[146]

At the beginning of the new parliament session, German deputies submitted remarkable proposals for the regulation of education on the basis of national self-government. In fact, they meant a personal autonomy where one of the projects stated, among other things, that: "1. Individual nations in the Czechoslovak Republic shall be constituted as bodies qualified for having rights. 2. The national register shall serve as a basis for membership in a nation."[147] However, these proposals aimed at widening the rights of minorities were rejected and legal rules adopted from 1926–1928 rather restricted the rights of minorities.

One of the most significant legal rules governing the status of minorities was the Government Language Order of 1926. The unstable political situation of the Czechoslovak Republic had a negative impact on its enactment. The collapse of the so-called red-green coalition (created mainly by Social Democrats and Agrarians) in 1920 actually marked the end of relatively friendly Czech approaches to minorities, because the weakness of government coalitions and concerns over strengthening the role of the nationalist National Democracy hampered making concessions, as well as the creation of a consistent government conception of nationalities' policy. In the following years and, in fact, to the end of the First Czechoslovak Republic, "individual steps in the nationalities' policy resulted from current political constellations and compensatory deals among parties, where nationalities/political aspects were clearly sacrificed for social/political priorities."[148]

This situation reflected also in the implementing Governmental Order for the Language Act of 1920, the passage of which had been delayed for six years. According to the first version from the summer of 1920, the order permitted, for example, the use of minority languages in official internal dealings, while later versions completely abandoned this idea. In its final wording of 1926, the Language Order represented a significant narrowing of the conception of

---

145   Národní archiv v Praze (NA), collection Ministerstvo vnitra, stará registratura (MV), box 502, file 20.
146   See for example Kárník, *České země v éře první republiky*, vol. 1, p. 376ff.
147   Peška, *Kulturní samospráva národních menšin*, p. 73.
148   Kučera, "Koncepce národního státu Čechů a Slováků," p. 606.

the Language Act of 1920. The Language Act permitted interpretation favourable to minorities, which had been the original intention of the government at the beginning of the Czechoslovak Republic, but also an unfavourable interpretation, which was the final result. Yet this issue lay in the power of the government only, since the law set more or less just a framework.[149] Members of minorities presented legal arguments, too, claiming that a constitutional Language Act should be followed by implementing legislation, and only then could the government issue its order. So they required that the parliament, now including minorities, could decide the matter and the executive, which could rightfully be expected to be always subject to key Czech interests, should be strongly restricted in its independent decision making.

The process of enactment of the Governmental Order was symptomatic, too, as the Prime Minister, Antonín Švehla, likely forced it because the Germans were to join the government soon and the approval of a step so unfavourable for minorities would hardly be conceivable then. Other similar interferences occurred, such as the promotion of the Czechs among the official workforce, favouring the Czechs in land reform, etc. Social Democratic ministers refused to sign the Order and the Supreme Administrative Court found some of the provisions to be unconstitutional. The Germans sharply protested and claimed that the order was contrary to the Minorities Treaty of St. Germain. They also mentioned Švehla's promise that the order would be debated in the constitutional committee of the Czechoslovak National Assembly before its passage. There were demonstrations and bloody clashes in the border areas, probably the hardest filibustering in the Czechoslovak parliament in the interwar period, and, after a long time, the German camp started to act in unity again.[150]

This Germans' militant stance did not last long, and on the contrary, German parties soon joined the Czechoslovak government. It stemmed from the complicated political situation of those days, when the Czech right wing needed support for the law on grain tariffs, which had been refused by the left wing. Thanks to the extraordinary political intelligence of Švehla, the leader of the Agrarian Party, in the new right wing government two German parties met the National Democrats who used to declare that if the Germans ever joined the government, they would start a revolution! The Germans obtained two Departments (public works and justice); however, it was not an attempt at achieving a Czech-German balance, but rather a pure purpose-created coalition. Yet the German share in the government of the Czechoslovak state, where they represented a quarter of the population, was quite rightful and just, and it is possible "to talk about a turnaround which

---

149 Kučera, *Minderheit im Nationalstaat*, pp. 87–97.
150 On policy of "negativism" see Beneš and Kural, *Facing history*, pp. 80– 83.

might even be described as historic – after dozens of years of a split during the Habsburg Monarchy and in the Czechoslovak state, the Czechs and the Sudeten Germans once again find a common language and a table where they sit to administer state matters."[151] President Masaryk acclaimed the German participation in the government and called it his most beautiful day since the foundation of the Czechoslovak Republic.

The results of German participation in the government, however, were by no means brilliant for the minorities.[152] If perhaps the Germans had been promised autonomy when they were enticed into the coalition, such a promise was forgotten very quickly. On the contrary, the status of minorities was weakened namely in the administrative reform of 1927. For their approval of very unpleasant measures, German activist parties were rewarded by political deals typical of the First Czechoslovak Republic. For example, the Germans obtained increased state funding for German schooling and they coerced negotiations to remedy encroachments on the Germans in state administration, police, and army. In spite of these partial advantages it was "actually surprising that the newly born government activism even managed to survive this hit below the belt."[153]

An important question relating to the status of minorities was administrative reform. When the establishment of regions – never accomplished in the Czech lands – was abolished, the lands were retained and mainly democratic principles of territorial self-government were restricted. The reform was not designed directly against minorities, although the national issue influenced it strongly, but minorities could exert their influence in territorial self-government, and particularly the Germans perceived it as a seed of autonomous institutions. However, now the powers of state bodies in relation to self-governance increased, which resulted in the growing influence of Czech bureaucracy, which subsequently clearly prevailed.[154]

During the adoption of the Regions Act in 1920, the constitutional committee of the Revolutionary National Assembly agreed with the government that the reform should be implemented within five years. Later, however, the ideas of the National Democracy, which officially resolved that it would not admit the implementation of the Regions Act and primarily the creation of two German regions, were gaining more and more support. In the end, the same approach was supported by the pivotal Agrarian Party, although national arguments did not play an important role for it.[155]

---

151   Kural, *Konflikt místo společenství?*, p. 66.
152   Klepetař, *Der Sprachenkampf in den Sudetenländern*, p. 136ff.
153   Ibid., p. 69.
154   César and Černý, *Politika německých buržoazních stran*, pp. 389–390; Kural, *Konflikt místo společenství?*, pp. 68–69.
155   Peroutka, *Budování státu*, vol. 3, pp. 1021–1022.

In 1926, the new government worked out a draft of a Bill on the organisation of political administration and opened political negotiations. The most significant points were the unification of administration within the Czechoslovak Republic, the cancellation of regions and re-introduction of lands, subjecting self-government in districts and lands to the state and thus final removal of duality, strengthening of police and penal competences of administrative bodies, and last but not least, strengthening the position of the government and bureaucracy. This so-called Organisation Act was later adopted and promulgated as Act No. 125/1927 Sb. The main inventors of the Act were National Democrats, for whom its enactment meant the victory in a long lasting fight against the establishment of regions. "So it certainly was not a coincidence that the reporter in the House of Deputies was Karel Kramář as one of the co-authors of the Act, which was consequently sometimes referred to as the so-called 'Kramář Act'."[156]

Political negotiations concerning the Organisation Act were rather difficult, as the reform faced the resistance of many political parties, including coalition parties. All German parties, including government parties, opposed the law, too, since it was not favourable for this minority: it brought the non-existence of two German regions as well as the liquidation of Silesia with its German-Polish majority. While non-government parties could attack the reform virulently, German activist parties found themselves in a difficult situation, because with regard to their partners in the government coalition they had to agree with the prepared reform, but at the same time it was necessary to take heed of their concerned followers and not to support it openly.[157] The main role in the enforcement of the reform played the attitude of Agrarians who supported the regions' reform until 1926, when negotiations on the new government had begun and the parties, with which they wanted to make the coalition, maintained a negative attitude towards regions (National Democrats, members of the People's Party, and Hlinka's Slovak People's Party). Later, support for the Organisation Act was gained also from other coalition parties, mainly German, which found their participation in the government more important than an issue of administration[158], yet parliamentary debates were not spared difficulties when there were loud obstructions and even brawls.

Unlike the Regions Act of 1920, which meant a serious intervention in the organisation of the administration, the new Act, formally passed as its amendment, was rather a set of measures regulating current conditions

---

156 Karel Schelle, "Příprava zákona o organizaci politické správy z roku 1927," in *Pocta prof. JUDr. Karlu Malému, DrSc., k 65. narozeninám*, ed. by Ladislav Soukup (Prague: Karolinum Press, 1995), p. 297.
157 César and Černý, *Politika německých buržoazních stran*, pp. 390–392.
158 Kural, *Konflikt místo společenství?*, p. 68ff.

surviving (in the Czech lands) from the time of the Habsburg Monarchy. Namely the position of citizens in administration was weakened dramatically.[159] Proposals aimed at enforcing the idea of regions (zhupas), either to enable the resolution of the national question or because of too large territories of lands, weren thus not successful in the period of the First Czechoslovak Republic.

An important legal regulation related to the status of minorities was the Government Regulation of 1928 governing the use of languages in land and district councils, which introduced in districts with a high share of the minority population (over 75 per cent) quite an equal position for both the minority and the state language; however, it unfortunately did not serve as a basis for a more substantial regulation of language law.[160] Moreover, this equality applied only in some matters.[161] This Regulation was the last one which strongly affected the legal status of minorities; it was thus stabilised and did not change much until the end of the First Czechoslovak Republic with the exception of, for example, the unimpressive development of case law of the Supreme Administrative Court. Some attempts occurred in 1935–1938 period of crises, but they failed to be implemented in practice, as we will explore in more details in the following part of the book.

Among the most important initiatives in the 1920s was that of the President in the National Assembly on the 10th anniversary of the establishment of independent Czechoslovakia. Masaryk recommended changes to the Constitutional Charter of 1920 and to other laws enacted at the beginning of the Czechoslovak Republic, which in his opinion had been hastily made, were vague, and were full of mistakes, which were not unjustified claims. Masaryk then recommended the establishment of autonomy, which he understood principally as vast self-government. However, the proposal was not carried out.[162] Leading Czech political parties were convinced that after the ten years of existence of the Czechoslovak Republic, the legal status of minorities was stable, as the main legal regulations were created in 1918–1920 and then also in 1926–1928. Although changes were considered many times, in the political situation of the First Czechoslovak Republic – fragmented as regards nationalities as well as political parties – it was hardly possible to implement them, because it had not been possible to reach a wide enough consensus. The situation, where the majority was content and decent conditions were provided for the minorities, lasted to the end of the 1930s; then pressure coming rather

---

159 Jiří Hoetzel, *Nová organisace politické správy* (Prague: Spolek československých právníků Všehrd, [1927]), pp. 8, 13–19, 27.
160 Kučera, "Koncepce národního státu Čechů a Slováků," p. 607.
161 Zdeněk Peška, *Národní menšiny a Československo* (Bratislava: Právnická fakulta University Komenského, 1932), pp. 166–167.
162 Kural, *Konflikt místo společenství?*, pp. 70–71.

from abroad started the process of changes, which, however, resulted in the disintegration of independent Czechoslovakia.

2.2 STATISTICS ON MINORITIES IN THE CZECHOSLOVAK REPUBLIC

Before embarking on legal regulation it is necessary to explore the statistics, their significance, and underlying legal aspects. The total number of members of (national) minorities in Czechoslovakia was crucial for their status and the influence they exercised on the state. The possibility of using one's own language in communication with public authorities, in schools, and in many other situations was conditional on the territorial distribution of minorities. The question of the numbers of minority members appears simple, but in practical terms it was sometimes very complicated, both with regard to individuals and to entire groups. The statistics of minorities must be examined together with many related issues, such as national affiliation and assimilation. The distribution of minorities in the country should also be outlined, in particular with regard to potential alterations of state borders or the creation of closed single-nation administrative units. In many countries minority statistics were massively manipulated, which today seems rather absurd. Czechoslovakia successfully avoided these pitfalls, although it did not always proceed entirely objectively either. The key issue, which has been raising heated discussions since the times of the First Czechoslovak Republic up until now, is the question of the decrease of minority members – both in relative and absolute terms (which was quite common, though, in Central and Eastern Europe in the interwar period) – and the extent to which this was due to state policy.

First it is necessary to briefly address a few theoretical issues, because even seemingly very abstract matters played out substantially in the interwar period. For example the existence of the Jewish nation was significant, as the recognition of the Jewish nation (i.e. the possibility to declare Jewish nationality during the census) in Czechoslovakia, unlike in the Habsburg Monarchy, weakened the position of the German minority. At the time of the First Czechoslovak Republic this ostensibly abstract theory was seen to have impacted practical matters (E. Rádl, J. Slavík, Z. Nejedlý, T.G. Masaryk, Z. Fierlinger etc.), which was recognized even by jurists (E. Sobota, Z. Peška).

When using such words as nation, minority, etc. it is necessary to realise that there is no widely recognised accurate definition of these notions, and various authors approach those notions in very different ways. From among various definitions of a nation we must distinguish notably an objective approach (nationality is determined by objective features – language, ethnicity, etc.) and a subjective approach (what is decisive is a personal, subjective feeling).[163] Similarly, the definition of a minority, the classification of minorities, etc. are currently covered by extensive scholarly literature.[164]

At the time of the First Czechoslovak Republic a few crucial theoretical issues emerged, stirring up many heated debates. One of the most important issues was the very existence of the ruling Czechoslovak nation.[165] While some people clearly meant a single nation, others interpreted this term – which was used in legislation and in the Constitutional Charter of 1920 (Preamble stated: "We, the Czechoslovak nation, seeking to reinforce the perfect unity of the nation . . .")[166] – only as an expression of equality of the Czechs and Slovaks, i.e. two nations.[167] Such seemingly theoretical issues could be easily used or abused in politics, even on an international level, because it was naturally quite crucial what proportion of the Czechoslovak population was taken up by the ruling nation. World politics offered rather curious cases too. For example during the negotiations of the Peace Treaty of Trianon, the Hungarians argued that the Slovaks were divided into two races, a Western and an Eastern race, which had a distinct language and a way of life.[168]

The crucial question of the First Czechoslovak Republic was whether the very numerous Germans could be at all regarded as a minority in Czechoslovakia. It was a question of whether this sizeable group, which had previously enjoyed a dominant position, could be downgraded to an inferior position and after the foundation of the Czechoslovak Republic be possibly restricted in their use of language before public authorities. In this connection, the possibility to establish "state of nations" or "state of nationalities" were frequently discussed, but these concepts were defined in various different ways. From the legal point of view (for example according to leading Czech expert Emil Sobota) a state of nations was one whose legal system preferred a particular nation, while a state of nationalities maintained equality of all nations. In Czechoslovakia there were both elements of equality and provisions about the preferred position of the Czechoslovak nation (and of the Ruthenian nation in Sub-Carpathian Ruthenia), and the minorities were granted minimum legal standards – the national and nationality approach were said to be overlapping.[169]

---

163   See for example Eric J. Hobsbawm, *Nations and Nationalism since 1780: Programme, Myth, Reality*, 2nd ed. (Cambridge: Cambridge University Press, 2012), esp. pp. 8–14.
164   See for example Miroslav Hroch, *V národním zájmu* (Prague: Nakladatelství Lidové noviny, 1999), p. 141ff.
165   For the Slovak interpretations see Krajčovičová, "Slovakia in Czechoslovakia, 1918–1938," p. 139ff.
166   For the text of the Constitution of 1920 in English see *Constitution of the Czechoslovak Republic*, introduction by Jiří Hoetzel and V. Joachim (Prague: Orbis, 1920).
167   Emil Sobota, *Republika národní či národnostní?* (Prague: Čin, 1929), p. 13.
168   Jaromír Korčák, *Geopolitické základy Československa* (Prague: Orbis, 1938), p. 67.
169   Sobota, *Republika národní či národnostní?*, pp. 11–12; Leo Epstein, *Der nationale Minderheitenschutz als internationales Rechtproblem* (Berlin: Engelmann, 1922), p. 8.

After the brief outline of the related issues we can now embark on the basis for minority statistics – the census of population. Traditionally, this ostensibly objective collection of data was also affected by politics and Central Europe was not the exception.[170] In the 19th century questions were raised at international statistical congresses as to whether it was at all appropriate to ask about a language during a census of population. In addition, many countries were dealing with a political problem concerning the question to what extent a national affiliation was determined by a language. During the Austria-Hungary the question about the language of intercourse was asked in the census of population in Austria, while in Hungary the relevant question centred on the mother tongue. The first reliable ethnicity statistics for the western part of the Habsburg Monarchy were compiled by the Austrian government during the census of population in 1880.[171]

While during the census in 1869 no box for language and nationality was provided, in the census of 1880 the language of intercourse was introduced. Although such language could not adequately show one's ethnic identity, the politicians, demographers and the public accepted the information provided about the language of intercourse as a declaration of one's national affiliation. It was important that only one language could be stated, even though bilingualism was quite common back then. Major nationalist disputes were said to have occurred in connection with the declaration of one's language in the census.[172] In the Czech borderland regions German employers and municipalities pressured local Czech minorities, and their numbers in the official statistics were therefore (according to the Czech side) significantly lower than in reality. As a result, in 1900 and 1910 Czech associations carried out a private census of Czechs living in municipalities controlled by Germans. After the establishment of Czechoslovakia the possible ways of replacing the Austrian concept of language of intercourse were debated and disputed in the Committee of the State Statistical Council (in which Germans were also represented, e.g. professor of German University in Prague Heinrich Rauchberg).[173] Finally it was in principle agreed that each person was to declare his or her national affiliation himself/herself – which was in line with the subjective approach as opposed to the objective approach that had been pursued in the Habsburg Monarchy. This approach was strongly opposed by the Germans, who (quite understandably) feared that their position would be weakened once the Jewish

---

170 See for example Zeman, *The Making and Breaking of Communist Europe*, pp. 27–36.
171 Ibid.; see also G. B. Cohen, *Politics of Ethnic Survival*, pp. 65–68.
172 Ibid., esp. p. 69ff.
173 Professor Heinrich Rauchberg dealt with the statistical question of Czech-German relations for a long time and he is author of important book entitled *Der nationale Besitzstand in Böhmen* published already in 1905.

nationality had been recognised (which was not the case in the Habsburg Monarchy).[174]

In reality, problems occurred notably in situations where regulations made it possible to objectively determine nationality to a certain extent, which was generally done in favour of the ruling nation. The relevant law was framework Act No. 256/ 1920 Sb, of 8 April, implemented by Governmental Order No. 592/ 1920 Sb. of 30 October. In 1930 changes were introduced by Act No. 47/1927 Sb. on population census and Governmental Order No. 86/1930 Sb. on population census.[175] Under Section 20 (1) of Order No. 592/1920 Sb. nationality was to be determined with great care and according to the reality. A citizen's own declaration could be altered by the census commissioner (Section 20 (3)) if it was apparently false, and if the citizen disagreed it was up to the superior political office to make a final decision. This provision speaks for the objective approach as it stipulates that a particular fact may be determined in an official manner, even against the citizen's will. That was criticised for example by prominent jurist Emil Sobota, who pointed out that an objectively ascertainable fact such as nationality should be clearly defined and spelled out. The directions for the completion of the census form described nationality as "tribal affiliation," which, however, provided little explanation, and nationality was not defined by the legislation. There were only regulations essentially stating what nationality was not – nationality could not be defined by religion, race or language.[176]

According to the population census of 15 February 1921, the composition of the population of Czechoslovakia was as follows: 65.5% Czechoslovaks (out of that approx. 14.5% Slovaks), 23.3% Germans, 5.6% Hungarians, 3.4% Ruthenians and Russians, 1.3% Jews (problematic statistics), 0.5% Poles. The population census of February 1921 was challenging. For example, representatives of both the ruling nation and minorities organised trips, visits, and similar events in order to increase the share of their ethnic group in particular municipalities. There were local riots and complex legal disputes over the nationality of certain individuals, which in some cases had to be resolved by the Supreme Administrative Court. The persons concerned were mostly native Czechs who had been living in a German environment for a long time and declared German nationality, but the census commissioners asserted

---

174 Antonín Boháč, *Národnostní mapa republiky československé* (Prague: Národopisná spol. československá, 1926), pp. 9, 15–16; Peška, *Národní menšiny a Československo*, pp. 131–135; Jaroslav Bubeník and Jiří Křesťan, "Zjišťování národnosti jako problém statistický a politický," *Paginae historiae* 3 (1995), pp. 127, 137–138; Hassinger, *Die Tschechoslowakei*, p. 134ff.

175 Jaroslav Bubeník and Jiří Křesťan, "Národnost a sčítání lidu: k historickým souvislostem polemiky mezi Antonínem Boháčem a Emanuelem Rádlem," *Historická demografie* 19 (1995), pp. 120–121.

176 Sobota, *Republika národní či národnostní?*, pp. 7–10.

Czech nationality in their case. In Slovakia there were Slovaks claiming to be Hungarians (according to the state authorities). Such mild forms of favouritism towards the ruling nation greatly irritated the minorities which had been used to being favoured during the Habsburg Monarchy. The census was therefore strongly opposed in Parliament by the Germans and Hungarians and the German representatives sent a memorandum to the League of Nations claiming duress.[177] From the European perspective, however, the results of the census in the First Czechoslovak Republic could be in general regarded as relatively objective.[178]

The irritation of minorities after the census of 1921 was primarily caused by the finding that their numbers had considerably decreased compared to 1910. Although other new states experienced similar developments, it could appear that this fact is a valid argument against the minority policy and law of the First Czechoslovak Republic. Therefore, at least the situation of the Germans should be explained in more detail. The decrease in the number of minority members was in no way caused by manipulated statistics or pressure during the census. While it is possible or even probable that statistics were manipulated – which happened in almost all so-called successor states and in many other states to a very large extent – in Czechoslovakia such interventions were only marginal.[179]

The decrease in the numbers of minority members was significant, e.g. the number of Germans in the Czech lands decreased by 517–519,000 between 1910 and 1921, falling to 2,973,000, which represented a decrease from 34.95% to 30.28%. The real causes of the decrease were primarily much greater war casualties of the Sudeten Germans (130,000) compared to the Czechs. Another cause was the move of around 43,000 Jews from the German nationality to the Jewish nationality and 54,000 Germans moved to the category of foreign nationals. Another important factor, in particular from the long term perspective, was a lower birth rate of Sudeten Germans. Also, the question about the language of intercourse was not included in the census, which eliminated certain former advantages of the German language which was used in the course of employment by some non-Germans. In other words, minorities lost some of their former privileges rather than being discriminated against. Germans opposed the statistics in Czechoslovakia, claiming that a higher number of voters voted for German parties using secret ballot than the number of Germans suggested in the census (32.48% as opposed to 30.28%). The Czech

---

177   Boháč, *Národnostní mapa*, p. 17.

178   Bubeník and Křesťan, "Národnost a sčítání lidu," pp. 130–131.

179   Václav Kural, "Lidský potenciál sudetských Němců a vznik Československa," *Slezský sborník = Acta Silesiaca* 89, no. 2 (1991): pp. 94–96.

authors, however, emphasise an older age structure of the Germans as the main cause, with a higher number of voters over 21 years.[180]

Other minorities experienced a certain decrease between 1910 and 1921 as well. Particularly interesting was the development of the Poles, whose number was reduced to 53.4% compared to 1910. In Moravia the decrease represented 86.06% (in absolute terms 12,844), in the Teschen (Těšín-Cieszyn) district 49.81% (68,824) – the number of Czechs was increased by 56.92% (in absolute terms 64,431).[181] Thus, major changes occurred on the Czech-Polish ethnic border. The Polish expanded in the second half of the 19th century, but the expansion was over still during the Habsburg Monarchy, and the Czechs started consolidating their position as evidenced by the population census of 1910. The foundation of Czechoslovakia obviously increased assimilatory powers of the Czech environment: a Polish worker from Galicia willingly accepted the Czech language as a symbol of a higher culture. Numerous Slonzaken *(TN: Šlonzáci: inhabitants of the Ciezsyn district with their own distinct culture and language)* turned to the Czechs and, in addition, many Polish immigrants from Galicia (formerly part of unitary Cisleithania) failed to obtain citizenship.[182]

In connection with the radical change of the Polish-Czech ethnic border, the problem of assimilation potential moved to the forefront, concerning also other minorities and isolated groups of the ruling nation in the minority territory. It is a very complicated issue where the success of the assimilation policy (which was not implemented in Czechoslovakia) is conditional on many factors – primarily on "national mobilisation," the attitude of the parent nation, and the difference in the level of cultural development of the minority and majority. If the minority is on a higher cultural level, or presumably on a higher level, then assimilation can hardly be successful.[183] As the Germans and Hungarians generally looked down on the Czechs and Slovaks, they would only rarely break away from these formerly ruling "lordly" nations. The exceptions were persons ambivalent as to their nationality or a few German "islands" in an overwhelmingly Czech environment. Moreover, unlike some democratic countries (e.g. France), Czechoslovakia did not pursue an assimilation policy.

However, for example in the initial period of the state's existence, an idea emerged to deal with the nationality challenges by way of administrative measures. The so-called Regions Reform of 1920 *(TN: župní reforma, Zhupa*

---

180   Kural, *Konflikt místo společenství?*, pp. 85–87.
181   Ibid., p. 219; Tadeusz Siwek, Stanisław Zahradnik and Józef Szymeczek, *Polská národní menšina v Československu 1945–1954* (Prague: Ústav pro soudobé dějiny AV ČR, 2001), p. 11.
182   Boháč, *Národnostní mapa*, pp. 77–78; Dan Gawrecki, "Polská menšina v Československu 1918–1938," in Valenta, Voráček and Harna, *Československo 1918–1938*, pp. 620–628.
183   See for example Hroch, *V národním zájmu*, p. 149ff.

Reform) which was designed to introduce a radical administrative reform and thus substantially modify the whole state's organisation (but was never implemented), was often accompanied by chauvinist opinions instead of reasonable arguments. The plans to divide Czechoslovakia into new administrative units (regions – *zhupas*) were substantiated by national interests and concerns about the weakening position of one's own nation: "In this way our Czech minorities in the Karlsbad (Karlovy Vary) and Česká Lípa regions will disappear, to be replaced with a nest of irredentists, but if we place the Germans into Czech regions, we will tear them apart."[184] Some ideas about the consequences of territorial re-organisation were rather humorous: "The town of Jihlava will be completely wiped out from the Czech region and in 20 years the Jihlava region will be assimilated beyond recognition."[185]

Nowadays, when miniature, almost vanished communities such as the Cornish people are experiencing a revival in Europe, it is difficult to understand that such ideas appeared in the interwar period. But back then the ideas about assimilation of large ethnic groups (e.g. of the whole Czech nation) were quite commonplace. During WWII, for example, the Czechoslovak Government-in-Exile was considering the expulsion of the majority of Germans while retaining approximately one million Germans to be assimilated. The postwar "re-slovakisation" (where the majority of Hungarians declared Slovak nationality out of fear of expulsion or discrimination) showed how realistic such ideas were. Once the situation was stable again an overwhelming majority of them turned back to their original nationality.[186] Irrational ideas and concerns about the fate of the Czech nation or, on the other hand, about the fate of minorities resonated with authors who were otherwise quite objective. Even the slightly reinforced position of a competitor nation or essentially insignificant misunderstandings could grow to become insurmountable conflicts. It is a lack of objectivity which in many cases was and still is crucial in minority disputes.

It is necessary now to discuss some minorities in Czechoslovakia individually. In the case of the German minority, particular attention should be paid to its territorial distribution. Although the Germans in Czechoslovakia represented one of the largest European minorities, according to the Czech authors they could not create a separate, unitary territory because their distribution was fragmented, as they lived in many different parts. In some cases they lived in little pockets surrounded by the state nation. Disputes over the borders and territorial organisation of the Czech lands were, together

---

184 This opinion was voiced during the debate on the Constitution and other major laws at the Constitutional Committee of the National Assembly, APP, RNA collection, box 33, file 1277, "153th meeting of the Constitutional Assembly on February 19, 1920, morning," p. 36.
185 Ibid., p. 35.
186 Karel Kaplan, *Pravda o Československu 1945–1948* (Prague: Panorama, 1990), pp. 116–118, 128–129, 133.

with language issues, some of the most important minority problems of the First Republic. According to the voices from the Czech side, after the annexation of the Sudeten Germans to Germany, a meaningless, indefensible border would have been created and soon the whole country would have become part of the German Empire. Moreover, between the Czech and German regions there were strong economic, transport and family ties. For example, prominent expert Emil Sobota claimed: "they are so interwoven that they cannot be separated nor granted autonomy."[187] Such an unequivocal opinion by an objective author was not unusual at that time. A Czech geopolitician curiously addressed concerns about an enclosed German territory or autonomy in the Czech lands by referring to overpopulation and non-existing colonies, which aroused a fanatic interest even in small territories, often in single villages. "The Czechs hate the idea that the territories where Germans live would constitute a special part of the Czech lands, a separate property. This Czech tenacity is incomprehensible for Frenchmen, Englishmen or Italians; only a German would understand."[188]

In the interwar period the Czech nation progressively expanded into some formerly German regions, which was largely a natural process (that had started as early as in the Habsburg Monarchy) rather than an outcome of the state policy. The most significant Czech expansion was seen in the region between Chomutov and Ústí nad Labem. Despite this process and the position of the state nation it was still possible to identify Czech communities with a pro-German attitude – e.g. the Hlučín region where the population (the so-called "Moravci") spoke Czech but, for instance in 1925 elections, two thirds of the population voted for German parties, and during censuses many declared German nationality.[189]

Gradual and very slow assimilation took place in the case of German "islands" and minorities in the Czech territory. During the Habsburg Monarchy the Germans controlled many mixed municipalities due to undemocratic franchise, but the changes to the laws on elections to the municipal self-government of 1919 (Act No. 75/1919 Sb.) brought about a new situation, which affected the choice of nationality declared by people. Previously, Czech urban inhabitants had been temporarily denationalised, which was redressed during the 19th century, but in Moravia and Silesia denationalisation lasted much longer, as the large Jewish minorities were strongly pro-German. The new electoral procedure as well as recognition of the Jewish nationality caused rather remarkable changes in many cities. For example in Hodonín (in 1900 a largely German town according to the statistics) the German population

---

187 Sobota, *Národnostní autonomie v Československu?*, pp. 11, 8–10.
188 Korčák, *Geopolitické základy Československa*, p. 123.
189 Boháč, *Národnostní mapa*, pp. 19–20, 30, 38ff., p. 76.

represented only 8% in 1921 (and the Jewish approximately 4%). A similar situation could be observed in Frýdek.[190] Generally, this largely natural process of the gradual decline of the German positions, which started in the 19th century and was apparent, *inter alia*, in the economic sphere, provoked a defensive response from the Germans (e.g. seeking autonomy or secession), preventing a peaceful resolution of the problems in the Czech lands.

The Hungarian minority should also be briefly discussed. At the time of the Kingdom of Hungary the Slovak nation was severely hungarianised – which was successful mainly in eastern Slovakia where the sense of national identity was rather less developed. There, the Slovak municipalities were hungarianised with great speed during the decades before the war, with the turning point being the year 1918 when the whole process was halted and partly reversed. The city of Košice pertinently illustrates this development – until 1880 it had a largely Slovak population; in 1910 the Slovak population represented only 15%, in 1921 62%. Relatively large Hungarian minorities (but also local majorities, e.g. Zvolen, Banská Bystrica, etc.) also existed inside the Slovak territory, primarily in the cities, which was due to the previous Hungarianisation and pro-Hungarian attitudes of the Jews which were maintained during the First Czechoslovak Republic at least in eastern Slovakia.[191] Žitný ostrov (the Great Rye Island) represented an interesting issue, as it used to be almost entirely Hungarian, but during the First Czechoslovak Republic colonisation was commenced. A number of Slovak and Czech settlements were established on the subdivided land of large farm estates, which considerably altered the ethnic set-up of the region.[192] To conclude, the strengthening of the Slovaks' positions and the loss of former supremacy irritated the Hungarian minority, which was unwilling to tolerate the new situation. Nevertheless, the impact on the overall stability of Czechoslovakia was considerably less significant compared with the German minority. Obviously, this was partly due to the fact that the proportion of minorities in the population of Slovakia was smaller than in Bohemia, and thus "national rights were not exploited so extensively so as to gain political advantage, and were not instrumental in the destabilisation of the state, as was the case in Bohemia."[193] The year 1918, the Peace Treaty of Trianon, and the break-up of the Kingdom of Hungary were shocking and traumatic experiences for the

---

190   Ibid., pp. 97–103; Kořalka, *Češi v habsburské říši a v Evropě 1815–1914*, pp. 147ff.
191   Boháč, *Národnostní mapa*, pp. 124–130; Kocsis and Kocsis-Hodosi, *Ethnic Geography of the Hungarian Minorities*, p. 54ff.
192   Boháč, *Národnostní mapa*, p. 114; Pavol Martuliak, "Kolonizačná akcia pri I. pozemkovej reforme na Slovensku," in *Československá pozemková reforma 1919–1935 a její mezinárodní souvislosti* (Uherské Hradiště: Slovácké museum, 1994), pp. 81–85.
193   Michal Kaľavský, "Postavenie národných menšín na Slovensku v rokoch 1918–1938," *Slovenský národopis* 39 (1991), p. 152.

Hungarians (in whichever successor state they lived), which they did not overcome throughout the interwar period.

The case of the Hungarian minority illustrates an interesting problem of migration of non-ruling nations. During the Habsburg Monarchy Vienna and Budapest were immensely popular, attracting Germans and Hungarians respectively, as well as other nations, which led, *inter alia*, to the establishment of a very large community of Viennese Czechs, who were under pressure by German nationalists. However, that role was now partly taken over by Prague. While the Germans had been, since the time of the Habsburg Monarchy, very numerous in Prague and Bratislava, the Hungarians generally only started coming to Bohemia after the establishment of independent Czechoslovakia. Notably the intelligentsia and university students were heading to Prague, which became one of the centers of Hungarian culture in Czechoslovakia.[194] This development luckily did not bring about any national conflicts, although migrations, primarily those affecting ethnic borders, generally represent the most dangerous triggers, often initiating disputes. Temporary migrations also cause hostility, in particular in the case of the state nation's members who are posted to work as civil servants, police officers, judges, gendarmes or teachers in minority regions. The issue of Czech experts in Slovakia, i.e. where the second strand of the state nation lived, was a delicate and very significant question, given the numbers of experts involved. Notably in the 1920s experts often used the Czech language regardless of an appropriate official procedure, and it was only in the 1930s that they usually used the Slovak language.[195]

Sub-Carpathian Ruthenia represented a specific problem for the interwar Czechoslovakia. While the Ruthenian nation was supposed to have autonomy in their territory and special privileges similar to the status of a state nation, outside their territory they had the status of a national minority.[196] In practical terms, however, this led to many difficulties as the Ruthenians had an unclear national orientation; some favoured Greater Russia, others Ukraine or Ruthenia, and the border with the Slovaks – a state nation – was unclear. The Slovak and Ruthenian dialects passed into one another imperceptibly and nationality was often confused with religion, as the Slovaks were predominantly Roman Catholics and Ruthenians were mostly Greek Catholics (Uniates). During censuses the language/nationality data constantly changed in many regions, and as a result it was necessary to take into account religion

---

194 Petr Sadílek and Tamás Csémy, *Maďaři v České republice 1918–1992* (Prague: Svaz Maďarů žijících v českých zemích, 1993), p. 68.

195 Jan Rychlík, "Teorie a praxe jednotného československého národa a československého jazyka v 1. republice," in *Masarykova idea československé státnosti ve světle kritiky dějin* (Prague: Ústav T. G. Masaryka, 1993), pp. 73–77.

196 Sobota, *Republika národní či národnostní?*, p. 14.

in order to determine the real national border. Thanks to their more advanced culture the Slovaks often assimilated the Ruthenians, resulting in high numbers of Slovak Uniates.[197]

A very interesting minority issue represented the Jews: both as a religious minority and as an independent nation (nationality).[198] A large proportion of this religious group very fiercely rejected the idea of the restoration of their own nation, preferring assimilation with the Germans and Hungarians, and later also with the Czechs. It was a large minority and its economic and cultural influence was even more important – in 1921 there were more than 354,000 persons of the Jewish religion and over half of them declared affiliation with the Jewish nationality, which was recognised by the First Czechoslovak Republic. Most Jews, however, were largely ambivalent as to their nationality and they often passed from one nation to another, weakening the German minority during the early years of Czechoslovakia. While the Jews in Bohemia predominantly sought assimilation with the Czechs or Germans, further east a larger proportion of the Jews declared affiliation with their own nation. In western regions of the state the Jews only represented a small proportion of the population (Bohemia 1.2%, Moravia and Silesia 1.4%) and the proportion had been decreasing from the 19th century on. By contrast, in the eastern regions of Czechoslovakia their numbers were substantial (Slovakia 4.5%, Sub-Carpathian Ruthenia 15.4%. In many towns the Jews represented a remarkably strong minority, e.g. Prešov 20% Jews and out of them 11% declared affiliation with their own nationality), Stropkov 44% (43%), Humenné 40% (18%). In Sub-Carpathian Ruthenia the Jews lived in compact areas, forming Jewish "islands," especially in Mukačevo with almost 48% of Jewish population.[199]

In the First Czechoslovak Republic the Gypsies (nowadays called the Roma) represented an interesting but marginal issue. Few people declared Gypsy nationality (8,728 in 1921, i.e. 0.06%), but their numbers were undoubtedly much higher, in particular in eastern regions of Slovakia. Since they do not have a distinct religion, unlike the Jews, it is difficult to determine their actual numbers. Their numbers were low in Bohemia, Moravia and Sub-Carpathian Ruthenia, but in Slovakia there were municipalities with over 10% of the population declaring Gypsy nationality – in Ruskovce village (under the Vihorlat mountain) the proportion amounted to 33%.[200]

---

197 Boháč, *Národnostní mapa*, p. 19, 131–132; Korčák, *Geopolitické základy Československa*, p. 147–148.
198 Aaron Rabinowicz, "The Jewish Minority: Legal Position," in *The Jews of Czechoslovakia; Historical Studies and Surveys*, vol. 1 (Philadelphia: Jewish Publication Society of America; New York: Society for the History of Czechoslovak Jews, 1968), p. 155ff.
199 Boháč, *Národnostní mapa*, pp. 148–160.
200 Ibid., pp. 162–165.

The second census of the interwar period was conducted in December 1930 according to slightly amended legislation – Act No. 47/1927 Sb. The concept of nationality for the census was altered to correspond more closely with the "mother tongue."

The results were as follows: The total number of population in Czechoslovakia reached 14.729 million (13.613 in 1921). The number of people who claimed Czechoslovak nationality rose from 8.02 milion in 1921 to 9.757 milion in 1930, while the German minority reached 3.3 million, Magyar minority 719 000 (decrease from 762 000 in 1921), Polish minority 100 000 (to compare with 110 000 in 1921), Jewish minority (nationality) 205 000 and Ruthenian 569 000. 61 000 people declared "other" minority. The results of the census were published also in form of maps showing the distribution of minorities according to political and judicial districts. The maps with French, German and English references were officialy handed over to the foreign legations to Prague and used to illustrtate the Czechoslovak minority policies.[201]

In general it is apparent that the statistics of national minorities in the First Czechoslovak Republic represented a significant problem which was, *inter alia*, due to the fact that many very different nations lived next to one another – beside the Germans or Czechs also ambivalent Ruthenians or scattered Jews and Gypsies who were not recognised as a nation in many other countries. The affiliation of some large groups was unclear, and unclear was also the very concept of the state nation. This complex situation had to be addressed by legal regulation which recognised the existence of minorities. During the actual population census, whose outcomes relating to the national set-up frequently provoked heated discussions, the First Czechoslovak Republic largely tried to proceed in a fair manner, unlike many other countries.

2.3 REGULATIONS GOVERNING THE STATUS OF MINORITIES

In the interwar period, as well as today, the most important minorities were national minorities, in general regarded as identical to language minorities according to the Czechoslovak legislation. Consequently, the concept of minority law generally denotes the same thing as the law of national minorities.[202] During the First Czechoslovak Republic the legal status of minorities was regulated by both national and international law. In interwar Czechoslovakia the influence of international law on national legislation was significant, even crucial – because the provisions of the Minorities Treaty of St. Germain were recepted by the Czechoslovak constitutional acts.

---

201 The National Archives, London (TNA), collection Foreign Office (FO) 925/20125.
202 *Slovník veřejného práva československého*, vol. 2 (Brno: Polygrafia – Rudolf M. Rohrer, 1932), p. 573.

During the First Czechoslovak Republic the legal status of minorities was regulated by minority law which in practical terms corresponded to nationality law because religious and racial minorities only played a marginal role in the Czechoslovak law. For example, prominent expert E. Sobota provided this definition: "Nationality law is conceived as a body of rules governing the relations which result from the existence of nationalities in a state."[203] Equally important was his observation that the legal status of minorities is also affected by the rules which do not form part of the nationality law or minority law. "Hence, nationality law is not entirely identical to the body of rules which bear on the nationality policy. The realities of life can assign a major national significance to a rule which concerns and regulates an entirely different field of social phenomena, very distant from nationality. For example, the legislation on the land reform."[204] While many legal regulations are easy to identify, others can be singled out only with difficulty. In many cases only certain provisions impact the minorities.[205]

When analysing the nationality law (just as in any other branch of law) it is necessary to determine how the whole issue should be organised and which legal regulations should be regarded as the core elements. It is a complex problem, and Czechoslovak jurists of the interwar period resorted to various methods. For example, in one of his books Emil Sobota proceeds as follows: "Nationality law, as laid down by the Constitution or other acts, is of two kinds: firstly the regulations granting more favourable treatment to the members of the Czechoslovak nation, and secondly the regulations assuring total equality of the nationalities. The former category primarily comprises rules about the use of languages in communication with public bodies."[206] However, such basic subdivision is far from exhaustive, giving rise to specific groups which fall outside the subdivision, and it must be emphasised that the author uses a completely different subdivision in his other works.

Another prominent expert, Cyril Horáček, uses a different basic subdivision: "In the Czechoslovak nationality law two kinds of regulations should be distinguished: language law and the rules assuring protection of national and racial minorities. The Constitutional Charter largely amalgamates both issues in its Title VI, but . . ."[207] The difference from Sobota's opinion as stated above is seemingly negligible; what is problematic, though, is the fact that Horáček understood the difference between language law and minority protection as

---

203   Sobota, *Národnostní právo československé*, p. 1.
204   Ibid.
205   Emil Sobota, "K pojmu národnostního práva," *Národnostní obzor* 4 (1933–1934): pp. 222–224.
206   Sobota, *Národnostní autonomie v Československu?*, p. 30.
207   Horáček, *Jazykové právo československé republiky*, p. 11.

a difference between individual (language) rights and collective (minority) rights, which is not in line with the approach of other authors.[208]

Many similar examples are available to illustrate the various (and incompatible) approaches to interpretation and subdivision of nationality law, as almost every author had his own conception and a single author sometimes inconsistently pursued various approaches in his works. Even prominent authors frequently display a certain lack of organisation when analysing the issue in question, notably on the very general level. This was caused by a complex combination of national and international law where it is not clear which one prevails, as well as by a lack of clarity as to which regulations belong to the nationality law. Also, certain unclarified theoretical questions (e.g. the definition of a nation) played an important role, as well as issues which require a complicated historical explanation in order to be fully understood (e.g. disputes over the state language or official language). Czech lawyers of the inter-war period particularly struggled with the issue of "Minorities Treaty of St. Germain" (the so-called "Little Treaty" of Saint-Germain-en-Laye of 10 September 1919 concluded between the Principal Allied and Associated Powers and Czechoslovakia, see also I.4.), which was a very peculiar piece of legislation aiming to set out basic national rules to govern the legal status of minorities.[209] As professor František Weyr aptly observed, the idea of an international treaty taking precedence over sovereign national law was a curious novelty, inconsistent with contemporary legal logic. To illustrate how the issue was misused for political purposes it is worth mentioning that he was criticised as a national egoist for this observation by many foreign lawyers, notably from Germany.[210]

When aiming at a unifying approach, the reception of the Minorities Treaty of St. Germain into the body of nationality law remains problematic, *inter alia* because Title VI of the Constitutional Charter of 1920 was drafted according to that Treaty. Consequently, some authors regarded an analysis of the Minorities Treaty of St. Germain as a key element for the interpretation of minority-nationality law.[211] Moreover, the analysis of the Minorities Treaty was not easy and it was (in practical application) closely linked to the international situation rather than based on legal logic. Other authors combined an analysis of Title VI of the Constitutional Charter with the

---

208 Ibid. These views are rejected by for example Sobota, *Národnostní autonomie v Československu?*, p. 29; Peška, *Národní menšiny a Československo*, p. 126.
209 For its text in English see Beneš and Kural, *Facing history*, document no. 1, pp. 295–296.
210 *Slovník veřejného práva československého*, p. 578.
211 For example Weyr, *Slovník veřejného práva československého*, entry "Menšiny." For modern approach see Malý, "Sprache – Recht und Staat," p. 271, where the Minorities Treaty of St. Germain was designated as the baseline for regulation.

Minorities Treaty analysis[212], while many other authors marginalised[213] the Treaty, which is not surprising since the treaty is so difficult to deal with. There are instances of legal interpretation where the author states that the Minorities Treaty of St. Germain takes precedence over all Czechoslovak law and in the same paragraph the author says that the Constitution is invariably the basis of Czechoslovak law, without any further explanation of the inconsistency of such statements. Obviously, the present work does not attempt to evaluate logical or stylistic qualities of experts from the interwar period, but tries to explore the key problem of the regulation governing the legal status of minorities – i.e. that the very basis of the regulation was problematic and questionable. While contentious issues are common in law, they usually do not affect such fundamental matters.

As previously suggested, the approach to the interpretation of nationality law is not a simple or clear matter. In this book the whole issue will be subdivided into three parts – besides this general part which will also explore the rules impacting the minorities essentially indirectly. Only domestic regulation will be discussed now, as the international law (i.e. the Minorities Treaty of St. Germain) will be discussed separately due to its specific features. The three parts that the domestic nationality law may be divided into are: language law, minority educational and cultural law, and the issue of autonomy. Although this subdivision was not traditionally used as the methods were very wide-ranging, it corresponds to the usual classification. In particular language law was a fairly stable precept – it was the largest and the most researched topic from the minorities domain which provoked considerable interest in jurists. By contrast, the issue of autonomy was rather controversial and the relevant fragmented legal rules were interpreted in various ways by various authors – some of them regarded them as a specific basis of the autonomy of minorities in Czechoslovakia, while others completely rejected the idea. Equally controversial was the incorporation of Sub-Carpathian Ruthenia into minority issues, etc.

A very important issue of nationality law is the definition of a nation and nationality. The law in interwar Czechoslovakia failed to provide a general definition: the concept was partly defined in a few isolated places in the legal order only for specific purposes, and each time differently. The Constitutional Charter of 1920 stated "citizens irrespective of their nationality, language, religion, and race" (Section 130) and the Protection of the Republic Act (No. 50/1923 Sb.) stated "groups of inhabitants for their nationality, language, race, or religion" (Section 14 (2)). Therefore, it may be possible to conclude

---

212 Horáček, *Jazykové právo československé republiky*, p. 11; Peška, *Národní menšiny a Československo*, pp. 127–131.
213 For example Emil Sobota in his works.

that the definition of nationality did not correspond to the differences in terms of language, religion, or race. Apparently, according to the wording of the legislation, nationality was not inherently linked to a language – unlike in other parts of Central Europe.

Governmental Order No. 601/1920 Sb. implementing the Constitutional Act on the Acquisition and Loss of Citizenship (Act No. 236/1920 Sb.) provided a merely demonstrative list of documents proving that a person "is a Czechoslovak citizen by language and race (e.g. documents regarding the attendance of Czechoslovak schools, a declaration about the use of the Czech or Slovak language in the population census, etc.)" (Article 3 (4) (d)). Thus, the facts in question were of an objective nature. While the regulation governing the population census was based on a subjective affiliation with a nation – i.e. freely expressed by the respondent – there were efforts to determine those facts objectively. However, neither the Population Census Act No. 256/1920 Sb. of 8 April 1920 nor the implementing Governmental Order No. 592/1920 Sb. defined the concept of nationality, even though, pursuant to Section 20 (1) of the Order, the relevant authorities were supposed to thoroughly determine such facts: "The data on nationality shall be determined with great care and according to the reality." Only "Directions" for the completion of census forms and "Instructions" for census bodies, which were not published in the Collection of Laws, indicated that "nationality shall be understood as tribal affiliation, with the mother tongue being its major external feature." However, since tribal affiliation was never defined, the definition was not very useful.

The case law of the Supreme Administrative Court[214], primarily concerning the disputes over the population census, helped to stabilize the concept of nationality in practical situations. The decision of 1 December 1924 (No. 21.982/23, Collection of Decisions by Dr. Bohuslav, No. 4173) was important for the determination of nationality based on tribal affiliation – i.e. based on one's origin: "The origin is not the only objective feature of nationality: if in doubt, nationality can be determined on the basis of various objective features, such as upbringing, language of communication, tribal affiliation, and the language of intercourse of other family members, etc." In reality, objective determinations were in some cases preferred over subjective declarations about one's affiliation with a nation, in particular where officials (census commissioners) tried to make the inhabitants sign up to the state nation against their will, which obviously provoked criticism from the minorities. Nevertheless, such practices were approved by the Administrative

---

214 Peška, *Československá ústava a zákony s ní souvislé*, vol. 1, pp. 324–325; Sobota, *Národnostní právo československé*, pp. 16–17.

Court[215] (a decision of 10 February 1923, No. 10.967/22, Collection of Decisions by Dr. Bohuslav No. 1952): "Therefore, it is incorrect to believe . . . that as regards the box "nationality," solely the person concerned decides about the nationality to be stated, since such person is required to state such nationality as appropriate, based on the assessment of objective features relevant for the determination of nationality."[216]

The complexities of the nationality law can also be illustrated by the concept of affiliation with a language group (the Czechoslovak language, minority languages) which only had a bearing on the language law branch. Such affiliation was considered an objective fact, and a voluntary signing up to a particular language represented only one of the features of that affiliation. A false declaration was subject to a procedural fine. As a result, objective determinations were clearly preferred over subjective declarations about a person's affiliation with a minority. One of the few instances where a person's declaration could not be reviewed[217] was set out in Section 6 of the Rules of Procedure of the Chamber of Deputies (No. 325/1920 Sb.): "Before the deputies enter the assembly room [upon their election] they shall declare their nationality in the Office of the Chamber."

Even the Minorities Treaty of St. Germain, which so strongly impacted the nationality law of the First Czechoslovak Republic, failed to provide a definition of the nation or nationality. Certain indications for determining nationality were provided in the bilateral treaties concluded with Austria (7 June 1920, published in the Collection of Laws No. 107/1921 Sb.) and Germany (No. 308/1922 Sb.) – aiming at the interpretation of the words denoting nationality in the Peace Treaties. Under Article 9 of the Treaty with Austria "in practical situations language shall be generally considered as the most important feature of nationality." Under Article 2 of the Treaty with Germany: "The determining feature shall be the fact of whether the person concerned has been speaking the Czechoslovak language as the mother tongue since childhood." That provision was used to determine the affiliation with the "Czechoslovak race and language." However, it is questionable to what extent those treaties can be regarded as part of the Czechoslovak law, and, therefore, whether these attempts at definitions should be at all taken into account.[218]

To sum up, there was no general definition of the affiliation with a nation in the Czechoslovak legal order. The non-existence of key definitions is not unusual in law, but in the case of nationality law that deficiency was added

---

215 Sobota, *Národnostní právo československé*, p. 109.
216 *Sbírka nálezů Nejvyššího správního soudu ve věcech administrativních: nálezy z roku . . .*, ed. by Josef Václav Bohuslav, (Prague: Právnické vydavatelství (V. Tomsa), 1920–1934), pp. 321–323, quotation p. 321.
217 Sobota, *Národnostní právo československé*, p. 18.
218 Ibid., p. 16.

to many other shortcomings, further intensifying many unclear elements of this particular legal branch.

The Constitutional Charter of 1920 was the basis for the nationality law and, in general, for the law in the First Czechoslovak Republic.[219] However, the minority law as laid down by the Constitution was partly inconsistent with the Minorities Treaty of St. Germain. The Preamble to the Constitutional Charter started with "We, the Czechoslovak nation, desiring to consolidate the perfect unity of the nation, . . . to contribute to the common welfare of all citizens of this state . . ." Thus, the Constitution referred to a nation[220] (we can leave aside the issue of the Czechoslovak nation) rather than reading e.g. "We, the citizens," as in the present Constitution of the Czech Republic. However, it mentioned an effort to contribute to the welfare of all citizens – i.e. also (national) minorities. Nevertheless, the distinction between civic and national constitutions, with a preamble serving as an important indicator, is not very clear, and as a result there is no need to discuss this issue any further. What is important is that in its Title Six the Constitution guaranteed most of the obligations concerning minority law in almost identical wording as in the Minorities Treaty of St. Germain, although some differences, as we will explain below in more details, occurred. Minorities, however, – notably the Germans – refused the Constitutional Charter of 1920 as an imposed instrument, as they had not participated in its drafting. This issue, together with other aspects connected with the adoption of the constitution, is discussed in detail in the chapter dealing with historical development.

In the brief Preamble the following statement may be found: "We, the Czechoslovak nation, declare that we will endeavour to carry out this constitution as well as all the laws of our country in the spirit of our history as well as in the spirit of the modern principles embodied in the slogan of self-determination." In fact, that is a paradoxical statement, as large minorities in Czechoslovakia invoked the right to self-determination, but its practical application would probably have put an end to the Czechoslovak Republic. However the Czech experts of the interwar period interpreted the

---

219   Ibid., pp. 68–74; František Weyr, *Soustava československého práva státního*, 2nd ed. (Prague: Fr. Borový, 1924), pp. 80–82, 391–398; Horáček, *Jazykové právo československé republiky*, pp. 11–16; Epstein, *Studien-Ausgabe der Verfassungsgesetze*, pp. 204–208. On the rights of minorities in constitutions see Jean A. Laponce, *The Protection of Minorities* (Berkeley: University of California Press, 1960), pp. 43–67.

220   Karel Malý, "Vznik ČSR a problematika státního občanství," *Právník* 127, no. 10 (1988): p. 911; Jelena Serapionova, "Národnostní práva podle ústavy Československé republiky roku 1920," in *Kroměřížský sněm 1848–1849 a tradice parlamentarismu ve střední Evropě: sborník příspěvků ze stejnojmenné mezinárodní konference konané v rámci oslav 150. výročí říšského sněmu v Kroměříži 14.–16. září 1998 = Der Reichstag von Kremsier 1848–1849 und die Tradition des Parlamentarismus in Mitteleuropa: Sammelband mit Beiträgen der gleichnamigen inaternationalen Konferenz veranstaltet im Rahmen der Feierlichkeiten anläßlich des 150. Jahrestages des Reichstages von Kremsier, 14.–16. September* (Kroměříž: KATOS, 1998), p. 77.

right to self-determination as solely the right for nations (the Czechoslovaks) and not for minorities. They argued that the application of that right to minorities would, in the case of Czechoslovakia, have led to the creation of defunct borders, which would subsequently have endangered or made impossible the republic's existence, preventing the self-determination of the Czechoslovaks.

As was already mentioned the protection of minorities was enshrined in Title VI of the Constitutional Charter, but some important and relevant provisions could be found elsewhere as well. Article IX of the Constitutional Act promulgating the Constitutional Charter stipulated that "all provisions in violation of this Constitutional Charter and of the republican form of government shall be deemed invalid." Because the status of minorities was primarily governed by the Constitution, the regulations enacted at the time of Habsburg Monarchy were usually repealed by this provision. The new principles of the Czechoslovak Constitutional Charter were thus the basis for further provisions, acts but also ministerial ordinances and instructions.[221]

The autonomy of Sub-Carpathian Ruthenia[222] was laid down in the Title I -General Provisions – of the Constitutional Charter (Section 3 (2), which stipulated: "An integral part of this unit [Czechoslovakia] shall be, based on a voluntary accession under the Treaty between the Principal Allied and Associated Powers and the Czechoslovak Republic in Saint-Germain-en-Laye of 10 September 1919, the autonomous territory of Sub-Carpathian Ruthenia which shall be granted the largest autonomy consistent with the unity of the Czechoslovak Republic." The Constitution directly refers to the Minorities Treaty of St. Germain, which was (and largely still is) rather unusual in the law. What the declared "largest autonomy consistent with the state's unity" was supposed to look like, in practical terms, was hard to say. The explanatory memorandum read: "The Ruthenian nation south to the Carpathian Mountains . . . joined our country, deliberately establishing with us a unitary state rather than a federation or confederation."[223] Sub-Carpathian Ruthenia was to have their own Assembly (Diet) competent to adopt laws in the fields of languages, education, religion, etc. As regards autonomy, the reality was, however, totally different, which was mainly due to the complicated situation in this area.

Similarly, Section 106 (2) of the Constitutional Charter affected minorities as it guaranteed the protection of life and freedom for all inhabitants

---

221 See extensive edition of documents Josef Harna and Jaroslav Šebek, *Státní politika vůči německé menšině v období konsolidace politické moci v Československu v letech 1918–1920* (Prague: Historický ústav AV ČR, 2002).

222 Peška, *Národní menšiny a Československo*, pp. 204–219.

223 *Tisky k těsnopiseckým zprávám o schůzích Národního shromáždění československého*, vol. 9, *Rok 1919–1920* (Prague: [Tiskárna Poslanecké sněmovny], 1920), print no. 2421, p. 3.

of Czechoslovakia irrespective of their origin, citizenship, language, race or religion. This provision was very close to the provisions of Title VI, *inter alia* due to its relation to the Minorities Treaty of St. Germain. The difference was that it applied to the whole population rather than just the citizens as in Title VI. According to the explanatory memorandum[224], the provision implemented Article 2 (1) of the Minorities Treaty. The Constitution even contained an unusual direct reference to international law: "Derogations from this principle are only permissible where allowed by the international law."

Most provisions dealing with minorities were concentrated in Title VI. of the Constitutional Charter entitled "Protection of minority nations, and religious and racial minorities" (Sections 128–134). The explanatory memorandum[225] emphasised that the designation "minority nations" rather than "nationalities" was used deliberately in the heading. It explained that in the Kingdom of Hungary the minorities were humiliated by "being deprived of the status of a nation and reduced to mere nationalities."[226] The constitutional committee drafting the Constitution is said to have tried to avoid this pitfall. However, prominent jurist professor František Weyr, for example, declared the distinction between minority nations and nationalities incorrect and useless.[227] Again, there is a lack of clarity over certain theoretical issues. The Constitutional Charter of 1920 failed to list minority nations because, as pointed out in the explanatory memorandum, this issue was difficult to address scientifically. It was emphasised that the very concept of a nation was not precisely defined and there were some other problems – e.g. whether the Jews represented a nation. Another contentious legal issue was the question of whether Title VI of the Constitutional Charter was directly binding. While the Supreme Administrative Court held that it was not binding, many experts disagreed.[228]

Section 128 laid down the principle of equality of citizens, regardless of whether they were affiliated with a minority, which only reiterated the provision on the equality of all citizens. In subsection 3 free use of all languages was set out, both in private settings, business, and other areas. However, under Subsection 4 the rights listed in Section 128 could be restricted "by reason of public order, state security, and effective supervision," where appropriate, by an ordinary act. Section 129, governing language law, referred to a special constitutional Language Act, which was adopted together with the Constitutional Charter (Act No. 122/1920 Sb.) as its part.

---

224 Ibid., p. 32.
225 Ibid., p. 21.
226 Ibid. For the situation in the Kingdom of Hungary see for example Hronský, *The Struggle for Slovakia*, pp. 14–15, 35–37.
227 Weyr, *Soustava československého práva státního*, p. 394.
228 Peška, *Československá ústava a zákony s ní souvislé*, vol. 1, p. 326 claimed that it was binding.

Particularly important was Section 131, governing the minority educational system – already in existence in the Habsburg Monarchy – as opposed to Section 132 under which minorities were entitled to a reasonable share of costs incurred on education, religion, and charity from public budgets. This new precept adopted in accordance with the Minorities Treaty of St. Germain gave rise to many controversies. For example, professor František Weyr concluded that minorities should have their own organisations for the administration of such funds. "It appears to require that these minorities be constituted as corporations, which applies accordingly to all other rights which are collective by their nature."[229] Thus, this prominent jurist reached an important conclusion which was, however, not widely accepted. The relationship between individual and collective rights in Title VI was a controversial issue on which experts could not agree. Some experts considered solely collective rights (Sections 131 and 132) as the actual protection of minorities, as opposed to individual rights (Sections 128 and 130).[230] Unlike sections 128–133 which protected only minorities, Section 134 prohibiting forcible denationalisation applied to all nations, as emphasised by the explanatory memorandum to the Constitution.[231] This seems relatively meaningless, but in reality there was a curious problem of the denationalisation of Czech minorities in borderland regions, which caused quite a stir among the Czech public, sometimes bordering on hysteria.

The key issue of Title VI of the Constitutional Charter was its relation to the Minorities Treaty of St. Germain (published in the Collection of Laws No. 508/1921 Sb.). Under Article 1 of the Treaty its fundamental provisions prevailed over the Constitution. "Czechoslovakia undertakes that the stipulations contained in Articles 2 to 8 of this Title shall be recognised as fundamental laws and that no law, regulation, or official action shall conflict or interfere with these stipulations, nor shall any law, regulation, or official action prevail over them." The explanatory memorandum to the Constitution[232] recognised that Sections 128–132 were adapted in accordance with the Minorities Treaty. However, the relation between the Minorities Treaty and the Constitution and the significance of the Treaty for the domestic situation was rather controversial. Section 128 was drafted in accordance with Article 7 (1) – (3) of the Treaty, Section 129 in accordance with Article 7 (4), Section

---

229 Weyr, *Soustava československého práva státního*, p. 398; Fritz Sander, *Die Gleichheit vor dem Gesetze und die nationalen Minderheiten* (Prague: [Lese- u. Redehalle d. dt. Studenten], 1937), pp. 9–10.
230 Weyr, *Soustava československého práva státního*, p. 395; Václav Pavlíček, "K ústavním aspektům práv menšin po vzniku Československa," in Valenta, Voráček and Harna, *Československo 1918–1938*, p. 598.
231 *Tisky k těsnopiseckým zprávám*, vol. 9, print no. 2421, p. 21; Peter Mosný, "Postavenie národnostných menšín v právnom poriadku predmníchovského Československa," *Acta Iuridica Cassoviensia* 15 (1990), p. 21.
232 *Tisky k těsnopiseckým zprávám*, vol. 9, print no. 2421, p. 21.

130 in accordance with Article 8, Sections 131 and 132 in accordance with Article 9. However, the wording in the Constitution did not precisely copy the wording of the Treaty – e.g. the important provision of Section 128 (4) providing for the restriction of rights by way of a piece of legislation was not set out in the Minorities Treaty. Sections 131 and 132 were incorporated into the Constitutional Charter although the corresponding provision of the Treaty was not designated as fundamental law, and consequently may have not had a constitutional character.[233] Czech experts usually claimed that the provisions were incorporated into the Czechoslovak Constitution to the minimum extent required, but some German experts argued that some inadmissible, restrictive provisions were included too.[234]

Even though the provisions of Title VI were, as the explanatory memorandum explained, based on the Minorities Treaty, i.e. implementing international obligations, many Czech jurists tried to emphasise that such provisions were not included due to external pressure, but rather "constituted a logical part and followed from other provisions of the Constitutional Charter, and they would have been incorporated even if such commitments had not existed."[235] This opinion was partly justified, for example with regard to Sections 131 and 132, which were incorporated into the Constitutional Charter although they were not designated as fundamental laws by the Treaty. However, the explanatory memorandum did not quite agree: "Sections 128–132 provide the minimum standards that have to be granted, in accordance with the Saint-Germain Minorities Treaty, to the nations which represent minorities in our state."[236]

Hence, there was a politically sensitive, contentious question about the extent to which the protection of minorities was imposed by the Great Powers – which had a bearing on any potential intervention from abroad in the future. In general we can accept the opinion, common at that time, that the constitutional rules of Czechoslovakia had a legal force and a binding character exclusively based on the will of the national legislature, and the existence of the international commitments of Czechoslovakia had no significance for their validity. The supreme courts also adopted the view that the protection of minorities and language law was not based on international commitments but rather on the Constitution, just as any other legal rules. The Supreme Administrative Court expressly ruled: "A treaty concluded between states gives rise to rights and duties of contracting states among one another, as

---

233 See for example Klepetař, *Der Sprachenkampf in den Sudetenländern*, pp. 127–129; Epstein, *Studien-Ausgabe der Verfassungsgesetze*, p. 204ff.; Malý, "Sprache – Recht und Staat," pp. 272–273.

234 Franz Adler, *Grundriß des tschechoslowakischen Verfassungsrechtes* (Reichenberg: Stiepel, 1930), p. 120.

235 Horáček, *Jazykové právo československé republiky*, p. 12; Kučera, *Minderheit im Nationalstaat*, p. 33ff.

236 *Tisky k těsnopiseckým zprávám*, vol. 9, print no. 2421, p. 21.

well as, possibly, to rules of international law, but never to rules of domestic law which would directly, and in a binding fashion, govern the relationship between the state and its citizens" (ruling of 29 March 1921 No. 13.297/20, Collection of decisions by dr. Bohuslav, administrative series No. 786). "The right to use a minority language in the Czechoslovak Republic may only be based on the Language Act of 1920 . . . , and not directly on the provisions of the Saint-Germain (Minority) Treaty."[237]

As a result, the provisions of the Minorities Treaty of St. Germain only represented an international commitment[238] which put considerable restrictions on the legislators with regard to the protection of minorities, including language law, but only on the level of international law. According to Czechoslovak jurists of the interwar period, a valid law could be adopted which would be in contravention of the Minorities Treaty, but the state would breach an international commitment, facing sanctions under international law. The intervention of the treaty signatories would probably make the legislature repeal the provisions conflicting with the treaty. But in the interim, the law conflicting with the international commitment would probably be valid.[239]

The interplay between the Czechoslovak legal order and international law provoked complex scholarly and political discussions influenced by nationalism. A particularly courageous and radical opinion was outlined by professor František Weyr in one of his fundamental works.[240] In his view the provision of the Minorities Treaty of St. Germain, according to which a part of the treaty should be recognised as fundamental law with absolute priority, was "a commitment which was theoretically unfeasible and practically meaningless."[241] He justified his claim by highlighting the existence of the sovereign Czechoslovak legal order, the non-existence of the international legal order (he indicated that the Covenant of the League of Nations was just the beginning), and by the fact that there was "an erroneous effort to establish a normative body which would be at the same time an obligated body, which is impossible as the normative body may not oblige itself in this role."[242] He engaged in polemic with another prominent expert, professor Jiří Hoetzel, who regarded international treaties as a legal commitment of the state concerned. "Hoetzel's opinion would require express restriction of the

---

237 Sbírka nálezů Nejvyššího správního soudu, vol. 3, pp. 319–321.
238 As contrasted with Antonín Hobza, "Publikace a platnost mírových smluv v čsl. republice," Právník 62 (1923), pp. 17–22.
239 Even the advocates of the state's sovereignty were aware of the risk of international sanctions. Horáček, Jazykové právo československé republiky, p. 16.
240 Weyr, Soustava československého práva státního, pp. 80–82.
241 Ibid., p. 80.
242 Ibid., p. 81.

National Assembly's competence to be set out in the Constitutional Charter, so that no law (not even a constitutional act) could stipulate anything that would be in violation of the provisions of international law (treaties)."[243] As there is no such express provision in the Constitution, domestic law prevails. According to professor František Weyr, it could be changed *de lege ferenda*, but it is impossible that both international law and domestic law prevail and, therefore, the Minorities Treaty only contains a moral commitment. This statement provoked harsh criticism by some German experts who liked to question Czechoslovakia's sovereignty in favour of the international protection of minorities (of course, mainly the German minority).[244] In particular a non-lawyer reader should bear in mind that while there tend to be numerous seemingly fundamental, but only theoretical, discussions notably in the area of constitutional and international law, the number of ambiguities surrounding minorities was truly very high.

Highly important for the status of minorities was the protection of minorities – the protection of nations and of the affiliation with those nations.[245] The protection was laid down by the Constitution, as well as by criminal law and other rules. The relevant provision of the Constitutional Charter was Section 106 (2) which ensured life and freedom to all inhabitants of Czechoslovakia, and Section 128 (1) which ensured the equality of citizens. Moreover, those rules were derived from the Minorities Treaty of St. Germain. Section 134 of the Constitutional Charter provided protection against forcible denationalisation. Penal protection was primarily laid down in Section 14 of the Protection of the Republic Act of 19 March 1923 (No. 50/1923 Sb.).[246] Under that section a person was subject to prosecution if they publicly induced others to commit acts of violence or other hostile acts, or if they incited hatred against individuals or groups by reason of nationality, language, race, or religion (Subsections 2 to 4). Subsection 5 provided an interesting definition of the crime: "A person who publicly denigrates the republic, a nation, or an ethnic minority in a brutal or seditious way so that such conduct may affect the republic's dignity or endanger general peace within the republic or the republic's international relations." According to the explanatory memorandum (Print No. 4021) such conflicts could have serious consequences. "Undoubtedly, religious and nationality disputes have intensified in the postwar period, and have come to endanger peaceful political as well as economic life, paralysing the successful development of the state. The bill does not pretend to conceal the fact that such disputes have existed and will exist and cannot be

---

243 Ibid., p. 81.
244 *Slovník veřejného práva československého*, p. 578.
245 Sobota, *Národnostní právo československé*, pp. 18–21.
246 Klepetař, *Seit 1918*, p. 188ff.

eliminated." Penal protection was also granted by the Act against Oppression and for the Protection of Freedom in Public Assemblies of 12 August 1921 (No. 309/1921 Sb.) – Provision of Section 1 (2) dealt with a strike or lockout where it targeted individual employees on ethnic, religious, or political grounds.[247]

There were also some other means which served to protect the affiliation with a particular nationality. The Act on Industrial Committees of 12 August 1921 (No. 330/1921 Sb.) provided protection of workers or employees in Section 3 (1) (g) – (aa) against discharge where such discharge was obviously due to, *inter alia*, affiliation or not with a national or religious community or organisation. The so-called Perek Provincial Act No. 4/1906 of Moravian Provincial Code (Part II, Section 20) ensured the protection of children against denationalisation in Moravia through the compulsory public educational system, as ordinarily only children who spoke the language of instruction were admitted to a general school (*Volksschule*).[248] The act No. 205/1925 Sb. in its Section 53 provided for the protection of nations against prejudicial treatment which could occur in connection with the distribution of seats during the election to the National Assembly.[249]

Highly significant for the protection of minorities was the issue of citizenship[250] which could not be addressed by Czechoslovakia alone and in an arbitrary fashion, but, notably at the beginning of the republic's existence, in agreement with other countries. The Allies also recognised the importance of this issue, which has led to a minor amendment to the Minorities Treaty of St. Germain (Articles 3–6). The objective was to ensure that Czechoslovakia (but also other successor states namely Poland) would not be able to refuse to grant citizenship to the minority members, as notably political rights were, pursuant to domestic legislation and the Minorities Treaty of St. Germain, only vested in the citizens. On the other hand, there was an effort to prevent undesirable citizenship (after the state borders had been significantly altered) with respect to an affiliation with a nationality – i.e. recognition of the right of option. That was provided in the Peace Treaties with Germany (Article 85), Austria (Article 80), Hungary (Article 64), in the bilateral treaty with Austria (Article 9), the Minorities Treaty of St. Germain, and other treaties. Domestic legislation contained a similar provision – Section 4 of the Constitutional Act on Citizenship and the Right of Abode of 9 April 1920 (No. 236/1920 Sb.). This constitutional act, implemented by the Governmental Order of 30 October

---

247 Certain controversial issues, Josef Zelenka, "Terror," part 2, *Právník* 60, no. 11 (1921): pp. 336–337.
248 Sobota, *Národnostní autonomie v Československu?*, pp. 39–40.
249 The act gained recognition even abroad as an interesting way of ensuring a balanced distribution of national communities, Laponce, *The Protection of Minorities*, p. 127.
250 See for example Peška, *Národní menšiny a Československo*, pp. 183–203; Peška, *Československá ústava a zákony s ní souvislé*, vol. 1, pp. 137–138, 806; Malý, "Vznik ČSR a problematika státního občanství," p. 915ff.

1920 (No. 601/1920 Sb.), laid the foundations for the national regulation of citizenship, which was, however, substantially influenced by international law.

The Czechoslovak legal order also contained regulations governing the specific status of the state nation. Some authors regarded that as a specific protection of the state nation.[251] One of those regulations was embodied in the first Act on the Establishment of the Independent Czechoslovak State (No. 11/1918 Sb. z. a n.) – the words "on behalf of the Czechoslovak nation" in fact designate the Czechoslovak nation as a state-constituting nation. Similarly, the Preamble to the Constitutional Charter reads "We, the Czechoslovak nation." "While we may dispute the normative character of such sources, they very effectively help to provide some explanation."[252] The definition of the state nation placed all the other citizens in the position of minorities.

Some rather particular provisions of the Czechoslovak legal order laid down sanctions against persons who behaved in a hostile manner towards the Czechoslovak nation during WWI. Section 9 of the Act on the Confiscation of Large Land Property (No. 215/1919 Sb.) presupposed that a special piece of legislation would provide for confiscation without compensation of land from *inter alia* persons who were guilty of serious misconducts towards the Czechoslovak nation during the world war. However, the special piece of legislation was never adopted and the Compensation Act (No. 329/1920 Sb.) failed to implement that design. Sanctions against persons hostile towards the Czechoslovak nation were also presupposed in the Act on Taking over Military Personnel and Modifying Maintenance Rights, of 19 March 1920 (No. 194/1920 Sb.), which stipulated in Section 4 (2) – (3) that professional soldiers would be deprived of maintenance rights where "an investigation shows that their conduct during the war was detrimental to the Czechoslovak nation or its members, proving their hatred towards the Czechoslovak nation, or that by persecuting the Czechoslovak nation or its members they sought to acquire special personal advantages or benefits. Where such persons . . . have already been admitted into the armed forces of the Czechoslovak Republic, they shall be dismissed." However, such legal provisions had a very limited practical impact.

The Czechoslovak legal order of the interwar period also contained a few rather controversial provisions which showed a peculiar concern for the perceptions of the state nation. The Act on the Names of Cities, Municipalities, Villages, and Streets, etc. of 14 April 1920 (No. 266/1920 Sb.)[253] stipulated in its Section 7: "It shall be prohibited to continue using the present names of

---

251 Sobota, *Národnostní právo československé*, pp. 19–20.
252 Ibid., p. 20.
253 Kučera, *Minderheit im Nationalstaat*, p. 298, he makes very ironic comments ("kakanische" Symbolik).

streets and public places which are inconsistent with the history and external relations of the Czechoslovak nation, in particular those which evoke persons who have demonstrated hostile attitudes towards the Czechoslovak nation or associated nations, or those which evoke subversive events." Section 10 prohibited the use of such names in the future. This represented an attempt at a radical departure from one's own recent history, imposed by the statutes. Pursuant to the Supreme Administrative Court decision such unacceptable names generally included the names of Austrian monarchs (Decision of 16 September 1924, No. 15.756, Collection of decision by dr. Bohuslav, administrative series No. 3904): "Naming a street after a former Austrian monarch may be regarded as inappropriate under this section." Such provisions were, according to the authors of this book, inappropriate, as they unnecessarily irritated major minorities which had no reason to perceive their own history in a negative light. It is quite curious that this legal protection was granted to the allies too ("the associated nations").

Section 1 of the Act on the Removal of Inappropriate Names of 14 April 1920 (No. 267/1920 Sb.) was unnecessarily controversial as well: "It is not allowed to refer to any bodies, legal entities, companies, public premises, plants, institutes, products, etc. publicly (for the public) by names which evoke the government of the Czechoslovak lands before 28 October 1918, or which are inconsistent with the direction and spirit of the foreign relations of the Czechoslovak Republic, or which evoke persons who have demonstrated in any way hostile attitudes towards the Czechoslovak nation or associated nations, or which evoke subversive events." The explanatory memorandum[254] exacerbated the poorly drafted provision by defining names which could hurt the feelings of the majority population: "This generally includes any and all allusions to the Habsburg Dynasty and Austrian Empire, as well as any names associated with the foreign policy of the former Austro-Hungarian Empire, in particular the expression of sympathy to the nations which had been hostile to the Entente Powers."[255] Such hostile nations – primarily the Germans and Hungarians – represented almost 30% of the state's population. This statute touched on many practical areas – for example a trademark was deleted from the register because it contained the Austrian Empire's coat of arms (Decision of the Supreme Administrative Court of 14 December 1922, No. 19.125, Collection of decisions by dr. Bohuslav, administrative series No. 1751).[256]

A free choice of names was, according to the authors of this book, unnecessarily restricted by special legal provisions. Although legal rules concerning inappropriate names represented a minor issue which had little practical

254 *Tisky k těsnopiseckým zprávám*, vol. 10, print no. 2802.
255 Ibid., p. 1.
256 *Sbírka nálezů Nejvyššího správního soudu*, vol. 4b, pp. 1459–1462.

impact on the minorities, it significantly affected their prestige ("national pride") which tends to be of major importance in such issues. While the above mentioned rules punishing hostile conduct towards the Czechoslovak nation, as well as many similar legal rules which have not been mentioned here, delivered no real benefit for the ruling Czechoslovak nation, they aroused feelings of hostility and estrangement on the part of minorities. It is not surprising that these ill-conceived statutes were adopted by the Revolutionary National Assembly at the very last moment.

This fight over street names, the national perspective affecting the appropriateness of certain names, and displaying state symbols was part of a tradition which is the subject of ridicule by many historians. However, such major disputes over trivial issues or issues of prestige have always been very numerous in the case of national conflicts. Alongside the criticism of rather controversial legal rules, it is necessary to outline the practical arrangements too. During the initial stages of the existence of the Czechoslovak state, when such legal rules mostly came into being, the state authorities were quite cautious. For example, in May 1919 some soldiers wished to rename their barracks (using the name of Hussite leader Jan Žižka), but the Ministry of Defence rejected their proposal as it feared nationalist incidents. "As regards German towns, it is significant that such inscriptions would be permanently subject to attacks and violent acts by the Germans, would be constantly stained and damaged; therefore it is questionable whether such inscriptions should be allowed to give rise to riots which could surely be anticipated in this transitional period. The Ministry of National Defence raised the example of Liberec, where the presence of the coat of arms of the Czechoslovak Republic on the city hall building led to much friction among the public."[257] In this way, the Czech nationalist initiatives, which often initiated the above mentioned legal rules, had corresponding counterparts in the tempestuous emotions among the minorities.

Some legal rules clearly preferred the state nation, and the state nation was also favoured by other legal rules which did not directly concern minorities or nationalities. Although such rules are not part of the nationality law, they are important for minorities. Therefore, many legal rules impacted the nationality policy even though they dealt with a different topic.[258] In the first place, there were statutes regulating the land reform, because the owners affected by the reform were predominantly affiliated with minorities rather than the state nation. Another example was the settlement of war loans

---

257 Letter of the Ministry of National Defence no. 17769 of May 27, 1919 for Administrative Board of the Ministerial Council: Národní archiv v Praze (NA), collection Předsednictvo ministerské rady, box 3295, file Zákaz označovati . . . [Prohibition of Placing Inscriptions . . .].

258 Sobota, *Národnostní právo československé*, pp. 1–2.

which had been subscribed significantly more often by the Germans and Hungarians than by the Czechs and Slovaks.

The nationality element – i.e. the preferential treatment of the state nation – was even more pronounced in the case of laws providing compensation to the participants in the (first) resistance, as basically only the members of the (now) ruling nation took part in the resistance: Act on the Compensation for the Victims of Political Persecution during the War 1914–1918 of 15 April 1920 (No. 333/1920 Sb.) and legionary statutes. Legionaries were granted considerable advantages under acts No. 282 and No. 462 of 1919. They were entitled to 50% of posts of servants and supervisors with state authorities, enterprises and institutions funded by the state. Legionaries were preferred over other applicants when applying for jobs with state authorities, courts, state civil guards, and financial guards. Thanks to these laws the proportion of the Czechs in state administration was greatly increased – but the official justification for the restriction of the minority members was their alleged lack of language skills of Czech and Slovak as the official languages. It was the struggle to secure posts in public administration which most worried the German minority, apart from language and educational issues.[259] Thus, the minority policy found its way into certain statutes on the position of civil servants. For example, the Act laying down Provisions for Civil Servants and Officers of the Former Hungarian State of 15 April 1920 (No. 269/1920 Sb.) was influenced by the fact that Hungarian employees at first refused to take the oath of allegiance after the establishment of the Czechoslovak Republic.

Other regulations touching on the status of nationalities included the Act on the Relationship between Prague Universities (No.135/1920 Sb.), named "Lex Mareš" after its sponsor. The Act renamed the Czech University as Charles University; Charles University was declared to be the successor of the university founded by Charles IV in the 14th century.[260] In 1925 special Act on Public Holidays and Commemorative Days (No. 65/1925 Sb.) was enacted and some other less important laws and especially implementory legislation followed. To sum up, a substantial number of regulations either directly or indirectly addressed, albeit fractionally, the issue of the legal status of minorities. The approach to these issues varied depending on one's attitude to the Czechoslovak state – some nationalist jurists from the minorities circles tended to regard very many regulations as having a negative influence on the minorities. In such disputes the nationalist perspective often prevailed over the scientific viewpoint. "Exploring such moments and selecting on

---

259 Zdeněk Deyl, *Sociální vývoj Československa 1918–1938* (Prague: Academia, 1985), p. 34; Kučera, *Minderheit im Nationalstaat*, pp. 24 and 246–297.
260 For the documents see Jan Krčmář, *The Prague Universities: Compiled according to the sources and records* (Prague: Orbis, 1934), esp. pp. 25–31.

their basis legal regulations relevant for the nationality policy is the task for a writer – a politician, but not for a lawyer."[261]

Besides legal rules which were to a certain extent less favourable for the minorities, there were also some other regulations relevant for the status of minorities. Some of them were in fact advantageous for the minorities in that they ensured equality – e.g. regulations on the composition of public bodies and franchise. For example, although the rules on the composition of certain public and advisory bodies did not expressly provide for the representation of minorities, such representation was guaranteed in the institutions divided according to nations (e.g. universities, trade corporations, etc.) – even though such representation was not proportional: e.g. the State Statistical Council (Act No. 634/1919 Sb.), the State Trade Council (Act No. 59/1920 Sb.), the Advisory Body for Sports (Act No. 616/1920 Sb.), etc.

Highly significant were legal rules providing for franchise in Czechoslovakia, based on proportional representation. This was not restricted to Parliament (Constitutional Charter of 1920, Title II., the Chamber of Deputies: Act No. 123/1920 Sb., the Senate: Act No. 124/1920 Sb.), but covered local self-government as well (e.g. municipalities: Act No. 75/1919 Sb.) and other bodies (delegates to general meetings, boards of directors and supervisory committees of sickness insurance funds and companies: Act No. 689/1920 Sb. and No. 221/1924 Sb., the committee and board of directors of the Central Social Insurance Company: Act No. 221/1924 Sb., trade communities: Act No. 217/1923 Sb., industrial committees: Act No. 330/1921 Sb., etc.). According to Czech experts of the interwar period, the principle of proportional representation was one of the most important guarantees of the protection of minorities.[262] However, it should be emphasised that, unlike smaller minorities, the German minority would probably not have been prejudiced by the majority electoral system. Also, it should be pointed out that the Czech representatives gerrymandered the election results in order to weaken the position of the Germans, which was quite striking, for example, in the case of the attempted administrative reform. At any rate, the state's democratic character enabled the minorities to exercise their franchise and subsequently to participate in the government and self-government, which was in general rather unusual in the interwar period.

Legal rules concerning the economy were particularly significant for the status of minorities, which had to do with the previous economic superiority of the Germans and Hungarians and the efforts of the Czechoslovak ruling

---

261 Sobota, *Národnostní právo československé*, p. 2.
262 Similarly, protection was guaranteed against infringements that could occur when dividing seats on the basis of the remaining votes, Laponce, *The Protection of Minorities*, p. 127; Sobota, *Národnostní právo československé*, pp. 1–2.

elite to change that. In this complex area the actual legal regulations (which did not explicitly mention minorities) were not so important as were their purpose and practical arrangements. This specific issue must be addressed in a comprehensive and thorough manner, as it was in the economic area where minorities lost their traditional positions most markedly, primarily during the land reform. Immediately after the establishment of the Czechoslovak Republic the German-Austrian and Hungarian business and aristocratic classes maintained, in the Czech lands and in Slovakia respectively, the strongest positions in industry, agriculture, and business, which endangered the primacy of the Czech nation in the new Czechoslovak state. Moreover, Czechoslovakia had initially strong economic ties with Vienna and Budapest – i.e. with the countries which were potentially hostile due to the minority issue.

According to Czech historian V. Lacina "in order to compete the Czech and Slovak bourgeoisie could rely on the state's economic policy which considerably weakened the economic positions of the German bourgeoisie and aristocracy through monetary policy, nostrification (*TN: forcing certain companies to transfer their head offices to the territory of the new state*), land reform, and other measures."[263] This struggle to put an end to German and Hungarian economic supremacy, which was passed off as a great national work was often portraied as a "satisfaction for the Battle of White Mountain of 1620" and greatly resonated with the public immediately after the war. Economic interventions were being prepared by the domestic resistance even before the fall of the Habsburg Monarchy, in particular the scheme of the so-called Draft Fundamental Act (divided into a political and economic strand) which was, however, never approved or even discussed by Parliament after the establishment of the Czechoslovak Republic. The vast majority of proposed measures were implemented by way of separate regulations during the first two years after the war. The Draft Fundamental Act highlighted the importance of interventions which aimed to weaken the position of the German bourgeoisie and aristocracy.[264]

After the establishment of Czechoslovakia the monetary reform and later monetary policy were generally the most important instruments of the state's economic policy. In addition, in the first years there were measures in place to ensure the economic independence of the Czechoslovak Republic and the hegemony of the Czechs, such as nostrification in industry and banking, as well as the land reform in agriculture. Nostrification, which forced certain companies to transfer their foreign head offices to the territory of Czechoslovakia, significantly reinforced the influence of the Czech capital in major businesses in Czechoslovakia – the Czech capital acquired an interest

---

263 Vlastislav Lacina, *Formování československé ekonomiky 1918–1923* (Prague: Academia, 1990), p. 7.
264 Ibid., pp. 7 and 61–63.

in the majority of nostrified businesses, and in many nostrified businesses the Czech capital gained decisive influence. In this way, nostrification, which was meant to release the Czechoslovak Republic from the economic influence of Vienna and Budapest, introduced complex mechanisms to promote the participation of the Czech capital, and consequently rearranged the powers of individual nations within the Czechoslovak economy, weakening the Germans and Hungarians. The persons concerned were mostly foreigners, i.e. citizens of newly established Austria and Hungary, but that was largely irrelevant in terms of the influence of the nations within the state. Overall, through monetary reform, nostrification, and repatriation of the capital the Czech business elite managed to eliminate German and Hungarian supremacy in industry, business and banking, and to effect large capital and property transfers to their own benefit. On the other hand, it should be emphasised that the strengthening of the Czech positions in the economy was a long-term process which had started at the time of the Habsburg Monarchy, and that the Germans themselves were largely responsible for the weakening of their positions. Notably during the crucial initial stages after the establishment of the Czechoslovak Republic the Germans felt distrust and antipathy toward Czechoslovakia, and lesser participation of the German capital significantly contributed to a reinforced Czech position within the new state's emerging economy.[265]

While the crucial influence of the German capital was weakened, it remained greater than what the proportion of the minority to the population would suggest. Thus, in many prominent businesses (notably in the mining and metallurgy industry) the German language remained as the official language, and Germans often held dominant positions in businesses with a predominantly Czech workforce. "Managers of mines and ironworks who were in charge of production tended to prefer German workers, assigned better paid work to them, and did not dismiss them among the first ones to be dismissed . . . , etc."[266] In this way, the members of the largest German minority managed to maintain, at least partially, their advantageous position in the private sector, unlike in the public sector.

As in the case of industry and business, at the beginning of the existence of independent Czechoslovakia agricultural property was largely held by the Germans and Hungarians. One third of all land belonged to large farm estates which were predominantly owned by German and Hungarian aristocracy and the Catholic church. The land reform, in addition to its national significance, also aimed at social aspects because the rural population had struggled with

---

265 Lacina, *Formování československé ekonomiky*, pp. 91, 100, 109 and 125; Kárník, *České země v éře první republiky*, vol. 1, pp. 213–220.

266 Deyl, *Sociální vývoj Československa 1918–1938*, p. 40.

a shortage of available land.[267] A peculiar side effect of the land reform was the Czechisation of part of the aristocracy living in Czechoslovakia (in particular the houses of Lobkowicz, Colloredo-Mansfeld and Schwarzenberg). These aristocrats also tried to become closer to the most influential Czech Agrarian Party. Thanks to their connections at the Land Office, at the Prague Castle, and at the Agrarian Party, a part of aristocracy managed to avoid land reform rather successfully.[268] An important element of the reform was the colonisation of sparsely populated borderland regions, mainly in Slovakia. The colonists were almost invariably Czechs and Slovaks who were financially supported by the state, which irritated the minorities, although the actual scale of the operation was rather limited.[269]

Agrarian reforms, which took place after WWI in Czechoslovakia, Poland, Romania, Lithuania, and other countries, were often criticized as measures targeted against minorities.[270] Many complaints against land reforms were dealt with by the League of Nations, which struggled with their resolution due to the complexity of the issues in connection with specific technical and agricultural matters. Minorities invoked minority treaties and referred to land reforms *inter alia* as violations of internationally guaranteed equality of citizens. Unlike many other issues which provoked criticism of the new so-called successor states by the international community, these interventions were largely considered as justified by other (mainly western) countries, aimed at consolidating the social situation in rural areas. According to one of the directors of the Minority Section of the League of Nations, Pablo de Azcárate, the land reforms negatively affected the minorities as a natural consequence of the historical development, because previously the ruling nations had been preferred and after the war they became minorities. He went on to designate the reforms as the basis for the economic and social consolidation of those countries, and he considered it preposterous if the minority treaties had not allowed such measures as violations of equality. Although in some countries the reforms were accompanied by unfair treatment, this expert indicated that in Czechoslovakia the agrarian reform was conducted in the fairest manner.[271]

---

267 For legal aspects see Kuklík, *Czech law in historical contexts*, pp. 91–92. For political and social aspects Kárník, *České země v éře první republiky*, vol. 1, pp. 453, 470, 479–488.

268 Lacina, *Formování československé ekonomiky*, pp. 125, 129.

269 Martuliak, "Kolonizačná akcia pri I. pozemkovej reforme," pp. 81–85.

270 In more details for example Wojciech Roszkowski, *Land Reforms in East Central Europe After World War One* (Warsaw: Institute of Political Studies, Polish Academy of Sciences, 1995).

271 Azcárate, *League of Nations and National Minorities*, pp. 62–64: "I feel that the state which carried out agrarian reform with the greatest justice to its minority was Czechoslovakia" (pp. 63–64).

2.4 LANGUAGE LAW

Language law, i.e. legislation concerning the possibility to use the mother tongue when approaching authorities and within the scope of their activities, created, in common practice, essentially the most important, as well as the most extensive, part of national minority law.[272] Before an overview of the First Czechoslovak Republic legislation we first have to refer to the historical development of the issue, which is, in connection with the language law, of major influence. Without the knowledge of a number of circumstances relating to the times of the Habsburg Monarchy quite a few elements of the law of the Czechoslovak Republic cannot be fully comprehended.[273]

In Austrian part of the Habsburg Monarchy the language issue was regulated by Article 19 of the "Fundamental Law of the State" (Act No. 142/1867, Austrian RGBl), which granted all nations equality – also when using their own languages. This brief provision, though, was interpreted quite differently and gave rise to conflicts which sometimes had to be resolved out in the streets! Germans, holding the position of the ruling nation, claimed that this was just a general principle which had to be amended to be actually implemented.[274] Using these arguments they tried to keep the prerogative position of the German language over the Czech language in the Czech lands. Disputes arose e.g. over the concept of "all customary languages in the country" – which should all possess equality "in school, office and public life" (Article 19, section 2). In accordance with the opinion advocated by some courts, with which German nationalists agreed, the German language was commonly used in the entire territory of the Czech lands, while the Czech language was used only in some areas, and not within districts inhabited by a German majority even though settled by a relatively strong Czech minority.

There were two major issues surrounding the conflicts concerning the language of state administration. First: the differentiation between the external and internal official language. Second: how this issue should be regulated – by an Act of Parliament (or Provincial Diet), by a regulation, or just by internal ordinance.[275] Meanwhile the Czech language was usually accepted

---

272 See for example Peter Mosný, "Poznámky k jazykovému právu v Československu 1918–1938," in *Minority v politike: Kultúrne a jazykové práva*, ed. by Jana Plichtová (Bratislava: Česko-slovenský výbor Európskej kultúrnej nadácie, 1992), pp. 112–113.

273 Even during the times of the Habsburg monarchy the old history, sometimes back to the 12th century, was used as an argument supporting language disputes, Jan Kapras, *Přehled vývoje české jazykové otázky* (Prague: R. Brož, 1910).

274 See *Slovník veřejného práva československého*, p. 62ff.; or Klepetař, *Der Sprachenkampf in den Sudetenländern*, pp. 35–126.

275 Of major importance was namely the so-called Pacák's Proposal of the Language Act from the end of the 19th century – Allgemeines Verwaltungsarchiv Wien, collection Ministerium

in dealing with the parties (external official language), within the scope of internal official language – that is the language used while working in the office or the language serving as the communication between the authorities themselves – the exclusiveness of the German language was maintained in the Czech lands. Czechs generally acknowledged the overall communicative function of German within the Habsburg Monarchy, yet still its prevailing position in the inner administration in the Czech lands, in which this was the language of a minority, had been ravishing when comparing the position of Polish in Galicia or even Italian (in the Habsburg Monarchy spread just a little) in Dalmatia and other areas had the status of internal official languages. The possibility to use Czech in Silesia was far more restricted than it was in Bohemia and in Moravia.

Attempts for acquiring the equality of the Czech language in the Czech lands gave rise to conflicts lasting till the end of the Habsburg Monarchy and Austrian governments, both of which attempted to solve this issue by regulations or acts by which means they entered skating on very thin ice. In 1897 the so-called Badeni Decrees for Bohemia and Moravia were issued – decrees of the Ministers of the Interior, Law, Finance, Commerce and Ploughing (No. 12, Bohemian Provincial Code, No. 29, Moravian Provincial Code) regulating the usage of languages in proceedings of courts, state Prosecuting Attorney's Offices, and inferior authorities. The Badeni Decrees significantly expanded the rights of the Czech language not only in the inner bureaucracy but they also initiated huge riots amongst Germans, especially in Vienna (i.e. outside the Czech lands), which resulted in the resignation of the government and the withdrawal of the Decrees. Later governments sought to establish mono-lingual regional administrative districts (negotiations were held e.g. in 1903 and 1909) and the language issue became connected with the proposed regional administration. German parties generally tried to make German codified as a state language by which it would be ensured the predominant position once and for all.

A different situation could be found in connection with self-government, where the major importance in the usage of language was granted by the established practice of the Supreme Administrative Court and the Court of the Empire (Reichsgericht). Self-governing corporations possessed the right to independently establish their language of agenda, but they were also obliged (according to Article 19, the Fundamental Act of the State No. 142/1867 Austrian R.G.Bl.) to accept petitions in other languages common in the relevant country. Whereas the Court of the Empire acknowledged Czech and German as common languages within the whole of Bohemia, the Supreme

des Innern, Präsidiale 3–1848–1918, box 73, where lots of files relating to the proposal can be found – P.Nr.2056/M.J. 1899 [P.No.2056/Ministry of Justice 1989], 2350/M.J 1989, 2657/M.J./99.

Administrative Court assessed the common language essentially just for the territorial district of the given self-governing corporation. This discrepancy gave rise to many conflicts. This generally led, in the issue of the usage of languages in self-government, to wilfulness resulting in chaos.[276]

In Hungary the legislation was quite different. The state language was Hungarian under Act No. 44/1868. The option of using minority languages was even more restricted by later acts as well as by practice.[277]

Language law, being in force during the interwar period in the Czechoslovak Republic, was based on the Constitutional Charter and above all on the Language Act of 29 February, 1920 (Act No. 122/1920 Sb.), together with implementing regulation from 1926 (No. 17/1926 Sb.) ; but what has to be taken into concern is also the complicated situation of the first year and a half after the establishment of the Czechoslovak Republic. October 1918 entailed, in contrast with the majority of other legal branches, a significant change in the language issue. According to the so-called Reception Act "the existing provincial and Empire acts and regulations remain in force" (Article 2, Act No. 11/1918 Sb.), but the rules not reflecting the existence of an independent state could not be subsequently applied, such as rules restricting the use of the Czechoslovak language, so the Czechoslovak government had to deal with this issue with no delay. "Ministerial Council at the meeting held on 22 November 1918, agreed that all autonomous self-governing offices' inquiries should be answered in their own language, while state offices should communicate only in Czech."[278]

The key language issue had been solved mainly by the Supreme Administrative Court in its principal resolution from the 19 March 1919[279]: "By the nature of the Czechoslovak state as the national state, . . . which was stated in the Act of 28 October 1918, No. 11/1918 Sb., a logical legal consequence may be implied – that the Czech (Slovak) language is the language in which the state and its respective bodies express their will and exercise their rights."[280] The court referred to certain legal rules already issued by the new state, as was namely the Reception Act No. 11/1918 Sb. It particularly pointed out radical Section 3 of Act No. 64/1918 Sb. concerning the extraordinary temporal provisions in Slovakia – "In Slovakia the office agenda is carried out in Slovak. As

---

276 See for example Allgemeines Verwaltungsarchiv Wien, collection Ministerium des Innern, Präsidiale 3–1848–1918, box 73.

277 *Slovník veřejného práva československého*, pp. 63–64; Wenzel Frind, *Das sprachliche und sprachlich-nationale Recht* (Vienna: Manz, 1899), pp. 311–342; Horáček, *Jazykové právo československé republiky*, pp. 38–40.

278 Národní archiv Praha (NA), collection Ministerstvo vnitra – stará registratura, box 502, file 8 File Předsednictvo ministerské rady, Pres. No. 1519 27.11.1918 for the Ministry of the Interior].

279 Decision of the Supreme Administrative Court No. 73/1918, *Sbírka nálezů Nejvyššího správního soudu*, vol. 5; see also Kučera, *Minderheit im Nationalstaat*, p. 17ff.

280 *Sbírka nálezů Nejvyššího správního soudu*, vol. 1, pp. 557–558. Adoptio Plenissima.

for the right to use other, in Slovakia indigenous, languages, a special decree will be issued."[281]

The preference of the state nation was expressed very clearly in this controversial finding of the Supreme Administrative Court. "Members of other national tribes, incorporated into the territory of this state, are not eligible to claim, in connection with their national rights, more than the rights ensuring them to live their own national life and use their own language, supposing that these rights can be guaranteed by the national state without losing its own national character." The Court might have paradoxically referred to Article 19 of Austrian Fundamental Act of the State, No. 142/1867 Austrian R.G.Bl., which according to the so-called Reception Act (No. 11/1918 Sb.) remained to a limited extent in force. In accordance with the resolution of the Supreme Administrative Court it followed, for national minorities, that they "were provided with, once they were recognised as a national minority, within the given territorial district in which they could be considered a national minority, while dealing with all authorities for this district established and competent, the possibility to seek and find rights." A territorial district meant a judicial district. This resolution enforced the priority of the state nation, which can be found natural; still, minority rights were sometimes restricted very harshly. Above all, the protection of language rights, when dealing with administrative bodies as well as courts, was declared to minorities just in those judicial districts where they constituted at least half of the population, and nowhere else! Moreover, minority protection was only applied to citizens, and whoever claimed these rights for himself had to prove his citizenship. Generally until the Language Act became effective, i.e. till 6 March 1920, the recepted regulations from the time of the Habsburg Monarchy was still in force (for the territory of Slovakia Act No. 64/1918 Sb. applied), but the privileges of German and Hungarian were transferred to Czech and Slovak, and the possibility to use minority languages when dealing with authorities were to be rather restricted, according to the finding of the Supreme Administrative Court – the usual practice, however, was quite different.

Even at government offices, including the key Ministry of the Interior, the limit of 50% led to a certain embarrassment, since 25% had been considered before and most frequently the limit wouldn't get above 20%. "While

---

281 *Slovník veřejného práva československého*, p. 65. It is necessary to add that section 3 of Act No. 64/1918 was quite a controversial provision. The decree which should regulate the use of other languages in Slovakia had never been issued.; as explained by Horáček, *Jazykové právo československé republiky*, pp. 124–125 with reference to Hausmann "In reality the language issue had never been settled and the regulation of section 3 of the cited Act of 10 December 1918, if it was made public at all, was rarely applied in practice and fell into oblivion!" From the legal point of view this is a really shocking statement which still, considering the chaos of the early stages in Slovakia, may match the reality.

the specific language issues were regulated at the interministerial meetings so far, in some cases (the issue of public notices, forms, announcements on premises, etc.) the limit of 20% was considered."[282] The finding of the Supreme Administrative Court of 19 March 1919, concerned only state administration and not self-government, which usually operated the way it used to be during the Habsburg Monarchy,[283] and also for a number of specific branches another solution was chosen, when e.g. in accordance with the decree of the Ministry of Postal Services of 22 March, 1919, the language for postal stamps was chosen, basically, on the basis of 20%; plenty of other similar details were being resolved at the same time.[284] Incidentally, a number of state agencies used German as the only language because many clerks had no knowledge of a single Czech word, and that was mostly tolerated: "I would excuse this to a limited extent but just for a certain time, . . . but even in this case it has to be taken into account that they will not process the agenda in German forever and that they should take care to learn Czech very diligently."[285]

The stabilisation of language law regulations was accomplished after the enactment of the Constituional acts on 29 February 1920. The Czechoslovak language law of the interwar period was extremely detailed and complex, however, our interpretation is not intended to examine details but rather to point out basic elements and problematic issues. The Constitutional Charter itself contained a number of provisions concerning the use of languages. Mainly according to Section 128 (3) citizens were allowed to "within the framework of general acts, freely use any language in private and business interactions, in the issues concerning religion, in press and publications, or during public meetings." Besides specific provisions regulating the use of languages, Section 129 referred to a special act forming part of the Constitution and regulating the principles of language law. According to some opinions the Constitutional Charter also determined the concept of language law, by which we understand only those legal rules "which regulate the use of languages in those relations for which the principles are set out in the Language Act."[286] This legal institute will not cover the rules regulating the use of language in private, business, and other spheres, according to Section 128 of the Constitutional Charter. The major subject matter of the legislation of the Language Act No.122/1920 Sb. were the principles of language use in

---

282 Národní archiv v Praze (NA), collection Ministerstvo vnitra, stará registratura (MV), box 502, file 10, doc. MV no. 12687/1919 from April 2, 1919.

283 With the inception of the Republic this led to a number of conflicts between the state and self-governing corporations with a German majority – for example Národní archiv v Praze (NA), collection Předsednictvo ministerské rady, box 3295.

284 Národní archiv v Praze (NA), collection Ministerstvo vnitra – stará registratura, box 502, file 1.

285 Ibid., file 5, Presidium zemské správy politické v Praze (no. 335518) from October 18, 1919 for the Ministry of Interior.

286 *Slovník veřejného práva československého*, p. 66.

the following spheres: determining the language of the state – that is, the language of state authorities when performing their administrative power and within the course of their other activities, and also the language which could be used by individuals when interacting with the state and state authorities, guidelines regulating the use of languages in connection with self-governing authorities, representative bodies, and public corporations.[287]

The base of language law was constituted by "the Act passed on 29 February 1920, in accordance with Section 129 of the Constitutional Charter, by which the principles of language law in the Czechoslovak Republic are determined" (Language Act No. 122/1920 Sb.).[288] This was the Constitutional Act in accordance with Section 129 of the Constitutional Charter, and it should be remembered that, taking into consideration its rigid character, that on the grounds of the political situation as well as of the nationality issues of the First Czechoslovak Republic, it was practically unalterable. It laid down the principal that Czechoslovak was the state, official language of the Czechoslovak Republic.

When determining the principles of language law, law makers took into account the obligations of the Czechoslovak Republic resulting from the Minorities Treaty of St. Germain which contained certain provisions regarding the language issue . Thus Section 1 of the Language Act followed Article 7 (4), of the Minorities Treaty. Even though "the Saint-Germain Treaty, which the law maker tried to follow as strictly as possible, did not provide many guidelines for regulating the subject matter by the national legislation," according to the opinion of experts "the wording of this Treaty is of a high importance when interpreting potentially controversial parts of the Act."[289] Still, as the Supreme Administrative Court pointed out in its finding of 29 March 1921 (No. 13.297/20, Collection of decisions by dr. Bohuslav, administrative series No. 786),[290] the right to use a minority language could only be derived from the Language Act of 1920 and not directly from the Minorities Treaty of St. Germain.

The key issue, when forming the act, as also stressed by the explanatory memorandum of the Constitutional Committee,[291] was to adjust the

---

287 Emil Sobota, *Výklad našeho jazykového práva* (Prague: Ústřední dělnické knihk. a naklad. Ant. Svěcený, 1926), p. 5. As distinct from some other countries, the Czechoslovak constitutional law tried to precisely ensure the right to use the language, Laponce, *The Protection of Minorities*, p. 57.

288 The analysis of the so-called Hartmann Act, Antonín Hartmann, *Předpisy jazykového práva* (Prague: Československý Kompas, 1925), pp. 28–77; Sobota, *Národnostní právo československé*, pp. 75–89; Sobota, *Výklad našeho jazykového práva*; Leo Epstein, *Das Sprachenrecht der Tschechoslowakischen Republik* (Reichenberg: Gebrüder Stiepel, 1927), pp. 47–136; Peška, *Československá ústava a zákony s ní souvislé*, vol. 2, p. 1768; Malý, "Sprache – Recht und Staat," p. 273ff.

289 Weyr, *Soustava československého práva státního*, p. 400.

290 *Sbírka nálezů Nejvyššího správního soudu*, vol. 3, pp. 319–321.

291 *Tisky k těsnopiseckým zprávám*, vol. 9, print no. 2442.

requirements of minorities to the most extended possibility of using their languages with the interest of the state that the authorities would not be overwhelmed by the extraordinary usage of a variety of languages. "This is not the national-political approach, but just a simple requirement that the state administration be organised effectively, reflecting the needs of the citizens." "Seeking the compromise of the needs of citizens and the interest of the state, the Constitutional Committee restricted its memorandum on what the actual and indispensable requirement of the state was; the result of this was that the state language was not empowered with such far-reaching and unnecessarily extended means of preference of actual usage in the same way as German was actually used in Austria and Hungarian used by law in Hungary."[292] It should be added that the reality did not always correspond to these beautiful words of law makers and that the preference of the state language was significant.

Right with the beginning of the effect of the Language Act of 1920, the controversial term of the Czechoslovak language appeared;[293] still, as the explanatory memorandum[294] stressed, the Constitutional Committee had no intention, by using this term, of taking a stand on – or even of acting on dispute – whether Czech and Slovak were independent languages. Another particularly important term followed instantly – "state, official language of the Czechoslovak Republic,"[295] by which it was meant the Czechoslovak language. This apparently not a crucial term gave rise to conspicuous debates and also caused significant obstacles when passing the law. It was also related to the Minorities Treaty of St. Germain, which stated the "langue officielle," and that was translated in the original Czech version of the Minorities Treaty as the "administrative" language, but the translation in the collection says "official."

The dispute over whether the Czechoslovak language should be the "state" or "official" language gave rise to magnificent conflicts when the Language Act was formulated. Some political parties attached great importance to the explicit announcement of Czechoslovak as the "state" language, significantly greater than to the actually important detailed list of its particular preference. This peculiar conflict may be understood just from the historical point of view, since at the times of the Habsburg Monarchy, German nationalist parties, against the resistance of Czechs, promoted the explicit proclamation

---

292 Ibid., pp. 1–2.
293 Horáček, *Jazykové právo československé republiky*, pp. 18–23. Principally, in the Czech lands, the office agenda should be carried out in Czech and in Slovakia in Slovak, but within the Czech environment the substitution of standard Slovak with Czech was considered for a long time – up until 1930, Rychlík, "Teorie a praxe jednotného československého národa," p. 69. Czech officers in Slovakia then, and for a long time, preferred Czech.
294 *Tisky k těsnopiseckým zprávám*, vol. 9, print no. 2442, pp. 2–3.
295 Klepetař, *Der Sprachenkampf in den Sudetenländern*, p. 14; Horáček, *Jazykové právo československé republiky*, pp. 24–37; Kural, *Konflikt místo společenství?*, pp. 35–37.

of German as a state language ("Staatssprache"), by which they thought that it would reach the legal entitlement to preferences that, so far, it had held only factually. No concrete requirements enforcing the impact of German were in question and so this was just a formal argument. Due to this the state language became a very well-known term, and many people falsely thought that this was a coined and framed term, which contained, without any additional legislation, important privileges. This caused persevering disputes which, according to the opinions of a number of experts in law, were of no legal importance. On the basis of the proclamation of the language as the state language, only the general preference favouring the Czechoslovak language might have been deduced in controversial matters.[296]

Section 1 of the Language Act of 1920 further defined the use of the Czechoslovak language. "Czechoslovak is primarily the language, 1st in which, with the exception of other provisions . . . all the agenda of courts, offices, institutions, businesses and administrative bodies of the Czechoslovak Republic is carried out,[297] as well as public notes and outer markings, 2nd in which the main text of state notes and banknotes is formulated, 3rd which is used by the armed forces during their command and as the language of administrative service; when dealing with a team not knowing this language, Hungarian may also be used." This list was only demonstrative, and while interpreting controversial matters, the state language was in common preference. The Language Act mentions the agenda (ad 1.) and did not explicitly distinguish between the internal and external office agenda, as it was applied, even though more in reality than by law, at the times of the Monarchy. Considering the fact that Section 1 regulated the office agenda to be carried out, generally, in the Czechoslovak language and Section 2 admitted the exceptions just for the internal agenda of state courts, offices, businesses, and others, the internal agenda was carried out exclusively in the state language. These provisions did not relate to the self-government which was regulated quite distinctively by other legislation.

Of major importance was Section 2, introduced by the words referring to the Minorities Treaty of St. Germain – "On national and language minorities (Title 1) the following provisions are in force:" Section 2 in particular represented the key issue of minorities' languages[298] – that is the possibility of members of minorities to use their own language. This whole matter was perhaps too extensively complex and for authorities or courts it meant a tough

---

296 Weyr, *Soustava československého práva státního*, pp. 401–403. Accordingly also Hartmann, *Předpisy jazykového práva*, pp. 30–31; Epstein, *Studien-Ausgabe der Verfassungsgesetze*, pp. 261–262.

297 Klepetař, *Der Sprachenkampf in den Sudetenländern*, p. 134; Horáček, *Jazykové právo československé republiky*, p. 45–47.

298 Peška, *Československá ústava a zákony s ní souvislé*, vol. 2, pp. 1774–1786; Horáček, *Jazykové právo československé republiky*, p. 57.

proposition. "Courts, administrative offices, and representative bodies of the Czechoslovak Republic, the powers of which administer the judicial district, in which, according to the latest population census, at least 20% of the citizens of the same but other than Czechoslovak language are . . . obliged to accept from members of this language minority filings in their language and to issue the settling of these filings not only in the Czechoslovak language but also in the language of the filing." The possibility of the members of minorities to use their own language when approaching the state offices depended on the quantity of the (relative) nationality in the given district. The possibility to use one's own – minority – language was outlined as an exception from the principle of carrying the office agenda in the state language, which was effective throughout the entire territory.

The major issue concerning the Language Act was the limit of 20%, which might be considered as relatively liberal,[299] as the explanatory memorandum (print No. 2442/1920) did not forget to remind: "It should be remembered that the draft of many variations, the selection of which provides an outline of the history of the language issue so far, was chosen so that it would be the most convenient to the minorities." Most important was that the limit of 20% was determined individually for each judicial district, and so a minority did not have to constitute one fifth of the citizens of the whole state; on the other hand, large minorities in Czechoslovakia had the possibility to use their own language when dealing with authorities just in those districts were they exceeding the 20% limit. The obligation to accept as well as to administer filings in the minority language (and, simultaneously, in the state language) did not relate just to the offices of the district level, but to all offices of a higher level, including central ones, once their competence covered the district of a 20% of minority. As members of a minority language were considered not only natural persons but also legal entities (resolution of the Ministry of Justice of 28 July 1922, No. 28.856/22), so even they acquired the possibility to use a minority language. In connection with the problem who was the member of a minority language group and what rights he acquired, lots of judicial decisions were quickly issued (mainly by the Supreme Administrative Court),[300] out of which the complexity of the issue could be observed.

Other provisions of Section 2 admitted that the decree determined some districts in which the issuance of a ruling could only be carried out in the minority language and the state language would not simultaneously have to be used. This was certainly applied only to specific cases for which the

---

299 Horáček, *Jazykové právo československé republiky*, pp. 57–59; Klepetař, *Der Sprachenkampf in den Sudetenländern*, p. 141ff.

300 See Hartmann, *Předpisy jazykového práva*, pp. 46–63; Peška, *Československá ústava a zákony s ní souvislé*, vol. 2, pp. 1775–1786.

possibility to use a minority language existed, since the state language was preferred throughout the entire territory. For instance, even in purely German areas only the members of the German minority could use German, whereas others had to act in the state language. Section 2 also contained other provisions (e.g. on a criminal action filed in a minority language) and generally the whole matter was rather complicated, as it can be observed from commentaries on the act and further analyses. In numerous cases even the state offices produced significant incompetencies! For instance, in accordance with the last subsection of Section 2, in judicial districts with a minority of at least 20%, the minority language should be used on public notes, outer markings of state courts, offices, and administrative bodies – but only next to the state language, which could not be omitted, which constituted the general concept of the Language Act of 1920. "Nevertheless, it was observed that in the notices, mainly in 'the Official Notice,' on a daily basis, the judicial notices of some courts were published only in minority languages. . . . So I demand that inferior courts (offices) be strongly notified on this imperative statutory instrument" (Decree of the Ministry of Justice of 12 September 1922, No. 41.106/22)[301].

The number of language law issues was disputable, as e.g. if the foreigners were the subjects of the advantage of Section 2.[302] A number of legal experts discussed this issue in their treatises, as well as the Supreme Court and the Supreme Administrative Court, both of which took mutually different approaches, and also, last but not least, the Ministry of Justice. This, e.g., in its Decree of 2 November 1924, No. 40.958/24, dealt with the factual issue which, after the on-going disputes, had appeared before this instance. This issue did not concern a regular matter but its prolonging and complex legal settlement was, unfortunately, rather characteristic in connection with the language law disputes, and so we have decided to give it closer attention. It is also of some interest that the decree referred to the Minorities Treaty of St. Germain as a key argument – this was, paradoxically, common in the First Czechoslovak Republic language law, even though the interpretation of this rather peculiar international legal institute was not, particularly in details, either solid or unambiguous.

The Ministry of Justice was resolving the issue of whether the claimant, born in Chile, who was not a Czechoslovak citizen and claimed that his mother tongues were Spanish and German, was entitled to use German while dealing with the state organs in accordance with minority provisions of the Language Act. The Ministry took the position that it could not be

---

301 Quoted according to Hartmann, *Předpisy jazykového práva*, p. 67.
302 See Epstein, *Studien-Ausgabe der Verfassungsgesetze*, pp. 263–265; Peška, *Národní menšiny a Československo*, pp. 155–158.

acknowledged (because of the validity of the Language Act) that someone could be a member of two or more languages, and the claimant would state Spanish as the first language. This language, as opposed to German, did not fulfil the requirement of the 20% limit in the given judicial district, the claimant did not hold Czechoslovak citizenship, and as such he was forced, when dealing with authorities, to use the state language. The overall analysis of the matter was very complex,[303] but today it is not essential which way the issue was solved, but mainly that the conclusion was that language law was frequently too complex. The common administrative practice (and courts – even the Supreme Administrative Court were wasting time) then had to deal with complicated and trifling details – e.g. if someone could hold two language affiliations – and the question arises why these issues were not resolved somewhat more liberally.

The preference of the state language, as the above mentioned case illustrated, significantly added to the complexity of this issue, since it was not, for example, possible to freely decide to use a minority language (in this case German) not even in those regions where the authorities otherwise accepted the given minority language and it would therefore not constitute a problem from an administrative point of view. Czechoslovak politicians were afraid that in the districts where German (or even Hungarian) could be used, this language would be preferred by members of other minorities, foreigners, and maybe even other state citizens, which would disrupt the national character of the state and weaken its status in the eyes of the allies.

Section 3 comprised the issue of self-governement: " i.e. self-governing offices, representative bodies, and all public corporations[304] in the Czechoslovak state."[305] An explanatory memorandum (No. 2442/1920) explained why the liberty to choose the use of languages was not granted to the organs of self-government: "To grant the self-governing offices and other public corporations the complete freedom of self-determination in connection with the language issue after the experience procured in the Habsburg Monarchy and during which the concept of self-determination, in the language issue, was frequently substituted by pure despotism, seriously endangering the functioning of the state administration, this is not possible." The experience with frequent chaos and despotism from the times of the Monarchy served as a considerable inspiration when forming language law. The state

---

303 Hartmann, *Předpisy jazykového práva*, pp. 41–42.

304 It related even to churches and so it linked the complicated language law to the complex legal regulation concerning the relations between the state and the church (e.g. the issue relating to Register records), see for example Peška, *Československá ústava a zákony s ní souvislé*, vol. 2, pp. 1789–1790.

305 Epstein, *Das Sprachenrecht*, pp. 111–117; Horáček, *Jazykové právo československé republiky*, p. 82–83; Peška, *Československá ústava a zákony s ní souvislé*, vol. 2, pp. 1789–1791.

language was at an advantage[306] – similarly as in other sections of the Language Act – since the self-government was obliged, in the entire territory of the Czechoslovak Republic, to accept filings in this language and to enable the use of this at meetings, while minority languages held these rights only under the conditions set out by Section 2 (the minimum of 20% minority in a territorial district, and others).

For minorities, Section 5, which specifically guaranteed them a minority educational system, was of major importance. The following Section 6 regulated the complex language issue of Sub-Carpathian Ruthenia:[307] "The Assembly (Provincial Diet), which will be established for Sub-Carpathian Ruthenia, will have the discretion to regulate the language issue for this territory by the means conformable with the idea of the unity of the Czechoslovak State (Article 10 of St. Germain Treaty)." So again, the Language Act refers to the Minorities Treaty of St. Germain. How the language issue could be regulated in a way conformable with the unity of the state was not clear, and so the problem gave rise to various discussions. The idea was promoted that it would not be admissible for the local language to possess the status of an exclusive state language, but the possibility was that it would be equal to the Czechoslovak language. The nation of Sub-Carpathian Ruthenians was not supposed, in any case, to be considered (on the territory of its own autonomy) a minority. According to Section 6 (2), until the Provincial Diet was established, "this Act should be applied, still with respect to specific language relations within the territory." This verbal trickery did not belong to those of a clear meaning and the Assembly (as well as the entire autonomy) was not established. The language of Sub-Carpathian Ruthenia was targeted by a number of other provisions contained in other legislation, whilst it is of some importance that these could not agree on its designation. In some places it was being referred to as a folk language, while other citations would use "Russian (Ruthenian)," only "Russian" language of the Assembly (Provincial Diet), and others.[308] In practice the issue was extraordinarily complex and disputable, since in reality the Ruthenian literary language had not been ready to be used. It balanced between Russian, Ukrainian, and local dialects. Czechoslovak administrative bodies then showed tendencies to rather prefer Czech.

"Conflicts accompanying the use of language at courts, when dealing with offices, institutions, business, and state authorities, as well as with self-governing offices and public corporations, shall be settled by the competent state bodies observing these matters as parts of state administration

306 Criticised by German experts: Schranil, *Gutachten zur tschechoslowakischen Verwaltungsreform*, p. 51.
307 Horáček, *Jazykové právo československé republiky*, p. 101.
308 Hartmann, *Předpisy jazykového práva*, p. 73; Národní archiv v Praze (NA), collection Ministerstvo vnitra – stará registratura, box 502, file 31.

separated from the issue of which this has arisen."(Section7).[309] This seem-ingly hardly understandable provision was similarly, as many others, (e.g. the issue of state-national language) the result of the on-going practice which the Czech lands experienced in connection with language disputes, as the explanatory memorandum (print No. 2442/1920) reminded: "The pro-vision of this section reflects the experience that by connecting the language issue with the subject matter of the dispute, which the administrative body has to settle, many legal inaccuracies and significant damage to the parties were caused." According to the judicial practice during the Monarchy, the judge could, while adjudicating on rather immaterial issues, simultaneously ruled on the language, i.e. the constitutional right of the party, against which there was no appeal. Supervising bodies of the previous Austrian judicial administration then in language disputes refused to take action referring to the independence of the court, even though this was mostly a matter of judicial administration.

"Comprehensive complementation of this Act will be carried out by the decree issued by the executive branch of the state" as stipulated by Section 8.[310] As we have already pointed out such an executive regulation was post-poned until 1926 and constituted a very significant political issue. However, the original ideas supposing that a special language decree would soon come into existence did not materialized.[311] "In view of this, neither the individual ministries nor subordinate offices may, before the actual issuance of the gov-ernment decree itself, . . . by their own orders or dispositions, start to imple-ment the Act by any means,"[312] since it could result in chaotic practice and also be understood as determining the future government decree. Administrative bodies were to follow the current practice as specified e.g. by the Ministerial Council resolution of November 1919. But the original premise was not met and the situation led to a great deal of equivocality as to how to simply still apply the general Language Act. According to the ruling of the Supreme Ad-ministrative Court, the fact that language decrees were not issued yet did not prevent the Act from being effective.[313] This Section 8 also enabled that during the first five years after the Language Act became effective, the decree would enable exceptions "necessary in the interest of ongoing and undisturbed

309 See for example, Peška, *Československá ústava a zákony s ní souvislé*, vol. 2, pp. 1793–1801.

310 Klepetař, *Der Sprachenkampf in den Sudetenländern*, p. 33; Horáček, *Jazykové právo československé republiky*, p. 117.

311 Národní archiv v Praze (NA), collection Předsednictvo ministerské rady, box 1714, file Zákon, jímž se stanoví zásady jazykového práva [The Act Regulating the Principles of Language Law], Ministerstvo spravedlnosti no. 7561 from March 10, 1920.

312 Ibid., file Zákon, jímž se stanoví zásady jazykového práva, Předsednictvo ministerské rady no. 8798/20, Government meeting resolution, March 19, 1920.

313 *Sbírka nálezů Nejvyššího správního soudu*, vol. 6a. [Judgment from March 11, 1924, no. 4150, no 3348], pp. 606–610.

administration," which according to the fact that this was a Constitutional Act, meant a peculiar extension of powers of the executive; meanwhile it was not stated which provisions might be suspended.

According to the last Section 9, the Language Act became effective as from the day of its promulgation – i.e. from 6 March 1920. By this Act all language decrees in force before 28 November 1918 were repealed. This provision gave rise to huge discussions in which some of the authors questioned the grammatical content itself and claimed that not all the regulations were repealed but just those which were in contradiction with the Language Act.[314] Judgements of the Supreme Administrative Court were not consistent when deciding about the extent of derogatory clause. Similarly, the Supreme Court in its holding expressed the view according to which one of these provisions had not been repealed by Section 9. These inconsistent judicial decisions, constituting one of the many of language law issues, frequently gave rise to huge criticism by the experts.[315]

Language law rules mainly consisted of, besides the actual Language Act, government decrees issued to implement this Act. Temporarily, and only for Slovakia, this was the decree No. 27/1924 Sb., which regulated the use of languages in connection with regional councils, regional committees, and district committees established in Slovakia (according to the decree No. 310/1922 Sb.). The language issue was interlinked with the issue of public administration, and so after the failure and cancellation of the regions' (zhupas') reform, the decree regulating the use of the language also disappeared. Of major importance during the First Czechoslovak Republic was Governmental Order No. 17/1926 Sb. by which "the constitutional Language Act was implemented for the Ministry of the Interior, Ministry of Justice, Ministry of Finance, Ministry of Industry, Commerce and Trade, Ministry of Public Works, Ministry of Public Health and Physical Education, for public corporations, submitted to the ministries in the Czechoslovak Republic as well as for the local government bodies." The Order No. 229/1928 Sb. which regulated the use of languages for provincial and district representative bodies as well as for provincial and district commissions, was also very important. It concerned the self-government established under Act No. 125/1927 Sb., on the organisation of political administration which eliminated the regions' (zhupas') reform. By this alteration of public administration the above mentioned Order No. 27/1924 Sb. became obsolete, as well as some other provisions of Order No. 17/1926 Sb.[316]

---

314   Hartmann, *Předpisy jazykového práva*, p. 77. On the contrary e.g. Horáček, *Jazykové právo československé republiky*, pp. 122–124.
315   Horáček, *Jazykové právo československé republiky*, p. 122.
316   *Slovník veřejného práva československého*, p. 67.

Of these orders the most important was the very extensive Governmental Order No. 17/1926 Sb.[317] It regulated, usually in detail and casuistically, a great number of language issues – e.g. register records, official seals, language examinations, and the language of the gendarmerie and customs service. Of major importance was the complex regulation of the possibility of minority members to deal with authorities in their own language. If minority members approached a Government office[318] in their own language (they could still use the preferred state language), then there were three levels relevant to the extent of their entitlement in accordance with the quantity of minority members in a given territorial district. The definitions and specifications contained in the order were extremely complicated and also bound by the Language Act, and so the following interpretation is significantly simplified. In judicial districts with a minority not exceeding 20% of the population, the courts, offices, and representative bodies of the Czechoslovak Republic carried out the administration only in the state language. There were attempts to enable the members of minorities at least a certain amount of communication in their own language, but usually only in those cases when they did not possess at least a certain command of the state language. So the crucial issue was the division of the Czechoslovak Republic into judicial districts. Living in the territories where not a single minority reached 20% were also, according to the statistics from the second half of the 1920s, besides about 7 million members of the state language users, 134,000 of German language users, 51,000 of Hungarian, and 12,000 of Polish languages users.

Real minority protection – meaning the possibility of minority members to use their own language while dealing with authorities – covered, to put it in a simple way, judicial districts with a minority of at least 20% (the limit of two-thirds denoted an even higher level), in the territory, of which resided approximately 753,000 members of the German minority, 252,000 of the Hungarian and 45,000 of the Polish minority. In these areas, while administering the filings in connection with which the member of the minority possessed the right to the hearing in his own language, minority as well as state languages were simultaneously used. The highest degree of protection of minority languages related to judicial districts with at least two-thirds minority members, in the territory of which resided approximately 2,244,000 members of the German language minority, 435,000 of the Hungarian and 19,000 of the Polish language minority. Here, principally (concerning the matters with specific relation to members of minorities), the decisions, findings,

---

317 Klepetař, *Der Sprachenkampf in den Sudetenländern*, pp. 144–145; Sobota, *Národnostní právo československé*, pp. 38–42.
318 Sobota, *Výklad našeho jazykového práva*, p. 7.

hearings, agenda minutes, and file records were carried out only in the language of the minority.[319]

Governmental Order No. 17/1926 Sb. also regulated the position of minority languages within the sphere of self-government, where the limits distinguishing different levels of the use of minority languages were set to 20% (that means identical with state administration) and 50% (as opposed to two-thirds). Again, this concerned a huge set of provisions which were rather difficult to understand. The Order also regulated the issue of minority languages when approaching public corporations (distinct from self-government). Once their competence encompassed districts with minorities, then the protection of minority languages, equal to that provided by bodies of the republic, was guaranteed.

After the reform of the state administration under the Organisation Act of 1927, the regulation concerning higher levels of self-government – district and provincial offices – was changed by Governmental Order No. 229/1928 Sb. The levels were set to 20%, 50% a 75%. With the exception of the internal agenda of section bodies, for the bodies of self-governing corporations, the same rules as for the state administration were applied (Article 10).[320]

Generally it can be observed that the territory of the Czechoslovak Republic consisted of the unilingual areas of Czechoslovak language and areas of minorities, where different levels – usually two – of protection of minority languages existed. Within the territory of minorities, matters related to minority members were handled, apart from in the state language, either in the language of the minority or, to a certain extent, only in the minority language. But the state language also held important privileges in areas with a significant majority of minority languages. "In order to allow the use of a minority language, there had to be tracked, in connection with the "minority territory," some abstract relation (as a result of a general district affiliation of the administrative body handling this territory) and also some actual relations (reflecting the consequences of the matter being disposed of in this territory). There had to be some kind of personal relation established should the party be the user of the same language, i.e. the nationality for which the given territory is specified as a minority territory."[321]

Should we consider the language Governmental Order No. 17/1926 Sb. and, after all, language law as a whole,[322] then we have to stress that this regulation, together with the language legislation for territorial and district

319   Statistics according to Sobota, *Národnostní právo československé*, pp. 38–42.
320   Peška, *Národní menšiny a Československo*, pp. 166–167.
321   Sobota, *Národnostní právo československé*, p. 34.
322   See for example Kural, *Konflikt místo společenství?*, pp. 93–95; Kučera, *Minderheit im National-staat*, pp. 187–298.

representative bodies, i.e. Order No. 229/1928 Sb[323], was to a huge extent the manifestation of Czech nationalism and as such it did not contribute to the understanding with minorities. The language issue, which on its own grounds was very complex, became by the Order No. 17/1926 Sb. even more complicated. Within the sphere of the internal official language (Czechoslovak law, however, did not acknowledge this term) the principle of the prevalence of the state language was thoroughly carried out, and, moreover, in a very complex and barely comprehensible way. Even more complex and elaborate was the regulation of the external language since this, when actually applied, created an intricate structure which was still enforced even when dealing with subtle details and thus gave rise to the minority aversion. There were efforts to promote the state language in regulations (and this was one of the reasons of their over-complexity), since in the Language Act of 1920, also with respect to the Minorities Treaty of St. Germain, the preference of the Czechoslovak language was not determined so significantly. The preference of the state language sometimes went so far that the Supreme Administrative Court held this unlawful, in some cases.[324]

After language Orders enacted in 1926 and 1928 no further legal provisions were issued. There were however attempts for alterations, mainly after 1936, until the end of the First Czechoslovak Republic, but with no success. Language law, to a certain extent, was still developing – mainly because of the efforts of the rulings of the Supreme Administrative Court.[325] Nowadays, the approach to this legal area is rather negative. "Language law, this most enormous branch of nationalities law of the Czechoslovak Republic, (otherwise generally modest and better than in other countries of Central Europe) has to be considered as its most incompetent part."[326] The Minorities Treaty of St. Germain was observed but language law did not satisfy "the needs and feelings of minorities and as such could not positively attract them for the Czechoslovak state. That is why it is the source as well as the object of competent criticism of a number of authors (Veith, Seibt, Franzel, Klepetař, also Rádl and – even sporadically – Sobota)."[327] This relatively harsh criticism of one of the most profound experts – historian Václav Kural, who explicitly characterised language law as unjust – may be considered excessive, but in many aspects it can unfortunately be agreed with – e.g. when he classifies it,

---

323   See for example Peška, *Národní menšiny a Československo*, pp. 166–168.
324   Ladislav Prokop, "Čtyři léta jazykového nařízení," *Národnostní obzor* 1 (1930–1931): pp. 33–34; Peška, *Národní menšiny a Československo*, pp. 138–140.
325   See for example Kučera, *Minderheit im Nationalstaat*, pp. 187–188.
326   Václav Kural, "Jazykový problém a jazykové právo v ČSR 1918–1938 z hlediska česko-německého," *Slezský sborník = Acta Silesiaca* 89, no. 1 (1991): p. 37.
327   Kural, "Jazykový problém a jazykové právo," p. 37; see also Kučera, *Minderheit im Nationalstaat*, pp. 307–308, overstressing the element of prestige.

from the point of view of administration, as impractical. On the other hand it should be kept in mind that the resolution of these matters always constitutes, in any single state with minorities, a rather complex issue for which the ideal solution might be impossible to find, if it exists at all.

2.5 SCHOOL AND CULTURAL NATIONALITIES LAW

The mutually interconnected issues of education and culture were of crucial importance for the existence of national minorities. Legislation, for the most part, did not distinguish the status of the state nation and of minorities. From the very extensive regulation of education we are going to examine just some provisions dealing with the existence of various nations in the state and their practical implementation. Within the cultural sphere such legal rules could hardly be tracked at all, and, moreover, the entire branch was regulated only as a framework. That is why we will discuss this issue relatively briefly.

The school educational system should first be considered at the times of the Habsburg Monarchy, since its legislation, for the most part, was adopted by the Czechoslovak Republic. School education – that is, the issue of languages at schools – was, at the times of the Habsburg Monarchy[328], regulated by Article 19, section 3 of the Fundamental Act of the State No. 142/1867 Austrian R.G.Bl., and further by Act No. 62/1869 Austrian R.G.Bl., which related to primary schools, i.e. elementary schools providing compulsory education ("Volkschule"), secondary town schools ("Hauptschule") and educational institutions. As for secondary comprehensive schools ("Klassische gymnasium"), and universities, the Act was not passed and the whole issue was regulated by the legislation of the Habsburg Monarchy. However, secondary schools ("Realgymnasium") were regulated by provincial legislation. So it is obvious that the division of legislative competences within the school education area was not a simple issue. Relevant legislation left the promotion of schools, including the position of nations in their educational scheme, to the discretion of the relevant offices. Generally, at the times of the Monarchy, the position of individual nations, from the point of view of schooling, was very solid, but some negative elements could also be found; for example, Czech minority education in German territories was in a fairly bad position. In Slovakia, before the foundation of the Czechoslovak Republic, the Hungarian language possessed the overall predominant position and, in reality, Hungarianisation took over, strongly supported by administrative offices. Their actions in disposing of matters were frequently

---

328 See mainly Burger, *Sprachenrecht und Sprachgerechtigkeit.*

irrespective of laws which would otherwise have, at least to some extent, protected minorities.[329]

The reception of legal rules followed 28 October 1918 and the so-called Reception Act of 1918, but still from 1919–1920 a number of generally binding legal acts were passed. These regulated the whole sphere of education with a new and rather different approach. The interpretation of the issue for minorities was crucial and minority education, thus, throughout the whole era of the First Czechoslovak Republic, attracted enormous interest from citizens. "It is exactly the issue of minority education which can demonstrate the position of nationalities, minorities in the bourgeois Czechoslovakia, because this issue tackles their whole civic base."[330] Of key importance is the issue of legal practice, since there could be huge discrepancies between the law in books and the law in action (i.e. its implementation).[331]

Generally it has to be pointed out that the legislation of the minority issue in the sphere of education was highly distracted[332]. Even in this sphere there were international obligations, contained mainly in Articles 8 and 9 of the Minorities Treaty of St. Germain, which were recepted into the Constitutional Charter (Sections 130 and 131) as well as into the Language Act (Section 5). According to Section 130 all state citizens (still within the framework of general acts) could establish, rule, and govern schools and other educational institutions, and were allowed to freely use their own language and practice their religion. Section 131 of the Constitutional Charter guaranteed the children of citizens using a language other than the state language, within the territories where they constituted a significant number of the population, the right to obtain public education in their own language. The teaching of the state language, however, could be imposed as obligatory. The Language Act of 1920 in Section 5 then followed Section 131 of the Constitutional Charter: "Education at all schools containing members of minorities is provided to these in their own language, and cultural institutions established for minorities are to be administered in this language (Article 9 of Minorities Treaty of St. Germain)." Disputes had arisen concerning the term "to be administered," which some restrictively interpreted[333] using the treaty between the Czechoslovak Republic and Austria, signed in Brno on 7 June 1920 (No. 107/1921 Sb.):

---

329 Struggle for Czech schools in borderland regions see for example František Bělehrádek, "Zákony o školství národním a jejich změny," *Česká Revue* 14 (1921): p. 26; Sobota, *Národnostní právo československé*, p.12.

330 Milan Kocích, "Poznámky k právní úpravě školské, osvětové a spolkové činnosti národnostních menšin v buržoasní ČSR," in *Sborník prací z dějin státu a práva* (Prague: Univerzita Karlova, 1979), p. 156.

331 Ibid., pp. 156–157.

332 Sobota, *Národnostní právo československé*, pp. 44–47; Peška, *Československá ústava a zákony s ní souvislé*, vol. 2, pp. 1722–1740.

333 Hartmann, *Předpisy jazykového práva*, p. 72.

"The right, given to language minorities . . . , so that they could freely use their own language in these schools and educational institutions, concerns only the language of education and the internal school language, and not the language used when dealing with offices, which is regulated by the general provisions concerning the use of languages" (Article 17 (3)).

The entitlement of children of citizens using languages other than the Czechoslovak language to be educated in their own language was provided within the framework of general acts, i.e. the general legislation regulating education (usually there were no special legal provisions). This was principally represented by the Act No. 62/1869 Austrian R.G.Bl., on the promotion of elementary schools, secondary town schools, and educational institutions, which was, after the establishement of the Czechoslovak Republic, amended by the Act No. 189/ 1919 Sb. on national schools and private educational and upbringing institutions. It was the Act No. 189/1919 Sb., as amended, which formed the basic legal rule for the organisation of the so-called minority schooling[334] – it has to be stressed, however, that what was understood by national minority in this act was a minority in a specific, individual municipality, not a minority in the whole Czechoslovakia as the wording of the Constitutional Charter and other acts would suggest. Minorities, as stated by this act, were also members of the state nation, once they happened to be, within the school district, in a numeral minority.[335]

The key provision of Act No. 189/1919 Sb. was set out by its Section 1: "A public national elementary school may be established in any community in which reside, according to the three-year average, at least 40 children subject to compulsory schooling, unless there is a public school, within the schooling administrative community, providing education in the language which is the mother tongue of these children." Section 2 then enabled the similar promotion of a public town school ("Hauptschule"). The explanatory memorandum of the Educational Committee of the Revolutionary National Assembly (print No. 718/1919), justified these provisions by the prolonging negotiations concerning the establishment of minority schools (usually in connection with Czech minorities in the borderlands), which might commonly last for years, and sometimes for decades, which indeed gave rise to many conflicts. "After the establishment of the Czechoslovak Republic, the parents, residing in places where there was no proper attention given to national schooling, firmly sought improvement. At some places they did not hesitate to use self-support." The whole educational system was supposed

---

334 The concept of 'minority' was not mentioned in the Act No. 189/1919 Sb., it was incorporated into the amendment to the Act No. 292/1920 Sb.

335 Horáček, *Jazykové právo československé republiky*, pp. 106–107; Bělehrádek, "Zákony o školství národním a jejich změny," p. 116ff.

to be reformed within a close time period, but the situation in this sphere became so unstable that a new act was immediately passed: "Educational acts and their amendments and interpretations in the educational system have created so complex and chaotic a situation that there is an urgent need to thoroughly revise the educational legislation and cooperate with the lawmakers to rework the legislation in accordance with the changing circumstances." This legislation, within the environment of the First Czechoslovak Republic, was not put through, similarly as it happened in many other legal branches. So this act, certainly not the best one, which was intended to serve as a certain temporary legal regulation, then became effective. The crucial practical problem of the act was represented by the fact that the promotion of new public schools with state support was made optional, and so preference was clearly and straightforwardly given to schools providing education for members of the state nation in the areas in which they constituted a numerical minority. The act which should have officially, according to the Czech politicians and lawyers of the intrerwar period, protected, among other things, the rights of minorities, in fact favoured the Czechoslovak nation, and doing so it used the assets of all the citizens, i.e. also of the German and Hungarian tax payers.

In accordance with Section 5, the ministry could, exceptionally, promote schools, according to Sections 1 and 2, even in cases where there were fewer students than required. Of particular importance was Section 6, according to which personal costs as well as material expenses for schools promoted pursuant to the law should be covered by the country. Schools were subject neither to local nor to district school boards. Lots of disputes (and, subsequently, a wide range of judicial decisions of the Supreme Administrative Court)[336] were caused by Section 7, which for the schools being established, including the lodging of their employees, enabled the expropriation of buildings or construction sites or the enforcement of a lease contract. "Even the room serving a particular school . . . might be, in a case needed, taken over by a forced tenancy for another school (minority school), unless by the loss of these premises the operations of the first mentioned school is not endangered;" (finding of the Supreme Administrative Court of 17 March 1923, No. 4080, Collection of dr. Bohuslav, administrative series No 2100).[337] The support of the so-called minority schooling (ironically used, in reality, mainly to favour the Czech nation) by the state was far-reaching and extensive.

Private schools and educational institutions were regulated by Sections 10–13, and they were supervised by the state administration (Section 10). Of crucial importance for private national schools was the so-called right of the

---

336   Sobota, *Národnostní právo československé*, pp. 56–61.
337   *Sbírka nálezů Nejvyššího správního soudu*, vol. 5a, pp. 636–637.

public – this was the authorisation to issue certificates with a validity equal to those issued by public national schools; this authorisation might have been granted to them by the state, in accordance with the law.

This rather peculiar act (mainly when we consider the actual application) became effective only in the Czech lands (Section 15), since in Slovakia there should have been a regulation specifying from when this act would have become effective, issued later, but this was never issued. The act was later partially amended by Act No. č. 292/1920 Sb., to regulate the school administration and Act No. 295/1920 Sb. on National Schools and Private Schools and Educational Institutions.[338]

Language issues at schools were regulated by a number of other legal regulations. Amongst these belonged, for example, acts and regulations establishing universities, trade and technical schools, and other types of educational institutions where the language of education was specified – for example, Act No. 50/1919 Sb., to promote the second Czech University in Brno, Act No. 197/1919 Sb. to promote the Jan Hus Czechoslovak Protestant Theological Faculty, and Act No. 375/1919 Sb. to promote the Czechoslovak State University in Bratislava. Among these regulations also belonged provisions regulating the language of examinations at universities (e.g. Governmental Orders No. 122/1919 Sb. , 353/1919 Sb. and 214/1921 Sb.), and also provisions stipulating the knowledge of the educational language when evaluating the teachers' qualifications for primary and town schools in Slovakia (Act No. 276/1920 Sb.).

In connection with minority issues there were also provisions specifying languages which were to be taught at schools as foreign languages; this naturally has to be distinguished from the key language issue, i.e. in which language education is provided: mainly Act No. 73/1922 Sb., which regulated education in modern languages, Act No. 137/1923 Sb., on teaching of the state language as well as of languages of national minorities at secondary schools and educational institutions. This issue was traditionally complicated by the fact that contrary to German – that is the language of the minority but simultaneously the predominant language in Central Europe – Czech was the state language, but was usable abroad to only a limited extent. It has to be stressed that the Minorities Treaty of St. Germain explicitly enabled the Czechoslovak Republic to impose Czech as the obligatory language at schools (this resolution was adopted by the Constitutional Charter), but this never happened, with the exception of secondary schools where, with regard to Czech schools, German was, reciprocally, made obligatory. Minority issues were also dealt with by provisions (Section 20) of Act No. 4/1906, Moravian Provincial Code (the so-called Lex Perek – Perek's Education Act), recepted by

---

338 Kocích, "Poznámky k právní úpravě školské, osvětové a spolkové činnosti," pp. 159–160.

the Czechoslovak Republic, which required a knowledge of the language in which education is provided by children attending the school.[339]

Referring to the school system it is necessary to consider not only the legislation itself, but also its actual application, as, for example, in the case of the so-called Czech minority schools in borderland regions. After all, in contrast with other issues of minority law (e.g. language law), the field of education may be critically evaluated due to relatively precise statistics. From the Habsburg Monarchy the Czechoslovak Republic took over an educational system with a very unbalanced structure – extremely advanced and prolific (even in comparison with western countries) in the Czech lands and underdeveloped in the Slovakia and Sub-Carpathian Ruthenia. A specific problem of the Czechoslovak educational minority policy was created by the crucial German issue. Germans, still from the time of the Habsburg Monarchy, possessed the best educational facilities, and that is why financial aid from the state targeted mostly the educational systems of other nations. This was frequently understood as a type of discrimination by the German minority. Moreover, its population growth was the worst out of all the nations of Czechoslovakia, which led to a great reduction in the number of children and so to another pressure for the restriction of German schooling. Therefore the quantity of German schools and classes (besides technical schools) was reduced, even though it stayed higher than it would be relevant to the proportion of Germans in the population. The average number of pupils for one class was still dropping (thanks to the significant decrease of pupils exceeding the process of the reduction of schools), so the quality of schools was improving in principal. However, it should be impartially stated that the educational system promoted the Czech nation. So already with the end of the 1920s the original German edge was being caught up with, and sometimes slightly overrun by the facilities of Czech (not Slovak) schools. Needless to say, Germans did not have to send their children to Czech schools, where they would have to face the process of assimilation, since only approximately 2–3% of German children attended non-German schools (out of which number nearly half of them attended schools providing education in more than one language). Germans in the Czechoslovak Republic – as the only minority – had at their disposition their own universities, namely the university in Prague and technical universities in Prague and Brno; meanwhile the number of their students was higher than it would be relevant to the proportion of Germans in the population. The minority educational system for universities was pretty unique in Europe, though on the other hand, it had already existed from the times of the Habsburg Monarchy.[340]

---

339 Horáček, *Jazykové právo československé republiky*, p. 107; Emil Sobota, "Čtvrt století Perkova zákona," *Národnostní obzor* 2 (1931–1932): pp. 88–99.

340 Kural, *Konflikt místo společenství?*, pp. 97–99; Andreas Reich, "Das tschechoslowakische

The above mentioned, so-called minority schools in the Czech lands, promoted under Act No. 189/1919 Sb., instituted a discrepancy within the Czechoslovak school and education law. These schools were promoted in districts where elementary and town schools already existed, but, at the same time, a minority using a different language than that used in these schools resided there. This might even contain (in the community by number minority) a group of members of the state nation. The so-called minority schools were funded by the state, and in reality this was applied almost exclusively to Czech schools, whose number was, for example in 1930, around 1400; meanwhile German schools only numbered 23! This discrepancy hugely irritated the Germans.[341] State minority schools were frequently placed into borderland German communities where only a limited number of Czech families resided. "The policy in the sphere of the so-called minority schools was very unfortunate, since these schools were basically discretionally (and often with a close cooperation with the Czech 'defence associations') promoted directly by the state: out of 1139 . . . only 20 German and 2 Polish schools."[342] Their real importance for strengthening the Czech national position, as the Czech nationalists probably wished, was in reality very marginal meanwhile, they contributed significantly to the negative approach of minorities towards the Czechoslovak Republic.

Apparently the key issue of the inter-war minority educational system involved neither school facilities, which were generally at a very high level in Czechoslovakia, nor the so-called minority schools under Act No. 189/1919 Sb. These were marginal problems; the major one was mainly constituted by the school administration, that is by its (very powerful at the time of the Habsburg Monarchy) self-governance, which was getting restricted. "The Czechoslovak educational system, even though based on previous Austrian legislation (Czech Provincial Acts No. 17/1873 and No. 46/1890, Moravian Provincial Act No. 4/1906), modified the adopted principle of administration, keeping centralistic and bureaucratic views, by which, to a certain extent, limited the administration of schooling with the aid of local, district, and provincial school boards."[343] Meanwhile in Cisleithania these administrative bodies were divided into nationality sections; in the Czechoslovak Republic this was mostly abolished and substituted by a proportionate representation. That is why, from the middle of the 1920s, proposals for reform started to

Bildungswesen vor dem Hintergrund des Deutsch-Tschechischen Nationalitätenproblems," *Bohemia* 36, no. 1 (1995): pp. 19–38.
341 Kural, *Konflikt místo společenství?*, p. 101; Kocích, "Poznámky k právní úpravě školské, osvětové a spolkové činnosti," pp. 157–158.
342 Kučera, "Koncepce národního státu Čechů a Slováků," p. 608.
343 Kural, *Konflikt místo společenství?*, p. 100. Differently Malý, "Sprache – Recht und Staat," pp. 272, 274.

occur, mainly from the initiative of the Germans, in which, for example, the school administration ruled by elected representatives should be segmented according to nationality. None of these plans had been realised.[344] "The reverse side of the coin was the actual reduction of school self-governance, which in the end survived only in a formal position. We might assume that providing school autonomy" will not endanger the state.[345] School administration, even without any certain kind of cultural autonomy, functioned, from the point of view of minorities, relatively affirmatively, but on the other side it brought to them (mainly to Germans) a certain frustration connected with the incapacity to independently administer their own matters. What was in question was mainly the nonexistence of the so-called cultural autonomy, which was a highly popular institute in Europe at this time, even though it was accompanied by lots of weaknesses, as is explained in further chapters of this book.

As for a general overview of the minority educational system – from the quality of schools, the high percentage of pupils eligible to attend schools providing their own educational language, etc., it is obvious that the legislation and, to a certain extent, the actual application, acknowledges sufficient support from the state. Even from the side of national minorities, usually ready to harshly criticise almost anything, the legislation was generally accepted with no major reservations (except some clamours from Hungarians).[346] "The school educational policy was, undoubtedly, the jewel of the Czechoslovak nationalities legislation, mainly when the German schooling is taken into consideration."[347]

Elementary and secondary schools formed the base for extraordinarily important public educational and cultural life in these times, as well as for the functioning of the associations of minorities. Minority schools functioned as the major centres of cultural and association institutions – for example, libraries, theatres, and other associations, the activities of which were traditionally very influential and powerful.[348]

Cultural issues legislation was frequently rather extensively interlinked with the regulation of education (for example, Constitutional Charter of 1920, Sections 130 and 131). The basic framework, in the very same way as in the case of education, was set by certain provisions of the Minorities Treaty of St. Germain and the related legislation laid down by the Constitutional Charter. However, the legislation was not too extensive and so many issues remained completely non-regulated, which is, in connection with culture, fairly natural.

---

344 Kural, *Konflikt místo společenství?*, pp. 100–102.
345 Kučera, "Koncepce národního státu Čechů a Slováků," pp. 607–608.
346 Kocích, "Poznámky k právní úpravě školské, osvětové a spolkové činnosti," pp. 159, 162.
347 Kučera, "Koncepce národního státu Čechů a Slováků," p. 607. Similarly, for example, Brügel, "The Germans in pre-war Czechoslovakia," pp. 184–185.
348 See for example, Peška, *Národní menšiny a Československo*, pp. 178–183.

One of the few legal regulations dealing with this issue was the Act No. 430/1919 Sb. on public community libraries,[349] which also regulated the issue of minority libraries, or special minority sections of general libraries. The act was implemented by the regulation No. 607/1919 Sb. and also No. 212/1921 Sb., which, however, did not relate to minority issues. Similarly to the educational issues, the legal regulation of minority issues was incorporated into general legislation. "In political municipalities with national minorities a special library or a special minority section of a general library shall be established" once the number of members of a minority in a municipality reaches the required level (Section 2 of the Act No. 430/1919 Sb.). This imposed the obligation to the municipality, which also covered the expenses in connection with public libraries "as a due municipal expense"(Section 5). Section 7 contained another important organisational resolution: "For the minority library (even though it is only a mere section of a general library), a special library board is to be established, all the members of which shall be members of the national minority for which the library is promoted." By "minority" was meant, under this act (in accordance with the Act No. 189/1919 Sb. regulating the minority school and educational system), the minority in the municipality. The most important fact was that the establishing of libraries was mandatory and finances were strictly specified, and so in practice the act was not misused in favour of other nationalities (contrary to the Act No. 189/1919 Sb.) or circumvented. Facilities of minority libraries as well as libraries serving the state nation were at a very high level in the First Czechoslovak Republic.[350]

The cultural and public enlightenment life of minorities was influenced not just by schools and libraries but was also shaped by theatre, the minority press and, above all, associations. Minorities disposed of the net of permanent and other types of theatre; they also published a daily press in a huge edition, as well as magazines and books. Legislation concerning the activities of associations and other cultural issues was extensive and, at the same time, was influenced only marginally by minority and national issues (let us mention, for example, the provision specifying that nationality associations could only be established as literary or educational ones), and so it will not be discussed here. The influence of the minority issue on press law or on the law on associations, and mainly on its actual implementation, is of a certain importance, but a similar situation was relevant to other Czechoslovak legal branches in the interwar period; so for even a minimal overview of the framework of the influence of nationality issues on all the branches, there is insufficient space available here.

---

349 Sobota, *Národnostní právo československé*, pp. 64–68.
350 Kocích, "Poznámky k právní úpravě školské, osvětové a spolkové činnosti," pp. 159, 163.

2.6 THE PROBLEM OF AUTONOMY

Autonomy has been discussed in various contexts now as well as at the time of the First Czechoslovak Republic, and the concept is sometimes understood rather widely and sometimes, conversely, very narrowly. In the inter-war period, a territorial autonomy was usually distinguished which corresponds with the currently used concept, along with a cultural autonomy, a peculiar institute which is rarely discussed nowadays. Up to the present there has been no generally accepted definition of territorial autonomy. However, there are some common traits shared by autonomous units which are usually regions of a state featuring national, ethnic, or cultural differences. Such units acquired varied powers of internal self-governance and did not split from the state to which they belong. There are even autonomous units with their own legislative and judicial power over local matters. Territorial autonomy was far from common in inter-war Europe, nor was it generally promoted by Minority Treaties, but there were exceptions, such as Sub-Carpathian Ruthenia.[351] Cultural, or in another terminology, personal autonomy entailed certain legal institutes which enabled the minority to administer some matters by itself – usually education, culture, and other similar affairs. However, the conceptions of inter-war authors varied significantly, so the cultural autonomy cannot be precisely defined.[352]

The problem of the autonomy of minorities in the First Czechoslovak Republic consisted of various elements, and it is important to stress from the start that the Czechoslovak lawyers of the interwar period were of very diverse opinions indeed. Principally we can consider three main spheres: firstly, there were certain effective minor elements of essentially cultural

---

351 Josef Mrázek, "Ochrana menšin z hlediska mezinárodního práva," *Právník* 132, no. 6 (1993): pp. 489–492; Jaroslav Kallab, "Otázka ochrany menšin jako problém mezinárodního práva," in *Problém ochrany menšin*, ed. by Alois Hajn (Prague: Orbis, 1923), pp. 32–34; Scheu, *Standard ochrany národnostních menšin v rámci Rady Evropy*, p. 12.

352 It is important, and often difficult, to distinguish a so-called nationalities' self-government (a specific type of, or according to some experts a part of cultural/personal autonomy) from a common self-government organised on a territorial basis. Put simply, in the case of nationalities' self-governance the territorial self-government is subdivided according to the affiliation of an individual to a nation, so it is divided not only territorially, but also personally. Thus in practice the territorial self-government in multinational regions operates in independent national sections. A complete cultural/personal autonomy then exists, if such individual national sections have at the top a single national state-wide organisation. The distinction between a nationalities' self-governance and a self-government certainly becomes slightly blurred, if the territorial self-government districts include just one nationality. That is why some authors did not recognise such a distinction with reference to the undisputable fact that even a common self-government was a support for the national interests of individual nations. This explanation is just a simplified scheme to clarify the following text also because the theory and terminology of cultural autonomy was not uniform.

autonomy in the Czechoslovak law in the interwar period[353], as well as efforts to broaden them. Secondly, it was the (territorial) autonomy of Sub-Carpathian Ruthenia which the Czechoslovak Republic promised to create in accordance with the Minorities Treaty of St. Germain and which, however, was not realised before 1938. A third sphere might be possibly determined, but the then lawyers usually did not classify it as a problem of autonomy. It was a question of territorial self-government, namely the endeavour at an administrative reform featuring the idea of zhupas, or regions, as a basis of some kind of territorial autonomy. By this example it is possible to show how unclear the terminology was. Many Czechoslovak politicians admitted the creation of an extensive self-government at the level of zhupas/regions which would also create the basis for the national life of minorities, but they principally opposed the territorial (nationalities') autonomy, although in the terminology used by many experts there is no difference between such self-governance and autonomy. Therefore it is necessary to very carefully examine what exactly the period terms and political requirements meant.[354]

Interestingly, the idea of national autonomy, like many other elements of minorities' law, originated essentially in Habsburg Monarchy. Initially, it was brought about by the socialists, and the autonomy of nations became the leading principle of the Austrian Social Democracy, which included this idea in its platform at the Brno congress in 1899. Socialist theoreticians Karl Renner and Otto Bauer devoted several books to the issue.[355] Renner underlined two chief principal elements of such autonomy, namely national registers, that is permanent lists of persons according to their nationality, and the creation of nationally uniform administrative units (regions).[356] Some states followed these theories in the inter-war period in the 1920s. Most of them organised autonomy exclusively on a personal basis (cultural autonomy – Estonia 1925, Germans in Latvia, Slovenians in Austria – Carinthia), and Poland combined it with territorial self-governance (Act No. 90 regulating self-government in duchies from 26 September 1922).[357] However, neither in Poland nor in Latvia was autonomy brought to life; in Estonia the principle of cultural autonomy contained in the constitution of 1920 was realised only after protracted

---

353 They were also described as e.g. national or nationalities' self-government. Different authors were using different, essentially non-standardised terms – so in this book we use the terms cultural or national autonomy, national or nationalities' self-government, etc. interchangeably, having regard to possible specific nuances.

354 Kural, *Konflikt místo společenství?*, p. 71.

355 Malloy and Palermo, *Minority Accommodation through Territorial and Non-Territorial Autonomy*, pp. 125–127.

356 See Karl Renner, *Das Selbstbestimmungsrecht der Nationen in besonderer Anwendung auf Oesterreich* (Leipzig: F. Deuticke, 1918).

357 Malloy and Palermo, *Minority Accommodation through Territorial and Non-Territorial Autonomy*, pp. 95–97 and 140ff.

negotiations in the years 1921–1925, and Austria, which was considered to be an almost perfect panacea by many in the Czechoslovak Republic and in Europe generally, provided an especially striking example of the existence of troublesome elements in cultural autonomy.[358]

The introduction of cultural autonomy in Austrian Carinthia paradoxically became the means of weakening the local Slovenian minority, which was a grotesque twist of the meaning of this remarkable institute. Austrian German parties, including the nationalist ones, without the knowledge of Slovene deputies, pushed through the Assembly of the Carinthian Land in June 1927 the law which should have introduce cultural autonomy for the Slovene minority. The law faced the sharp resistance of the Slovenes, namely because the affiliation to the autonomous minority was based exclusively on the person's own request – voluntary registration and entering in the public nationality register was required. That would naturally lead to duress, only few would register in practice, and the Austrian Germans would claim that there was only a minimum of Slovenes. Schooling was regulated rather unfavourably for the minority, too.[359]

In the time of the Habsburg Monarchy the idea of nationalities' autonomy did not gain ground; however, certain elements of this kind emerged[360] mainly in the legislation of the provinces in Cisleithania, while in Hungary no similar elements took ground. But we should remember the extensive autonomy of churches which, for example, ran many schools. Within churches in Hungary even minorities could partially live their national lives.

The so-called fundamental schools [fundamentalky] from 1871 were usually considered to be the first attempt at enforcing the principle of national autonomy in the supreme provincial bodies of the Czech lands. The Provincial Assembly of the Czech land (Czech Diet) adopted the law on nationalities' curias of the Assembly, and such a division was designed to protect the rights of nations. But in spite of the fact that it was a government Act, it was not granted assent by the monarch, mainly due to the German opposition. Its conception was to a certain extent accepted in Moravia in 1905 (Provincial Act No. 1/1906 Provincial Code) in the so-called Moravian Pact. However, the Provincial Assembly (Diet) was not divided into two national curias, but into three, including the curia of farmers owning large areas of land, which strongly weakened the principle of national autonomy. Thus a fixed percentage of deputies of the Assembly of different nationalities was created for good, and the Czech-German question was excluded from the election

---

358 Peška, *Kulturní samospráva národních menšin*, pp. 9–10, 26–29; articles on cultural autonomy by Zdeněk Peška in *Národnostní obzor* 1 (1930–1931): pp. 30–33, 192–198, 267–271.
359 Peška, *Kulturní samospráva národních menšin*, pp. 47–58.
360 Sobota, *Národnostní autonomie v Československu?*, p. 18ff.

fight[361] which had previously significantly worsened the relations between the two groups of citizens.

Minor elements of nationalities' self-governance gained ground in the Czech lands namely in lower level self-governing bodies, in particular in education.[362] Under Provinicial Act No. 17/1873 of the Czech Provincial Code school councils in communities were divided into Czech and German council (Section 7). In communities with both Czech and German schools where it was impossible to delimit the territory of school districts, special local school councils were established for Czech and German schools. District school councils were also divided into Czech and German ones (Section 21). A similar regulation was later introduced in Moravia (Provincial Act No. 4/1906). The provincial school council was divided into Czech and German sections – Provincial Act No. 46/1890 in Bohemia, Provincial Act No. 4/1906 in Moravia. The composition of the provincial school council was very complicated from the point of view of nationality, which is by no means unusual in the area of the legal status of minorities. The significance of these principally minor provisions, most of which were taken over by the Czechoslovak Republic, was highly appreciated by jurisprudence in the inter-war period, perhaps too highly: "Apparently, nationalities' self-governance penetrated into the school administration in a very far-reaching manner."[363]

The influence of nationalities' self-governance was significantly lower in other areas of self-government than in schooling. One of the few examples was the division of the Czech agricultural council into Czech and German sections under Provincial Act No. 20/1891 (identically in Moravia according to Provincial Act No. 40/1897). Medical chambers were also divided into Czech and German sections – in Bohemia it was laid down by the regulation of the Minister of the Interior No. 9826 (Provincial Act No. 84/1894) of the 19th of August 1894, in Moravia by the regulation of the Governor (Provincial Act No. 23/1906) of the 10th of February 1906.

The elements of national autonomy in the Austrian public administration during the Habsburg Monarchy were much smaller than in self-government. According to some authors a peculiar institution of the Minister-Compatriot was such an example, but it was denied by others. An isolated (and practically unimportant) element of national autonomy, more or less accepted by legal experts, was the so-called Schönborn language regulation (No. 1874) of 3 February 1890. It effectively divided positions at the High Court of the Czech land in Prague on the grounds of knowledge of provincial languages. However,

---

361 Sobota, *Národnostní autonomie v Československu?*, pp. 19–20; Křen, *Konfliktní společenství*, pp. 323–325; Peška, *Kulturní samospráva národních menšin*, pp. 14–18.

362 Peška, *Kulturní samospráva národních menšin*, pp. 18–23; see also Horáček, *Jazykové právo československé republiky*, pp. 40–41; Kořalka, *Češi v habsburské říši a v Evropě 1815–1914*, p. 164ff.

363 Peška, *Kulturní samospráva národních menšin*, p. 23.

it was very disadvantageous for the Czechs and as such it was cancelled as early as on 30 January 1919 by the regulation of the Minister of Justice (No. 56/1919 Sb.).[364]

After its foundation Czechoslovakia generally took over the mentioned minor elements of cultural autonomy, yet some changes occurred because, for example, the Assemblies of Land (Provincial Diets) were abolished along with their division into nationalities' curias in Moravia. The regulation from the times of the Habsburg Monarchy was retained in self-governing corporations, so agricultural councils and medical chambers were still divided according to nationalities, but the newly established chamber of engineers (Act No. 185/1920 Sb.) was not divided like that, although proportional representation of nationalities on its board was guaranteed.[365]

The strongest elements of nationalities' self-governance were retained in education, but significant changes occurred even there. The self-government was restricted (both the general self-government of schooling and the elements of nationalities' self-governance in it), but this regulation from Bohemia and Moravia spread principally to the entire territory of the state (Act No. 292/1920 Sb.). Previously obligatory nationality sections in school councils turned into facultative. Under Act No. 189/1919 Sb. so-called minority schools were established (in practice, however, mainly for the members of the state nation) which were administered by special local school committees composed only of the representatives of the relevant nation. Provincial school councils were to be substituted (under Act No. 292/1920 Sb.) by regional (zhupa) school councils undivided on the grounds of nationality. But the regional school councils were never established and the provincial school councils, sectioned along the nationality principle, continued their operation in the Czech lands. For the most part Act No. 292/1920 Sb. considerably restricted the domain of self-government in education, particularly the higher education matters were moved from the provincial school council to the ministry, so only elementary and town schools, as well as the so-called minority schools, remained in the scope of self-governance.[366]

In education, a miniature element of national self-governance won recognition even in higher education institutions, which were autonomous in themselves. It was the empowerment (laid down by Act No. 79/1919 Sb.) for German faculties to elect their own high disciplinary board (Section 8).[367] Nationalities' self-governance was newly introduced in the administration of public libraries in the Czechoslovak Republic. Minority libraries, or at least

---

364   Ibid., pp. 23–25; Sobota, *Národnostní autonomie v Československu?*, p. 19ff.
365   Sobota, *Národnostní právo československé*, pp. 47–48.
366   Sobota, *Národnostní autonomie v Československu?*, pp. 40–41; Peška, *Kulturní samospráva národních menšin*, pp. 60–61.
367   Peška, *Kulturní samospráva národních menšin*, p. 62.

sections of libraries, were established in communities with national minorities as well as special library councils, all of whose members belonged to the respective national minority.

Zdeněk Peška, an important expert on the law of the inter-war period, elaborated a remarkable comparison of small-scale elements of self-governance or autonomy in the Czechoslovak law with the well-operating autonomy in Estonia.[368] Based thereon he came up with four main features that were missing in the law of the inter-war Czechoslovakia so that the cultural autonomy could have been fully implemented: 1. there was no permanent record of members of individual nations (national registers) – the only such record was the obligation of members of the parliament, regional (non-established) and land councils, and members of district committees to register their nationality before they first entered the floor. Although, e.g. the Language Act of 1920 spoke about members of the minority language, there was no permanent and impartial register. Also missing were the central authorities of individual nations (2nd main feature), which would administer their education and cultural establishments. Furthermore, there were neither independent bodies in the Czechoslovak law which would administer schools other than elementary and town schools (3), nor the financial independence of self-governing bodies and the right to tax the members of their nation (4).

Zdeněk Peška emphasised that even through quite small changes, national cultural self-governance could be easily implemented on a large scale. According to him, the cultural self-governance would not have meant a risk to extensive dilution of state administration. He concluded: "It is necessary to consider the cultural self-governance of national minorities to be a sound and beneficial principle whose implementation would bring many advantages to the Czechoslovak Republic: calming down the national squabble, extending self-governance in educational affairs, de-bureaucratisation and decentralisation."[369] Projects of cultural autonomy were debated in the Czechoslovak parliament several times, namely in 1925. The Czechoslovak Social Democratic Party then declared the minorities' cultural self-governance as its requirement in September 1930.

The term cultural autonomy, or self-governance, is not strictly defined; some authors insist that there was cultural autonomy at the time of the First Czechoslovak Republic. Allegedly, there was cultural, language, education, and religious autonomy established under the Minorities Treaty of St. Germain. It is the vast cultural autonomy for minorities on the grounds of the Constitutional Charter and the Language Act of 1920 that is talked about, still

---

368 Peška, *Kulturní samospráva národních menšin*, pp. 60, 62–63, 65; see also Peška, *Národní menšiny a Československo*, pp. 222–223.
369 Peška, *Kulturní samospráva národních menšin*, p. 77.

within the system of a unitary state, i.e. without political or administrative autonomy.[370] However, what is meant when speaking about the cultural autonomy there is rather the "ordinary" self-governance (e.g. educational), while it was usually a particular national self-governance, i.e. personal autonomy, that the term denoted in the inter-war period. If we look at the "ordinary" self-governance, then its influence in the Czechoslovak law of the iterwar period was undoubtedly significant (however, it being a broad issue, it cannot be dealt with minutely in this book, apart from a few details). On the other hand, the self-governance was, compared to the times of the Habsburg Monarchy, fairly limited. Thus, it could hardly become a national pillar for minorities as was the case of the Czechs in Cisleithania, and the term "autonomy" is quite an overstatement for the circumstances of the Czechoslovak Republic.

Connected with the issue of autonomy it is also necessary to point to the noteworthy Section 132 of the Constitutional Charter, under which the minorities had the right to an adequate portion of financial means. "If in towns and districts in which a considerable portion of Czechoslovak citizens are settled who belong to religious, national, and language minorities, certain amounts of money should be expended on education, religion, or charity from public funds, such as the state budget, municipal budgets, or other public funds; these minorities are guaranteed, in compliance with general acts applicable to public administration, an adequate participation in emoluments and use." Experts on law were at their wit's end with this provision, which was based on the Minorities Treaty of St. Germain, which however only spoke about a decent share, and they often avoided this provision in commentaries to the Constitution by staying silent.[371]

On the other hand, some authors connected this provision of the Constitutional Charter and the Minorities Treaty of St. Germain with a far-reaching interpretation in which they even referred to it as the grounds of autonomy. They inferred that for due reallocation of this finance devolving on individual minorities, there must be an organisation similar to, for example, a personal autonomy. From an ambiguous and marginal provision within the framework of international legal protection (taken over to the Constitutional Charter) they inferred the establishment of some autonomous structures, which was one of the most important and radical features of the protection of minorities that changed its conception in many aspects. Similar, a fairly strained interpretation of legal rules is not unusual in the law of minorities. Implementing regulations to Section 132 were not adopted, perhaps partially

---

370 Malý, "Sprache – Recht und Staat," pp. 272, 274.
371 Sobota, *Národnostní právo československé*, pp. 49–50; Peška, *Československá ústava a zákony s ní sou-vislé*, vol. 1, pp. 329–330.

except for the Act on Municipal Public Libraries of 22 July 1919 (No. 430/1919 Sb.), which accurately determined financial means for minorities' libraries administered by members of minorities.

In Czechoslovakia there was (or rather should have been) real (territorial) autonomy. It was Sub-Carpathian Ruthenia,[372] which was a national autonomy – the autonomy of the nation Sub-Carpathian Ruthenians. It relied on the Minorities Treaty of St. Germain and on Section 3 of the Constitutional Charter. It applied to issues of language,[373] schooling, religion, and local administration, as well as to other matters that central laws would delegate to autonomic legislation. Thus, it was supposed to have both administrative and legislative powers. Regulations governing the administration of the area were the General Statutes (No. 26.536/19 of the Ministerial Council) for organisation and administration of Sub-Carpathian Ruthenia, which was attached to the Czechoslovak Republic by the decision of the Paris Peace Conference, and the Governmental Order No. 356/1920 Sb.[374]

Seemingly, nothing prevented bringing the autonomy to life, at least from a legal point of view; after all, there was an obligation flowing from the Minorities Treaty of St. Germain and even domestic regulations emerged. However, the existence of legal regulations themselves is not sufficient for the actual operation of an autonomic territory; this concerned many other minority issues, too. In fact, the situation in the area was utterly chaotic; furthermore, it was an extraordinarily underdeveloped territory (most Ruthenians were illiterate), as well as being nationally ambivalent, which was crucial to the minority issue. With respect to these circumstances, many legal regulations could not operate in practice at all. To illustrate, under Article II Subsection (c) of the General Statutes, the Slovak-Ruthenian border should have been specified more accurately: "As a part of the Ruthenian nation forms a minority in the Slovak territory, determined by the peace conference, the Czechoslovak government recommended to representatives of both nations that they agree on a possible incorporation of the respective Ruthenian area to Ruthenian autonomy." Who was supposed to be these said representatives was a slight mystery. It was similar in the case of Article III, Section 2: "The common language shall be the language of instruction, as well as the official language in general." However, it was not clear in practice which language was meant, which caused numerous problems.

The autonomy had not been implemented up till the Munich Agreement of 1938, and according to a finding by the Supreme Administrative Court it

---

372 See for example Peter Mosný, *Podkarpatská Rus: Nerealizovaná autonómia* (Bratislava: Slovak Academic Press, 2001).

373 On language law Horáček, *Jazykové právo československé republiky*, p. 101ff.

374 Sobota, *Národnostní právo československé*, pp. 48–49; Peška, *Národní menšiny a Československo*, pp. 204–219.

was Governmental Order No. 356/1920 Sb. which was binding: "Thus, it is these regulations which are authoritative with respect to the extent of the autonomy of Sub-Carpathian Ruthenia until such time when other definitive regulation is adopted." (the finding of 2 November 1921, No. 13.031, Collection of decisions by dr. Bohuslav, administrative series III.)[375] Failure to implement the autonomy raised doubts, but, taking into account problematic circumstances in the respective territory, the attitude was understandable, which was usually recognised even by foreign countries.

For example, Pablo de Azcárate, a worker and later a director of the Minorities Section of the League of Nations Secretariat visited the region in the spring of 1923 and came to a conclusion that anyone who had objectively looked into the situation must have sustained the arguments the Czechoslovak government had brought against the immediate implementation of the autonomy, which would have meant, according to him, that the power would have rested in the hands of local Hungarians who had traditionally controlled the territory and were responsible for the underdevelopment of the Ruthenian peasants. In his opinion it was necessary first (before the implementation of the autonomy) to help that nation develop. He also appreciated the progress after the area was attached to Czechoslovakia, which was clearly visible during his visit. The issue of the autonomy of Sub-Carpathian Ruthenia, directly enshrined in the Minorities Treaty of St. Germain, showed, according to him, how dangerous it was to put plans and visions on paper in international treaties irrespective of their practicability.[376] This is quite an objective assessment because Minorities Treaties were adopted hastily, and almost nothing was known about this territory at the time of its incorporation into the Czechoslovak Republic under the so-called St. Germain Minorities Treaty. Azcárate's quite minutely described opinion also proved that competent officials, although from far and culturally different foreign countries, in responsible efforts for understanding, which however was often lacking, had a chance to prudently assess the local situation, as it is visible from his criticism of Hungarian endeavours to implement and afterwards to seize control of the autonomy.

Considerable, although different, risks would have been entailed if autonomies strived for by some minorities in the Czechoslovak Republic, namely by the Germans, had been successfully brought into being. Especially in the case of the Germans, the required autonomy could have actually been just an initial stage leading to the secession from the state and possibly to control of the Czech basin being taken by Germany. This manifested itself particularly markedly in a bill proposed to the parliament by the Sudeten German Party

---

375 Sbírka nálezů Nejvyššího správního soudu, vol. 3, pp. 804–807.
376 Azcárate, League of Nations and National Minorities, pp. 40–42, 85–88.

in April 1937. Although the project proceeded from the conception of personal autonomy, it would have resulted in a complete separation of the Germans and Czechs, and representatives of individual national groups would have gained total control over the members of their nationality. The scheme was impractical in many aspects; moreover, it was in deep contradiction with the principles of democracy. Its result would have been the total disintegration of the state, which also was its clear objective.[377]

A question per se that was related to the issue of autonomy was the reform of administration, namely the so-called "zhupas" (regions) reform. Also nowadays it is often mentioned in connection with minorities, but the knowledge of this rather complicated issue is missing many times; therefore, let us pay attention to it more thoroughly, also for the reason that it is worth noting how significantly this matter was influenced by the nationalities issue in the 1920s. It was assumed that self-government, which should have operated at the level of regions, would be virtually a substitute for unimplemented autonomy, especially for the most numerous and key German minority; however, even the rather limited regional self-government prompted serious worries in Czech nationalists which contributed to the failure of this new, radical conception of the organisation of public administration.

However, fear of the irredentism of minorities was not the only reason for the failure of the administration reform; it was rather caused by an intricate aggregate of political, financial, organisational-administrative, and other difficulties. Ideas from the beginning of the Czechoslovak Republic regarding possible radical reforms of the state and the society, a part of which was the regions' reform, failed. The Act on regional and district authorities of 1920, which was to bring radical changes, was after all perceived as the first step towards the transformation of public administration. Soon afterwards the reform of the lowest component of the administration – municipalities (first reformed already in 1919), should have followed, as well as the reform of the central bodies (established in 1918).[378] Such far-reaching ideas, however, like in the case of many other branches of law, did not break through.

The reform of regions was governed, in compliance with the Constitutional Charter, by statutes, namely by Act No. 126/1920 Sb., on the establishment of regional and district authorities in the Czechoslovak Republic (the Regions Act),[379] and by Act No. 158/ 1920 Sb., on administrative justice administered by district and regional courts as well as by Act No. 330/1920 Sb.

---

377 Emil Sobota, *Zákonodárné návrhy Sudetoněmecké strany s hlediska demokracie* (Prague: Jan Laichter, 1938); Laponce, *The Protection of Minorities*, pp. 90–91.

378 *Tisky k těsnopiseckým zprávám*, vol. 9, print no. 2422, p. 7; Laštovka, *Zákon župní*, pp. 7–15.

379 Laštovka, *Zákon župní*, pp. 7–15; see also Baxa, *Zákon o zřízení župním a jeho nedostatky; Tisky k těsnopiseckým zprávám*, vol. 9, print no. 2422 – there is also a governmental explanatory memorandum (pp. 45–81).

of 14 April 1920, on the election to regional boards and district committees. It was necessary to prepare the reform, which required further laws. Some details were reserved for decrees or special internal regulations.[380] The most important ones comprised: Governmental Order No. 310 of 26 October 1922, which implemented the regional system in Slovakia and Governmental Order No. 290 of 21 September 1922, on the rules of procedure at regional and district authorities.[381] The reform required a lot of preparatory work and so the date of effect of the Regions Act had not been determined beforehand and the government should have decided thereon in the form of a decree (Article 1), which was quite an unusual approach.

The Regions Act was rather radically against traditions and it anticipated an extensive reorganisation of public administration that should have been based on completely different grounds. That would have changed the entire republic, and even more, the status of minorities. The dualism of administration in the Czech lands should have been eliminated through the amalgamation of state administration with self-governance. The most important element of administration until then – the lands – should have disappeared and been replaced by regions ("zhupas"). The Act anticipated unification of administration in the entire territory of the Czechoslovak Republic; however, new authorities took over the competences of the old ones, which were significantly different in Cisleithania and in Hungary (Sections 4–6).[382] Thus, there were many provisions in the law (in particular Section 8) which authorised the government, or the Ministry of the Interior, to make changes in competences, particularly in the first five years of the effectiveness of the Act; compliance with the Constitutional Charter was questionable in the case of some of these provisions.[383] Great leeway of the executive when implementing laws was common at the time of the First Czechoslovak Republic (e.g. implementing regulations to the Language Act of 1920, decisions on the effectiveness of the Regions Act), and it negatively impacted the status of minorities many times.

The internal administration in Czechoslovakia should have been carried out by regional bodies and by district bodies subordinate thereto unless the administration was vested in other bodies (Section 1). Districts were responsible for the supervision of municipalities. The Act should have applied to

---

380 See for example Vratislav Kalousek, "Přehled zákonodárné činnosti ministerstva vnitra v prvém tříletí," *Věstník ministerstva vnitra republiky Československé* 3 (1921): p. 410.

381 For regulations regarding the organisation of political administration in the Czechoslovak Republic see for example Jan Říha, *Organisace politické správy v republice Československé* (Prague: Československý Kompas, 1928), pp. 993–999.

382 Karel Laštovka, "K otázce postupu při provádění zákona o župních a okresních úřadech," *Věstník ministerstva vnitra republiky Československé* 2 (1920): pp. 285–286.

383 Schelle, *Vývoj správy v předválečném Československu*, pp. 176–178.

the entire territory of the Czechoslovak Republic except for the capital city of Prague. There were debates incited by the issue of the status of Sub-Carpathian Ruthenia and its autonomy, as it was not clear whether or not the act applied to it.[384]

Besides the territorial division of regions, it was chiefly the question of the participation of citizens in administration that was of key importance with respect to minorities. It was broad competences to independently administer their own affairs at a regional level that should have been, according to some important politicians, a certain substitute for the autonomy for minorities, which however incited strong opposition on the part of Czech nationalists. However, self-governance was actually fairly limited, a fact which used to be ignored at the time of the First Czechoslovak Republic. When criticising the weak influence of self-governing units, which could have been used by minorities to live their own national lives, it is not about the subjective assessment of what influence the self-governance should have had, although the author would recommend that it be extended, but rather about the fact that it was officially and demagogically promised, e.g. during debate in the parliament, although the reality was different. The key matter of the organisation of public administration may illustrate the important aspect of the operation of the legal status of minorities, especially if we become aware of the fact that the reform eventually did not take place, and in 1927–1928 strong centralisation occurred.

In regions, and similarly in districts, the self-government was represented by regional councils and committees; there were the issues of their establishment, competences, and the relations to the governor of the region and other state officials. Regions should have been headed by governors of the region and districts by chiefs of the district, who were both state officials. They even had a right to vote in the bodies of the self-government (Sections 20 and 26 of the Regions Act). Moreover, the government originally wished that regional councils would consist of not only members elected by citizens, but also of some appointed by the Minister of the Interior. However, this idea failed in general and was only implemented in Slovak regions. Regional authorities answered directly to the Ministry of the Interior, which had vast powers, even the power to dissolve the regional council at its own discretion (Section 61).

It is obvious that the ideas that regions would in a way be a substitute for the autonomy were somewhat exaggerated, and that the influence of the state was far-reaching. Moreover, the territorial division of regions was being rigged in an effort not to allow minorities to gain a majority in any

---

384 See for example Laštovka, *Zákon župní*, p. 28; František Weyr, *Československé právo správní* (Brno: Nákladem Čes. akadem. spolku Právník, 1922), p. 129.

of them. Despite that, the regions reform was eventually not put into practice, due among other things to opposition by the Czech nationalists, and
it was replaced by the Act on the Organisation of Political Administration
(No. 125/1927 Sb.), which further reinforced the role of the government and
bureaucracy. In spite of the considerable impact of the minorities issue on
the organisation of public administration, it cannot be said that the most
significant cause of the failure of the regions reform was nationalism. It
was rather the aggregate of economic, administrative, political, and national reasons. Particularly in the case of public administration, but also
in the case of other minorities' issues, such interconnectedness should not
be ignored.

2.7 DEVELOPMENT IN THE SECOND DECADE
OF THE CZECHOSLOVAK REPUBLIC 1929–1938

In the first decade of the Czechoslovak Republic many principal legal regulations were enacted, including those which laid the basis of the legal status of
minorities. This development was studied in the previous section, in which
we focused our interest on the circumstances of the origination of legislation
and namely their consideration in the Czechoslovak parliament. The development in the second decade of the Czechoslovak Republic was different.
Endeavours at making substantial changes in the legal status of minorities
were not successful, yet this period may not be omitted. We will, however,
focus on the problems of the application of law to the minority issue and on
unsuccessful efforts to change legal regulations, which were often exacted
by the deteriorating international and internal political situation of the First
Czechoslovak Republic.

The main aspect of the legal development in this period was facing up
to the crises – first economic, later political. The legal order had to respond
to the complicated situation of the Czechoslovak Republic too. Not only in
Czechoslovakia, but in other democratic states generally, the power of the
executive branch increased by means of secondary legislation which made
it possible to cope flexibly with the catastrophic economic situation.[385] Also,
statutes providing for possible crackdowns against political parties, the
principal regulation of armed forces, and other legal regulation reacting
to the strengthening of anti-Czechoslovak forces were adopted. At the end
of the First Czechoslovak Republic an important feature of the legal status
of minorities was the endeavour on the part of the government to swiftly
accommodate the demands of the German minority in particular. These

---

385   In more details Kuklík, *Czech law in historical contexts*, p. 98ff.

questions will be explored in this chapter devoted to the second decade of the inter-war period. As a limiting factor we took the administrative reform, approved in 1927 and implemented in 1928, as the last realised and strong – if indirect – intervention in the legal status of minorities.

An important question which needs to be explored is the minorities' attitude to the Czechoslovak Republic. Minorities – namely the key German group – had only reluctantly become reconciled with their inclusion in Czechoslovakia after 1918. In the 1920s, however, German representatives found their way to compromises (so-called "activist" policy) with the Czechoslovak state, which was symbolised by German ministers joining the government in 1926, where they stayed until 1938.[386] It should be noted that in spite of the obliging approach of German activism the Czech side was not willing to make many concessions which would change the existing legal status of minorities. In fact, the administrative reform actually meant fewer possibilities for minorities to decide their affairs in self-government.

In the first provincial elections carried out according to the new arrangement of public administration in December 1928, however, German activist parties reached comparatively handsome results, which many researchers describe as wonderful with regard to the preceding steps of the government, which had weakened the status of minorities.[387] Similar results were also brought by the crucial German minority in parliamentary elections in October 1929.[388] This situation, when before the beginning of the Great Depression the Germans in the Czech lands were contented with their political parties willing to co-operate with the Czechs, shows that ideas of a permanent, strong resistance by this minority against Czechoslovakia or their legal status are just fiction. The disastrous consequences of the economic crisis in German regions as well as the influence of Nazi Germany were much more important for the future success of the Sudetendeutsche Partei (SdP). Before the crisis, even the nationalist, or we may call it the Nazi party, the Deutsche Nationalsozialistiche Arbeiterpartei (hereinafter refered to as DNSAP), may have considered its involvement in the activist camp.[389] Similarly, other minorities were prepared to make at least partial compromises with the Czechoslovak Republic then. Traditionally, the Hungarian minority had the worst relation to Czechoslovakia "when . . . attempts at activism of any kind in Hungarian bourgeois parties were nipped in the bud, which was due to direct interferences from Hungary."[390] The elections in Sub-Carpathian Ruthenia in 1929

---

386 Beneš and Kural, *Facing history*, pp. 83–85.
387 Kárník, *České země v éře první republiky*, vol. 1, p. 407.
388 Ibid., p. 559.
389 Johann Wolfgang Brügel, "Noch einmal: Zur Frage der Deutschenvertreibung aus der Tschechoslowakei," *Bohemia* 4, no. 1 (1963): p. 395.
390 Juraj Purgat, *Od Trianonu po Košice* (Bratislava: Epocha, 1970), p. 70.

showed that among Ruthenians there was quite a big number of those who trusted the Czechoslovak Republic, and many hoped that with the support of the Czechs their region would successfully develop.[391]

Problems related to the national issue emerged also in the most successful years of the First Czechoslovak Republic, not only in the context of minorities but also in connection to the second state-constituting nation – the Slovaks. An interesting problem from the point of view of law was the co-called vacuum iuris. Vojtech (Béla) Tuka, constitutional law expert and an important representative of Hlinka's People's Party, published as an editor-in-chief of daily Slovák on 1 Januay 1928 a peculiar article entitled "Vacuum Iuris." He claimed there that there was a secret amendment to the Martin Declaration of 30 October 1918 which provided that Slovakia was joined with the Czech lands for only ten years.[392] Unless a new Constitutional Act had been adopted by 30 October 1928, the vacuum iuris should have come and the laws of Czechoslovakia, including the Constitutional Charter of 1920, would cease to apply on the territory of Slovakia. Other participants denied the existence of such an amendment to the Martin Declaration, and from the point of view of the constitutional system of the Czechoslovak Republic the idea was absurd. Nevertheless, it was a dangerous attack against the very foundations of the Czechoslovak state, and it occurred at the time when the 1927 campaign against the "unjust" Trianon Peace Treaty, launched by a British press magnate Lord Rothermere in his London paper, the Daily Mail, and challenging the shattering of traditional Hungary, was not yet over.[393]

The article caused fierce conflicts in the Czechoslovak parliament, and the situation was even more complicated by the fact that the Hlinka People's Party participated in the government coalition, which consequently fell apart. Tuka was sentenced to fifteen years of imprisonment in the middle of the elections campaign in October 1929 and Hlinka immediately summoned two ministers from his party away from the government. Ludaks were not willing to distance themselves from this blatantly anti-Czechoslovak action, which provoked annoyance among Czech politicians and almost aversion against the main Slovak party.[394] Tuka gained the reputation of a national martyr among many Slovaks; however, in reality he was a Hungarian agent, which was proved much later. The disagreement between the Czechs and the Slovaks influenced

---

391   Magocsi, "Utváření národní identity," p. 121.
392   Mikuláš Teich, Dušan Kováč and Martin D. Brown, eds., *Slovakia in History* (Cambridge: Cambridge University Press, 2011), p. 147.
393   András Bán, *Hungarian-British Diplomacy, 1938–1941: The Attempt to Maintain Relations* (London: Routledge, 2004), pp. 14–16.
394   Ibid.; see also Antonín Klimek, *Velké dějiny zemí Koruny české*, vol. 14 (Prague: Paseka, 2002), pp. 236–237.

the partially interconnected problem of minorities. We made this digression to the Czech-Slovak problems to show how a fairly absurd issue was able to complicate the situation in the Czechoslovak Republic. A great response to rather crazy arguments is typical of nationalities', hence minorities' disputes. This example shows that the state was not completely stabilised yet and that many of its foundations were challenged more than once.

Considering that relations between the state nations – Czechs and Slovaks – were far from ideal, it comes as no surprise that relations towards minorities were not based on mutual trust, but rather on suspicion; thus results could be achieved only if both parties were open to compromise. The legal initiatives of minorities frequently sparked mistrust on the part of the government, and, unfortunately, often rightfully. For instance, Czech politicians were concerned when on 4 April 1930 the representatives of all German parties – including governmental – along with the representatives of the Hungarians, Poles, and Ruthenians, presented in the National Assembly (Czechoslovak Parliament) a proposal for the establishment of a special Minorities Committee. It would consider minorities' grievances in all objectionable matters and submit relevant proposals designed to settle national and political divisions in the state to the National Assembly (proposal No. 413 of 1930).[395] The proposal was prepared by the German Christian Socialists, namely by Felix Luschka. Czech deputies kept deferring the debate on the proposal and in the end it was not debated at all. This proposal was condemned even by the moderate Czech press as canvassing against the Czechoslovak Republic, but some Czech politicians, for example from the Czechoslovak Social Democracy, recognised its justness.

Czech nationalism manifested in the pressure of the public, or rather the press, to not make concessions to minorities had a very negative impact on the situation in Czechoslovakia. Chauvinism among the Czechs was weaker than, for example, among the Germans, as nationalists were generally satisfied with the creation of a relatively large "Czech" state, yet it cannot be underestimated. According to some historians[396] particularly the Czech National Democrats and the so-called League against the Tied Ballot, composed of radical socialists headed by Stříbrný and fascists, provoked nationalist conflicts with the intent to damage the political line of the President, which underlined their co-operation with German activist parties.

---

395 Felix von Luschka, "Im Parlament der Ersten Tschechoslowakischen Republik: Erinnerungen eines sudetendeutschen Abgeordneten 1920–1938," *Bohemia* 4 (1963), p. 250; Klimek, *Velké dějiny zemí Koruny české*, vol. 14, p. 70.

396 See for example Věra Olivová, *Československé dějiny 1914–1939*, vol. 1 (Prague: Karolinum Press, 1993), pp. 202–203.

One of the most significant incidents of the time was the argument over German sound films.[397] In 1930, sound films started coming to Czechoslovakia more frequently, which brought up the question of their language version. German prevailed in Central Europe, and even Hollywood exported and distributed films in the region in the German language. On 23 September 1930, the League against the Tied Ballot used the success of a German film to incite unrest in Prague, where a mob demolished and robbed two cinemas and looted German and Jewish shops. The police response was lax[398] and riots were not suppressed until as late as 25-26 September. The reaction of the Mayor of Prague, Karel Baxa, was shameful too, as he described the demonstrations as respectable and expressed his approval, which caused problems for Czechoslovakia at an international level, for example in the League of Nations. In Germany, counter-actions were organised, including a boycott of Czechoslovak goods which was quite successful. As is the case in many other minorities' questions, the problem is more complicated and cannot be generally reduced to unrest caused by fascists and Czech nationalists; according to some people the real cause of the riots was a fight among rival film distributing companies who did not hesitate to use such odd methods to crush their competitors.[399]

Now we shall move to the question of the legal status of minorities at the end of the 1920s. The main problem traditionally consisted of language law, in those days particularly the application of language Govrnmental Order No. 17/1926 Sb. However, other legal issues were discussed throughout the entire period of the First Czechoslovak Republic. In Czechoslovakia and generally all over the world a reform of the system of international protection of minorities which would have an impact on national law was being considered. Complicated negotiations were held on the floor of the League of Nations primarily in Madrid in 1929; however, they did not bring any enhancement of the international protection of minorities, partly due to resistance on the part of states, such as the Czechoslovak Republic, which had accepted Minority Treaties. Those were rather theoretical discussions for the Czechoslovak lawyers,[400] while the application of the language Governmental Order

---

397   Zdeněk Kárník, *České země v éře první republiky*, vol. 2 (Prague: Libri, 2002), pp. 142–144; Dagmar Moravcová, *Československo, Německo a evropská hnutí 1929–1932* (Prague: Institut pro středoevropskou kulturu a politiku, 2001), pp. 137–139, 176–181, 198–217.

398   Wenzel Jaksch regarded this as a countenance of Prague police and portrayed similar problems of interwar period as expression of Czech chauvinism, Wenzel Jaksch, *Europe's Road to Potsdam*, trans. and ed. by Kurt Glaser (New York: Praeger, 1964), p. 221ff. However, it is not possible to ignore the strong influence of the nationalist right wing in the police force, which later showed in their attitude to minorities.

399   Moravcová, *Československo, Německo a evropská hnutí 1929–1932*, pp. 179–181, 199–202. The author is, however, sceptical of the explanation of the "film affair" as an incident caused by competition.

400   German lawyers in Czechoslovakia usually supported the strong reinforcement of international interventions in national law, for example Johann Jarolim, "Die Reform des Minderheitenschutzes

No. 17/1926 Sb. represented a substantial practical problem. Related legal issues show how complicated the language law is. The regulation itself was casuist and covered many surprising details, but its application required the clarification of many apparently commonplace matters. The natural problem of the use of minority languages in official dealings was made more complicated by the complex system of Czechoslovak language law, which was often influenced by a rather small-minded effort to assert the priority of the state language, that is, mainly of Czech over German.

The key role in the development of language law after the passage of principal legislation was played by the case law of the Supreme Administrative Court, which underwent a relatively significant change in certain areas of the language question. "In the past two years [1928–1930] the Supreme Administrative Court had more opportunities than ever before to consider complaints from the area of language law, and it made several principal decisions, which resolve hitherto disputable legal questions."[401] The main practical disputes arose over the interpretation of the term "bodies of the state" in language legislation, which included public notaries, land surveyors, authorised civil technicians and mining engineers, district and community state doctors, etc. One of the duties of these persons was to take an examination in the state language, which German lawyers (such as Spiegel and Epstein) considered as unlawful. Ministry regulations ordering such examinations provoked so many complaints, for example from German civil technicians, that the Czech side believed it was an organised pressure action. Unfortunately, it frequently happened that such principally marginal questions were made political. The Supreme Administrative Court examined the legal situation of individual professions and sometimes it accepted (mainly German) complaints – in specific cases; for example in the case of civil land surveyors, it decided that they were not bodies of the state in the sense of the Language Act of 1920.[402]

The Supreme Administrative Court decisions concerning the power of the government to pass orders regulating the use of language in self-governing bodies were much more significant, even from the point of view of legal theory. The key subsisted in the interpretation of Section 55 of the Constitutional Charter which was, not incidentally, to be found at the beginning of part three regulating the governing and executive power: "Orders may be issued only for the purpose of implementation of a specific act and within its

von Dr. Heinrich Rauchberg, Professor an der Deutschen Universität in Prag," *Juristen-Zeitung für das Gebiet der Tschechoslowakischen Republik* 12 (1931): pp. 38–39.

401 Felix Stein, "Zur Frage der Sprachenrechte der Reichsdeutschen und Österreicher in der Tschechoslowakischen Republik," *Juristen-Zeitung für das Gebiet der Tschechoslowakischen Republik* 9 (1928): pp. 158–160; Cyril Horáček, "Nová judikatura nejvyššího správního soudu z oboru jazykového práva," *Právník* 69, no. 8 (1930): p. 241.

402 Horáček, "Nová judikatura nejvyššího správního soudu," pp. 241–245.

scope." The Supreme Administrative Court maintained the position that the government is bound by Section 55 of the Constitutional Charter in the case of language law in spite of the constitutional nature of the Language Act, which in its Section 8 empowered the government to make a more detailed regulation of implementation. But the court interpreted Section 55 specifically for this case: "The scope in the sense of Section 55 of the Constitutional Charter is to be understood here as including the spirit of laws . . . the spirit of the Language Act is to be understood as principles, which can be obtained from the Language Act by abstraction, and according to the resolution of the plenum of the Supreme Administrative Court, the principle of preponderance of the state language is such a principle. As a result, the government, when regulating the use of languages in self-governing bodies, may exceed the positive restriction which Section 3 [of the Language Act of 1920] imposes with respect to the state language."[403]

Such interpretation obviously extended the position of the state language beyond the scope of constitutional laws. If we keep in mind that the basis of the legal status of minorities, including language law, was given to Czechoslovakia by the international treaty which had priority over all laws and official measures, then it is disputable whether the Supreme Administrative Court had the capacity to make such an extensive interpretation with reference to a "spirit of the Act." It is a question of whether at the beginning of the 1920s, when there were fears (later dispelled) that the League of Nations would consistently supervise adherence to the rights of minorities embodied in the Minorities Treaty of St. Germain, the court would resort to such a legal interpretation. In this case the problem consisted of the use of an arguable method of legal interpretation in a disputable case rather than a breakthrough in the conception of the minorities' rights; however, a willingness to quite arbitrarily use arguments, such as the spirit of laws, in the sensitive area of nationalities was slightly dubious. Moreover, these cases meant further, if minor, restriction of self-government in the Czechoslovakia, which was a step back in the process of democratisation in comparison to the strong self-government in the period of the Habsburg Monarchy. "These decisions of the Supreme Administrative Court represent a principal change in its opinions regarding the use of language in self-governing bodies and public corporations. Previously, the Supreme Administrative Court had the opinion (e.g. in its finding No. 3892 of 27 March 1928) that the Language Act principally recognises the freedom of language self-determination of such corporations and that it is possible to limit their self-determination only in cases explicitly mentioned in the Language Act of 1920, i.e. within the scope of Section 3 of the Language Act. . . . Thus, a dramatic change occurred in the

---

403 Horáček, "Nová judikatura nejvyššího správního soudu," p. 247.

interpretation of the Language Act when compared to older case law of the Supreme Administrative Court."[404]

In Czechoslovakia the language issue had always been very sensitive, and it easily inflamed tempers. Even in professional legal texts, such as in the journal Právník (The Lawyer), we can find contributions strongly influenced by nationalism whose diction can be either shocking or laughable. Such was, for example, a discussion about a Prague Czech atorney at law who had been appointed to represent ex officio a poor German and had refused the case, claiming his lack of knowledge of the German language; the Bar Association in Prague later administered a disciplinary punishment to him. This provoked a passionate response from Dr. Václav Perek, a former counsel and Moravian deputy and a distinguished expert in language issues. He strictly condemned such treatment, which was allegedly in breach of language acts and in his opinion denied the endeavours of generations of Czech lawyers and politicians to enable the Czechs never to be forced to speak German: "In this struggle [in the times of the Habsburg Monarchy] where our revivalists Palacký and Jungmann excelled on the Czech side . . . blood was shed, prisons were filled, and the Czech people were dismissed from public service."[405] A representative of the Bar Association placidly responded to this fiery article which was in fact inspired by only a minor organisational matter.[406] He pointed out that an ex officio appointed legal counsel, defence lawyer, or guardian may commonly be of different ethnic origin than the client, and that it is virtually impossible to appoint a lawyer of the same nationality, as in the case of Hungarians in the Czech lands or foreigners from the regions outside of Central Europe. So the counsel may not refuse such an assignment and it is his responsibility to overcome the language barrier, or at least to make an attempt at overcoming it in an appropriate way. He justified this duty of the members of the Bar Association by a complicated legal analysis. The case may have been assigned to a lawyer having a good command of the German language, but an immediate refusal for lack of knowledge of the language without any attempt to help the client was not deemed acceptable. Actually, it was a dispute over a minor matter, but Dr. Perek's reaction was inadequately sharp, which, unfortunately, was common in minority disputes on the Czech side and maybe even more so on the German side.

This presentation of some legal issues at the end of the 1920s and of contemporary scandals was rather critical to the Czechoslovak Republic. Our goal was to draw the attention to many shortcomings in the legal status of

---

404 Horáček, "Nová judikatura nejvyššího správního soudu," pp. 248, 249.
405 Václav Perek, "Jazyková otázka v advokátní komoře pražské," *Právník* 69 (1930): p. 182.
406 Arnošt Weinfurter, "Slovo k 'jazykové otázce' v České advokátní komoře," *Právník* 70 (1931): pp. 323–326.

minorities and the general social atmosphere of relations among nations in the Czechoslovak state, which was far from ideal and which often complicated the practical application of law or endeavours to improve it.[407] However, these problems were mostly just trifles, and with regard to what was to come in just a decade, or in comparison with the current situation in many other countries, the life of minorities in the Czechoslovak Republic was more favourable. In many aspects, such as the tradition of usually non-violent conflict resolution, a guarantee of civic rights for all citizens, and other life security, it followed the life conditions of the Habsburg Monarchy, or at least the Cisleithan Regions.

We shall now move from the analysis of some legal questions from the end of the 1920s to one of the key events of the inter-war period not only in Czechoslovakia, namely the Great Depression. It brought an economic disaster of unthinkable size, resulting in terrible social disruption, followed in many countries by a political collapse. The crisis arrived in Czechoslovakia slightly later, however, the recovery was slower than was the world-wide average, and it objectively depended too much on the boom of the arms industry. Obviously, the most important aspect for us is the impact of the economic disaster on minorities and their relationship to Czechoslovakia, particularly in the case of the key German group.

The economic crisis affected the entire world, but in case of Czechoslovakia the worst economic and social impacts were frequently seen in regions with a German majority. The main reason for the partially different economic development of the borderland and the upcountry of the Czechoslovak state was the dissimilar structure of the economy. Borderland regions, inhabited primarily by Germans, depended much more on light industry, often outdated and mainly export-oriented.[408] And it was foreign commerce which dropped much deeper worldwide than production; Czechoslovak exports were affected very strongly even in international comparison (in 1933 they dropped to 28.56 per cent of the Crown value in comparison with 1929). This led to social catastrophe, which was related mainly to unemployment in the borderland regions, but the German capital was also badly affected, which contributed to the future anti-Czechoslovak German national front of businessmen and workers. Comparing Czechoslovakia, unable to overcome crisis, and the success of Nazi Germany, which rid itself of the most feared scourge, i.e. unemployment, thanks to the boom of the arms industry and a quite low average living standard, became an important aspect.[409]

---

407 See also Johann Wolfgang Brügel, *Czechoslovakia before Munich: The German minority problem and British appeasement policy* (Cambridge: Cambridge University Press, 1973), pp. 136–149.

408 Radomír Luža, *The Transfer of the Sudeten Germans: A Study of Czech-German Relations, 1933–1962* (London: Routledge, 1964), pp. 14–15.

409 See for example also Beneš and Kural, *Facing history*, pp. 90–92.

Unemployment hit Czechoslovakia very strongly indeed, and it is estimated that half or even more than half of those unemployed were Germans. Overcoming the crisis slowly meant that high unemployment in German regions continued much longer than in Czech ones. According to some estimates the unemployment rate of Sudeten Germans was among the highest in Europe.[410] It led to horrible social consequences in the form of suicides, an increase in the occurrence of tuberculosis, etc. All the Germans likely believed that the Czechs were at least partially at fault. It is rather complicated to assess this question objectively. The main reason for the disaster in the borderland was the structure of its economy; for Czechoslovakia, which had tried to follow a relatively liberal economic policy for quite a long time, it was difficult to change this primary fact. The minister of social affairs at the time of the crisis was Ludwig Czech, representing the German Social Democracy, so the Germans could hardly challenge the distribution of social benefits from the point of nationality. Yet it should be noted that the Czechoslovak state could have done more for its borderland. For example, the policy favouring Czechs in civil service caused many bad feelings, particularly during the crisis, as in 1930 there was a 15 per cent share of Germans in judiciary and public administration, a 12.5 per cent share in posts and railways, and only in education (23 per cent) did it correspond with the share of the population. We should mention another important negative aspect: support was provided to businesses, including those owned by Germans, but German industrialists complained that banks, usually in Czech hands or in those of friendly allied foreigners, thus strengthened their dominion. The granting of public procurement contracts did not look trustworthy from the point of view of the nations either,[411] but the problem there subsisted rather in clientelism and common corruption, which objectively favoured the nation holding stronger positions in state power than in intentional discrimination against any nation.

As in other countries, the result of this economic and social catastrophe was the growth of political extremism – either right or left wing, represented by the Communists. The strongest extremism could be found among German workers, which reinforced the Nazi DNSAP along with the success of the almost twin party – the NSDAP in Germany.[412] The DNSAP presented its requirements, which at least officially did not endanger the unity of the Czechoslovak state. In 1930, the party repeated its resolution requiring the

---

410 For the fugures see ibid., p. 91.
411 Christoph Boyer, "Přidělování státních zakázek v ČSR ve 30. letech – prostředek likvidace sudetoněmeckého hospodářství?," in *Ztroskotání soplužití*, ed. by Jörg K. Hoensch and Dušan Kováč (Prague: Ministerstvo zahraničních věcí České republiky, 1993), pp. 123, 139.
412 On the origins of DNSAP and its influence upon Nazism see interesting account in Zeman, *The Making and Breaking of Communist Europe*, pp. 39–41.

Assembly of the Sudeten German Land, the creation of the office of the President of the Land, etc., drawing inspiration from the status of Sub-Carpathian Ruthenia, which had never been implemented. In the end of 1931 and beginning of 1932, local elections were organised in many places, where the DNSAP reached significant success; in some areas it gained the majority of German votes. The government tried to cover up the results, defiance against this radical party grew even among German activist parties, and measures designed to enable actions against the Nazi and other opponents of the Czechoslovak democracy were looming.[413]

In the period of economic and emerging political crisis, the government parties decided to make a number of significant interventions in the system of the state. In the economic area it was the Parent Act No.95/1933 Sb., debated in summer 1933 but proposed since 1930. The Government was entrusted with the power to enact by-laws having the force of Acts of Parliament which empowered the government to make orders having the force of law without the approval of the parliament. It applied exclusively to economic issues, however, and in many heated discussions voices could be heard saying that it should apply to political life, too, and sometimes quite far-fetched opinions, completely transforming the state system, came up. The Parent Act was met with strong opposition in the government coalition and even more so in extremist parties, when e.g. the Communists spoke of the founding of a fascist system. The Act, hastily passed on 9 June 1933, meant a certain restriction of democracy and to some degree excluded the parliament from decision-making in the area of the economy. The government had to submit the orders to the parliament for approval, but the parliament usually did not consider them at all. The orders lost validity only upon express refusal by one of the houses, which was quite exceptional.

Originally, this power of the government should have lasted only until 15 November 1933, but it was prolonged every year up until June 1937! Three hundred and six orders were made under this empowerment. According to the economic history expert Vlastislav Lacina[414], system in Czechoslovakia approached the state monopolist forms of fascist states due to these interventions and drifted away from West European democracies, where the division of power into executive and legislative persisted even in the economic field. It is disputable how strong a restriction of democracy the Parent Act and the following regulations actually meant. The strongest interventions occurred in agriculture, which was caused by the key position of agrarians in the

---

413   Ferdinand Seibt, *Německo a Češi* (Prague: Academia, 1996), p. 300; Luža, *Transfer of the Sudeten Germans*, p. 20.

414   Vlastislav Lacina, *Velká hospodářská krize v Československu 1929–1934* (Prague: Academia, 1984), p. 170.

political system; many regulations were related to social care, and only a few to industry, which had to manage by itself. Undoubtedly, the Parent Act was just a part of the measures aimed at "strong democracy,"[415] which in the political area was mainly a series of acts passed from July to October 1933. Unlike in many other states these measures were not abused to destroy democracy.

One of the first and more significant measures having an impact on the political scene was the amendment No. 88/1933 of the Rules of Procedure of the House of Deputies of 30 May 1933. Its purpose was, among others, to prevent deputies' excesses during sessions, to ensure at least a minimum attendance of deputies in sessions, and to prevent the circumvention of censorship by reading articles which had previously been confiscated – and to provide them with immunity for distribution in this way. The actual effect of the Act, however, was relatively low. On 28 June 1933, Act No. 108/1933 on the Protection of Honour was passed, whose provisions were relatively flexible, while at the same time the sanctions were very stringent in certain cases. On 10 July 1933, three important amendments were passed. The amendment of the Act on Emergency Measures of 1920 (amendment No. 125/1933 Sb. of Act No. 300/1920 Sb.) was passed, which extended the scope of acts carrying emergency measures as well as imposed more stringent sanctions for violations. On 10 July 1933, a so-called Small Press Act was passed, which was designed to prevent "press exuberance" – namely Act No. 126/1933 changing and amending press laws. Some of its provisions were broadly formulated and enabled abuse in the form of the restriction of the availability of newspapers, which might have resulted in bankruptcy. On the same day the Protection of the Republic Act was amended (amendment No. 124/1933 Sb. of Act No. 50/1923 Sb.), again in the direction of the significant extension of sanctions for acts against the state. Lesser measures of a similar nature could be found in other laws then passed, such as in the Act regulating the prosecution of acts against the state committed by public servants or in the changes of the rules of local elections. Acts protecting the republic, including the regulation of armed forces, were passed in the following years; however, some measures could not be enforced, such as the Registration of Political Parties Act (in November 1934), which would compel them to express their positive relation to the state.[416]

Probably the most significant – and from the point of view of its conception for Czechoslovak law, the most revolutionary – was Act No. 201/1933 of 25 October 1933, regulating the suspension of the activities of political parties

---

415 On the "democracy of strong hand" see for example Lipscher, *Verfassung und politische Verwaltung*, p. 149ff.

416 Kárník, *České země v éře první republiky*, vol. 2, pp. 137–139, 261.

and their dissolution, which caused the largest conflicts in the society.[417] It was dramatically new from the point of view of the legal regulation of political parties during the Czechoslovak Republic as well as during the Habsburg Monarchy, because the hitherto legal order principally ignored the existence of parties in spite of their extraordinary importance for the state and its constitutional system. Political parties were existing entities and according to case law, they did not have the nature of artificial legal persons. The law permitted vast inroads on political parties, such as the seizure of their property and stopping their press, as well as actions against associations, business companies, and cooperatives linked to them, regardless of the fact that the parties did not exist in the eyes of the law. Upon the dissolution of a party, the members of all representative bodies elected on their tickets, including the parliament, lost mandates, and the alternative members could not take their seats (Section 16). Thus the electors of such parties lost their representation to the next election, which was an exceptional restriction of the mechanism of a parliamentary democracy.

The opportunity to dissolve political parties was used in 1933 against the DNSAP Nazi party, but this case had an earlier pursuit in interventions against the Volkssport organisation,[418] which raised an enormous response and contributed to the passage of laws prosecuting acts against the state in 1933. Verband Volkssport, i.e. the Union of the People's or rather National Sport, was supposed to engage in tourism, biking, and all kinds of sports. In reality it was a paramilitary organisation based on military principles, which was permitted by authorities on 18 April 1929, even though its nature was recognisable from the beginning. In October 1930 it became a part of DNSAP; apart from a legal structure it built an illegal one, it was managed according to the leader system, its members wore uniforms inspired by the Nazi SA, and the organisation terrorised political opponents and smuggled leaflets and allegedly also weapons from Germany. State authorities monitored the activities of Volkssport and restricted them from 1930; in 1932 there was a wave of arrests and on 22 February the official dissolution took place. In the summer of 1932 a big trial of the members of Volkssport was held in Brno, where all seven defendants were convicted of conspiracy against the Czechoslovak Republic.[419] The trial was met with a lively response even abroad; the German press in Czechoslovakia mostly spoke against the trial, but the leading representatives of parties (with the exception of DNSAP) acted cautiously.

---

417 Ladislav Vojáček, "K právní úpravě postavení politických stran v I. ČSR," in *Aktuální otázky českého a československého konstitucionalismu: Sborník příspěvků z vědecké konference věnované prof. JUDr. Bohumilu Baxovi* (Brno: Masarykova univerzita, 1993), pp. 287–295.

418 See for example Kárník, *České země v éře první republiky*, vol. 2, pp. 123–128; Luža, *Transfer of the Sudeten Germans*, pp. 63–70; Wiskemann, *Czechs and Germans: A Study of the Struggle*, p. 139.

419 Kural, *Konflikt místo společenství?*, p. 117 describes the sentences as harsh and partially disputable.

However, the following process against the Jungssturm raised much stronger protests.

The investigation during the prosecution of Volkssport indeed came close to the leaders of DNSAP, who started considering the option that they should rather officially dismiss the party. They also tried to unify the German parties, possibly under the DNSAP leadership, which the other parties refused, and they perhaps even covertly enjoyed the imminent liquidation of a dangerous competitor. The key moment came when five DNSAP deputies were accused under Section 2 of the Protection of the Republic Act No. 50/1923 Sb. and the parliament discussed stripping them of immunity in February 1933. But the German parties refused to vote for stripping and thus the trust of the Czechoslovak parties to activism suffered a serious blow. DNSAP continued its activities against the state and prepared to go underground. It was precisely this situation which was the main cause for passing a series of Acts and amendments prosecuting actions against the Czechoslovak state mainly in July and October 1933. The Act regulating the suspension and the dissolution of political parties was passed in the end of October 1933, particularly because it provided the opportunity to dissolve the DNSAP, which was achieved on 11 November together with the suspension of the activities of the *Deutsch Nationale Partei* (DNP) – right wing nationalist party.[420] Vast interventions permitted by law were performed, such as stripping the deputies of their mandates. Thus the ascent of Nazism in the Czechoslovak Republic was temporarily stopped; however, the fact that crucial laws were passed hastily and almost ad hoc in a crisis situation showed the instability of Czechoslovakia and the weaknesses of the legal order, which lacked sufficient instruments at that time. Moreover, the Nazis furtively moved from the dismissed parties to the newly formed future SdP, although its recognition was accompanied by many complicated reversals. But the ascending German Nazism was only one of the threats that Czechoslovakia faced then; relations with the Slovaks were also deteriorating, which was manifested by the so-called Pribina celebrations, Czech fascism was on the increase, and traditional threats posed by the Communist Party of Czechoslovakia (CPC- KSČ), Hungarian revisionism, and other minor conflicts often linked to a nationality or a minority problem persisted.[421]

The recognition of the SdP – originally *Sudetendeutsche Heimatfront* (SHF), led by Henlein as the largest German and consequently the largest minority party, and unfortunately and not surprisingly also the main internal threat to the republic – was rather complicated. This topic has been thoroughly

---

420 Vojáček, "K právní úpravě postavení politických stran v I. ČSR," p. 293; Goswin von Dewitz-Krebs, *Das verbotene Parteiverbot: ein theoretischer Beitrag*, vol. 3/1 (Göttingen: Dewitz-Krebs, 2003).
421 Kárník, *České země v éře první republiky*, vol. 2, pp. 131–142, 164.

researched by historiography[422] and it is not very interesting from the point of view of law, perhaps with the exception of the problem of Henlein party's constant hovering on the verge of being prohibited by the state. It is obvious that speculations about this potential strict intervention were much more influenced by topical political considerations than by legal rules; Henlein manoeuvred very shrewdly among the German and Czechoslovak parties and succeeded in avoiding a principal conflict with the state. The fact that legal issues are affected by political influence at the highest political level, however, is not unusual even in more stable democracies than was the Czechoslovak Republic in the interwar period.

The international situation strongly impacted the development of the issue of DNSAP and SHF (SdP) in the Czechoslovak Republic, as is commonly the case in the minorities question. At the beginning, after the instalment of Nazism in Germany in January 1933, concerns over this threat caused efforts to carry out strong and swift actions, whose important part were the laws and amendments prosecuting activities against the Czechoslovak state of 1933; in later years, however, the fears of Germany rather prevented radical steps and pushed Czechoslovakia into agreements with other minorities, which had strong support abroad.

It was namely Poland with which Czechoslovakia had fairly decent relations when the post-war conflict concerning the common frontiers was overcome; Warsaw appreciated the good status of the Polish minority, which was not particularly numerous but was concentrated in a strategic area. Teschen (Cieszyn) Poles were under the strong influence of Warsaw, obviously much more so than was the German minority under the influence of Berlin (at least before 1937). It is noteworthy that already from the year 1921 the Polish representation had relied on the expectation that the Czechoslovak Republic as well as Austria were countries that would not last long and would perish as a result of external and internal pressure.[423] In the years 1932 to 1934 there had been alliance negotiations between Poland and the Czechoslovak Republic, but in 1934 Warsaw decided to change their policy; they oriented towards Germany and Czechoslovakia became one of their main adversaries. Local policymakers in the Teschen area started a campaign for unification with Poland; they co-operated with the Polish secret service and even performed terrorist acts, though luckily not on a very big scale. They, for example, destroyed Czech schools and state or Czech symbols. The 1935 elections brought success to Polish nationalists and Communists, who fostered both social and

422   Ibid., pp. 183–202; Kural, *Konflikt místo společenství?*, p. 121ff.; Wiskemann, *Czechs and Germans: A Study of the Struggle*, pp. 137–206.

423   Václav Žáček, *Češi a Poláci v minulosti*, vol. 2 (Prague: Academia, 1967), p. 534; see also John W. Wheeler-Bennett, *Munich: Prologue to tragedy*, 2nd ed. (New York: Duell, Sloan & Pearce, 1963), p. 282ff.; or Wiskemann, *Czechs and Germans: A Study of the Struggle*, p. 235.

national radicalism there. The Czechoslovak Republic tried to negotiate with Poland and mention the decent status of the Polish minority, but for Warsaw, which, for example, supported the anti-Czechoslovak broadcasting from Katowice reminiscent of the style of the Nazi broadcasting from Leipzig, the question of the Polish minority was just an excuse and, of course, no agreement could be reached.[424]

Sub-Carpathian Ruthenia was a peripheral part of Czechoslovakia, which in comparison to the Czech lands and even to Slovakia was very poor and backward; e.g. illiteracy in Czechoslovakia persisted only there. An affiliation to Czechoslovakia had brought enormous cultural enhancement to the region, however, autonomy guaranteed by the Minorities Treaty and the Constitution was put off. At the beginning a justification for it existed, recognised even by the League of Nations, because the self-government would most probably be controlled by local Hungarians; but as the Ruthenian elites grew this situation appeared more and more problematic. Similarly to other, not only minority problems, a difficult feature of Czechoslovak democracy manifested itself here: because of the need to engage almost all parties loyal to the state in government, it was very difficult to push any principal changes through, such as autonomy in this case.

The question of autonomy was further complicated not only by the backwardness of the region, with a large number of Hungarians and nationally conscious Jews, but also by the undecided national orientation of the Ruthenians. The government in Prague wavered among the support for the Russian, Ukrainian, or Ruthenian language and did not show any significant preference to any. Although local elites became increasingly irritated, the majority of the population remained faithful to Czechoslovakia, which they considered a guarantee of future development and a shield against other countries, which would probably treat Ruthenians less favourably.[425] Like in other regions of Czechoslovakia, local irredentists enjoyed support from abroad; from the mid-1930s Poland also supported a pro-Hungarian orientation there as they strived to weaken the Czechoslovak state, which was perceived as a competitor.[426]

A huge minority conflict where both Czech and German nationalists "distinguished themselves" was a so-called "insigniade,"[427] which grew into vast unrest in the end of November 1934. The gist of the dispute was the question of whether the successor of the traditional Charles University was the Czech

---

424 Jaroslav Nebeský, "Polská menšina na československém Těšínsku," *Zahraniční politika* 15 (1936): pp. 95–111, 196–205; Kárník, *České země v éře první republiky*, vol. 2, pp. 223–224, 499.

425 Kárník, *České země v éře první republiky*, vol. 2, pp. 254–255; Magocsi, "Utváření národní identity," pp. 120–123.

426 Žáček, *Češi a Poláci v minulosti*, p. 554.

427 Kárník, *České země v éře první republiky*, vol. 2, pp. 269–280.

or the German University in Prague. Nationalist, Professor František Mareš, initiated the adoption of Act No. 135/1920 Sb. on the Relationship between Prague Universities (a so-called Lex Mareš), which was passed hastily like many similar ill-conceived measures at the very end of the term of the Revolutionary National Assembly on 19 February 1920 and which determined the Czech University to be the lawful, exclusive heir of Charles University. One of the consequences was that the German University was obliged to hand in their traditional symbols – so-called insignia. However, they did not render them in spite of all the efforts of the Czech side, and discussions about whether the German University was also the successor of Charles University continued.[428]

In 1933 Professor Karel Domin assumed the office of the Rector of Charles University and started phased steps to get back the insignia – first of all, he ensured the entering of the official seat of University – Carolinum, where they had been deposited as the property of the Czech University in the land register. This development caused a number of ever sharper conflicts fostered by the press, which did not stop even when the new rector assumed his office. On 20 November 1934, Professor Jan Krčmář, the minister of education and a law Professor, issued a decision that Section 5 of Act No. 135/1920 Sb. should be enforced. The Rector's Office of the German University refused to deliver over the insignia and German students, very often right-wing and nationalist or Nazi oriented, occupied the Carolinum to prevent the rendering, which led to clashes with Czech students. The situation resulted in vast unrest, where mobs and nationalist groups of armed troublemakers, attacking the left-wing oriented people, participated rather than students, and which claimed 180 injured persons. In the end, the insignia were delivered with much merrymaking, but they were not practically used by academics anyway. It was a typical case in many respects of minority disputes in inter-war Czechoslovakia, also from the point of view of legal aspects. The conflict was mostly just a matter of prestige, yet it raised vast unrest, where moderate representatives, such as the president, most members of the government, and mainly the parties on the left[429] were shouted down by chauvinists on both sides, who abused a principally academic matter for riots and for drawing attention to themselves. The legal issues were peculiar, too, but not unusual in the environment of the Czechoslovak Republic where the passage of a law affected by nationalism was not followed by its complete implementation, and the deferring of the solution finally caused many problems amplified by the lack of willingness of the German University to submit to a legal intervention.

---

428   Krčmář, *The Prague Universities*, pp. 25–31.
429   Kural, *Konflikt místo společenství?*, p. 134.

A significant breakpoint in the development of the German question within the Czechoslovak Republic represented the parliamentary elections in May 1935, which many researchers (probably justly) recognise as the beginning of an open crisis of Czechoslovakia. The key role was played by the extraordinary, even shocking when compared to the previous election, success of SdP, the party which was negativist in relation to Czechoslovakia in spite of its declarations. There were discussions before the elections about whether the SdP (then SHF) should not be prohibited, a question which had been discussed in corridors ever since its foundation. In April 1935 the government discussed the matter, and all but the agrarians were for the official dismissal of the party; then the government took an unusual step and sent the Prime Minister Jan Mapypetr and Edvard Beneš to Lány to enquire about the president's opinion. Masaryk did not recommend dismissal, probably as he was concerned over the possible underground activities of the Henlein Party members and was perhaps relying on Henlein's moderation. Such discussions did not conform to the legal order and there was a threat of scandal before the elections, so the government officially, but not truthfully, disclaimed discussions about the prohibition of SHF as well as the president's intervention.[430]

The SdP achieved enormous success in the election, approximately two thirds of the Germans, and in some districts more than 80 per cent voted for it, but a precise statistic is not available. Thus this party, in fact totalitarian, gained control over the majority of the German population, which, however, was still used to a democratic government and cohabitation with the Czechs and the Czechoslovak Republic; the SdP therefore had to slowly recondition their electorate, to weaken the competing parties and to prevent their revival, often by force or later even by terror. According to Wenzel Jaksch, however, the success of the SdP in the borderland regions could have been significantly higher considering the depth of the crisis. The SdP became an important part of the political scene in Czechoslovakia, and in spite of its growing radicalism and often almost overbearing behaviour, discussions of banning it must have been put off. The success received a response abroad, too, and many influential journalists, among others, came particularly from Britain and ensured a good position for Henlein on the international scene.[431] Immediately after the elections the SdP mounted its political offensive where it proposed the participation of the party in the government, astonishingly increased the number of its members, and disdained and ridiculed the German activist parties. But it also introduced in the Czechoslovak Republic the

---

430 There have been speculations of certain senility of Masaryk, which was responsible for his approval of SHF-SdP participation in elections but, for example Kárník, *České země v éře první republiky*, vol. 2, pp. 192–193 refuses that.

431 See Houžvička, *Czechs and Germans 1848–2004*, pp. 191–202.

demeanour inspired by Nazism, such as the oath of loyalty and obedience to the party and to Henlein required from the elected senators and deputies. Yet in 1936 it had to tackle internal disagreement caused by conflicts between old Nazis and the so-called Kameradschaftsbund. The strengthening of the SdP, supported by the persistent disastrous economic situation in the borderland regions, continued. The unemployment rate remained much higher there than in the Czech regions, where it was no longer so apparent.[432]

The leaders of the Czechoslovak state were aware of the critical trends, although the election of the new president, Beneš, showed that Czechoslovak Republic and its traditional policy still enjoyed significant support. Jan Malypetr became the Prime Minister after elections in May 1935, but as early as in November he was substituted by a Slovak Agrarian, Milan Hodža, the first person of non-Czech origin in this office. From the establishment of Czechoslovakia Hodža was recognised as a supporter of regionalism and decentralisation, which was beneficial for minorities. Neither German opposition nor Hungarian parties were overly satisfied with Hodža: "Although it was generally known that the government had made preliminary reviews of the extensive minority memoranda, and the preparation of legal unification of all minority legislation and regulations had begun with the aim of elaborating them in a uniform nationalities statute, none of the minority parties cherished the illusion that the government as a whole would like to engage in a clear pro-minority policy, let alone in the trends towards decentralisation."[433] Prague proceeded relatively slowly as usual; however, partial steps in the direction of decentralisation and the extension of the rights of minorities were made. They stemmed from government analyses prepared on the grounds of meticulous inter-departmental research of the situation of minority rights carried out in 1935–1936. Responsible politicians were fully aware of the necessity of a compromise with minorities, certainly the most influential besides Hodža was Beneš, who recommended a more liberal application and the corrections of some laws, in particular the Language Act, consistent implementation of proportionality in state administration, and in the distribution of public funds as well as the strengthening of self-government, although at the same time he rejected territorial self-governing units which in his eyes posed a threat to the Czechoslovak Republic.[434]

In the proposed legislation, however, provisions against powers hostile to the state prevailed, such as the extension of the legal force of the Act

432 Kárník, *České země v éře první republiky*, vol. 2, pp. 495–528, 551–556.

433 Luschka, "Im Parlament der Ersten Tschechoslowakischen Republik," p. 263; László Szarka, "Národnostní statut a rozpory mezi Benešem a Hodžou 1935–1940," *Střední Evropa* 8, no. 26 (1992): p. 50.

434 Szarka, "Národnostní statut a rozpory mezi Benešem a Hodžou," pp. 50–53; Sobota, *Národnostní autonomie v Československu?*, pp. 60–61.

regulating the prohibition and dissolution of political parties. The government requested the extension in November 1935 and had to face protests not only from minorities, but also from the Communists and the Social Democrats referring to legal assessments stressing the mistakes and shortcomings of the law. The adoption of a stringent law on the registration of political parties was considered, which would make it possible to deny key registration to existing political parties. Only parties registered with the Ministry of the Interior could thus participate in elections, but the registration would be decided by the government. Another group were laws regulating and strengthening the armed forces. This vindicatory approach failed to intimidate the SdP or other negativist parties; rather, it perhaps weakened the remaining German activism.[435] This process was sometimes criticised as a destruction of the rule of law.[436]

We should now deal comprehensively with laws regulating armed forces. Not only is it one of the least researched topics, it is also an extremely complicated one; historians are frequently almost at a loss when it comes to it. One of the problems consists in the effort to interpret some legislative regulations only from the point of view of the then situation – e.g. the influence of Henlein's success or other minority conflicts – with no regard to long-term aspects. One of the key elements was a so-called Machník decree, which is an extraordinarily difficult legal problem which can hardly be understood without a knowledge of the international protection of minorities, both from the point of view of its formal framework and of its practical application. The legal regulation of armed forces was rather complicated in itself, and from the point of view of inter-war law it was almost unique, because the army had a peculiar and independent position.

The crucial legal regulation of armed forces was certainly the Defence of the State Act No. 131/1936 Sb. The question of how much the law was influenced by a rather acute crisis of Czechoslovak state has provoked discussions among historians, and its provisions are often assessed or criticised as a manifestation of so-called strong democracy. These opinions, sustained by a minimum knowledge of the development of legal regulation of armed forces, are relatively exaggerated, and they ignore the fact that the Defence of the State Act had been prepared for a long time. "The original bill was prepared at the National Defence Ministry as early as in 1926; when the Inter-departmental Body for the Defence of the State (IBPS) was established, which consisted of the representatives of the Board of the Ministerial Council, all ministries,

435 Klimek, *Velké dějiny zemí Koruny české*, vol. 14, pp. 432–433.
436 But such criticism often came from members of minorities having a negative attitude to the state. For example for the criticism of the amendment of the Protection of the Republic Act see Fritz Sander, "Spionagegesetz und Rechtsstaat," *Prager Juristische Zeitschrift* 16, November 1, 1936, pp. 621–626.

the Office of the President of the Republic, and the Supreme Auditing Office, the bill was discussed in this body, namely in its legal commission."[437] If we compare the final wording of 1936 with older preliminary materials, in particular with the draft bill including the explanatory report of 1930, we can see that some elements were included in the period of endangering of Czechoslovakia, but the conception of the Act is analogous and the effect of the threat posed namely by Nazi Germany should not be overestimated. After all, the siege of the Czechoslovak Republic by states which did not treat it in a very friendly was a permanent condition. "The preparation and provision of the defence of the state is the leading idea and purpose of the draft bill of the Defence of the State Act [prepared in 1930]. Submitting this bill, the government only fulfils its duty resulting from the responsibility for the state and its independence, unity, entirety and democratic and republican form."[438]

Prior to the adoption of the Defence of the State Act, the Czechoslovak Republic did not have a law consistently regulating the defence of the state and particularly its timely and efficient preparation. Besides the Armed Forces Act No. 193/1920 Sb. there were only partial laws, some of them taken over from the times of the Habsburg Monarchy. The style of legal regulation was original in many respects; one could be surprised by the Post Pigeons Act No. 2/1924 Sb., and legislation for the internal regulation of the department could be almost laughable for a modern day lawyer.[439] The legal regulation of armed forces in the inter-war Czechoslovakia actually represented a very specific branch of law, almost unique in a democratic state. The Defence of the State Act of 1936 newly introduced e.g. some new bodies and the armed alert of the state,[440] while the Constitutional Charter of 1920 made no mention of it. In fact it was full of significant exceptions from generally applicable law. However, it is of principal importance to note here that such a situation was (and frequently still is) common in other democratic states, and the criticism of some rather tough provisions calls for objective comparison.

The need for a clear regulation of the defence required many years of preparation of the Defence of the State Act, which was made more difficult

---

437 Jaroslav Vorel, *Zákon o obraně státu* (Prague: Čin, 1936), p. 3.

438 The draft bill of the Defence of the State Act with the explanatory report as they were debated in IBPS on December 1, 1930 (the Ministry of the National Defence, the main staff, the general secretariat of IBPS – Appendix to ref. No. 1286/expl. gen. secr. 1930), printed leaflet, p. 1.

439 Vorel, *Zákon o obraně státu*, p. 3; Robert Steiner, "Der strafrechtliche Gehalt des Staatsvertei-digungsgesetzes," *Juristenzeitung für das Gebiet der Tschechoslowakischen Republik* 17 (1936): pp. 161–165, 169–173; and 18 (1937): pp. 15–19, 36–48, 81–91.

440 Criticism by German lawyers, e.g. Fritz Sander, "Verfassungsrechtliche Bemerkungen zum Staatsverteidigungsgesetze," *Juristen-Zeitung für das Gebiet der Tschechoslowakischen Republik* 17 (1936): p. 110; rather sharp criticism can be found in Wiskemann, *Czechs and Germans: A Study of the Struggle*, pp. 238–239 (otherwise assessing Czechoslovakia mostly positively), "The practice of the Defence Ministry continued to be fairly chauvinistic . . ." (p. 239).

by the progressing Nazism and negativism of the German minority. At the beginning of 1936 the bill was completed, approved by the Inter-departmental Body for the Defence of the State and then by the Supreme Council for the State Defence, and on 13 March 1936 by the government, which submitted it for consideration to the parliament. The House of Deputies passed the Act on 30 April and the Senate on 13 May, both chambers by an overwhelming majority. It became effective on 23 June 1936.[441] Such a detailed timeline is not pointless, as from the end of January the very important case of the so-called Machník decree started evolving: the SdP challenged the state scheme of allocating the armaments contracts and tried to provoke a big international scandal. The time connection with the preparatory work on the Defence of the State Act was by no means a coincidence; after all the SdP quickly obtained secret documents, including the Machník decree itself.

We will dwell a little longer on the so-called Machník decree[442] because it is a remarkable case illustrating many problems of the subject of minorities in the First Czechoslovak Republic, including its legal aspects. The name Machník decree was given to the written appeals sent to companies interested in public procurement contracts at the end of 1936 by the National Defence Ministry, headed by František Machník.[443] The ministry requested that the companies take certain measures affecting the nationality structure of their employees, particularly that the number of employees of the Czechoslovak nationality be at least equal to the share of the state nation in the population of the respective region. Foreign employees and persons supporting political parties hostile to the state were to be dismissed. These requirements quickly leaked to the public and were sharply criticised by the German press, including pro-government. From 26 January ample articles emerged in the press.[444] The SdP took advantage of the fact that Czechoslovakia was bound by the Minorities Treaty of St. Germain and filed a complaint with the League of Nations at the end of April, where they attacked Czechoslovakia for excluding Germans from public procurement. The case is very complex and should be

---

441 Vorel, *Zákon o obraně státu*, pp. 3–4; Wiskemann, *Czechs and Germans: A Study of the Struggle*, p. 241.
442 Archiv Ministerstva zahraničních věcí (AMZV), collection II. sekce – Společnost národů, box 697, "Menšiny RČS – Stížnost sudetských Němců (Henlein)" ["Minorities of the RCS – Complaints by Sudeten Germans (Henlein)"]; see also *Sudetendeutsche Beschwerde an den Völkerbund über den Erlaß des Ministeriums für nationale Verteidigung der Tschechoslowakischen Republik betreffend die Vergabe staatlicher Lieferungen* (Karlsbad: Karl H. Frank, 1936); César and Černý, *Politika německých buržoazních stran*, p. 408.
443 František Machník was a MP for the Agrarian Party since 1925, an ardent propagator of civil defence and horse riding. Defence Minister from June 4, 1935 to September 22, 1938. He strived to strengthen the ability of Czechoslovakia to defend itself. According to Wiskemann, *Czechs and Germans: A Study of the Struggle*, p. 238 Machník issued his decree independently of other members of the government.
444 Some German articles were reprinted in *Sudetendeutsche Beschwerde an den Völkerbund*, pp. 20–61.

evaluated from diverse aspects – from the point of view of long-term trends in the allocation of public procurement contracts to Germans, then from the loyalty of this minority to the Czechoslovak state, and mainly from the legal aspects of this measure.

Public procurement based on objective criteria is a challenging task in democratic states, and the Czechoslovak Republic struggled due to the complicated ethnic set-up; traditionally every achievement by one of the nationalities, e.g. concerning a street sign or an office post, led to some friction. The problem was exacerbated by the undeniable fact that, compared to the Czechs or Slovaks, the German population paid higher taxes owing to their higher living standards, and from the time of the Great Depression, which persisted in the borderland regions during the whole of the 1930s, the entire region required enhanced state economic assistance. Hence, it is difficult to establish what proportion of public contracts should have been awarded to German companies, as the proportion of the population is not the only relevant criterion.[445] Christoph Boyer, a German researcher, recently concluded that German companies were indeed disadvantaged to a certain extent, but that unsuccessful competition was often caused by the worse performance of the German companies. The German companies often failed to submit proposals for tenders, and their price quotations tended to be 20% higher than those of the Czech companies. Public administration insisted on cost-effectiveness, and the demands advanced by the German economic associations to make acceptable the more expensive bids of the German companies in order to support the borderland regions were, of course, resisted. A particularly complicated issue is the influence of corruption and lobbying – in this respect the state nation was undoubtedly in a more favourable position due to its stronger position within the administration.[446]

Objective public procurement (e.g. as regards Machník's decree) is further complicated by the issue of the problematic state integrity of the German minority – as a considerable proportion of public contracts after 1935 was done for the Ministry of Defence.[447] On the one hand, the sense of allegiance of this minority was largely non-existent, and on the other hand, when awarding public contracts the state authorities were under the influence of a certain hysteria caused by the fact that Czechoslovakia was surrounded by potential enemies. In order to illustrate the achievements of

---

445 According to the SdP figures the participation of the Germans in public procurement in German regions was indeed very low – in those regions, with the German population of 84.5% and the Czech population of 15.5%, the German companies allegedly only represented 16.1% in public procurement. These figures were used by the SdP for criticism of Czechoslovakia abroad, *Sudetendeutsche Beschwerde an den Völkerbund*, p. 90.
446 Boyer, "Přidělování státních zakázek v ČSR ve 30. letech," pp. 133–142.
447 Zdeněk Kárník, *České země v éře první republiky*, vol. 3 (Prague: Libri, 2003), pp. 76–77.

the German espionage in Czechoslovakia we could mention the construction of borderland fortifications which, according to counter-espionage services, brought about an avalanche of German spying, allegedly becoming a national hobby for Sudeten Germans. This situation directly motivated[448] the adoption of so-called Machník's decree. While it is clear that the Czechoslovak authorities were understandably concerned about the disloyalty of part of the German population, certain measures of Prague central bodies made the minority members feel that the interventions targeted all Germans. Before the elections in April 1935, certain rumours suggested that there were measures putting German companies at a disadvantage[449], but Bohumír Bradáč, the then Minister of Defence, issued a reassuring declaration.[450] However, so-called Machník's decree, which was issued later, was exactly the type of measure which caused concern to the Germans. Despite the justified distrust of the minority, it is clear that certain activities of the government were rather short-sighted, *inter alia* Machník's decree. "Adoption of laws and other measures related to the defence of the state was a highly sensitive matter. It was known that the measures were supposed to address the German threat and that they would severely affect the Czech borderland regions."[451]

The legal aspects of the the so-called Machník's decree should be discussed as well, since the edict is one of the most interesting legal issues of interwar Czechoslovakia. In this curious case, a specific part of domestic law – i.e. departmental legislation of the Ministry of Defence (with doubts surrounding the legal character of the so-called Machník's decree) – was combined with the peculiar system of international law governing the protection of minorities. The so-called Machník's decree consisted of letters from the Ministry of National Defence which were sent to 18 companies[452] on 24 and 28 January, advising them that the ministry would award the contract to them only if they, beside stipulated prices and quantities of goods, unconditionally agreed

448 Ibid., p. 469. However, the reality was probably more complicated.
449 The Ministry of National Defence (MND) tried to keep such measures secret – the conditions which were, in the purchase orders for the army, imposed by the MND on businesses which allegedly lacked some integrity generally included *inter alia* the following provision: "You are asked by the MND, under section 6 of the Protection of the Republic Act, to keep these conditions of the purchase order secret and to take appropriate measures in your business in order to maintain secrecy." Archiv Ministerstva zahraničních věcí (AMZV), collection II. sekce – Společnost národů, box 697, "Menšiny RČS – Stížnost sudetských Němců (Henlein)," k 25.300/36/II-4 Tajné [Secret], p. 2. Despite this warning the information leaked and in May 1935 Dr. Luschka participated in a Parliament interpellation and the union of German employees in industry and trade filed collective complaints.
450 Prager Tagblatt, January 26, 1936 – quoted according to *Sudetendeutsche Beschwerde an den Völkerbund*, p. 20.
451 Very accurately explained by Klimek, *Velké dějiny zemí Koruny české*, vol. 14, p. 419.
452 Archiv Ministerstva zahraničních věcí (AMZV), collection II. sekce – Společnost národů, box 697, "Menšiny RČS – Stížnost sudetských Němců (Henlein)," 113.196/1936, p. 2.

to some other conditions. "Make sure you modify the nationality set-up of employees in your enterprise so that: 1) the number of clerks of Czechoslovak nationality corresponds at least to the percentage of manual workers of the Czechoslovak nationality employed in the enterprise; 2) the number of manual workers of Czechoslovak nationality corresponds at least to the nationality set-up of the population in the region where the enterprise has its registered office. Moreover, make sure you substitute, as soon as possible, foreign employees with domestic workforce of Czechoslovak nationality and refrain from employing personnel (clerks and manual workers) who sympathise with political parties hostile to the state."[453] Such conditions were rather controversial, and even more peculiar was the fact that the enterprises concerned were supposed to respond immediately (i.e. by noon of 30 January). If they failed to deliver an unconditional agreement with these terms, the ministry would immediately award the contract to another company.

The fact that the Czechoslovak Republic was bound by the Minorities Treaty of St. Germain was crucial for the further development of the issue, as the treaty guaranteed the equality of minority members, and such stipulations were "recognised as fundamental laws and that no law, regulation, or official action shall conflict or interfere with these stipulations" (Article 1 of the Minorities Treaty). From the end of January harsh criticism appeared in the press, claiming that German companies were excluded by this measure, referred to as Machník's decree, from participating in public procurement, and that this policy deliberately targeted Sudeten Germans. The so-called Machník's decree was subjected to severe criticism by the German lawyers in Czechoslovakia and, together with the bill on the defence of the state which was being drafted, was described as an open move from the rule of law to a police state.[454]

This incident was controversial even on the Czechoslovak domestic political scene. On 2 March the government had to respond to parliamentary interpellations and did so rather awkwardly. It argued that military production had to be appropriately secured even during difficult times, which was not the case in some enterprises, in spite of warnings made by the Ministry of Defence. The exceptionally short time limit was allegedly only for registration purposes. Thus, the government did not deny the actual content of the decree.[455] Prime Minister Milan Hodža then allegedly promised German activists[456] help in redressing the injustice surrounding nationality issues in

---

453   *Sudetendeutsche Beschwerde an den Völkerbund*, p. 14.

454   Fritz Sander, "Der Machnik-Erlaß und die Verfassungsurkunde," *Prager Juristische Zeitschrift* 16, November 1, 1936, p. 268.

455   *Sudetendeutsche Beschwerde an den Völkerbund*, p. 71.

456   Klimek, *Velké dějiny zemí Koruny české*, vol. 14, p. 393; Jindřich Dejmek, "Britská diplomacie, Československo a Sudetoněmecká strana," *Moderní dějiny* 9 (2001): p. 180.

the field of military procurement, as well as promised to dismiss Minister of Defence František Machník. On 24 April 1936 the Sudeten German Party and the Carpathian German Party submitted a complaint to the League of Nations, primarily against Machník's decree. Subsequently, the Czechoslovak Republic had to defend itself in Geneva, and it used some rather curious arguments. The official reply by Czechoslovakia submitted to the League of Nations on 31 August 1936 *inter alia* explained that on 19 June the government adopted a resolution prohibiting the imposition of conditions in relation to the nationality of employees in companies which were involved in public procurement. The resolution also stipulated that no employee could be dismissed for their nationality.[457]

However, besides general declarations denying anti-German policy, the Czechoslovak Republic had to address Machník's decree itself. According to the Czechoslovak statement addressed to the League of Nations, no decree was ever issued – from the legal point of view the so-called Machník Decree did not exist. Apparently, there were certain unwritten practices relating to public procurement which never gave rise to any complaints. These directives were newly put into written form, but they did not represent an authoritative edict of the Ministry of Defence, and the measure lacked the interventive character typical of public law. Moreover, the directives were said to be applied in a very liberal way and the companies which expressly refused to comply with the conditions were not treated in a less favourable way. In addition, the directives were repealed by the new Act on the Defence of the State.[458] Such declarations presented by Czechoslovakia were unacceptable for the League of Nations, and in a letter of 18 May 1936 the director of the Minorities Section indicated that the Czechoslovak approach put in danger the employment opportunities of minority members who already struggled with high unemployment levels. He underlined the fact that such a letter from the ministry addressed to companies could cause fear of discrimination, even if the measure in question was not implemented: "Considering all the circumstances, the conditions imposed by the ministry tended to create a threat of the discriminatory treatment of a minority . . . the minority could believe that it was just the beginning of a series of discriminatory measures targeting this minority."[459] This revealed, besides peculiar departmental legislation, another major legal issue of this case – the insufficient detail of minority treaties. Considerations about the unacceptability of threats of discriminatory treatment could not be properly aligned with the minority treaties. Any attempt

---

457 Otto Novák, *Henleinovci proti Československu* (Prague: Naše vojsko, 1987), p. 89.
458 Archiv Ministerstva zahraničních věcí (AMZV), collection II. sekce – Společnost národů, box 697, "Menšiny RČS – Stížnost sudetských Němců (Henlein)," 24.237/1937 of February 19, 1937.
459 Ibid., 67.728/1936 (letter of the director of the Minorities Section at the League of Nations from May 18, 1936).

at arriving at such unacceptability through interpretation would represent extended interpretation of this treaty, which would not be possible due to its exceptional character in international law.

In addition to arguments about the factual non-existence of Machník's decree Czechoslovakia had to resort to more complicated legal reasoning. The main objection was the character of letters, i.e. neither laws nor orders, and in the Czechoslovak view the letters did not represent an official act, and therefore the Minorities Treaty of St. Germain was not applicable. Thus, such measures were subject to judicial review, but the Sudeten Germans who filed the complaint with the League of Nations failed to pursue the national judicial route first. An ensuing judicial decision would have been an official act that could be complained about. However, the Minorities Treaty provided very little, i.e. insufficient, legal regulation of procedural aspects, and therefore the Czechoslovak arguments are rather dubious. In general the Czechoslovak Republic claimed that the letters of the ministry did not have the character of an act which would be covered by the protection of minorities, and even if they did have such character, they would not be inconsistent with the Minorities Treaty of St. Germain. This is just a very simplified version of the Czechoslovak legal opinion which had some rather peculiar elements. "It is necessary to take the approach as if the letters had never been sent, because although a few letters had been sent by the Ministry of National Defence, the ministry acted, is acting, and will act as if such letters never existed."[460] However, after preliminary examination, the Minorities Section of the League of Nations secretariat found the complaint of the Sudeten German Party admissible and referred it for further consideration. Hence, it did not consider the Czechoslovak reasoning sufficient. According to the League of Nations, Machník's decree had the character of an official act, discriminating against minorities members.[461]

The main problem of the international protection of minorities, which played out in this case as well, was the politicisation of conflicts. In this way, the inadequate legal regulation[462] of the Minorities Treaty of St. Germain, which lacked sufficient detail, was in its application considerably influenced by political interests. During negotiations in Geneva, the SdP representatives quickly learned that the League of Nations would have to reject their petition (complaint). They tried to avoid this because the rejection would have put

---

460 Ibid., 113.196/1936 of August 29, 1936 (government comments on petition of April 24, 1936 for the Secretary-General of the League of Nations), p. 8.

461 Ibid., 84.051/1936 from June 23, 1936.

462 Another problem caused by the lack of clarity in minority treaties was the position of Germany, as the country had withdrawn from the League of Nations and thus should not have had a say in the discussions about minorities issues in this organization, ibid., 36.327/1937 and 36.328/1937; Jindřich Dejmek, *Historik v čele diplomacie: Kamil Krofta* (Prague: Karolinum Press, 1998), p. 105.

Henlein in a very awkward position after a previous large campaign, and the world press had a very strong base in Geneva. Therefore, the SdP promised to submit supporting documents to the petition, stating the practical impacts of the so-called Machník's decree. But as the decree had no actual impact, the necessary documents were not collected and no additional petition was drawn up. The rejection of the complaint was repeatedly postponed and the Czechoslovak diplomats understood that the British Foreign Office did not really care about Machník's decree but, by extending the proceedings, the British tried to impose concessions on Czechoslovakia so that the issue of the Sudeten Germans would not cause trouble for British politics.[463] Thus, at the international level Henlein relied mainly on British support. Eventually, in May 1937, the Committee for Minorities of the League of Nations declared that the complaint had been resolved by the Czechoslovak explanation, but the whole dispute strongly contributed to the internationalisation of the Sudeten issue.[464]

Evaluating the issues surrounding the so-called Machník's decree is complicated.[465] Apparently, it illustrates certain practices of the Ministry of Defence in the area of public procurement which were not very favourable for the German minority. Nevertheless, this issue was probably only a faux pas of the ministry which happened to be disclosed to the public in writing and which included certain unnecessarily strict provisions – in particular, outrageous time limits preventing the companies concerned from being able to reach a compromise. The considerations that the letters heralded a new policy in that area, and that it was only the fierce opposition of the German minority which prevented further application, are probably false, *inter alia* because the letters were drafted in a transitional period while the comprehensive act on the defence of the state was under preparation. Overall, it was a storm in a teacup, but the German minority responded very ferociously and the issue was discussed on the international level. The steps of the Ministry of Defence also illustrate certain arbitrary approaches to the legal order which subsequently had to be justified with great difficulty on the international level. The complexity of this legal issue has led to many errors in historical works – e.g. the so-called Machník's decree is sometimes referred to as a law.[466]

---

463 Archiv Ministerstva zahraničních věcí (AMZV), collection II. sekce – Společnost národů, box 697, "Menšiny RČS – Stížnost sudetských Němců (Henlein)," 24.237/1937 from February 19, 1937, p. 3; *Zahraniční politika 1937*, pp. 669–670; Sabine Bamberger-Stemmann, *Der Europäische Nationalitätenkongreß 1925 bis 1938: Nationale Minderheiten zwischen Lobbyistentum und Großmachtinteressen* (Marburg: Herder-Institut, 2000), pp. 371–375.

464 Dejmek, *Historik v čele diplomacie*, pp. 76–77; Josef Chmelař, "Československá zahraniční politika v roce 1936," *Zahraniční politika* 15 (1936): p. 730.

465 Klimek, *Velké dějiny zemí Koruny české*, vol. 14, p. 419 the measure is tactfully referred to as unfortunate and the tight deadline is being criticised.

466 Dejmek, "Britská diplomacie, Československo a Sudetoněmecká strana," p. 180.

While the so-called Machník's decree was of minor importance, the Defence of the State Act (No. 131/1936 Sb.)[467], adopted at this time, was a highly significant piece of legislation which regulated the Czechoslovak armed forces. Although the act itself was quite robust, its implementation required a number of additional governmental orders and other implementing regulations. The act was subject to severe criticism, e.g. by German lawyers who regarded it as a measure against minorities.[468] While it is true that in a situation of imminent danger to the Czechoslovak Republic many radical measures were needed or even necessary, the act in question contained certain controversial elements – historical works quite frequently mention the definition of so-called people lacking integrity; very important is also the provision for extraordinary delegation of powers to the government[469] and the possibility to carry out a measure designed for the period of state defence emergency even where the period of emergency had not been formally declared. All in all, there were quite a few extraordinary measures which were inconsistent with ordinary legal practices, making even the Czech lawyers rather uncomfortable.[470]

A fundamental issue was the so-called lack of integrity which could result in further potential interventions. The concept was defined in Section 19 (9): "A person shall not be designated as lacking integrity on the grounds of his/her affiliation with a particular language, religion or race. Persons lacking integrity shall be notably such persons who can be reasonably believed to have abused their position to the detriment of the state's defence." The definition was followed by a demonstrative list which was of a general nature, allowing for arbitrary interpretations. A more specific definition covered persons "who were members of a political party which was officially dissolved for its subversive activities after this act came into effect." However, this provision was also quite general (perhaps even elastic) and was incorporated into the bill only during its consideration in the National Assembly. Thus, the original idea allowing for an absolutely free interpretation as advanced by the armed forces was never adopted. The Committee on Constitutional and Legal Affairs

---

467   See for example Vorel, *Zákon o obraně státu*; Kárník, *České země v éře první republiky*, vol. 3, p. 481.

468   A number of scholarly articles were then published in German law journals, generally strongly criticising the Defence of the State Act. For example, three articles appeared in *Juristen-Zeitung für das Gebiet der Tschechoslowakischen Republik* 17 (1936).

469   Kuklík, *Czech law in historical contexts*, pp. 107–108.

470   See for example Jaroslav Pošvář, "Správní delikty podle zákona o obraně státu," *Právník* 75 (1936), pp. 421–424. This author concludes that "statutory penal sanctions provide the state administration, insofar as its competence applies, with all necessary means to ensure the objective of the act: the defence of the state." (p. 424). The Czech public as well as a part of the Germans, including lawyers, generally recognised the necessity of strict measures in order to ensure the state's defence. Robert Steiner, "Der strafrechtliche Gehalt des Staatsverteidigungsgesetzes," *Juristenzeitung für das Gebiet der Tschechoslowakischen Republik* 17 (1936): pp. 161–165, 169–173; and 18 (1937): pp. 15–19, 36–48, 81–91.

of the Chamber of Deputies examined the concept of "lack of integrity" as used in the bill, and concluded that while its precise definition was impossible, certain criteria should be included. Also, a provision was incorporated to prevent a designation of a person lacking integrity merely on the grounds of his/her being a minority member.[471] In spite of that, the practical application of this provision provoked many discussions and disputes, notably in relation to its application to the members of the German minority.[472]

From a legal point of view, extraordinary measures included Section 138 (1) as well: "Powers shall be delegated to the government to adopt, subject to presidential approval, governmental orders where a law would have been otherwise needed, in order to address extraordinary circumstances caused by the state defence emergency." The rationale behind it was the fact that although the act provided sufficient detail, it was necessary to include a separate general provision. In this way, the government would be authorised to take necessary measures in cases which had not been expressly spelled out. It was argued that during a state defence emergency the ordinary legislative activities of the Parliament or even the Permanent Committee could be made difficult, if not impossible. The following Section 139 allowed the measures which were to be carried out during a state defence emergency, and which seriously departed from traditional legal practices, to be carried out even outside the period of emergency, including those relating to the delegation of powers under Section 138! Section 139 provoked considerable debate in Parliament and certain restrictions were imposed on the authorisation of the government and ministries.[473]

The assessment of the Act on the Defence of the State is difficult. Many works unfavourable to interwar Czechoslovakia often contain almost a firm denial, such as the allegation that it was the supreme manifestation of Prague's offensive, nationalist, anti-German politics. These works speak, for example, about a formalistic democracy in the first Czechoslovak Republic with indication to Beneš's dictatorship aimed against the Sudeten Germans.[474]

---

471 Vorel, *Zákon o obraně státu*, p. 31; similarly, Machník's decree raised the issue of which parties could be regarded as hostile to the state, Sander, "Der Machnik-Erlaß und die Verfassungsurkunde," pp. 263, 266.

472 Boyer, "Přidělování státních zakázek v ČSR ve 30. letech," pp. 143–145 identifies problems with practical application since the authorities tended to arbitrarily extend the numbers of persons lacking integrity and often resorted to dubious information sources, including informants; specific examples are provided by Wiskemann, *Czechs and Germans: A Study of the Struggle*, p. 244.

473 Vorel, *Zákon o obraně státu*, pp. 172–173; criticised by e.g. Sander, "Verfassungsrechtliche Bemerkungen zum Staatsverteidigungsgesetze," pp. 110–112; or Fritz Sander, "Weitere verfassungsrechtliche Bemerkungen zum Staatsverteidigungsgesetze," *Juristenzeitung für das Gebiet der Tschechoslowakischen Republik* 17 (1936): pp. 138–139.

474 Friedrich Prinz, ed., *Deutsche Geschichte im Osten Europas: Böhmen und Mähren* (Berlin: Siedler, 2002), p. 393: „Prags offensive Nationalitätenpolitik auf Kosten der Deutschen kulminierte dann im Staatsverteidigungsgesetz . . .“; firm criticism is also voiced in the works of many inter-war

However, even more objective works frequently contain criticism of said Act. It is important to note that it was only the main one of the acts reinforcing the defensive capacity of the Czechoslovak state; subsequently, other laws were also adopted which secured *inter alia* also the funding of the armament programme.[475] Generally, it may be said that the act was necessary, but it contained some elastic provisions which could have been easily abused, even though the parliament somewhat relaxed the original draft in the end. The Ministry of Defence possessed a rather lax approach towards law, and it tried to act in accordance with its own needs and not to rely on legal regulations.[476]

This analysis of the regulation of armed forces was comprehensive and quite thorough, which was caused by its distinctive character and the fact that it had been minimally researched. Now, it is necessary to go back to the interpolitical development in Czechoslovakia at the time of evident threat to the republic. When analysing this issue we cannot go into particulars, which can be found in numerous historical works after all; we will only emphasise elements relating either to planned alterations of the legal order or to the application of legal rules in which the particular character of the status of minorities found expression.

The adoption of new regulations that formed the so-called strong democracy in which the regulations governing the armed forces had a significant share was understandably just one of the ways to face the threat to Czechoslovakia. Taking into account the weak position of the state in which there were large and quite disloyal minorities, and which was surrounded by inimical countries, it is logical that representatives of the Czechoslovak Republic tried to negotiate and arrive at a compromise even at the cost of sometimes surprising concessions. As for the international level, it was the relationship with Nazi Germany that was crucial. The Nazi regime was interested in negotiations with Czechoslovakia, particularly in the first years after its installation in 1933, because it was often in considerable international isolation. Prague was also aware of the need for reasonable co-existence with its largest

---

German lawyers, e.g. Sander, "Verfassungsrechtliche Bemerkungen zum Staatsverteidigungsgesetze," pp. 109–113; according to quite an objective work Wiskemann, *Czechs and Germans: A Study of the Struggle*, p. 241, the act was more radical than the Act on the Defense of the State of 1923 and than the Act on the Dissolution of Political Parties of 1933, although it did not introduce harsh sanctions. However, the author somewhat ignores the particularities of the legal regulation of armed forces, which commonly deviates from the usual regulation in democracies.

475 Klimek, *Velké dějiny zemí Koruny české*, vol. 14. However, it is also important not to overemphasise the impact of these laws.

476 See for example Boyer, "Přidělování státních zakázek v ČSR ve 30. letech," p. 130. There were frequent arguments of the Ministry referring to the security of the state, which requires secrecy (p. 123); the analysis of contradictions with the constitution, for example Sander, "Verfassungsrechtliche Bemerkungen zum Staatsverteidigungsgesetze," pp. 109–113; Sander, "Weitere verfassungsrechtliche Bemerkungen zum Staatsverteidigungsgesetze," pp. 137–140.

neighbour, especially at the time when it was gradually becoming a more and more dangerous threat to the Czechoslovak Republic.[477]

Regarding various negotiations, which often took place unofficially, it is important to mention primarily two meetings of President Beneš and an important German researcher in the field of geopolitics, Karl Haushofer, who was in touch with Hitler, at the end of 1936.[478] Besides the issues of the improvement of foreign trade, a non-aggression pact, and co-operation between Czechoslovakia and the USSR, it was chiefly the German minority that was discussed. The President highlighted that said group was not in any way oppressed whatsoever, and that it was a domestic matter of the Czechoslovak Republic. He unequivocally rejected territorial autonomy, and neither Haushofer considered it to be a viable requirement; thus, it was only cultural autonomy and its widening that were discussed. It must be noted again that from the legal point of view, cultural autonomy is a vague term and according to Beneš, the Germans in Czechoslovakia in fact had it. Prague was probably willing to review its foreign policy and *inter alia* restrict the activity of German emigration in the Czechoslovak Republic. It is arguable whether the negotiations were meant seriously on the German side or whether it rather was Hitler's favourite method subsisting in dealing with politicians opened to "appeasement" and preparing for aggression at the same time. Generally, it can be assumed that Hitler was indifferent to the welfare of the Sudeten Germans, a fact that was realised neither by representatives of the minority nor by emissaries, such as Haushofer. Hitler's willingness to negotiate drained away at the beginning of 1937, and the Fuehrer ranked Czechoslovakia among states which could have been treated from the position of force.

Efforts to react to the threat to the republic manifested themselves also at the domestic level. One of the crucial features of this new policy was an attempt to revive German activism.[479] The election defeat in 1935 was a severe blow to activist parties, so they then strove to do politics that would help them regain German voters. Generally, they followed a harder political line when asserting German national interests and rejected the previous, not very successful policy of small concessions. What was important was that new groups began to gain ground in those parties; they often comprised young politicians with an opposition attitude to old leaders of activist parties, like Wenzel Jaksch in particular. On 26 April 1936 Wenzel Jaksch, representing the German Social Democratic Party, Gustav Hacker, the Chair of Bund der Landwirte, and Hans Schütz, from Christian-Social Unions, put forward virtually

---

477 *Zahraniční politika 1937*, pp. 25, 670; Hans Lemberg, *Porozumění: Češi, Němci, východní Evropa, 1848–1948* (Prague: Lidové noviny, 2000), pp. 235–236.
478 See for example Klimek, *Velké dějiny zemí Koruny české*, vol. 14, pp. 446–448.
479 Kárník, *České země v éře první republiky*, vol. 3, pp. 78–80; Luschka, "Im Parlament der Ersten Tschechoslowakischen Republik," pp. 265–266.

identical requirements that had most likely been agreed upon beforehand. They demanded that a new line of activism be followed; in practice, the Germans were mainly supposed to gain a share in the operation of the executive. The fresh wind was clear also among Czech politicians, which showed particularly in speeches by President Beneš and Kamil Krofta, Minister of Foreign Affairs. From the governmental officials it was Krofta,[480] who probably favoured minorities most and wanted the Germans to be recognised as the second state nation. However, his opinions intensely irritated the Czech nationalist press. We have to note that the so-called recognition of the Germans as the second state nation, or the transformation of the national republic into the republic of nationalities, which had also been debated, is rather a declaratory statement that is not backed by an unambiguous, clear construction in law. The practical implementation of such official conceptions is therefore unclear. On the other hand, such a public declaration by the state could have meant a lot to the minorities issue that had always been influenced by prestigious questions.[481]

In December 1936, following certain preliminary negotiations, Prime Minister Milan Hodža invited the German parties to prepare the common programme.[482] In January 1937 he received representatives of activist parties. Among their main requirements there were the equalisation of German companies at granting public procurement contracts, the economic support of border lands, and reducing local unemployment. It was strongly demanded that the number of state servants from the ranks of minorities be increased so that it reflected the proportion of the nationalities in the state, whereas the burdensome language exams should have been curtailed. It flows therefrom that a significant part of the demands was comprised of economic issues. Further, it was demanded that education of all children in their mother tongue be secured, and that the social and health care of children be improved and administred by members of the same nationality; cultural facilities and public enlightenment organisations should also have been financially backed. The use of languages should have been regulated by, for example, amending the language regulations. Minorities' languages should have been used more in the parliament and a committee for receiving complaints about the non-observance of said principles should have been set up. Legal issues often concerned the elements of cultural autonomy; in the case of territorial autonomy even the German activists were probably afraid

---

480 Dejmek, *Historik v čele diplomacie*, pp. 40–41.
481 See for example Fred Hahn, "Bylo Československo 1918–1938 národní nebo národnostní stát?," *Střední Evropa* 10 (1994): pp. 25–35; Eliezer Yapou, "Autonomie, která se neuskutečnila: plány na autonomii Sudet z roku 1938," *Střední Evropa* 7, no. 20 (1991): pp. 42–60; Brügel, "The Germans in pre-war Czechoslovakia," pp. 176–178.
482 Václav Kural, *Češi, Němci a mnichovská křižovatka* (Prague: Karolinum Press, 2002), pp. 83–85.

of abuse by the Nazis[483], so they did not table this conception. An important fact was that the requirements did not mean any substantial restructuring of the legal order; they usually could have been implemented even without amending laws in effect, and they did not alter constitutional laws in any way whatsover. Economic crisis surviving in border lands contributed significantly to a substantial portion of economic requirements. Such ideas were quite moderate and accomplishable, although their realisation required time, which Czechoslovakia no longer had at its disposal.

On 18 February 1937, the Czechoslovak government issued a statement which posed the acceptance of a large portion of German requirements.[484] The agreement was of a huge psychological importance and represented, according to many historians, a shift away from the conception of the Czechoslovak Republic as a national state.[485] However, the actual fulfillment was often problematic. One of the weightiest requirements of the German minority was the proportional representation in authorities, but in the one-year period following the governmental declaration, the portion of Germans hired as new employees was usually lower than what would have corresponded to the share in the population, so present disparities in most offices did not disappear. The government was quite willing to fulfill the declaration from 18 February but the pace was scanty. Contributing factors to this were the slowness of bureaucracy, as well as its aversion to the steps favourable for the Germans, because the bureaucracy was often impacted by nationalism. Despite numerous practical difficulties caused by the shift in governmental policy, the progress was indeed obvious. To illustrate, according to the assessment by the Ministry of Foreign Affairs regarding the proportionate (from the national point of view) granting of public contracts, more were obtained in a few months than over many years, which, on the other hand, is not a very good advert for the state policy in this issue prior to 1937.[486] The new conception, referred to as "the 18 February policy"[487] was promising, beneficial for minorities, and open to further development, however, it was probably adopted too late and belonged among the last attempts to settle differences with the German minority at the domestic level.

The other possibility of how to settle the relationship with the German minority domestically besides the revival of the activist parties was an

---

483 See for example Jaroslav Šebek, "Masaryk, Beneš, Hrad a Němci 1935–38," in *T.G. Masaryk a vztahy Čechů a Němců (1882–1937)* (Prague: Masarykova společnost v Praze, 1997), pp. 249–250.
484 Wiskemann, *Czechs and Germans: A Study of the Struggle*, p. 255ff.
485 Boyer, "Přidělování státních zakázek v ČSR ve 30. letech," pp. 154–155; Hahn, "Bylo Československo 1918–1938 národní nebo národnostní stát?," p. 33; Sobota, *Národnostní autonomie v Československu?*, pp. 14–15; Lipscher, *Verfassung und politische Verwaltung*, p. 170ff.
486 Boyer, "Přidělování státních zakázek v ČSR ve 30. letech," pp. 157–158; Dejmek, "Britská diplomacie, Československo a Sudetoněmecká strana," p. 174.
487 Yapou, "Autonomie, která se neuskutečnila," p. 50.

agreement with the SdP. Even despite certain attempts, the chance to arrive at a compromise was minimal, which was clearly manifested in the politics of this party. As for legal issues, its attitudes, hardly compatible with democratic principles, manifested themselves particularly in legislative drafts which were sponsored by deputies for SdP in April 1937. They followed from Henlein's requirements[488] articulated in late February/early March 1937. At the congress of the SdP on 28 February he announced that the party would table its legislative drafts which would ensure a determinate national boundary and thereby halt the assimilation process, push through national self-governance for all nationalities in Czechoslovakia, and right alleged wrongs inflicted on the Germans after 1918. On 2 March, Henlein for the first time openly requested territorial autonomy and the recognition of the Germans as a cohesive unit, i.e. as a juridical person.

On 27 March 1937, deputies for the SdP introduced to the National Assembly six interconnected bills[489] which would have significantly changed the legal status of the Germans in Czechoslovakia and which might have brought about the liquidation of democracy, at least within the German minority. Let us analyse them in more detail, as they show the attitude of the SdP, which was not compatible with the principles of democracy in many aspects. Of those six bills, three, which formed a certain complex, established national self-governance, and the fourth widened the criminal protection of nationality, while the last two did not relate directly to the national issue. The first three bills were the drafts of laws on national unions, on nationalities registers, and on the constitutional court, which would have made it possible for national unions to propose repeals of laws for contradiction with the Constitutional Charter of 1920.

The basis for the definite separation of nations in the Czechoslovak Republic should have been nationalities registeres[490], i.e. registeres of members of nations. Strictly speaking, free choice of nationality was excluded. Everyone was supposed to register in the nationality register at the age of 18 and then he was not allowed to ever change the nationality. A citizen could choose, when registering in the register, a nationality other than that which he had belonged to since birth only after he had been completely and provably denationalised.

Based on the nationalities registers, national unions could have then been formed which would have obligatorily united all members of a particular nation.[491] Thus, they would not have been determined territorially but

---

488   Klimek, *Velké dějiny zemí Koruny české*, vol. 14, p. 476.

489   Kural, *Konflikt místo společenství?*, pp. 160–161; Sobota, *Zákonodárné návrhy Sudetoněmecké strany*; Sobota, *Národnostní autonomie v Československu?*, pp. 63–124.

490   Sobota, *Národnostní autonomie v Československu?*, p. 65.

491   Sobota, *Zákonodárné návrhy Sudetoněmecké strany*, pp. 10–11.

personally. Members of a respective nationality would have had to contribute financially to the costs of the autonomy, but they would have been rather passive subjects cared for by the union, in relation to which they would not have political rights; in particular they would not have been allowed to elect the management of the union. A union would have been headed by a speaker (Sprecher) and his deputy; the mode of their election or appointment might have been determined by the board consisting of parliament deputies and senators of the respective nationality. The competences of the speaker were defined very vaguely in the drafts, and they could have been extensively wide in practice. The conception of the Sprecher was thus legitimately understood as a potential implementation of the leader's principle by many critics and later researchers.[492] Also, it was not clear from the draft whether the unions would have the legislative power, so through using vague provisions there could have actually been elements of certain federalisation of the state introduced.

The other bill, which concerned the criminal protection of nationalities,[493] introduced criminal prosecution of even natural phenomena, for example voluntary assimilation was prosecuted. Particularly odd was the criminal protection of the so-called national dependency. If a certain work position or property (e.g. a flat) was held for 30 (and in some cases 20) years by members of the same nationality, then it was supposed to form a permanent part of the national dependency. Efforts by members of other nations to gain such a work position or property, although it was natural competition, was punishable. Such a legal instrument would have clearly meant complicated restrictions of the market and it would have actually implemented a peculiar national autarky, which would have moreover been determined not territorially but personally. These and many other ideas contained in proposals from the SdP caused opposition even among the members of minorities. As the German Social Democracy cited, there for example could have been different working hours and wage conditions in one enterprise depending on the nationality of a worker.

This analysis was rather detailed although the proposed bills were not, quite understandably, adopted. However, they are an interesting illustration of the SdP's attitude to law. What is noteworthy is the fact that the sponsors of those bills, as well as their supporters from the SdP, highlighted that the drafts were in compliance with the constitution in effect, or that they were regulations implementing it. In fact, however, the proposed bills were a clear derogation from constitutional law, and what is more, they would have probably enabled, by abusing numerous vague or questionable provisions, the

---

492 See for example Kural, *Konflikt místo společenství?*, p. 161.
493 Sobota, *Národnostní autonomie v Československu?*, pp. 80, 89, 104–105.

destruction of the democratic system.[494] Also, the sponsors' reliance on older ideas of autonomy was demagogical because those ideas usually comprised *inter alia* a free choice of nationality and the democratic construction of national unions, incl. the election of officials, and they should not have represented the autarkic separation of the economies of individual nations.[495]

Despite the negative attitude of the SdP towards the Czechoslovak Republic, the government made an effort to negotiate with Henlein.[496] Prime Minister Hodža was aware of the significant predominance of the SdP over all other German political parties, and it was also disputes inside his own Agrarian Party that caused trouble for him. That was the reason why he deciced, in September 1937, to start negotiations with Henelein and the SdP, although its attitude towards the state did not arouse undue optimism as far as a possible compromise was concerned. During negotiations, Hodža promised concessions, such as authorisation to create uniformed security organisations of the SdP and the holding of local elections. The elections were deferred due to the fear of the success of the SdP, because they would have enabled the party to gain control of local self-government in the borderlands, which could have been, after all, more threatening to Czechoslovakia than the multitude of SdP deputies in the parliament who used to be outvoted. As Václav Kural aptly discerned, Hodža proposed a gradually formed compromise during secret negotiations with Henlein. "At . . . the beginning there should not have been a bonfire of national laws, or reconstruction of the governmental coalition, but a small, inconspicuous breakthrough in the form of admitting Henlein Party members into the bodies of several big towns . . . , in which Hodža would call a local election. There, Henlein's people should have proven their abilities and loyalty to the state. It should have been similar in the case of state administration, into which Hodža promised to sneak them."[497] In fact, he wanted to make use of a traditional method of political horse-handling, which is an interesting illustration of a practical resolution of the legal status of minorities. However, in the end of 1937 there was a crisis in the SdP itself, which was caused by pressure exerted by old Nazis. Thus, on 19 November Henlein turned with a request for support directly to Hitler,

494 According to Luža, *Transfer of the Sudeten Germans*, p. 97 the implementation of the proposals would have broken up the state into nationalities fragments, which could have hindered the operation of state authorities; according to Wiskemann, *Czechs and Germans: A Study of the Struggle*, p. 258–259 in place of the so far quite centralistic policy of the state, such barriers would be created between invididual nationalities that usually do not exist even between citizens from different states.

495 Sobota, *Zákonodárné návrhy Sudetoněmecké strany*, pp. 20–23; according to Sander, *Die Gleichheit vor dem Gesetze*, p. 12 democracy in Czechoslovakia does not need to fall if, for example, autonomy resolves the national issue.

496 See for example Kárník, *České země v éře první republiky*, vol. 3, pp. 87–90.

497 Kural, *Konflikt místo společenství?*, p. 163.

to whom he wrote a memorandum in which he assured Hitler that Sudeten Germans were national-socialist oriented and organised.[498] He also asserted that he wished the Czech lands to be incorporated into the Reich. It was clearly a high treason, and later politics of the SdP should have only masked the true German interests.

A minority issue which the government was trying to resolve in this time of crisis was also the issue of Sub-Carpathian Ruthenia.[499] The autonomy, or rather self-governance, guaranteed by the Minorities Treaty of St. Germain and by the Constitutional Charter of 1920 had been deferred for a long time, and Czechoslovakia thus lost much of the popularity gained by improving the cultural level of the area. Negotiations with representatives of Sub-Carpathian Ruthenia took place in late 1936/early 1937. What manifested itself there was, *inter alia*, a sensitive problem within minorities issue, namely the difference between the national and administrative border. Politicians from Sub-Carpathian Ruthenia required that the east of Slovakia inhabited by Ruthenians be attached to their land, whereas they did not hesitate to also demand some territories with a hardly dubitable Slovak majority. Naturally, this requirement was not successful, which was also caused by the fact that Prime Minister Hodža, a Slovak himself, could not afford such a step.

The main, traditional problem of Sub-Carpathian Ruthenia was the national ambivalence of the citizens, which also caused a complicated fragmentation of the political scene. The government thus had problems finding representative leaders of the area with whom it would be possible to negotiate. At the time of Czechoslovakia being at stake, the government, however, decided to lead complicated negotiations whose main result was the act No. 172 / 1937 Sb., on the Interim Regulation of the Legal Status of a Governor of Sub-Carpathian Ruthenia, and on Related Organisational Measures. The key position, according to the act that should have been the first step towards the implementation of autonomy, was gained by the governor; however, some crucuial provisions were never put into practice. The gubernatorial council, in particular, which was an advisory body to the governor prior to the establishment of the Assembly (Diet) of Sub-Carpathian Ruthenia, had never been called. Some important local politicians thus declared the act a camouflage masking the unwillingness of Prague to indeed implement the autonomy.[500] Not even in Sub-Carpathian Ruthenia was the minorities issue hurriedly resolved during the time of threat to the state.

---

498 It is, however, questionable to what extent the SDP was under the influence of Hitler before November 1937, Seibt, *Německo a Češi*, p. 312; Luža, *Transfer of the Sudeten Germans*, p. 74.
499 See for example Kárník, *České země v éře první republiky*, vol. 3, pp. 566–567.
500 Klimek, *Velké dějiny zemí Koruny české*, vol. 14, pp. 471–472, 498; Magocsi, "Utváření národní identity," pp. 123–124.

3. THE MUNICH AGREEMENT AND SECOND WORLD WAR

3.1 THE MUNICH AGREEMENT

Growing tensions between the Czechoslovak state and its national minorities worsened at the beginning of the 1930s due to international crises in Central Europe. As part of its expansive policy, Nazi Germany, headed by Hitler, demanded fundamental changes in the position of the German minorities abroad[501] and German pressure on Czechoslovakia was misused also by Hungary (supported by Italy and personally by Benito Mussolini)[502] and Poland in respect of their minorities and still disputed frontiers.

The internal causes for the Czechoslovak minority crises were closely connected with the developments within the Sudeten German society and policy, which led to the above mentioned establishment of the Sudeten German Party (Sdp) chaired by Konrad Henlein. This party, with political and financial support from Nazi Germany, gradually became the leading political representation of the German minority in Czechoslovakia, and so-called "activist" German parties in Czechoslovakia, with the exception of the Social Democrats, were in steady decline.[503] The SdP misused not only the deteriorating economic situation during the Great Depression (which affected border regions with predominantly German settlement more than inland regions) but also some flaws and misconceptions in Czechoslovak minority policies only partially reflected by Hodža's government after February 1937.[504] Henlein was personally also very successful in gaining support for the Sudeten German "cause" during his propaganda tours to Britain in 1937-1938. His warm welcome was prepared also by the British Envoy to Prague Joseph Edison, whose despatches to the Foreign Office depicted Henlein as moderate

501 Anthony Tihamer Komjathy and Rebecca Stockwell, *German Minorities and the Third Reich: Ethnic Germans of East Central Europe Between the Wars* (New York: Holmes & Meier, 1980), esp. p. 110ff.; see also Beneš and Kural, *Facing history*, pp. 103-109.

502 See reports by Italian Envoy to Prague from 1938, Arcivio storico diplomatico, Rome, collection Affari politici 1931-1945 on Czechoslovakia, vol. (busta) 23 and 26; for the negotiations between Hungarian Foreign Minister Csáky and Mussolini at the time of Munich see Bán, *Hungarian-British Diplomacy*, pp. 45-46.

503 Brügel, *Czechoslovakia before Munich*, pp. 120-122.

504 Brügel, "The Germans in pre-war Czechoslovakia," pp. 182-187.

politician, who is trying to secure fair treatment for the Sudeten Germans oppressed by the Czechs.[505]

During 1938 the SdP presented far reaching proposals for self-determination, initially in the form of territorial autonomy and self-government.[506] The most severe conditions for Czechoslovakia to accept, including acknowledgement of different (i.e. Nazi) ideology of German national group, were set in the so-called Karlsbad Programme of 24 April 1938. At that time the policy of the Sudeten German Party and its leader Henlein was consulted directly with Hitler and other leading Nazis[507] and its aim was to cause an internal disruption of the Czechoslovak democratic system and state structure. Other minorities, especially the Hungarian and Polish ones, exercised pressure on the Czechoslovak Government as well, using the above mentioned interaction with the Governments of Hungary and Poland.

The Czechoslovak Government tried to react and prepared the Statute for National Minorities, the Language Bill and the Administrative Reform Bill.[508] Its aim was not only to consolidate the minority legislation but also to modernize and amend it. During the preparatory works the Czechoslovak Government tried to compare the position of national minorities and minority rights in selected European countries, including Poland and the Baltic states. The comparative analyses proved that the proposed legislation was, in the context of the late 1930s, quite liberal, and, if put into practice, it could lead to the transformation of Czechoslovakia from a centralized national state with minorities into more decentralized state with certain degree of autonomy for minorities. Another initiative concerning the rights of minorities was connected with the proposed "resuscitation" of the Constitutional Court.[509] However the proposals were rejected not only by the SdP (under the advice from Berlin)[510] but also by the British and French diplomacy as not far reaching enough and therefore not appeasing Hitler.[511]

The situation worsened after the Czechoslovak partial mobilization of armed forces to react to the alleged German military manoeuvres, when especially the British Foreign Office feared that the Czechoslovak-German

505 Mark Cornwall, "The Rise and Fall of a 'Special Relationship'? Britain and Czechoslovakia 1930–1948," in *What difference did the war make?*, ed. by Brian Brivati and Harriet Jones (Leicester: Leicester University Press, 1993), pp. 133–134.

506 Kuklík, *Czech law in historical contexts*, pp. 111–112.

507 Brügel, *Czechoslovakia before Munich*, p. 142ff.

508 In more details Jan Kuklík and Jan Němeček, *Od národního státu ke státu národností? Národnostní statut a snahy o řešení menšinové otázky v Československu v roce 1938* (Prague: Karolinum Press, 2013), text of the documents published as an appendix, pp. 293–433.

509 Ibid., pp. 194 and 315.

510 For the policy of SdP after the so-called Anschlus (annexation) of Austria see Detlef Brandes, *Die Sudetendeutschen im Krisenjahr* (1938 Munich: Oldenbourg, 2008), p. 57ff.

511 Kuklík and Němeček, *Od národního státu ke státu národností?*, pp. 190–193.

disturbances could lead to the European war. After its pressure the Czech-oslovak Government was prepared to accept mediation offered by the British Government in the form of a mission headed by Lord Runciman of Doxford.[512] Runciman arrived in Czechoslovakia at the beginning of August 1938, and his activity was embodied in a report presented to the British Prime Minister Chamberlain on 21 September 1938 advocating a plebiscite and transfer of a part of the Czechoslovak territory to Germany. The Su-deten German Party also rejected two other proposals by the Czechoslo-vak President Beneš although at the beginning of September 1938 he was prepared to accept almost all points of the above mentioned Karlsbad Programme.[513]

The international circumstances which led to the Munich Agreement could be characterized as being more due to the violent and aggressive nature of the international policy of Nazi Germany than to the misconceptions of the Czechoslovak minority policies. The aim of Nazi policy, embodied in the so-called Plan Green (Fall Grün), was to crush Czechoslovakia even in a mili-tary way, change its democratic regime and to see the Czech lands as a sphere of vital German interests.[514] This was followed by changes in the French policy towards Central Europe. The French were, from the very beginning of their existence, the main allies of the Czechoslovak state. After the Anschluss of Austria and after the fall of the last government of the Popular Front, the French Government, headed by Eduard Daladier, became more and more dependent on British policy.[515] The policy maintained by the British Prime Minister Chamberlain is usually depicted as a policy of appeasement.[516] Al-though there might be various reasons for such a policy, it should be noted that, as a result of this policy, the Czechoslovak Government was forced at first to yield to the pressure from the Sudeten German Party (including the fate of the Statute of nationalities, which was put into the cold storage) and later from Hitler in September 1938. The minority problem, depicted as a total failure of the concept of the Czechoslovak state, was used as a pretext for Nazi aggression in Central Europe.

---

512   For the Runciman mission including his report see recently Paul Vyšný, *The Runciman Mission to Czechoslovakia: Prelude to Munich* (Basingstoke: Palgrave Macmillan, 2003).

513   Jan Kuklík, Jan Němeček and Jaroslav Šebek, *Dlouhé stíny Mnichova* (Prague: Auditorium, 2011), pp. 35–38.

514   Ibid., pp. 33–34.

515   For the French policy during Munich see Robert J. Young, *France and the origins of the Second World War* (London: Macmillan, 1996).

516   For the British policy of "appeasement" see for example Robert A. C. Parker, *Chamberlain and Appeasement: British Policy and the Coming of the Second World War* (London: Macmillan, 1993); or Keith Robbins, "Britain and Munich reconsidered: a personal historical journey," in *Czechoslova-kia in a Nationalist and Fascist Europe 1918–1948*, ed. by Robert Evans and Mark Cornwall (Oxford: Oxford University Press, 2007), p. 231ff.

However, the ideas of territorial concessions as a solution to minority problems had deeper roots. In 1934 Professor C. A. Macartney, in his book *National states and national minorities* written for the Royal Institute of International Affairs (so-called Chatham House),[517] proposed not only the improvement of minority procedures under the League of Nations and possibly exchanges of populations, but mainly territorial changes (revisions) and concessions as possible solutions to the pressing minority problems of the interwar period in Central Europe. In his view, Central Europe was among the most convenient regions for application of this policy, especially in the case of borderlands with "solid blocks of minority populations."[518] Discussions within this unofficial think-tank for the British diplomacy also addressed other minority problems, including potential peaceful settlement of Polish-German and Czechoslovak-German disputes in the borderlands and the position of Hungary after the Trianon Peace Treaty.[519]

The atmosphere on the international scene in Europe deteriorated even more during September 1938 as a result of Hitler's threats to launch war against Czechoslovakia. As we have already pointed out, the pressure to solve Czechoslovak minority issues, especially the problem of the Sudeten German minority, served Hitler as an excuse for German aggression. As early as 19 September 1938, France and Great Britain in form of démarches by their Envoys to Prague demanded that Czechoslovakia cede the part of its territory settled by a majority German population to Germany.[520] Negotiations between Hitler and Chamberlain in Godesberg and Berchtesgaden, followed by a mission of Chamberlain's aide, Horace Wilson, formed the prologue to an international conference to officially solve the issue.[521]

On 29 September 1938 an international conference was called in the Bavarian capital of Munich to settle the so-called Czechoslovak crisis and, as mainly Chamberlain believed, to save European peace.[522] Czechoslovakia was not invited to take part in the conference and its representatives were waiting for the results in a hotel room. The Munich Agreement, concluded on 30 September 1938 by two authoritarian Powers – Germany (represented by Adolf Hitler) and Italy (represented by Benito Mussolini) and two western democracies – Great Britain (represented by Neville Chamberlain) and France

---

517 Royal Institute of International Affairs Archives, London (RIIAA) 16/7.
518 Carlile A. Macartney, *National States and National Minorities* (Oxford: Oxford University Press, 1934), pp. 427–430.
519 RIIAA, 16/17, 16/21 and 16/23.
520 See for example Keith Eubank, "Munich," in Mamatey and Luža, *A History of the Czechoslovak Republic 1918–1948*, pp. 248–249.
521 For documents see *Documents on British Foreign Policy*, 3rd series, vol. 2 (London: H.M.S.O., 1949); from the Czech point of view most recently Kuklík, Němeček and Šebek, *Dlouhé stíny Mnichova*, esp. p. 45ff.
522 Kuklík, Němeček and Šebek, *Dlouhé stíny Mnichova*, esp. p. 45ff.

(represented by Eduard Daladier), forced Czechoslovakia to cede almost one third of its territory, inhabited by more than 50 per cent of the German minority, to Nazi Germany; the territory has been known as the "Sudetenland" section of Czechoslovakia.[523]

According to the Agreement, there were four zones, which were gradually occupied by Germany; the final boundaries were to be decided by an international committee formed by the representatives of the four parties to the Agreement and one from Czechoslovakia.[524] The Munich Agreement included a guarantee to preserve the remaining Czechoslovak territory by two of the four signatory powers (Great Britain and France), and a promise of guarantee by the other two signatories (Germany and Italy) contingent upon the fulfilment of Polish and Hungarian demands concerning their minorities and their parts of the Czechoslovak territory.[525] In Munich Britain and France decided, having considered all wider implications of their appeasement policy, to support the solution to the minority issue subsisting in the forced cession of a part of the Czechoslovak territory settled primarily by the German minority (at least 50 per cent according to the results of census from 1910!) for the benefit of Nazi Germany. They did so also because they considered the system of minority treaties, made under the auspices of the League of Nations[526] as well as the Czechoslovak–German agreement on arbitration from 1925, to be rather ineffective and inapplicable.

The Czechoslovak Government, President Beneš and Minister of Foreign Affairs Kamil Krofta accepted the Munich Agreement with protest, because the settlement was made "without and against Czechoslovakia." Therefore Czechs are usually portraying the Agreement as the "Munich Dictate."[527] As Elisabeth Wiskemann rightly pointed out, virtually all Czechs (and some Bohemian and Moravian Germans) "felt emotional attachment to the traditional frontiers of Bohemia and Moravia, which except for the inroads of Frederick the Great, had remained unchanged for a thousand years."[528]

---

523 For Munich Agreement in English see *Documents on British Foreign Policy*, 3rd series, vol. 2, document no. 1225, pp. 627–629.
524 Kuklík, Němeček and Šebek, *Dlouhé stíny Mnichova*, esp. pp. 82–88.
525 Vít Smetana, *In the shadow of Munich: British Policy towards Czechoslovakia from the Endorsement to the Renunciation of the Munich Agreement (1938-1942)* (Prague: Karolinum Press, 2008), especially p. 69ff.
526 Mark Cornwall, "'A leap into ice-cold water': the manoeuvres of the Henlein movement in Czechoslovakia, 1933–1938," in Evans and Cornwall, *Czechoslovakia in a Nationalist and Fascist Europe 1918–1948*, p. 139ff.
527 This argument was formulated for the Nuremberg trial concerning the non-validity of the Agreement. The Munich Agreement was simply "dictated" to the Czechoslovak Government and people against their will, see *Český národ soudí K.H. Franka*, ed. by Karel Kajiček (Prague: Ministerstvo informací, 1946), p. 185.
528 Elizabeth Wiskemann, *Germany's Eastern Neighbours: Problems relating to the Oder-Neisse line and the Czech frontier regions* (London: Oxford University Press, 1956), p. 52.

Germany occupied all zones of the territory granted to them by the Munich Agreement despite stipulations in the agreement providing for plebiscites in certain zones vitally important for Czechoslovakia. Even those boundaries were exceeded, and further protests of the Czechoslovak Government were disregarded. The final settlement of the Czechoslovak-German frontiers was even more in Germany's favour than the initial proposals made by Hiter in Godesberg in September 1938.[529] The Czechoslovak Government was not given the guarantees promised in its new post-Munich frontiers and found itself defenceless in the "sphere of the most basic interests of the Reich."[530] On 20 November 1938 it concluded an agreement with Germany in Berlin on the question of citizenship, which confirmed the German state citizenship for the Sudeten Germans from the territories ceded to Germany, while Czechs in Sudetenland and remaining members of German minority were offered the possibility of a choice.

The Munich Agreement dealt with the position of other national minorities in Czechoslovakia as well, and, as a direct consequence of the Agreement, a part of the Czechoslovak territory was ceded to Poland (mainly the disputed Těšín territory and part of Orava and Spiš territory in Slovakia), and Southern Slovakia (around 10 000 km^2 with 850 000 inhabitants), with predominantly Hungarian population, was ceded to Hungary.[531] The cession touched also the territory of Sub-Carpathian Ruthenia, and towns of Užhorod, Mukačevo and Berehovo were handed over to Hungarian hands. The so-called First Vienna Award of 2 November 1938 reached in Belvedere Palace by representatives of the German and Italian Governments, which dealt with the Czechoslovak-Hungarian territorial disputes, was at that time seen from the British perspective (especially by Neville Chamberlain and Lord Halifax) not only as being "in full accordance" with the solution reached in Munich[532] but also as a redress for the territorial injustices of Trianon.

The acceptance of the Munich Agreement caused great changes not only in Czechoslovak foreign policy and its new orientation towards Germany but also in the pre-Munich liberal democratic political system. The so-called Second Republic (Czecho-Slovakia, as the country was known from October to March 1939)[533] also adopted autonomy for Slovakia and Sub-Carpathian Ruthenia and the concept of one political Czechoslovak nation was

---

529 For the maps see The National Archives (TNA), London, FO 925/ 2010.
530 Smetana, *In the shadow of Munich*, pp. 69–73.
531 See especially documents in Ladislav Deák, ed., *Viedenská arbitráž. 2. november 1938: Dokumenty*, 3 vols. (Martin: Matica slovenská 2002, 2003, 2005); for its text in English see *Reports of International Arbitral Awards*, vol. 28, United Nations Publications ([U.S.A.]: United Nations – Nations Unies, 2007), pp. 404–406.
532 Bán, *Hungarian-British Diplomacy*, pp. 45–46 and 110.
533 In more details Theodor Prochazka, "The second republic, 1938–1939," in Mamatey and Luža, *A History of the Czechoslovak Republic 1918–1948*, p. 255ff.

abandoned.[534] As a consequence also the position of minorities worsened and Munich simply represents a prologue to greater tragedies of WWII. The Munich Agreement was also not able to fulfil its aim to solve the Central European minority problems by "rationalisation of borders."[535] On the contrary, almost immediately after the Agreement had been signed on 30 September 1938, thousands of Czechs, German antifascists and Jews were on the move from territories ceded to Germany, many of them forcibly.[536] The Munich Agreement also caused severe economic losses and social problems and in relation to minorities it also transformed the position of Jews. Especially after the pogrom of the so-called "Kristalnacht" the Jews from Germany as well as from the newly acquired regions of the "German Reich" tried to find new routes of escape, and for the rest the discriminatory Nuremberg Laws applied.[537] On 17 May 1939 only around 5 800 Jews were registered during the official census in the so-called "Reichsgau Sudentenland."[538] The Jews were however discriminated also by the new nationalistic Government of the Second Czecho-Slovak Republic especially in respect to civil service and certain employments like medical doctors or attorneys at law.[539] The Czechs on the ceded territories established new minorities in hostile German and Polish environment (820 000 Czechs according to the informed estimates of V. Houžvička)[540] as did the Slovaks (but also some Czechs) in Hungary. The situation after Munich (and especially its consequences during WWII) proved that the cession of the territory as such (followed by forced migrations) was not a working solution to the complex minority situation of the Central Europe.

3.2 THE PROTECTORATE OF BOHEMIA AND MORAVIA

It was Hitler who decided that the crippled, post-Munich Czechoslovakia had no right to exist as an independent entity.[541] He again used the minor-

---

534 Valerián Bystrický, "Slovakia from the Munich Conference to the declaration of independence," in Teich, Kováč and Brown, *Slovakia in History*, esp. pp. 157–160.

535 Houžvička, *Czechs and Germans 1848–2004*, pp. 266–267.

536 Jan Benda, *Útěky a vyhánění z pohraničí českých zemí 1938–1939* (Prague: Karolinum Press, 2012), pp. 42ff.

537 Michael Marrus, *The Unwanted: European Refugees in the Twenties Century* (Oxford: Oxford University Press, 1985), p. 209ff.; see also Eva Semotanová et al., *Frontiers, massacres and replacement of populations in cartographic representation: Case studies (15th–20th centuries)* (Prague: Institute of History, 2015), p. 71.

538 Volker Zimmerman, "Pachatelé a přihlížející: Pronásledování židů v Sudetské župě," in *Terezínské studie a dokumenty*, ed. by Miroslav Kárný and Eva Lorencová (Prague: Academia, 1999), p. 136.

539 Theodor Procházka, *The Second Republic: The disintegration of post-Munich Czechoslovakia, October 1938–March 1939* (Boulder, CO: East European Monographs, 1981), pp. 58–59.

540 Houžvička, *Czechs and Germans 1848–2004*, p. 266.

541 Kuklík, *Czech law in historical contexts*, pp. 115–116.

ity issues (for this purpose there was still a small German minority left in the Czech lands) and the Czech–Slovak unsettled relations as a pretext. On 14 March 1939 Nazi emissaries pressed Slovak representatives to formally proclaim an independent Slovak state under the guardianship of Nazi Germany;[542] on 15 March 1939 Hácha, the President of the Second Czecho-Slovak Republic declared in Berlin that he "entrusted with entire confidence the destiny of the Czech people and Czech country to the hands of Führer of the German Reich."[543] On 16 March 1939 the German Protectorate of Bohemia and Moravia was established by Hitler's special decree.[544] The Protectorate became a part of the German Empire, but for international and propaganda reasons it was given an insignificant degree of autonomy.[545] Hitler appointed Konstantin von Neurath as "Reichsprotektor," the highest representative of the German Empire in the Protectorate. The Protector was entitled to issue special laws for the Protectorate and supervise the decisions of the Protectorate bodies.

The President of the Second Czecho-Slovak Republic, Emil Hácha, was appointed as the State President, i.e. the head of the autonomous Protectorate entity. There was the Government of the Protectorate and autonomous state administration at regional and local levels. The minority question in the Protectorate was transformed to the system of personal categories of inhabitants with the breach of principle of equality of citizens before the law. Three categories of citizens were classified in the Protectorate, with different law applying to each of them. These were as follows:

a) German citizens, with a privileged position, their own law and administrative and judicial bodies;
b) Protectorate citizens of Czech nationality, with a disadvantaged position;
c) Jewish and Roma (Gypsy) populations, for which even more punitive and discriminatory provisions applied.

This approach, closely connected with the Nazi racial philosophy, again brought the principle of personality of law into the legal system. In the Protectorate Germans tried to control all spheres of life of the Czech nation. Initially Germans concentrated their attention on the Jewish population; after introducing the principles of the Nuremberg anti-Jewish laws, freezing and confiscating virtually all Jewish property (so-called *aryanisation*), they started transporting Jews to the Ghetto in Terezín in November 1941, and later to extermination camps.[546] In case of the Protectorate a complicated system

542 Bystrický, "Slovakia from the Munich Conference," pp. 173–174.
543 Beneš and Kural, *Facing history*, document no. 5.
544 Ibid., document no. 6, pp. 300–302.
545 Kuklík, *Czech law in historical contexts*, pp. 116–119.
546 In more details Livia Rothkirchen, *The Jews of Bohemia and Moravia: Facing the Holocaust* (Lincoln: University of Nebraska Press; Jerusalem: Yad Vashem, 2005), pp. 98–187; Jan Láníček, *Czechs,*

of legal regulations and bodies was introduced by the Nazis, which applied a complex mechanism of confiscations, expropriations, forced gifts, stealing and other transfers of property, as well as the abuse of tax regulations, imposition of special charges on the Jewish communities and the use of forced labour.[547] Those issues had to be embedded in a wider context of anti-Jewish measures and, notably, the Final Solution to the Jewish Question designed by the Nazis.[548]

Jewish natural persons and legal entities were at first limited in the free usage of their property through the imposition of the Nuremberg Laws in the territory of the Protectorate in June 1939 (by special Konstantin von Neurath's decree on the Jewish property); it was possible to identify a corporation as Jewish even if it was only under the "Jewish influence," or if just one member of the Board was of Jewish origin. As early as March 1939, the first confiscations began to be pursued by special German State Police ("Gestapo" in German) commandos. The first period of anti-Jewish measures, until the end of 1940, was also connected with the promotion of Jewish emigration in accord with the Austrian model.[549] Those Jews who were given permission to leave the Protectorate were forced to pay a special emigration tax and transfer all their valuable property to the Nazis. This approach is therefore sometimes referred to as "the collection of ransom for life."[550] In 1940, the first series of laws adopted by the Protectorate Government on German order banned Jewish citizens from holding various professions and occupations, both in public and private sphere, and the Jewish population was subjected to many other prohibitions and persecution measures.[551]

When the possibility to move from the Protectorate ceased in 1940, the Jewish population was stripped of their property through a complicated system of German laws, especially with respect to real property, financial means, gold and other precious metals, objects of art, residential premises, insurance policies, etc.[552] Various forms of curtailment, removal from positions of

---

Slovaks and the Jews, 1938–48: Beyond Idealisation and Condemnation (Basingstoke: Palgrave Macmillan, 2013), especially p. 76ff.

547   Jan Kuklík et al., *Jak odškodnit holocaust? Problematika vyvlastnění židovského majetku, jeho restituce a odškodnění* (Prague: Karolinum Press, 2015), p. 98ff.

548   See for example Saul Friedländer, *The years of extermination: Nazi Germany and the Jews, 1939–1945,* (New York: Harper Collins Publishers, 2007); Semotanová et al., *Frontiers, massacres and replacement of populations,* pp. 68–71.

549   Dirk Rupnow, "'Zur Förderung und beschleunigten Regelung der Auswanderung . . .' Die Zentralstelle für jüdische Auswanderung in Wien," in *Ausgeschlossen und entrechtet, Raub und Rückgabe: Oesterreich von 1938 bis heute,* ed. by Verena Pawlowsky and Harald Wendelin (Vienna: Mandelbaum, 2006), pp. 13–30.

550   Kuklík et al., *Jak odškodnit holocaust?,* pp. 120–121.

551   Ibid.

552   Ibid., p. 98ff.; Alice Teichová, "The Protectorate of Bohemia and Moravia (1939–1945): The economic dimension," in Teich, *Bohemia in History,* pp. 289–290.

authority, forced sales, aryanisation and confiscation went along with mass deportations. Aryanisation of small and medium sized Jewish property was done in the Protectorate with the help of loans given by the German financial institutions.[553] Smaller property items were transferred from the Jewish also into the Czech hands.

German occupation bodies also tried to change the legal and actual position of Czech population. Czechs as the Slavonic race were treated as a kind of minority too, deprived of part of their rights. From 1942 Germans also used the compulsory work not only within the Protectorate but also on the territory of the German Reich. Around 400,000 Czech workers were sent to Germany to work in coal mines, iron works and other industries important to Nazi Germany. Germans used a system of slave labour within their concentration and extermination camps, which applied also to Jews from Czechoslovakia.[554]

The Czech population became a subject of Nazi persecutions as well. The first wave of persecutions came soon after the establishment of the Protectorate when Germans sent selected groups of former or presumed political opponents to jail and concentration camps.[555] After mass protests connected with the 21st anniversary of the Czechoslovak Republic on 28 October 1939, there were disturbances and bloodshed. After the shooting death of Jan Opletal, a medical university student attending the demonstration, another anti-German protest was called at his funeral; subsequently the Nazis decided to close down Czech universities.[556] The German occupation bodies gradually limited civic rights and freedoms for the Czech population; they introduced tough censorship, and Czech national cultural and sports associations were persecuted. The Nazis extended persecution also to the Catholic Church as well as to other churches and religious groups.[557] First plans for the solution of the "Czech problem" with the "intention to Germanize the territory (Raum) and people in Protectorate" were prepared by Konstantin von Neurath and his deputy K. H. Frank already in August 1940.[558]

---

553 See in more details Drahomír Jančík, Eduard Kubů and Jiří Šouša, *Arisierungsgewinnler: Die Rolle der deutschen Banken bei der „Arisierung" und Konfiskation jüdischer Vermögen im Protektorat Böhmen und Mähren 1939–1945* (Wiesbaden: Harrassowitz, 2011).

554 Wolf Gruner, *Jewish Forced Labor Under the Nazis: Economic Needs and Racial Aims, 1938–1944*, trans. Kathleen M. Dell'Orto (New York: Cambridge University Press, 2006), p. 162ff.

555 Radomír Luža, "The Czech resistance movement," in Mamatey and Luža, *A History of the Czechoslovak Republic 1918–1948*, pp. 150–151.

556 See František Buriánek et al., eds., *The 17th November: Almanac about the Resistance of Czechoslovak Students in the years 1939–1945* (Prague: Central Union of Czechoslovak Students, 1945), pp. 48–52.

557 See authentic account in *Two years of German oppression in Czechoslovakia* ([London]: Czechoslovak Ministry of Foreign Affairs, Department of Information, 1941), pp. 75–76.

558 For the Memorandum on a Method for the Solution of the Czech Problem and the Future Ordering of Bohemia-Moravain Territory (August 28, 1940) in English see Houžvička, *Czechs and Germans 1848–2004*, document no. 3, pp. 557–561.

On 28 September 1941 Konstantin von Neurath was replaced by Reinhard Heydrich, who was appointed the Deputy Reichsprotektor.[559] Immediately after his arrival in Prague, Heydrich proclaimed a state of emergency and hundreds of Czech participants in the resistance movement, members of the intelligentsia or those who committed "economic crimes" against the war economy were sentenced to death or sent to concentration camps by special courts operated by Gestapo.[560] Within the first 105 days of his brutal rule, 394 people were executed and 1,134 imprisoned. Heydrich prepared plans for the liquidation of most of the Czech people after an assumed victorious war combined with the Germanization and resettlement of the remainder of the population. The Czech lands were planned to become an integral part of the German Empire.[561] The concept of Germanization through resettlement of German peasants (as part of relocation of the so-called Volksdeutsche), which was already underway in Poland, was planned and to certain extend applied also in respect to the Protectorate.[562] Moreover, Heydrich proposed changes in the administration of the Protectorate to curtail its autonomy and to impose more effective forms of exploitation of the Czech labour force, industry and agriculture for German war needs. It could also be regarded as another part of the above mentioned policy of Germanization.[563] During Heydrich's rule in the Protectorate the forms of persecutions tightened. In addition to forced labour, various forms of confiscation and transfer of property from Czech and Jewish hands into German ownership were implemented.[564]

The peak of German persecution came after the successful assassination of Heydrich by two Czechoslovak parachuters sent to the Protectorate under a combined operation of the Czechoslovak resistance and the British Special Operations Executive (SOE), known under its code name Operation Anthropoid.[565] Heydrich's deputy, K.H. Frank, immediately announced a second martial law in the Protectorate, and a new series of executions began. The German revenge against Czech civilians had their most brutal expression in the fate of the villages Lidice and Ležáky. On 9 June 1942 the village of Lidice, as a result of false allegations that its inhabitants took part in the

---

559   Chad Bryant, *Prague in Black: Nazi Rule and Czech Nationalism* (Cambridge, MA: Harvard University Press, 2007), pp. 141–142.
560   See the publication by the Czechoslovak Government in exile, *On the Rule of Terror under the Regime of Reinhard Heydrich*, London 1941, especially pp. 18–24.
561   Bryant, *Prague in Black*, pp. 139–144.
562   Detlef Brandes, *Germanizovat a vysídlit: Nacistická národnostní politika v českých zemích* (Prague: Prostor, 2015).
563   Recently Patrick Crowhurst, *Hitler and Czechoslovakia in World War II: Domination and Retaliation* (London: I.B. Tauris, 2013), p. 194ff.
564   Kuklík et al., *Jak odškodnit holocaust?*, especially p. 98ff.
565   Recently Michal Burian, *Assassination: Operation Anthropoid 1941–1942*, 2nd rev. ed. (Prague: Ministry of Defence of the Czech Republic, 2011).

assassination of Heydrich, was eradicated from the map, all men found in the village were shot on the spot, and women and children sent to concentration camps, where the majority of children were killed. Ležáky, connected with the SOE operation with the code name Silver A, followed the same destiny two weeks later. Between 28 May and 3 July 1942 there were at least 1,288 executions; 653 more followed between July and December 1942. The rest of the war witnessed even more brutal ways of persecution by German judicial and police authorities. For example, between 1943 and 1945, on the basis of adjudication by German courts, the guillotine in the Pankrác prison in Prague decapitated 1,075 Czech civilians.[566]

3.3 INTERNATIONAL NEGOTIATIONS ON TRANSFER OF MINORITIES

The behaviour of the overwhelming majority of the German inhabitants of Czechoslovakia experienced at the time of Munich and the involvement of huge numbers of the Sudeten Germans in the persecutions in the Protectorate, but above all Nazi plans for the "final solution" to the Jewish and Czech questions during WWII influenced radical plans for the solution to minority problems not only among Czechoslovak exile politicians but also among other wartime Allies. Even stronger impulses for such radical plans were coming from the Polish side.[567] The most important factor for the solution of complex minority issues of Central Europe, including Czechoslovakia and Poland, were the negotiations of Allied war coalition.[568] The resettlements of populations, exchanges of populations or further territorial concessions were taken into account using also historical arguments and cases like the decision of Lausanne conference and Greek-Turkish exchange of populations after WWI despite the fact that it led to enormous human sufferings and its envisaged outcomes were doubtful.[569] When on 22 October 1943 leading British expert on transfers of population J.D. Mabbott prepared a position paper on the precedents for the proposed transfer, he dealt mainly with the lessons learned from Greek-Turkish and Greek-Bulgarian exchanges of population and Hitler's transfers of "Volksdeutsche."[570]

566 See account of German persecutions in *Český národ soudí K.H. Franka*, especially pp. 65–73.

567 In more details Jan Kuklík and Jan Němeček, *Frontiers, Minorities, Transfers, Expulsions: British diplomacy towards Czechoslovakia and Poland during WWII*, vol. 1 (Prague: Faculty of Law, Charles University Institute of History CAS, 2015).

568 Ibid., especially, p. 9ff.

569 See unpublished study *National Minorities* by J. D. Mabbott, chapter 9, Royal Institute of International Affairs Archives, London, 20/11a.

570 See his paper from August 10, 1942, TNA, London, FO 371, 34461, C 12352.

The eviction and resettlement ("transfer") of minorities was mainly discussed in connection with German minorities, because they were regarded as
one of the main causes of the war.[571] It is also necessary to take into account
that from the very beginning of the war Hitler (but also Stalin) used forced
migrations as a part of his wartime policies. Hitler's idea of the so-called
"Heim ins Reich" policy led to the resettlement of the Volksdeutsche – i.e. ethnic Germans from their homes in South Tyrol, the Baltic states, Eastern Europe
and the Balkans to the territory of German Empire.[572] The policy started in 1939
when a special decree was issued on the "return of Volksdeutsche," allegedly
endangered by assimilation policies. Germany also concluded special bilateral
agreements concerning the resettlement.[573]

Within a year and a half almost 800,000 of ethnic Germans were resettled, in some cases not entirely voluntarily. The policy of resettlement of the
"Volskdeutsche" was closely connected with the plan of "re- Germanization"
of the territory of so-called Warthegau (part of pre-war Poland directly ceded to Germany) as well as with the "General Plan Ost," according to which the
Polish inhabitants were to be settled in Siberia to make room for the Germans
(with possible selection of part of Polish population for Germanization).
Within a year Germans expelled over 1 million Polish people from the Polish
western areas.[574] Germans also used Polish inhabitants as a source for forced
labour and resettled them in the Reich. The total estimated number of forcibly moved Poles during the war is therefore close to 1.7 million.[575]

Supporting the restoration of Czechoslovakia within its pre-Munich
frontiers and of Poland with its western borders moved possibly up to the
Oder–Neisse line,[576] Britain and other major Allies were trying to find an alternative to minority policies of the interwar period; from May 1940, when
such an alternative was discussed within the Chatham House expert group[577]
and definitely from July 1942 the alternative was seen in the resettlement of
members of German minorities from Czechoslovakia, Poland and from other
countries in the Central and Eastern Europe to Germany.[578]

---

571   Ibid.; see also Detlef Brandes, *Der Weg zur Vertreibung 1938–1945: Pläne und Entscheidungen zum
      „Transfer" der Deutschen aus der Tschechoslowakei und aus Polen* (Munich: Oldenbourg, 2001).
572   Philipp Ther, *The Dark Side of Nation-States: Ethnic Cleansing in Modern Europe*, trans. Charlotte
      Kreutzmüller (New York: Bergham, 2013), pp. 90–95; see also Semotanová et al., *Frontiers, mas-
      sacres and replacement of populations*, pp. 46–47.
573   Kuklík and Němeček, *Frontiers, Minorities, Transfers, Expulsions*, pp. 9–10.
574   Piotr Eberhardt, *Ethnic groups and population changes in 20th century East Central Europe: History,
      Data and Analysis* (London: M. E. Sharp, 2003), pp. 122–124.
575   Dariusz Matelski, *Niemcy w Polsce w XX wieku* (Warsaw: PWN, 1999), pp. 198– 199.
576   Ther, *The Dark Side of Nation-States*, pp. 148–150.
577   See its memorandum on the transfer of minorities prepared by J.D. Mabbott, May 29, 1940; Kuk-
      lík and Němeček, *Frontiers, Minorities, Transfers, Expulsions*, document no. 1.
578   Kuklík and Němeček, *Frontiers, Minorities, Transfers, Expulsions*, document no. 3 and 4.

This approach of the Great Powers was based upon several reasons besides their belief that the transfer of German minorities would strengthen the position of the respective states in Central Europe, which could then cooperate in a federal union and effectively face the threat coming from Germany in the future, but according to British views also potentially from the USSR (reflection of interwar "cordon sanitaire"). In addition, the resettlement ("transfer") would eliminate a possibility that German minorities could again become a threat to European peace. Another reason was the fact that, having analysed the whole problem, the British Foreign Office concluded that no "revival" of the system of minority treaties would be feasible after WWII.[579] This was not only because the whole system failed even before WWII but also because Czechoslovakia, Poland and the USSR were strictly against its re-installation.[580] In respect to minorities the United States were interested mainly in the fate of the Jewish population. The issue of endangered international minority protection was behind the protests against the proposed transfers and exchanges of populations by those scholars who associated the protection of minorities mainly with the Jewish minorities and feared the rise of nationalism in Central Europe. In 1942 Mark Vishniak published a pamphlet for the Yiddish Scientific Institute in New York, entitled "The Transfer of Populations as a Means of Solving the Problem of Minorities," where he examined various arrangements for the exchange of populations carried out in the Balkans during and after WWI as well as the transfers made by Hitler in 1939–1940. He concluded that the policies of transfer offered no permanent solution to the minority issue, and advocated the protection of minorities "by an international status within the framework of a world-wide organisation."[581] In 1943 J. Robinson and O. Karbach published for the New York Institute of Jewish Affairs a book entitled "Were the minority treaties a failure?"[582] On 22 November 1944 the Post-war Planning Committee of the US State Department regarded the obligations arising from the minority treaties as still valid (mainly regarding Jewish minorities), but proposed their adaptation to new conditions. It was cautious in respect of the transfer of minorities and supported such a move only as an ultimate solution.[583] When the Foreign Office commented on the American proposals for "the international safeguard of human rights" in 1944[584] it still preferred its transfer schemes

---

579   Ibid., document no. 9.
580   Ibid., document no. 8 and 11.
581   See also Láníček, *Czechs, Slovaks and the Jews*, pp. 121–122.
582   Jacob Robinson et al., *Were the minority treaties a failure?* (New York: Institute of Jewish Affairs, 1943).
583   Inis L. Claude, *National Minorities: An International Problem* (Cambridge, MA: Harvard University Press, 1955), p. 225.
584   Alfred W. Brian Simpson, *Human Rights and the End of Empire: Britain and the Genesis of the European Convention* (Oxford: Oxford University Press, 2004), p. 212.

but it was obvious that the issue of the protection of minorities could not be eliminated; it was included in debates over the new conception of basic human rights within the preparation of a new international organization – the United Nations Organization.[585]

It is also true that the home resistance both in Poland and the Czech lands as well as exile Governments pressed the Allied Great Powers to adopt the policy of transfer of German minorities as a precondition for re-establishment of independent national states (or until 1943 possibly Central European Federation), but it was mainly the policy of the Great Powers which was playing the most important role.[586] The so-called "Big Three" had been considering the option of transfer throughout WWII and confirmed "in principle" their approval of its future implementation to the Czechoslovak and Polish side, even though they certainly differed in their conception of the goals which the transfer would achieve and in their reasons for finally expressing agreement to the measure as a component of Allied policy towards Germany.[587] The question must be seen in terms of a developing line of the policy, progressively responding to a whole series of international political factors, from the Atlantic Charter to the conferences in Teheran, Yalta and Potsdam.[588]

At a meeting of the War Cabinet the British Government declared its agreement to the "general principles of the transfer of German minorities" from the countries of Central and South-Eastern Europe after the war on the basis of a memorandum by Anthony Eden entitled "Anglo-Czechoslovak Relations" of 2 July 1942.[589] This was at a time when the Czechoslovak and British sides were seeking a compromise formula for the repudiation of the Munich Agreement (and therefore repudiation of cession of territory as a solution for the Czechoslovak minority dispute), and the memorandum explicitly confirmed the linkage.[590]

During May and June of 1943, the USA and the USSR confirmed that the policy of transferring the German minority should apply in the Czechoslovak and Polish cases after the war. The USSR in particular supported the Czechoslovak claims, including the transfer, as part of their expansion to Central Europe; the Soviet support of the pre-Munich Czechoslovak frontiers and the transfer of the German minority was confirmed to the Czechoslovak exile

---

585 Ibid.
586 Kuklík, *Czech law in historical contexts*, pp. 128–129.
587 Ray M. Douglas, *Orderly and Humane: The Expulsion of the Germans after the Second World War* (New Haven, CT: Yale University Press, 2012), pp. 7–38.
588 In more details Brandes, *Der Weg zur Vertreibung 1938–1945*, p. 271ff.
589 Kuklík and Němeček, *Frontiers, Minorities, Transfers, Expulsions*, document no. 3.
590 Jan Kuklík and Jan Němeček, "Repudiation of the Munich Agreement during the Second World War as seen from Czechoslovak Perspective," in *The disintegration of Czechoslovakia in the end of 1930s: Policy in the Central Europe*, ed. by Emil Voráček (Prague: Institute of History, 2009), p. 115.

President Beneš by the Soviet representatives during Beneš's visit to Moscow in December 1943.[591]

The delay in final decision on the transfer of German minorities was mainly due to the Polish question. The Foreign Office did not want to commit the British Government to the pre-war Polish borders.[592] Even though the British diplomacy was not prepared to recognise the Soviet annexation, there were widely held views within the Foreign Office that "the Poles would have to make large-scale concessions in the East."[593] The situation changed after the USSR entered the war when Ambassador Ivan M. Maisky, during his conversation with Anthony Eden on 4 July 1941, proposed an independent Polish state within its "natural" ethnographic borders.[594] Sikorski, on the other hand, demanded a proclamation of non-validity of the 1939 "occupation" of the Polish territory but was prepared to make certain territorial concessions in the East provided they were compensated in the West at the German expense.[595] A compromise was reached in the Polish-Soviet Treaty of 30 July 1941 accompanied by the British assurance not to recognise the changes in the Polish borders from 1939; however, Stalin made it clear to Eden during his visit to Moscow in December 1941, that the USSR wished to retain its territorial gains from 1939–1940, while Poland could be compensated in the West.[596] Moreover, the British assurance to Poland did not mean "any guarantee of future frontiers," which, as in the Czechoslovak case, had to be decided by the Peace Conference after the war.[597] As the adviser of the Foreign Office on Germany J.M. Troutbeck put it, the British were "committed to the principle (of transfer) but not to the method" until 1945. The USSR supported eviction and resettlement of Germans connected with the Polish claims for Oder–Neisse line, especially when the pro-Soviet Polish Committee of National Liberation was established in July 1944.[598]

The international dimension on discussions about the transfer intensified when the European Advisory Commission was established by the Big Three to prepare the Allied policies towards Germany and for a post-war Peace Conference. On 25 July 1944 the Commission asked the Czechoslovak and Polish exile Governments to present their conditions for armistice with Germany.

The large proportion of Czechoslovak claims, agreed by the Czechoslovak Government in exile on 24 August 1944 and presented to the European Advisory Commission on 23 November 1944 were based mainly on the Czechoslovak

---

591 Kuklík and Němeček, *Frontiers, Minorities, Transfers, Expulsions*, pp. 22–23.
592 Antony Polonsky, *The Great Powers and the Polish question, 1941-45: A documentary study in Cold War Origins* (London: London School of Economics, 1976), pp. 16–17.
593 Ibid., p. 17 and document no. 11.
594 Ibid., document no. 16.
595 Ibid., document no. 15.
596 TNA, London, FO 371, 31077, C 245.
597 Polonsky, *The Great Powers and the Polish question*, p. 18.
598 Kuklík and Němeček, *Frontiers, Minorities, Transfers, Expulsions*, p. 29.

view regarding the non-validity of the Munich Agreement as connected with the transfer of the German minority. The Czechoslovak Government especially demanded that Germany (and also Hungary) should "without prejudice to her responsibility, as defined in the armistice terms recognize . . . : a) nullity of the Munich Agreement of 29 September 1938, and the so-called Vienna Arbitrary Award of 2 November 1938, as well as all enactments arising from these Agreements and enactments, or others connected with them . . . ; b) nullity of enactments regarding the establishment of the Protectorate of Bohemia and Moravia . . . ; c) sovereignty of the Czechoslovak Republic over the territory within the frontiers before 29 September 1938, ensuing from the preceding points, and all other consequences ensuing from them." The minority question was proposed to be settled by the transfer not only of the German but also the Hungarian minority.[599]

The Czechoslovak arguments were not officially confirmed, and the final solution was left to the post-war negotiations, especially until the Potsdam conference. However the European Advisory Commission informally discussed the position towards the transfer and the British delegation was still guided by an important policy paper prepared by the Interdepartmental Committee on the Transfer of German Populations and submitted on 12 May 1944.[600] On 11 January 1945 the European Advisory Commission presented to the Czechoslovak Government its proposal for the unconditional surrender of Germany, which spoke about the German frontiers as they had existed before 31 December 1937.[601] Nevertheless it is important to note that the British Government, using arguments from Memorandum of the Foreign Office Research Department on German Eastern Frontiers from November 1944 submitted to the Post Hostilities Planning Committee of the War Cabinet,[602] was still counting not only on the transfer but also on minor territorial adjustments (corresponding with Beneš's ideas).

Nevertheless, the British standpoint agreed to by the War Cabinet in March 1945 meant an undertaking to allow the Czechoslovak bodies to exercise full state (administrative) authority in the territory defined by the pre-Munich frontiers.[603] Interestingly the British and Soviet Governments exchanged information on the Czechoslovak transfer and frontier questions even before the Potsdam conference.[604] In any case, from January 1944 at the latest, when it assessed Beneš's "Ten-Point Plan," the Foreign Office

---

599 Ibid., document no. 17.
600 Ibid., document no. 14; see also Houžvička, *Czechs and Germans 1848–2004*, pp. 300–301.
601 School of Slavonic and East European Studies, University College London, K. Lisický collection, box 14, vol. 4/1/2.
602 Kuklík and Němeček, *Frontiers, Minorities, Transfers, Expulsions*, document no. 16.
603 TNA, London, collection Cabinet Papers, CAB 121, 359 and FO 371, 47085, N 3159.
604 TNA, London, FO 371/47086, N 4867.

made a clear connection between the exercise of state sovereignty over the pre-Munich state territory (with possible "minor adjustments") and the transfer. This statement was confirmed in July 1944 during the preparation of the above mentioned memorandum on the eastern frontiers of Germany.[605]

After the establishment of what was known as the Lublin Committee of National Liberation in July 1944 and its recognition as the Polish interim government the issue of transfer of German population was viewed differently by the Czechoslovak and Polish exile representations, especially when the question of new borders started to collide with the Czechoslovak territorial claims in cases like Kladsko. Also the territorial disputes between both states concerning the Těšín territory complicated the initial collaboration on the preparation of transfer plans.

We have already mentioned that the principle of transfer conducted under international supervision was an important component of inter-Allied negotiations at the end of the war, especially in connection with the question of the final form of the Polish western borders.[606] The USA in particular was expressing a reserved attitude toward concrete plans for the transfer of German minorities in Europe as early as the beginning of 1945. Roosevelt and the State Department repeatedly stressed that the territorial changes (and interconnected transfers or exchanges of population) await "general post war settlement."[607] They also viewed the whole situation in the context of the transfer of Germans from other countries and the fate of all the refugees that occupation authorities in Germany would have to deal with as they flooded into the country. They intended to take into account the needs of the establishment of peace and security in Europe as a whole. However in December 1944 Roosevelt wrote to both Stalin and Churchill that the United States Government came to the conclusion that "the transfer of minorities in some cases is feasible and would contribute to the general security and tranquillity in the areas concerned." The USA was ready to "join in assisting such transfers."[608] This policy was mentioned in direct connection with the solution of post war Polish frontiers and Roosevelt expressly mentioned that this policy was already promoted by Eden (after his memorandum on the future of Germany was endorsed by the War Cabinet) during Moscow's talks of Foreign Ministers.[609] On the other hand Americans

---

605   TNA, London, FO 371, 39139, C 9093.

606   Polonsky, *The Great Powers and the Polish question*, pp. 42–44.

607   See for example Roosevelt's personal telegram to Churchill from December 17, 1944 (TNA London, FO 371, 39420, C 17459).

608   Ibid.

609   See memorandum by A. Eden on the future of Germany, from September 27, 1943 and War Cabinet conclusions from October, 5 1943 in Kuklík and Němeček, *Frontiers, Minorities, Transfers, Expulsions*, documents no. 6–7.

demanded the final decision on the transfer to be taken by the next meeting of the Big Three.

The USA also warned against implementation of any "unilateral act of transfer of large groups," and supported the principle that such transfer must be undertaken only after international approval, under international supervision, and gradually. This was the standpoint transmitted to the Czechoslovak Government in exile by the Chargé d'Affaires ad interim Rudolf Schoenfeld on 31 January 1945 in response to a Czechoslovak memorandum of 23 November 1944, and it came with the proviso that the USA would make further investigations into the question of transfer. It was for the same reason that the USA criticised the wild expulsions in May and June 1945 and several times repeated its demand that transfer be carried out under the supervision of the Great Powers and on the basis of agreement between them.[610]

3.4 POLICY OF EDVARD BENEŠ AND THE CZECHOSLOVAK GOVERNMENT IN EXILE RELATED TO MINORITIES

The German occupation was opposed by resistance movements organized both at home and abroad. The Czechoslovak resistance movement set re-establishing an independent Czechoslovakia as the common state of Czechs and Slovaks, and preferably in pre-Munich borders, as its aim. Those Czechoslovak politicians who went into exile after the break-up of Czechoslovakia considered the Munich Agreement void and not binding for Czechoslovakia from the very beginning because it represented serious violations of international law.[611] The establishment of the Protectorate was invalid under international law as well.[612] The leading role in the struggle to re-establish Czechoslovakia was played by the Second Czechoslovak President, Edvard Beneš, who resigned under German pressure after Munich on 5 October 1938.[613]

After the outbreak of WWII, Beneš and his followers were trying to establish a Czechoslovak Interim Government. The main aim of such a government was not only to represent the existence of an independent Czechoslovakia but also to start a political struggle to repudiate the Munich Agreement.

---

610 Ibid., p. 49.
611 Edward Táborský, *The Czechoslovak Cause: An Account of the Problems of International Law in Relation to Czechoslovakia* (London: H.F. & G. Witherby, 1944), especially pp. 5–25.
612 See arguments prepared for the League of Nations by Jan Kuklík and Jan Němeček, "Memorandum by Hans Kelsen on the Breaking up of Czecho-Slovakia," in *Das internationale Wirken Hans Kelsen*, ed. by Clemens Jabloner, Thomas Olechowski and Klaus Zeleny, Schriftenreihe des Hans Kelsen-Instituts 38 (Vienna: Manz Verlag, 2016)
613 Československá zahraniční politika v roce 1938, ed. by Jindřich Dejmek, *Dokumenty československé zahraniční politiky*, vol. 2 (Prague: Ústav mezinárodních vztahů, 2001), document no. 819, p. 489ff.

France and Great Britain were unwilling to support such schemes for Central Europe, and they allowed only for the establishment of the Czechoslovak National Committee to direct Czechoslovak military units politically.[614]

This transitional period ended when Winston Churchill became the Prime Minister and after the military collapse of France. In July 1940 the Provisional Czechoslovak Government in exile was recognized by Great Britain and the Provisional State Apparatus in Great Britain was established on the British soil.[615] During the process of recognition of the Czechoslovak exile Government the British Government made certain reservations concerning the juridical continuity of the Czechoslovak state and its future frontiers. It was clear that the British attitude towards the Munich Agreement was behind such reservations.[616]

On the occasion of the second anniversary of the adoption of the Munich Agreement, on 30 September 1940, Winston Churchill stated in the BBC Czechoslovak programme that the Munich Agreement was "destroyed" by Hitler after 15 March 1939. Churchill refused "to recognize any of the brutal conquests of Germany in Central Europe and elsewhere" and stressed that the British Government "have welcomed the Czechoslovak Provisional Government in this country, and that we have made the restoration of Czechoslovak liberties one of our principal war aims."[617]

Nevertheless, the British Government did not wish to commit themselves to recognize or support the establishment of any particular frontiers in Central Europe, and this covered the frontiers set as "a result of the Munich Conference." This standpoint was communicated to Beneš on 11 November 1940 by the Foreign Office.[618] The British decision regarding the Czechoslovak frontiers was thus postponed until the end of the war. Great Britain, for other reasons (e.g. the status of national minorities, position of Slovakia, position of other states in the region), did not intend to simply return the region to the status quo ante Munich.

Beneš tried to change the British attitude when he asked for *de jure* recognition of the Czechoslovak Government in exile in the spring of 1941.[619] The Czechoslovak position was strengthened after the German attack on the USSR. The Soviet Union immediately changed its relationship towards the "Czechoslovak case" and was prepared to recognize Beneš and his exile

614   Kuklík, *Czech law in historical contexts*, pp. 122.
615   Ibid., pp. 122–123.
616   Kuklík, Němeček and Šebek, *Dlouhé stíny Mnichova*, pp. 141–143.
617   Edvard Beneš, *The Fall and Rise of a Nation: Czechoslovakia 1938–1941*, ed. by Milan Hauner (Boulder, CO: East European Monographs, 2004), pp. 104–105.
618   Kuklík and Němeček, *Frontiers, Minorities, Transfers, Expulsions*, pp. 17–18.
619   Edward Táborský, "Politics in exile, 1939–1945," in Mamatey and Luža, *A History of the Czechoslovak Republic 1918–1948*, pp. 326–327.

Government in London. The Soviet recognition of the Czechoslovak exile Government in July 1941 implied the re-establishment of Czechoslovakia in its pre-Munich borders, which was confirmed by Stalin during his conversation with Anthony Eden in December 1941.[620] Britain accorded *de jure* recognition to the Czechoslovak exile Government on 18 July 1941 but was not prepared to withdraw its principal objections concerning the Czechoslovak frontiers.[621]

Starting from January 1942, Beneš and the Czechoslovak Government in exile drew a linkage between the non-validity of the Munich Agreement and the final settlement of the Czechoslovak frontiers.[622] Simultaneously they suggested the transfer of a substantial part of the German minority (and to certain extend also of Hungarian minority) from Czechoslovakia together with the cession of a limited part of the Czechoslovak territory.

For the British Foreign Office the question of "repudiation" of Munich was not only closely connected with the transfer of German minorities from Central and Eastern Europe but also with the proposed Central European Confederation, based mainly on cooperation between Czechoslovakia and Poland.[623] The British Government was prepared to repudiate Munich on condition that a compromise was found on the relationship between Czechoslovakia and the democratic representatives of its German minority, mainly with Social Democrat Wenzel Jaksch.[624]

Negotiations between Beneš and Jaksch in 1942 proved that even the democratic representatives of German minority with its programme of regional autonomy were not able to come to terms with the majority of Czechoslovak exile politicians. Jaksch refused even a limited transfer and negotiations reached deadlock. The situation changed dramatically after the assassination of Heydrich and especially after the unprecedented German retaliations against Czech civilians symbolized by the fate of the Lidice village. It helped the Czechoslovak Government strengthen its arguments against Munich and meant that the negotiations with representatives of German minority were postponed until a more convenient time, which in fact was never to come.

The Czechoslovak position was also strengthened again with the help of Soviet diplomacy. The re-establishment of a "strong and independent" Czechoslovakia in its pre-Munich borders was expressly confirmed by

---

620 TNA London, CAB 66/220 and FO 371, 31077, C 245, *Memorandum by the Secretary of State on Conversations with Stalin*, December 12–20, 1941.

621 Táborský, "Politics in exile, 1939–1945," p. 328.

622 In more details Smetana, *In the shadow of Munich*, p. 262ff.

623 See Memoranda on Central European Confederation and the Transfer of German populations, February 20, 1942 in Kuklík and Němeček, *Frontiers, Minorities, Transfers, Expulsions*, document no. 2.

624 Francis Dostál Raška, *The Czechoslovak Exile Government in London and the Sudeten German Issue* (Prague: Karolinum Press, 2002), esp. p. 179ff.

A. Bogomolov, Soviet Ambassador to the Czechoslovak Government in exile, and by the Soviet Minister of Foreign Affairs V. Molotov on 9 July 1942.[625]

The British were ready to denounce the Munich Agreement provided their different view concerning the initial validity of the agreement was not challenged. The British Secretary of State for Foreign Affairs, Anthony Eden, informed the British War Cabinet about the negotiations with the Czechoslovaks. We have already mentioned that the question of the non-validity of the Munich Agreement was directly connected with the proposals for the solution to the minority issues by eviction and relocation (transfer).[626]

On 5 August 1942 Eden handed a diplomatic note to the Czechoslovak Minister of Foreign Affairs, Jan Masaryk. According to Eden, the statement made by Winston Churchill on 30 September 1940 represented "the attitude of His Majesty's Government in regard to the arrangements reached in Munich," i.e. that "the Munich Agreement had been repudiated by the Germans." The British Government maintained its reservation concerning the final Czechoslovak frontiers but stated that, "in order to avoid any possible misunderstanding," the frontiers should be decided by the end of the war and "they will not be influenced by any changes effected in and since 1938." That same day Masaryk sent a reply to Eden in which he regarded the British note "as a practical solution of the questions and difficulties . . . maintaining of course our political and juridical position with regard to the Munich Agreement and the events which followed it" and declared that "between our two countries the Munich Agreement can now be considered dead."[627]

The Munich Agreement was repudiated (and declared null and void from the very beginning) also by the French National Committee headed by Charles de Gaulle in September 1942 and later also by the French Provisional Government in 1944.[628] Italy was the last party to the Munich Agreement to change its attitude towards the Munich Agreement during WWII. This was only after the Mussolini fascist leadership had been replaced, when the Italian Government proclaimed the Munich Agreement to be null and void from the very beginning. On 26 September 1944 the Italian Minister for Foreign Affairs Count Sforza also announced that the territorial changes between Slovakia and Hungary should be regarded as null and void as a direct consequence of Munich. The Italian proclamation on the Munich Agreement had wider consequences. It influenced Czechoslovak relations with the Holy See and

---

625 Kuklík and Němeček, *Frontiers, Minorities, Transfers, Expulsions*, p. 21.
626 Kuklík, Němeček and Šebek, *Dlouhé stíny Mnichova*, pp. 367–369.
627 Československá zahraniční politika v roce 1942, vol. 2, (1. 8. – 31. 12. 1942), ed. by Jan Němeček et al., Dokumenty československé zahraniční politiky B/3/2 (Prague: Ústav mezinárodních vztahů, Historický ústav AV ČR, 2015), document no. 219, pp. 10–12.
628 Kuklík and Němeček, "Repudiation of the Munich Agreement during the Second World War," pp. 117–119.

was used as a precedent for the Peace Treaty with Hungary after the end of WWII.[629] By 1944 both the Munich Agreement and Vienna Award concerning the Czechoslovak frontiers were declared null and void by its signatories, but the final frontiers of post-war Czechoslovakia and the position of its minorities were still to be decided.

The idea of the transfer of members of the German minority from Czechoslovakia can be traced back to the beginning of the home resistance movement, with the most radical support for the idea coming from the military segment of the resistance.[630] The first document which expressly mentioned the necessity to expel the German population from Czechoslovakia was a memorandum on the exchange of populations prepared for the political leadership of the non-communist home resistance movement by professor of constitutional law Zdeněk Peška in August 1939. Military organization called Obrana národa – Defence of the Nation was even more radical and its Moravian headquarters had prepared, as early as in 1939, an instruction on the expulsion of Germans; the instruction suggested that Germans would be evicted on 24 hour notice, allowed to take only 20 kilograms of their belongings and a limited sum of Reich marks.[631] It was a natural consequence of a programme of national resistance movement at home which also relied on the pre-Munich borders.[632] It is therefore important to note that it was the leadership of the democratically oriented home resistance movement, that came to the conclusion that the Czech-German issue could be solved only by choosing the most extreme option of expulsion employed entirely as an emergency instrument and as a safeguard for the Czech nation for the future, particularly in connection with the Czechoslovak-German borders.

The position of the Polish home resistance movement was similar. In July 1940 the Polish underground press demanded the "return" of the territory east of the rivers Oder and Neisse as an expression of "historical justice" with strategic consequences.[633] The Polish home resistance leaders advocated the expulsion of all Germans from this territory, pointing to methods the German occupation forces applied in Poland.[634]

---

629 Ibid., pp. 120–121.
630 Jan Kuklík, "Transfer or expulsion? The fate of the German minority in post-war Czechoslovakia from the Czechoslovak law point of view," in *War die „Vertreibung" Unrecht? Die Umsiedlungsbeschlüsse des Potsdamer Abkommens und ihre Umsetzung in ihrem völkerrechtlichen und historischen Kontext*, ed. by Christoph Koch (Frankfurt am Main: Peter Lang, 2015), p. 122.
631 Václav Kural, *Vlastenci proti okupaci: Ústřední vedení odboje domácího 1940–1943* (Prague: Karolinum Press, 1997), p. 38.
632 See Jitka Vondrová, ed., *Češi a sudetoněmecká otázka, 1939–1945: Dokumenty* (Prague: Ústav mezinárodních vztahů, 1994), document no. 6.
633 Kuklík and Němeček, *Frontiers, Minorities, Transfers, Expulsions*, p. 16.
634 Ibid.

Beneš on the other hand originally combined the principle of transfer with a possible cession of part of the Czechoslovak border territory; and this linkage was to persist in his proposals to various degrees until the very end of the war.[635] The cession of the territory was supposed to not only reduce the numbers of German population in the Czechoslovak Republic but also to justify the transfer of those leaders of the German minority who had committed the worst offences against the Czechoslovak Republic.[636]

As early as in February 1941, Beneš in his memorandum entitled "Czechoslovak Peace Aims" presumed "the relocation of population to the maximum possible extent" with respect to Germans, in addition to the transfer of Hungarians.[637] Czechoslovak demands against Hungary were based on the fact that Hungary ended up as a German ally, i.e. an enemy if considered from the perspective of the anti-German allies. However, in the case of Hungary, the Czechoslovak Government in exile preferred a combination of transfer and exchange of population as a more feasible solution.

On 6 January 1942 Beneš drew up a "Memorandum on the Question of the Borders of the Czechoslovak Republic." He ruled out the possibility of simply returning back to the concept of the "minority policy of the First Republic."[638] Essentially, he demanded the restoration of the pre-Munich frontiers while conceding "modifications of the former historic frontiers of the Republic in such a way as to cede to Germany a more substantial piece of the Czechoslovak territory in return for a significantly smaller piece of the German territory, an exchange that would automatically reduce the overall number of Germans in Czechoslovakia by a significant percentage in a peaceful way and without further sacrifices and sufferings for the population." According to Beneš, the number of Germans could be reduced in this way by 600,000 to 700,000. He intended to make the exchange of territory subject to the proviso "that approximately another 1,200,000 to 1,400,000 German-speaking inhabitants will be moved out of Czechoslovakia by transferring them to Germany and Austria." In support of this solution he referred to the Turkish-Greek exchange and transfer of populations after WWI. In overall figures, his proposal meant that 2,100,000 Germans would be resettled in Germany and that about 1 million German inhabitants would remain in Czechoslovakia. The transfer would be carried out in an organized way, with financial aid for the departing population, and would be internationally approved. Beneš also envisaged that the property of persons included in the transfer would, to a significant extent, satisfy the main Czechoslovak demands for reparations.

---

635 Kuklík, "Transfer or expulsion?," p. 126.
636 Bryant, *Prague in Black*, pp. 209–212,
637 Vondrová, *Češi a sudetoněmecká otázka*, document no. 88.
638 Ibid., document no. 80; see also Hoover Institution Archives, Táborský collection, box 6.

However, Beneš's proposals for the cession of a part of the territory, just like his proposal for Sudeten German "self-government" within the Czechoslovak Republic (combined with internal relocation), met with opposition not only in the home resistance but also in the Government in exile, with which he discussed his transfer plans both officially and unofficially.[639]

Although, as we have already mentioned, the British War Cabinet declared its agreement to the "general principle of the transfer of German minorities" from the countries of Central and South-Eastern Europe after the war already in July 1942, Beneš was informed that it does not mean "a bianco check" in minority questions. According to British diplomat Frank Roberts both Beneš and Jaksch were verbally and "extremely informally" informed about the British views on transfers and about the decision of the War Cabinet, which was "the only action in this respect."[640] However the British diplomacy confirmed to the Czechoslovak Government the linkage between the repudiation of the Munich Agreement and the transfer of German minorities.

Most radical positions in both the Czechoslovak and Polish exile environment were maintained by military representatives. In August 1943 General Bedřich Neumann-Miroslav proposed to Beneš to "get rid of approximately 2 million Germans and 400,000 Hungarians in four modifications: Plan A – Resettlement of minorities agreed by Allies without territorial compensation, Plan B – Combination of cession of territory with transfer, Plan C – Exchange of populations with Germany and Hungary and Plan D – Expulsion of minorities from Czechoslovakia during revolutionary period.[641] After discussion with Beneš the Czechoslovak commanders-in-chief agreed on the preference of a nationally homogenous state with a minority population of at most 10%.[642]

Beneš again brought a more lenient standpoint into the discussions. In his article for "The Foreign Affairs" he pleaded for the transfer of minorities and emphasised that Czechoslovakia did not wish to restore the international system of protection of minorities under the auspices of the League of Nations, but it would accept solutions agreed during a peace conference.[643]

In November 1943 Beneš prepared his "ten-point plan for the transfer of the German population from the Czechoslovak Republic," which he first put forward during his negotiations with Soviet leaders in Moscow and then presented to the Foreign Office.[644] This proposal already contained the principle that Czechoslovakia would decide through its own legislation on the question

---

639 See for example Luža, *Transfer of the Sudeten Germans*, p. 229ff.
640 TNA London, FO 371, 34396, C 416.
641 Kuklík and Němeček, *Frontiers, Minorities, Transfers, Expulsions*, p. 23.
642 Ibid.
643 Ibid., p. 19.
644 Hoover Institution Archives, Táborský Collection, box 8.

of the state citizenship of persons of German and Hungarian nationality, and in this way identify the category of people subject to future transfer. Loss of citizenship and therefore transfer was supposed primarily to affect active Nazis, like members of the Gestapo or representatives of the Nazi government in the Protectorate. It is necessary to note, that this so-called "guilt principle" was opposed by the British diplomats, mainly because of the feasibility of the transfer and because of the limited scope of these criteria.[645] By the end of 1943, in a short memorandum entitled "Some of the Main Principles for the Future Status of the Czechoslovak Republic," Beneš conceded the possibility of exchange of territory with Germany and Hungary and even the possibility that after the implementation of a transfer the Czechoslovak Republic would accept a regime to be stipulated for minorities in European states at the peace conference.[646]

The Soviet support of the pre-Munich Czechoslovak frontiers and the transfer of the German minority were confirmed to Beneš by the Soviet representatives during Beneš's visit to Moscow in December 1943. In Moscow Beneš also concluded the Treaty of Alliance, Friendship and Mutual Aid between the USSR and Czechoslovakia on 12 December 1943.

Because of the above-mentioned orientation on the USSR, the Czechoslovak Government in exile in London was forced to cooperate also with the Czechoslovak Communists, who had their exile centre in Moscow. By the end of 1943 the Czechoslovak politicians in exile in London came to terms with the Moscow Czechoslovak Communists on the programme for the post war reconstruction of the Czechoslovak state. Within a programme of profound economic, social and political changes, described as a "national and democratic revolution," there was also understanding on land reform, and confiscation of property of war criminals, home traitors, but also of Germans and Hungarians. The Czechoslovak Communists only gradually changed their originally cold reaction to the transfer proposals by Beneš and tried to put forward their own alternatives.[647] In fact, the exile leadership of the Communist Party of Czechoslovakia initially proposed that the German question be solved "as part of action taken to punish the perpetrators of the war and crimes against the Czechoslovak Republic, following the anti-fascist and anti-Nazi line."

Towards the end of 1943 the Czechoslovak Government in exile started preparations for a post-war Peace Conference. As we have already mentioned a large proportion of Czechoslovak claims were based mainly on the

---

645 This stance was confirmed by William Strang during his conversation with Ray Atherton, March 19, 1943 (TNA, London, FO 371, 34396, C 3518).
646 Kuklík and Němeček, *Frontiers, Minorities, Transfers, Expulsions*, p. 22–23.
647 Kuklík, "Transfer or expulsion?," pp. 127–128.

Czechoslovak view regarding the non-validity of the Munich Agreement connected with the transfer of the German minority and reestablishment of Czechoslovakia in pre-Munich frontiers. On the 5 January 1944 Hubert Ripka, State Secretary of Foreign Affairs, spoke "informally" on the transfer of German and Hungarian minorities with William Baker from the Foreign Office Research Department.[648] Ripka personally estimated that larger numbers of Sudeten Germans would be affected by the transfer than what Beneš predicted at that time (1.5 million) and spoke about 2 to 2.5 million. If such transfer was agreed to by the Great Powers, Czechoslovakia was prepared for smaller territorial rectifications. Ripka was aware of the economic losses associated with the transfer but he foresaw advantages in the long term perspective, especially regarding a homogenous character of Czechoslovakia. For the Hungarian minority (because of the claim for pre-Munich borders) Ripka advocated the combination of transfer with an exchange of populations (700,000 Hungarians in Slovakia and 350,000 Slovaks in Hungary). The Czechoslovak Government was also prepared for small rectifications of the pre-Munich borders in the case of Hungary.

In 1944 the Czechoslovak Government in exile realized that the problem of the Hungarian minority should be treated separately from the German minority. Considering Hungarians, the exchange of population as well as assimilation were considered; moreover, it was necessary to take into account a substantially different position with respect to the Hungarian issue expressed particularly by the American[649] and British sides.[650]

Not until February 1945 did the British side recognise Czechoslovak state power over the whole pre-Munich territory, i.e. within the borders between the Czechoslovak Republic and Germany as on 31 December 1937, explicitly including territories taken by Poland and Hungary. Britain considered it likely that if the Soviet Union would liberate these territories they would be rendered to Czechoslovakia. Before the end of WWII it was quite clear that the position of Hungary would essentially differ from that of Germany. This was shown during the negotiations with Hungary on the conditions for armistice concluded between the Hungarian Interim Government and

---

648   TNA, London, FO 371, 38928, C 643.

649   The State Department presumed that the pre-Munich borders between Czechoslovakia and Hungary would be restored, although with some rectifications, and preferred the exchange of population. See the proposal of the Advisory Committee of the State Department regarding the negotiations with Hungary, 1 May 1944; Ignác Romsics, ed., *Wartime American Plans for a New Hungary: Documents from the U.S. Department of State, 1942-1944* (Boulder, CO: Social Science Monographs; Highland Lakes, NJ: Atlantic Research and Publications, 1992), part 4, document no. 1.

650   In more details András Bán, *Pax Britannica: Wartime Foreign Office Documents Regarding Plans for a Postbellum East Central Europe* (Boulder, CO: Social Science Monographs; Highland Lakes, NJ: Atlantic Research and Publications, 1997).

representatives of the USSR, the USA, and Great Britain on 20 January 1945 in Moscow.[651]

The Czechoslovak exile diplomacy intended to enforce an adjusted version of conditions for armistice, which was debated in November 1944; diplomats tried to emphasise that Czechoslovakia as a victim of Hungarian aggression should be entitled to restore the borders before the Vienna Arbitration and to receive reparations. The transfer of the Hungarian minority was mentioned as preference, combined with a relevant exchange of population. Czechoslovak requirements were comprised in the despatch by H. Ripka addressed to Czechoslovak Envoy to Moscow Z. Fierlinger from 30 December 1944, clarified on 8 and 9 January 1945.[652] A Czechoslovak diplomatic note addressed to the Governments of the Big Three for their negotiations with Hungary referred to the *aide mémoire* of 24 August 1944.[653] Ripka primarily emphasised the fact that the outcome of the negotiations with Hungary would constitute a precedent for negotiations between the Allies on the issue of transfers.

Czechoslovak as well as Yugoslavian conditions for armistice with Hungary were debated during negotiations held in Moscow on 15 January 1945, chaired by V. Molotov and with participation of US Ambassador W. A. Harriman, British Ambassador J. Balfour and Z. Fierlinger. The formulation of an explicit principle of transfer and exchange of population was not included in the armistice conditions due to the negative position of both American and British representatives; however, it was admitted that the issue might be debated later.[654] Despite this partial failure, the armistice conditions nevertheless contained items important for Czechoslovakia. The Hungarian Government terminated the state of war with respect to the Allies and expressly with Czechoslovakia. Article 2 contained the essential Hungarian waiver of territorial benefits resulting from the Hungarian annexation of neighbouring states' territories in 1938; Hungary undertook to terminate the validity of all legal and administrative measures relating to its annexation of these territories. Article 19 declared the Vienna Arbitration Award to be null and void. Issues regarding a Czechoslovak share in Hungarian reparations

---

651 See "Agreement, with annex and protocol, signed at Moscow January 20, 1945;" Executive Agreement Series 456 in *Treaties and Other International Agreements of the United States of America 1776–1949*, ed. by Charles I. Bevans, vol. 3 (Washington, DC: Department of State Publication, 1969).

652 Jan Němeček et al., *Československo-sovětské vztahy v diplomatických jednáních 1939–1945: Dokumenty*, vol. 2 (Prague: Státní ústřední archiv v Praze, 1999), document no. 206, p. 426ff., and no. 225, p. 465ff.

653 See also TNA London, FO 371, 47130, N 1017. J. Balfour addressed in this sense the Soviet People's Commissariat of Foreign Affairs on December 9, 1944.

654 See Štefan Šutaj, *"Akcia Juh" – odsun Maďarov zo Slovenska do Čiech v roku 1949* (Prague: Ústav pro soudobé dějiny AV ČR, 1993), p. 7.

for war damage and Hungarian occupation of the Czechoslovak territory, as well as compensation of various property losses were solved. An Allied Control Commission was established to supervise the fulfilment of the armistice conditions. The Commission was chaired by Marshal K. J. Voroshilov, and was to solve certain issues regarding Czechoslovakia, such as repatriation and complaints raised by the Hungarian Government against "persecution" of the Hungarian minority in Slovakia.[655]

3.5 EXPULSIONS AND FORCED MIGRATIONS BEFORE THE POTSDAM CONFERENCE

Expulsions of German population, which is also known as "wild transfer" or "wild expulsion" began with the participation of Czechoslovak military and administrative bodies (officially called "evacuation") immediately after the cessation of wartime events and continued in many areas up to the Potsdam Conference and even after it.[656] Many Czechs were simply not willing to wait until organized resettlements were officially agreed and took part in "wild expulsions."[657] By the end of the war approximately 3.4 to 3.7 million German civilians resided on the Czechoslovak territory. Although most of them were permanently settled inhabitants; thousands refugees fled before the advance of the Red Army from Silesia and from eastern European territories. There were also German officials and soldiers, who were pre-war citizens of the German Reich. Expulsions and the above mentioned "evacuation" (eviction and resettlement) affected more than 700,000 Germans (and some estimates are even close to 1 million)[658], and involved crimes, violence and individual wrongdoings. Germans were forced to move mostly to the Soviet occupation zones in Germany and Austria (for example through train and lorry transports in Northern Bohemia or the infamous March of Germans from Brno).[659] It was mainly the end of the war, accompanied by acts of German terror, what provoked violent acts of revenge on the side of the Czech population.[660]

655   See for example diplomatic notes of July 26 and August 23, 1945 by the Hungarian Government to the Allied Control Commission. Besides, the Hungarian Government filed six other protests against allegedly bad treatment (TNA London, FO 371-48488).

656   Tomáš Staněk and Adrian von Arburg, "Organizované divoké odsuny? Úloha ústředních orgánů při provádění 'evakuace' německého obyvatelstva (květen až září 1945)," *Soudobé dějiny* 13, no. 3-4 (2006): especially p. 321ff.

657   Douglas, *Orderly and Humane*, p. 93ff.

658   Staněk and A. von Arburg, "Organizované divoké odsuny?, part 3, closing summary.

659   David Kovařík, "'Brněnský pochod smrti 1945': Mýty a skutečnost," in *Konec soužití Čechů a Němců v Československu: Sborník k 60. výročí ukončení II. světové války*, ed. by Hynek Fajmon and Kateřina Hloušková (Brno: Centrum pro studium demokracie a kultury, 2005), pp. 63–79.

660   In more details Tomáš Staněk, *Poválečné „excesy" v českých zemích v roce 1945 a jejich vyšetřování*, Sešity Ústavu pro soudobé dějiny AV ČR 41 (Prague: Ústav pro soudobé dějiny AV ČR, 2005).

The expulsions were followed by the seizures of German property. There were also attempts to intern German population including women, children and old people in special camps and impose other discriminatory measures.[661] This period is definitely one of the darker pages in Czech-German history and one should welcome the fact that a number of previously taboo subjects have been opened up and investigated, especially on the regional level. Without corresponding changes in the law, which moreover do not much differ from the legislative responses of the majority of the other occupied European states towards enemy property and the property of collaborators and wartime speculators[662], the situation on the ground would have been entirely out of control. It must also be realised that in the first weeks following liberation the primary concern was with the reconstruction and assertion of state power over a territory which had been under the control of enemy states for six years. The situation also differed on the territory liberated by the American army and on the territory under the Red Army control. Furthermore, many government decisions and laws issued at the time were corrected in the following period. In any case, guidelines intending to bring a definitive end to the initial phase of wild transfer and imposing an obligation "to respect those Germans citizens who remained loyal to the republic, actively participated in the struggle for the liberation of the republic or suffered under Nazi and fascist terror" were adopted by the Czechoslovak Government as early as 15 June 1945.

On the basis of recent historical research, it is also necessary to correct the persisting stereotype presented by the Sudeten German literature that speaks of hundreds of thousands of victims of the expulsions or even of the genocide of the German minority. The Czech-German Commission of Historians reached a figure of 25,000 to 30 000 victims.[663] The claims of genocide must be therefore rejected. On the other hand it must be admitted that the expulsions were exploited by Czechoslovakia and its military and administrative bodies to establish a *de facto* situation that the Potsdam Conference then had to take into account. Even in the period of "wild transfer" a necessary condition was the co-operation of the Soviet occupation authorities in the Soviet zones of occupation and to a lesser extent this is also true of the American, British and French authorities. The British zone, for example, was the main destination for those "Reich" Germans who had been domiciled there before the war and the British did not want to repatriate the Sudeten Germans from their zone to Czechoslovakia, whereas the French even

---

661 Beneš and Kural, *Facing history*, pp. 218–219.
662 Ibid., pp. 244–245.
663 Ibid., pp. 230–232.

expressed their will to except certain categories of Czechoslovak Germans into their zone of occupation.[664]

The period of wild expulsions is connected with discussions about an Act on the legality of acts connected with the fight for the restoration of the liberty of Czechs and Slovaks of 8 May 1946.[665] The provisions of this Act include the declaration of immunity from prosecution for acts that were "an expression of desire for just retribution for the acts of the occupying forces or their accomplices," in the period from Munich to 28 October 1945. The Czechoslovak Republic was blamed for not having legally ensured the punishment of "excesses" and manifest crimes against members of the German minority. The law in question, considered in terms of its purpose and wording was in no circumstance intended to cover crimes committed "for low and dishonourable reasons." A number of people who had committed post-war crimes against Germans were in fact brought to justice, although it must be admitted that far from every case concrete culprits were identified and punished and not all the punishments appear adequate from today's point of view.

3.6 THE POTSDAM CONFERENCE AND ORGANIZED TRANSFER OF GERMAN MINORITIES

Resettlement of German minorities from Central Europe in form of internationally organized transfer was finally discussed by the Big Three during the Potsdam Conference in July/August 1945. On 3 July 1945, the Czechoslovak Ministry of Foreign Affairs submitted memoranda to the Allies regarding the transfer of German and Hungarian minorities.[666] The Ministry referred to the above-mentioned memoranda and the *aide mémoire* of the Czechoslovak Government in exile from 1944. The post-war Czechoslovak Government proposed not only the transfer of German minority but also that talks should be held with the Allied Control Commission in Budapest to debate the Hungarian issue; the transfer was proposed to be pursued by means of the exchange of population since the Czechoslovak estimate suggested that about 345,000 Slovaks living in Hungary wished to return to Czechoslovakia. Under the memoranda, Czechs and Slovaks considered the transfer of both Germans and Hungarians to be "the basis for the future safety of the State" and to contribute to "the preservation of peace in Central Europe."

---

664 The Deputy Minister of Foreign Affairs V. Clementis discussed this possibility with French chargé d'affaires to Prague in July and August 1945 – Jan Kuklík and Jan Němeček, *Osvobozené Československo očima britské diplomacie* (Prague: Karolinum Press, 2011), p. 217

665 Beneš and Kural, *Facing history*, pp. 255–266.

666 TNA, London, CAB 121, 359.

Transfer of German minorities was confirmed by Article XII of the Potsdam Conference protocol of 2 August 1945 that declared resettlement of Germans from Poland, Czechoslovakia and Hungary in "an orderly and humane manner."[667] The transfer thus acquired an international legal basis and was regulated in detail by the decisions of the Allied Control Council for Germany, especially by its decision from 20 November 1945, which was communicated to the Czechoslovak Government, interim Polish Government, Allied Control Commission for Hungary and Allied Control Commission for Austria.[668]

The future of the Hungarian population living in Czechoslovakia and other countries neighbouring Hungary was not debated during the Potsdam Conference, nor was a final determination of Hungarian-Czechoslovak borders. The Hungarian question was reserved for solution at a separate peace conference, similarly to the question of Italy and other wartime satellites of Germany. It was clear that a bilateral agreement on the exchange of population endorsed by the Great Powers was a more preferred solution. After the publication of the outcomes of the Potsdam Conference, on 16 August 1945 the Czechoslovak Ministry of Foreign Affairs informed the British, USA and Soviet Embassies in Prague that he intended to commence direct negotiations with the Allied Control Commission in Budapest regarding conditions for potential exchanges of population with Hungary.[669]

Czechoslovak authorities planned that 250,000 Germans should be relocated in December 1945 and further 125,000 in January 1946 to end the main transfer by August 1946. The Czechoslovak Government discussed the transfer scheme on 14 December 1945.[670] However the food, weather and transport conditions in Germany delayed the beginning of "organized transfer." In the framework of the organised transfer, which began in January 1946 (although the first train with 495 "refugees" from "Eastern Sudetenland" was reported from Regensburg on 29 December 1945),[671] at least 1.5 million of Germans were resettled from the Czechoslovak Republic to the American occupation zone and 750,000 to the Soviet zone in Germany and by the autumn of 1946 the mass organized transfer essentially ended. In 1947 it was renewed only in a limited scale to the American and Soviet zones and around 200,000 Germans remained in Czechoslovakia.[672]

---

667 See Final protocol of 2 August 1945. *Documents on British Policy Overseas*, series I, vol. I, *The Conference of Potsdam July–August 1945*, London 1984, p. 1275 and *Foreign Relations of the United States. Diplomatic Papers: The Conference of Berlin (Potsdam Conference), 1945*, vol. 2 (Washington, DC: U.S. G.P.O., 1960), pp. 1511–1551; see also Beneš and Kural, *Facing History*, pp. 267–280.
668 TNA London, FO 371, 55390, C 304.
669 TNA London, FO 371, 48488, C 4830.
670 Beneš and Kural, *Facing History*, pp. 218 and 225–226.
671 TNA London, FO 371, 55390, C 170.
672 Beneš and Kural, *Facing History*, pp. 227–228.

A special Office for the Transfer of Germans was established as a joint authority of the Ministries of Interior and National Defence. On the local level the competences were given to national committees or administrative commissions in the border regions. The Ministry of Interior issued a circular concerning the beginning of mass transfer on 31 December 1945. Special Transfer Collection Centres (there were 107 of them) were established and the Czechoslovak authorities also issued guidelines concerning for example food ratios and personal property (from 30 to 50 kg and 1 000 Reich marks per person) of the transferees. There were also exemptions from transfer, for example for skilled workers needed for the Czechoslovak industry or for so-called "anti-fascists" identified by special commissions. Most of them were relocated to the Federal Republic of Germany by 1950/1951, including also the reunification of families. In April 1951 the policy of relocation was stopped by the Ministry of Interior and the policy was implemented by the national committees.[673]

For the actual implementation of the transfer, the Czechoslovak Government used orders, guidelines and other regulations issued by the Ministries of Interior and National Defence. There were also elements of the pre-Munich legal order, particularly the Act on Aliens No. 52/1935 Sb., the Governmental Order on Administrative Procedure No. 8/1928 Sb., and especially Austrian Act No. 88/1871 on Police Expulsion and Deportation. Czechoslovak authorities also used an agreement with the American organs (Soviets at the beginning stopped further transports from Czechoslovakia because of the situation in their zone) concerning the size of the transports, their numbers or medical services. Each train had its own self-administration.[674]

As a result of the decision of the Potsdam conference around 3.2 million Germans had to leave Poland too.[675] The so-called policy of "verification" of the Polish nationality (based in most cases on the testimony of three local Poles) and rehabilitation applied. For example in western Silesia 850,000 people were "verified" as Polish nationals and granted Polish citizenship. In reality between 1946–1947 only 2,170,000 to 2,400,000 Germans were resettled to Germany through the transfer schemes (hundreds of thousands of Germans fled before the transfer was started) and still around 300,000 remained in Poland by the end of 1947.[676]

Even more radical solution to the German question occurred in the liberated Yugoslavia, where the German minority was deprived of its civil rights

673 See circular instruction issued by the Reginal National Committee in Prague, 13 April 1951, Státní okresní archiv Kutná Hora, Fond Okresní národní výbor Kutná Hora 1945–1960, [District National Committee Kutná Hora 1945–1960], kart (Box) 244, sign. 573

674 Beneš and Kural, *Facing History*, pp. 226–227.

675 Maria Rutowska, Zbigniew Mazur and Hubert Orłowski, "History and Memory: mass expulsions and transfers 1939–1945–1949," *Biuletyn Instytutu Zachodniego* 21 (2009).

676 Eberhardt, *Ethnic groups and population changes*, pp. 139–140.

as early as November 1944, some 300,000 were expelled from the country, and their property was expropriated in favour of the Yugoslavian state. The expulsions of German population occurred also in Romania (250,000), even though they lacked the international approval.[677] In Hungary, the Provisional Government asked the Allied Control Commission for Hungary to approve of deportation of 200,000 to 300,000 Germans already in the spring of 1945 in connection with the proposed land reform. Following the Potsdam decision, 150,000 Hungarian Germans were transferred to the American zone in 1946 (starting in December 1945 with Germans from Tolna and Budapest)[678] and a year later, another 50,000 to the Soviet occupational zone in Germany. At the same time, transfers (or possibly evictions, expulsions, exchanges and replacements) of other nationalities – Polish, Ukrainian, Hungarian, Slovak or Italian – continued in connection with the territorial changes, Paris Peace conference of 1946 or even bilateral treaties.[679] Even the Western Europe (the Netherlands, Denmark) witnessed resettlements of the German population, though on a considerably smaller scale corresponding proportionally to the less numerous minorities. Other mass migrations of the German population amounting to approximately 800,000 people followed immediately after the war from the Soviet occupation zone to the West.[680]

The conduct of the Czechoslovak authorities, especially from the beginning of the organised transfer in January 1946, respected the decisions of the Allied Control Council for Germany and was in most cases in compliance with the international conditions for the implementation of transfer. This was confirmed by regular reports of the British diplomats who were especially concerned with this problem; the British consul Bamborough, for example, was sent to Karlovy Vary to report on the matter.[681] The transfer was organised using the limited resources of the time, the living conditions in the assembly camps were very harsh, especially in the winter of 1945/1946 and particularly for women and children, the food and clothes rations were inadequate, even though the Czechoslovak authorities used the material support of UNRRA for the transferees. Another problem was the separation of families in the course of the transfers.[682]

---

677 Marrus, *The Unwanted*, p. 329.
678 See report of Allied Control Commission, December 18, 1945 TNA London, FO 371, 55600, C 166. First estimates spoke about up to 500,000 of Hungarian Germans to be resettled.
679 Philipp Ther, "A Century of Forced Migration. The Origins and Consequences of 'Ethnic Cleansing'," in *Redrawing Nations: Ethnic Cleansing in East-Central Europe, 1944-1948*, ed. by Philipp Ther and Ana Siljak (Lanham, MD: Rowman & Littlefield Publishers, 2011), pp. 43-72.
680 Joseph B. Schechtman, *Postwar Populations Transfers in Europe 1945-1955* (Philadelphia: University of Pennsylvania Press, 1962), p. 299.
681 See P.Nichols'report of November 30, 1946, TNA London, FO 371, 56070, N 15858.
682 See e.g the Parliament Questions by MP Stokes October 30, 1946, TNA London, FO 371, 56070, N 14189.

4. CZECHOSLOVAK LEGISLATION CONCERNING MINORITIES 1945–1948

4.1 PRESIDENTIAL (SO-CALLED BENEŠ'S) DECREES

The Czechoslovak legislation concerning minorities is closely connected with the problem of the so-called Beneš's decrees or more precisely presidential decrees. Presidential decrees were first adopted by the Czechoslovak Government in exile, from 1940 to Mach 1945. They dealt mainly with the Czechoslovak Provisional State Apparatus in exile and with its preparations for the post-war re-establishment of Czechoslovakia.[683] From April 1945 they were drawn up by the relevant ministries and then debated and approved by the first post-war Government of the National Front, before being submitted to the President of the Republic for signature. These decrees were primarily instruments for carrying into effect the Governmental Programme announced on 5 April 1945 (the so-called Košice Governmental Programme).[684] This Programme promulgated profound changes in the Czechoslovak political, social and economic system, described as a "national and democratic revolution." Far reaching nationalization of industry, land reform, and confiscation of property of war criminals, home traitors, and also of Germans and Hungarians were proposed. The presidential decrees thus mainly symbolized "revolutionary changes."[685] Czechoslovakia was also re-established as a national state of Czechs and Slovaks, i.e. Slavonic nations, and changes in position of non-Slavonic minorities were therefore inevitable.

The draft of the Košice Programme had been prepared by the Communist Party, and the Communists reserved a key position in the new government for themselves. Zdeněk Fierlinger, left wing oriented social democrat and ardent collaborator with Soviets, became the Prime Minister. The main areas affected by the Governmental Programme implemented by the Presidential Decrees covered the changes in the Czech-Slovak relationship, the question of German and Hungarian minorities (primarily the confiscation of their property and deprivation of Czechoslovak state citizenship), the introduction of a new

---

683 Kuklík, *Czech law in historical contexts*, pp. 131–132.
684 Ibid., p. 140.
685 In more details see Vladimir Gsovski and Kazimierz Grzybowski, eds., *Government Law and Courts in the Soviet Union and Eastern Europe*, vol. 1 (New York: Atlantic Books; F.A. Praeger, 1959), pp. 228–229.

type of public administration in the form of so-called "national committees," the nationalization of major types of industry or banks, and the punishment of war criminals and traitors (retribution). In all of these areas, the Presidential Decrees brought in fundamental changes to the pre-Munich Czechoslovak legal order and can be regarded as the beginning of political, legal and social changes which resulted in the Communist takeover in February 1948.

The presidential decrees at first dealt with the fate of the property of persons of German and Hungarian nationality. So-called enemy property was "frozen" and put under the custody of the so-called national administration on the bases of presidential decree No. 5/ 1945 Sb. on the invalidity of certain property transactions at the time of loss of freedom (bases for the so-called restitutions) and on the national administration of the property assets of Germans, Hungarians, traitors and other collaborators from 19 May 1945.[686] Later the property assets were either confiscated, nationalized, or returned to the original owners (in case the property was confiscated because of political, national or racial persecution during the war). In all relevant decrees No. 5/1945 Sb. on national administration, No.12/1945Sb. on the confiscation of land property and No.108/1945 Sb. on (general) confiscation of enemy property and Funds of national renewal, the enemy property was defined as a property of German Empire, Hungarian State, Nazi Party and German (or Hungarian) legal persons, individuals of German (or Hungarian) nationality and those individuals of Czech or Slovak nationality, who were sentenced by people's courts as war criminals, traitors or collaborators. The measures taken against enemy property in the states previously occupied by Germany were linked to the principle of restitution of property appropriated by German occupying administrations during World War II and also with the question of reparations. It was not an isolated Czechoslovak case and it is in most of its aspects comparable with other European states.

Presidential decrees on national administration and confiscation of enemy property were related to the formulation of the relevant passages of the decrees on nationalization of industry, banks and private insurance companies (i.e. decrees No. 100–103/1945 Sb.).[687] Property that had already been nationalised was not confiscated. In the decrees on nationalization the definition of persons with no claim to compensation for nationalised property was the same as in decrees on confiscation or on national administration. There is also the explicit linkage between the questions of compensation for confiscation and nationalisation and enemy property in what are known

---

686 Beneš and Kural, *Facing history*, document no. 11.

687 Samuel L. Sharp, *Nationalization of key industries in eastern Europe* (Washington, DC: Foundation for Foreign Affairs, 1946), pamphlet no. 1, see especially Appendix Containing the Nationalization Decrees, pp. 13–21; see also Jan M. Michal, "Postwar economic development," in Mamatey and Luža, *A History of the Czechoslovak Republic 1918–1948*, pp. 438–442.

as the "compensation negotiations" held by the Czechoslovak Republic with such countries as the USA, Great Britain, France, the Netherlands or Switzerland.[688]

It is also impossible to ignore the fact that confiscation of property of German and Hungarian legal entities and natural persons was linked to Czechoslovak reparation demands for damages caused by the war and German occupation. The Great Powers asked all states occupied by Germany to give their preliminary estimate of damages by October 1945. As a result Czechoslovakia established a claim for 11,583.5 million USD (1938 value) at the Paris Reparations Conference.[689] The overall amount of Czechoslovak claims for reparation was later set at 19,471.6 million USD, regardless of any eventual further claims against Germany, for example claims relating to Munich. However Czechoslovakia was actually allocated only a minor part of the claimed amount by the Inter-Allied Reparations Agency and in direct restitution of Czechoslovak property.

The expulsion and resettlement of the Sudeten Germans was also used for radical land reform and redistribution of land. According to the presidential decree No. 12/ 1945 Sb. agricultural property was confiscated immediately and without any compensation.[690] The confiscated land vacated by the expellees was used for resettlement of the border regions by "Slavonic" (mainly Czech and Slovak) claimants of small and medium-sized farms directed by special Office for internal settlement.[691] During the first stage of the land reform also medium-sized agricultural farms of Czech and Slovak owners, who were justifiably, or sometimes mistakenly, accused of collaboration with Germans, were confiscated. The whole process of confiscation and resettlement was under the auspices of the Ministry of Agriculture and the local and regional national committees and it gradually changed the demographical situation in borderland of the Czech lands. Between 1945 and 1947 almost 1,400,000 hectares of agricultural land and 1,000,000 hectares of forests were confiscated. Until 1947 at least 150,000 new farmers with claims of 1,200,000 hectares settled in the borderland.[692]

688 Jan Kuklík, "Interference with proprietary rights between 1945 and 1948 and their reflection in so-called 'indemnity agreements' and in privatization and 'restitution' legislation after 1989," trans. Renata Hrubá, in *Czech law between europeanization and globalization: New phenomena in law at the beginning of 21st century*, ed. by Michal Tomášek (Prague: Karolinum Press, 2010), pp. 40–44.

689 In more details Jan Kuklík, *Mýty a realita takzvaných Benešových dekretů: Dekrety prezidenta republiky 1940-1945* (Prague: Linde, 2002), pp. 320–324.

690 For its text in English see Beneš and Kural, *Facing history*, document no. 13.

691 Alice Teichová, *The Czechoslovak Economy 1918-1980* (London: Routledge, 1988), pp. 96–97.

692 Tomáš Staněk, *Odsun Němců z Československa, 1945-1947* (Prague: Academia; Naše vojsko, 1991), p. 346.

For the definition of persons to be affected by the transfer the key measure was the Constitutional Decree No. 33/1945 Sb. from 2 August 1945 Sb."on the Czechoslovak state citizenship of persons of German and Hungarian nationality." The decree was prepared already in July but was signed by Beneš only after the Great Powers reached their agreement on the transfer of Germans at Potsdam.[693]

The decree on Czechoslovak state citizenship was under preparation by the Czechoslovak Government in exile and its successive versions developed in equivalence with the development of the above mentioned international negotiations on the transfer of the German and Hungarian minorities. The first proposals were thus based on the idea of linking forfeit of Czechoslovak state citizenship to such categories of German population as active Nazis or representatives of the occupation apparatus.[694] Some Czechoslovak politicians were more radical and demanded that the broadest possible group of the German minority should lose citizenship on the grounds of acceptance of the citizenship of enemy states and only anti-Nazis or active members of the resistance should retain the Czechoslovak state citizenship.[695] The preparations made in London as well as the comments of the home resistance and the regulations concerning the state citizenship issued from Munich until the end of the war were taken into account by the post-war government. The final version of the Constitutional Decree on the Czechoslovak state citizenship was debated by the Government between June and July 1945.

On 11 June 1945, i.e. before the final signature of the decree, the Government notified land and district national committees that "provisional certificates of state citizenship" could be issued. The rulings of the national committees were supposed to be based mainly on the so-called national and state reliability and on the examination of documents showing the domicile in the territory of Czechoslovakia obtained in the pre-Munich period, but not more than 10 years old.[696]

The constitutional decree on the state citizenship was based on the theory that from the point of view of the Czechoslovak law persons of German and Hungarian nationality had continued to hold Czechoslovak citizenship throughout the war years and this citizenship was only withdrawn by the decree itself. From the point of view of the Czechoslovak law the people in question therefore became aliens on the territory of Czechoslovakia on the date the constitutional decree was put into effect. The decree did not

---

693 For its text in English see Beneš and Kural, *Facing history*, document no. 17.
694 Karel Jech, ed., *Die Deutschen und Magyaren in den Dekreten des Präsidenten der Republik* (Brno: Doplněk, 2003), p. 530ff.
695 Kuklík, "Transfer or expulsion?," pp. 138–139; for documents see Vondrová, *Češi a sudetoněmecká otázka*, document no. 121–124.
696 Kuklík, *Mýty a realita takzvaných Benešových dekretů*, p. 282.

therefore affect German citizens who had possessed Reich German citizenship before Munich and in these cases the question was not one of transfer, but of repatriation. The "Sudeten Germans," who lost the citizenship, could be included in transfer to Allied occupation zones in Germany or Austria as persons who had forfeited Czechoslovak citizenship. While the Czechoslovak law recognised neither post-Munich legal changes nor the legal state established after 15 March 1939, it still had to derive consequences from the fact that the majority of Czechoslovak citizens of German and Hungarian nationality had actually become citizens of enemy states after Munich. The decree was based on the principle that state citizenship should be withdrawn from persons who after Munich or after 15 March 1939 became state citizens of the German Reich or Hungary, i.e. states with which Czechoslovakia was in a state of war.

On the other hand, from the very beginning of discussions on the decree there had been emphasis on the need to define the category of persons to which the provisions on loss of citizenship would not apply, especially those citizens who had remained loyal to the Czechoslovak state or in some cases fought for its liberation. The constitutional decree therefore defined the category of persons that would retain Czechoslovak citizenship and the category of persons who could reapply for Czechoslovak citizenship. Those persons who had shown that they remained loyal to Czechoslovakia would not forfeit citizenship. According to guidelines for the implementation of the decree issued by the Ministry of the Interior[697] this category covered, for example, a person who:

"1. had been, for political or racial reasons, imprisoned in a concentration camp or prison," or "had been otherwise persecuted by the Nazis for loyalty to the republic and loyalty to the Czech or Slovak people";

2. "had actively participated in struggles against Nazism and for the Czechoslovak Republic";

3. "had served in Czechoslovak or Allied units or in the home resistance" and 4. had not been a member of the SS, SA, SDP, NSDAP or other Nazi organisations. Emigration for racial or political reasons and subsequent political activity abroad, financing of the resistance and suchlike was also regarded as proof of loyalty to the Czechoslovak state. State citizenship was also to be retained by persons whose family members had been murdered for their anti-fascist activity or had died in concentration camps. As early as 13 November 1945, however, the Ministry of the Interior issued an executive order further stipulating that in considering the terms anti-Nazi or anti-fascist for the retention of state citizenship, account should be taken of "the whole thinking and behaviour of an applicant throughout his life, i.e. both in the

697 Ibid., pp. 283–287.

pre-Munich period and in the time of increased threat to the republic." Those Germans and Hungarians, "who at the time of increased threat to the republic identified themselves as Czechs or Slovaks in official declarations" did not forfeit citizenship.[698] For this reason we cannot speak of a blanket application of the principle of collective guilt, especially not in relation to this key decree although it is true that in the language of the period the concept of "punishing" the German minority that "betrayed the Czechoslovak state" or the using of transfer instead of criminal punishment in case of less serious crimes and misdemeanours appear frequently. In addition to legal concept and ideological and political justification one should also take into account the considerations of practical feasibility and speed of decision-making that were crucial in the situation immediately after the war.

In addition to the group of persons who retained state citizenship *ex lege*, there was another group of persons who could apply for the restoration of citizenship within a period of 6 months. This was a second category of German "anti-Nazis and anti-fascists," with individual cases to be determined on the basis of the judgment of special committees.[699] The details were set down in implementation orders and instructions of the Ministry of the Interior for land and district national committees.[700] Applications for the restoration of citizenship could not be accepted, however, "if the applicant has violated the obligations of a Czechoslovak state citizen." The latter category included people who had been members of the legislative body of an enemy state, its judges or senior state officials, army officers, members of Nazi parties or organisations, leading economic agents of German firms or members of the Sudeten deutschen Freikorps. Nor could state citizenship be restored to persons who had publicly expressed hostility to the Czechoslovak state, or were holders of honorary ranks or decorations "conferred by an enemy state or enemy institution" or who had "in any way collaborated with the enemy" or "had for themselves or persons close to them economically or financially exploited the conditions created by the occupation of the Czechoslovak territory by an enemy power." For the purposes of the decree, married women and under-aged children were to be assessed individually, but the decree stated that the applications for restoration of Czechoslovak state citizenship from the wives and under-aged children of Czechoslovak state citizens should be "judged generously," and until their applications had been processed they should be regarded as Czechoslovak state citizens. In practice serious problems soon appeared particularly in the case of mixed marriages and the Ministry of

---

698 Ibid.
699 David Kovařík, "Mezi mlýnskými kameny: Němečtí antifašisté v Československu v roce 1945," *Dějiny a současnost* 29, no. 4 (2007): pp. 41–43
700 Kuklík, *Mýty a realita takzvaných Benešových dekretů*, pp. 285–287.

the Interior therefore as early as 13 November 1945 issued instructions to the effect that a Czech woman should not lose Czech state citizenship simply because her husband had German nationality or citizenship; conversely the applications of German wives of Czech citizens should be settled quickly, and national committees should immediately issue them with certificates stating that until settlement of the application they were to be regarded Czechoslovak state citizens.

The period for the submission of applications to the district national committee for the restoration of Czechoslovak citizenship was set from 10 August 1945 to 19 February 1946. The district national committee was supposed to conduct the appropriate investigation. Applications were regarded as applications for the grant of Czechoslovak state citizenship and until they had been processed the applicant was naturally not regarded as a Czechoslovak citizen. The burden of proof was on the applicant. Recommended applications were forwarded to the Land National Committee or Slovak National Council for decision. Persons residing abroad had to submit their applications through Czechoslovak embassies.

The decree also imposed forfeit of Czechoslovak citizenship on Czechs, Slovaks and members of other Slav nations who at the time of increased threat to the republic had applied for the grant of German or Hungarian state citizenship without having been forced to do so by pressure or special circumstances.[701] On the other hand, the national committees were supposed to take into account the "methods and opinions of the occupiers," which often affected even Czechs and Slovaks who had not intended to become Germans or Hungarians voluntarily, or children, for example, who had no voice in the matter. Some of the cases were taken right up to the Supreme Administrative court, which issued some important rulings on the question.[702]

The key term for the application of the decrees concerning German property and state citizenship was German "nationality" for physical persons. The decrees did not define this term in detail, and the preamble to the constitutional decree on state citizenship stated that this was deliberate, since it was to be covered by "more flexible instructions, which must for example take account of the special Slovak problems" for Hungarian nationality.[703] For this reason the Ministry of the Interior in its executive instructions to the Land and District Committees on 24 August 1945 stipulated that for determining nationality it was necessary to look not just at data from the "census" of 1930, but also at police declarations, school applications, declarations for

701 Ibid.
702 Vladimír Mikule, "Die Dekrete des Praesidenten der Republik zur Stellung der Deutschen und ihre heutige rechtliche Bedeutung," in *Die Deutschen und Magyaren in den Dekreten des Präsidenten der Republik*, ed. by Karel Jech (Brno: Doplněk, 2003), pp. 186–189.
703 Ibid., document no. 8.10, pp. 344–345.

rations purposes, the origin of parents, school education and language used in private life. Special attention should then be devoted to participation in public life, specifically membership of political parties, associations, organisations and national churches. In judging an individual case, moreover, the national committee should not base its decision only on one of the types of evidence mentioned, but should assess them in their mutual connections. National committees were instructed to exercise particular caution in relation to the results of "the census in what was known as the Sudeten districts of 17 May 1939."

The Government Programme of 1945 provided also for the punishment of Nazi war criminals and collaborators with the representatives of Nazi occupation (so-called retribution).[704] There were three main presidential decrees on retribution – the Decree on Extraordinary People's Courts and Punishment of War Criminals, Traitors and Collaborators, the Decree on the Establishment of the National Court, and the Decree on Punishment of Petty Collaboration (i.e. on the punishment of certain transgressions against national honour).[705]

The crimes committed by Nazis were in most cases connected with the prosecution of officials of Nazi political organizations (like NSDAP and the Sudeten German Party) and members of the police or military elements of the occupational regime. Prosecution of Nazi war criminals was in compliance with the Charter for the International Military Tribunal in Nuremberg agreed to in August 1945.[706] Most of the crimes were punishable in accordance with the Czechoslovak interwar legislation (new crimes like denunciation, membership in Nazi organizations or participation in persecutions were also introduced) but the presidential decrees set more severe punishments, including the death penalty and forced labour in special camps; they established special courts with a fast-track procedure and limits on the rights of the accused. On the other hand, this was seen as an extraordinary measure for a limited period of time and for cases where facts could be proven without protracted proceedings[707] People's Courts were extraordinary courts presided over by a professional judge and consisted of lay judges chosen usually from credible members of the domestic resistance movement. The most important case heard by Czechoslovak People's Courts under the category of Nazi crimes was against K. H. Frank, responsible for the disintegration of Czechoslovakia and for a wide range of Nazi persecutions in the Protectorate, including the

704 See recently Benjamin Frommer, *National Cleansing: Retribution against Nazi Collaborators in Postwar Czechoslovakia* (Cambridge: Cambridge University Press, 2005), especially p. 63ff.
705 For their English translation see Ibid., appendix 1–3, pp. 348–373.
706 Arieh J. Kochavi, *Prelude to Nuremberg: Allied War Crimes Policy and the Question of Punishment* (Chapel Hill: University of North Carolina Press, 1998), pp. 224–226.
707 See also Kuklík, *Czech law in historical contexts*, pp. 141–143.

Lidice massacre. There were similar cases brought against members of the Gestapo or the Nazi Deputy Mayor of Prague, J. Pfitzner, which usually ended up with death penalties.

The punishments were severe especially in the initial phase of the retribution process and became milder in mid-1946, when lower officials were sometimes acquitted, and punishment was in many cases reversed to the transfer of these persons to the occupation zones in Germany, or convicted people were released earlier from jail and sent to Germany. There is a paradox that retribution in later stages was more severe regarding Czechs than Germans. Czechs were usually accused of various forms of collaboration, including political and economic help rendered to the occupation forces or profiting from the persecution of Jewish or Czech compatriots. There were special regulations regarding informants and denunciators.

There were also other presidential decrees connected with the legal position of the German minority. Decree No. 71/ 1945 Sb. introduced the general duty to work for those Germans, who were eligible for transfer and lost Czechoslovak state citizenship until the resettlement actually happened. The use of German working force was regarded as a tool to redress the war damages. However the general duty to work was enacted for all inhabitants of Czechoslovakia. Decrees No. 122–123/1945 Sb. closed down German university in Prague and German Technical Universities in Prague and Brno and it could be regarded as Czechoslovak response to the closing down of Czech universities in 1939 and Nazification of German academia after 1938.[708]

Many of the terms used in the presidential decrees (e.g. "enemies," "persons unreliable in relation to the state," "war criminals" or "traitors") and their implementation in practice reflected the inflamed national passions of the immediate post-war period; in many cases the decrees were abused and used in cases where they should never have been applied. Particularly in the immediate aftermath of the war there were cases of violence and homicides that can in no way be legally justified, and also seizures of property outside any framework of law at all. Some anti-German measures, including expulsion, were applied also to German speaking Jews and such policies were only slowly and gradually redressed.[709] As early as 8 June 1945 the Government published a proclamation on categories of persons to be exempted from measures against the Germans. The exceptions included: "1. Those who have returned from concentration camps and prisons if they had been placed there as a result of political or racial oppression, 2. Those who can be proven to have actively supported the Czechoslovak nation in the fight against Nazism, 3. Employees who are unconditionally necessary for maintaining the

---

708 Kuklík, *Mýty a realita takzvaných Benešových dekretů*, pp. 349–352.
709 See recently Láníček, *Czechs, Slovaks and the Jews*, esp. chap. 4.

operation of a factory." The state organs had an obligation "to provide these persons with personal protection and protection of their property."[710]

As we already mentioned, the period of 1945–1948 represents a tragic end to the coexistence between Czechoslovakia and its German minority population, which was fatally broken by Hitler already at the time of Munich. Expulsions and transfers of German population could be thus regarded, as Detlef Brandes put it, "delayed Czech alternative to the Dictate of Munich."[711]

4.2 HUNGARIAN MINORITY 1945–1948

Unlike the German population, with respect to which the Czechoslovak Government quite successfully managed to agree on conditions of its transfer to the Allied Zones in Germany, persons of Hungarian origin were not subject to a similar solution. On 27 February 1946, Czechoslovakia and Hungary signed an agreement on the exchange of population (published as No. 145/1946 Sb. to take effect on 15 May 1946); the agreement was to apply to Hungarians that had lost their Czechoslovak citizenship under Constitutional Decree No. 33/1945 Sb. The principle of transfer was rejected at the Peace Conference held in Paris in July and August of 1946.[712] The Czechoslovak Government reserved its right to relocate the population above the mutually agreed number with reference to Article VIII of the Agreement to the Hungarian territory; the Article allowed for the resettlement of those persons who had committed a crime under the Retribution Regulation of the Slovak National Council No. 33 of 15 May 1945. However, such possibility was limited as to the number of potentially relocated people.

Due to the fact that the Agreement affected only about 71,000 Slovaks and 89,000 individuals of Hungarian nationality[713], other modes of solving the minority issue were applied. The so-called *reslovakisation* enabled Hungarians who were, or discovered they were, of Slovak origin to apply for Slovak nationality.[714] If their application was decided affirmatively (their loyalty to

---

710 Kuklík, *Mýty a realita takzvaných Benešových dekretů*, p. 290

711 Detlef Brandes, "A müncheni diktátum egy megkésett cseh alternatívája," *Történelmi szemle* 38, no. 2–3 (1996): p. 228ff.

712 *Foreign relations of the United States. 1946, Paris Peace Conference: Documents*, vol. 4 (Washington, DC: US Gov. Print. Off., 1970), p. 727ff.

713 Árpád Popély, "Case studies 1944–1948: Czechoslovakia," in *Minority Hungarian Communities in the Twentieth Century*, ed. by Nándor Bárdi, Csilla Fedinec and László Szarka, trans. Brian McLean (Boulder, CO: Social Science Monogaphs; Highland Lakes, NJ: Atlantic Research and Publications, 2011), pp. 302 and 303; Štefan Šutaj, "Slovakia and Hungarian minority between 1945 and 1948," in *Key issues of Slovak and Hungarian History: A view of Slovak Historians* (Prešov: Universum, 2011), p. 227ff.

714 Šutaj, "Slovakia and Hungarian minority," p. 227ff.

the Czechoslovak State was considered primarily) these persons were not subject to deprivation of citizenship and to confiscation of property. Such policy resulted in the fact that the number of those claiming their Hungarian origin in Czechoslovakia temporarily (until the beginning of the 1950s) went down one third compared to the pre-WWII situation. The Government debated *reslovakisation* (combined with internal relocations within Slovakia) in June and August of 1946. The policy was prepared and implemented by the Ministry of the Interior in agreement with the Ministry of Foreign Affairs, the Interior Ministry Representative for Slovakia and the Office for internal settlement in Bratislava. Between 1946 and 1949 special Commission on Reslovakisation admitted almost 360,000 declarations.[715]

The legal status of the Hungarian minority was primarily settled by the Slovak National Council (SNC) and by those presidential decrees, which were valid for the whole territory of Czechoslovakia. Under legislation adopted by the Slovak National Council the property issues of Hungarian population were primarily treated. On 27 February 1945, the Council Presidium issued a Regulation for confiscation and swift redistribution of agricultural property of Germans, Hungarians, as well as traitors and enemies of the Slovak people (No. 4/1945 Sb. SNC). Slovakia, several months before the adoption of a proposed national law, applied its local law which was even retroactively amended as of 1 March 1945 by Regulation SNC No. 104/1945 Sb. of 23 August 1945.[716] According to this regulation agricultural property was confiscated immediately and without any compensation. Under this regulation Hungarians were divided into two groups: (a) those having Czechoslovak citizenship before the 1 November 1938 (i.e. one day before the First Vienna Arbitration Award); confiscation applied only to their property exceeding 50 hectares of land; and (b) persons without Czechoslovak citizenship who had arrived in the territory of Slovakia as part of the occupation administration; confiscation applied to all their property without any exception. Confiscated agricultural property (land) was under administration of the Slovak Agricultural Fund; it was included in the land reform and as such distributed among agricultural labourers, workers and small farmers. Preference was given to persons that had participated in the "National Liberation Movement," particularly soldiers and partisans (resistance fighters). An amendment of the Regulation from August 1945 expanded the scope of persons to be subject to confiscation, thus including persons politically unreliable in the meaning of SNC Regulation No. 50/1945 Sb. Citizenship of persons of Hungarian nationality was

---

715   Václav Průcha et al., *Hospodářské a sociální dějiny Československa 1918–1992*, vol. 2 (Brno: Doplněk, 2009), p. 136.

716   For details see Jozef Beňa, *Vývoj slovenského právneho poriadku* (Banská Bystrica: Iris, 2001), pp. 175-180.

governed by the above mentioned Constitutional Decree No. 33/1945. However, agricultural property of persons of Hungarian nationality who decided to accept a job offer in the Czech lands was not subject to confiscation and their estate was temporarily managed by administrators under SNC Regulation No. 50/1945 Sb.

Between 1945 and 1948 considerable numbers of Hungarians, who were not included in the exchange of population with Hungary, transferred or deprived of citizenship, and whose immovable property was subject to forced administration, arrived in the Czech lands. These people were involved in internal relocation or so-called diffusion and were supposed to be offered jobs in the Czech lands.[717]

In Slovakia, the Hungarian population was obliged to labour service under Presidential Decree No. 88/1945 Sb. governing the general duty to work. According to SNC Regulation No. 105/1945 Sb. SNC of 23 August 1945 establishing labour camps, Hungarians could be subject to forced labour in those camps if they failed to start, or stopped performing, their assigned work under the general labour service ordered by the Presidential Decree.[718] The Slovak National Council passed Implementing Regulation of the SNC Board No. 37/1946 Sb. (25 February 1946) governing the employment of Hungarians and Germans who lost their Czechoslovak state citizenship under Presidential Decree No. 33/1945 Sb. The main purpose of this regulation was to ensure that Hungarians deprived of their Czechoslovak citizenship would not be covered by legislation governing employment of aliens; on the contrary, they were subject to Decree No. 88/1945 Sb. This is how the legal position of Hungarians was different from that of the German population. It was also to ease their difficult situation until a decision on their citizenship was made. Within the general duty to work Slovak Hungarians were offered jobs in the Czech lands from the autumn of 1945, in particular in the borderlands. The objective was to supply a labour force in agricultural districts in regions from which Germans had been transferred or were preparing for transfer. Until the end of 1945 the procedure affected several thousands of Hungarians.[719]

After the above-mentioned Agreement on the exchange of population with Hungary came into effect and it became quite clear that a transfer of Hungarians would hardly be enforced, the Czechoslovak Government decided to relocate Slovak Hungarians to the Czech lands for work more extensively. This policy was considered by the Government on 16 July 1946, and later in

---

717   In more details Jan Kuklík, "Hungarian Population in the Czech Lands Between 1945 and 1949," *Acta Humana* 4 (2015).

718   Vladimír Varinský, "Nútené práce na Slovensku v rokoch 1945-1948," *Soudobé dějiny* 1, no. 6 (1994): pp. 724-736.

719   Helena Nosková, „Maďaři v České republice ve 20. a 21. století," in *Kdo jsem a kam patřím?* ed. by Dana Bittnerová and Mirjam Moravcová (Prague: Sofis, 2005), p. 104ff.

August in the light of news from the Paris Peace Conference. Relocating for the purposes of work in the Czech lands was closely linked to the above mentioned policy of *reslovakisation*, which was further acknowledged during Government meetings at the beginning of 1947 and the relevant directions were passed on 27 February 1947 (with stylistic modifications made in March). The whole initiative was implemented in the form of recruitment (on a voluntary basis), as a temporary measure (initially for one year) and was managed by the Government Representative for the recruitment of labour in cooperation with the Ministry of Social Affairs, the Board of Representatives of the Slovak National Council and the Settlement Office in Bratislava.

On 26 February 1947 the Government approved a resolution on the work of Hungarians in the Czech lands; it emphasised that further legislative measures should be taken, for example with respect to compensation for property, and acknowledged the voluntary basis of the action. However, the period of work of Hungarians was intended to be extended by 6 months. On 17 March 1945, the Government, relying on the report of its representative Okáli, confirmed the link between difficult talks with Hungary on the exchange of population on the one hand, and "work mobilisation" of Hungarians suitable for reslovakisation or not included in the exchange on the other.

A comprehensive report of the Deputy Prime Minister V. Široký for Rudolf Slánský of 3 February 1949 states that 44,000 Hungarians from 17 districts and 393 municipalities primarily from Southern Slovakia[720] (in reality it was an even higher number – up to 60,000) were relocated to the Czech lands for work between 1946 and 1948.[721] This measure was related to Presidential Decree No. 27/1945 of 17 July 1945 on the uniform governance of internal settlement. Settlement procedures in the country were governed by the Central Commission headed by the Minister of the Interior. Hungarians from Slovakia headed primarily to the borderlands. Most of them settled in the regions of Cheb, Sokolov, Loket; several hundreds of Hungarians were employed also at farms in the Czech inland regions. In the beginning of 1948 the total number of economic entities employing Hungarians reached 6,843.

Under Decree No. 88/1945 Sb. the position of Hungarians as employees was to be identical with that of persons of Czech or Slovak origin who were subject to labour service. However, the reality was often different. H. Nosková describes difficulties in the organisation of recruitment itself, the subsequent journey and assignment to work on site.[722] Hungarians were also not equipped with adequate clothing and shoes. However, they were provided

---

720   Ibid.; see also Šutaj, "Slovakia and Hungarian minority," p. 227ff.
721   Jan Křen, Dušan Kováč and Hans Lemberg, eds., *V rozdelenej Európe: Česi, Slováci, Nemci a ich štáty v rokoch 1948–1989* (Bratislava: Academic Electronic Press, 1998), p. 70.
722   Nosková, "Maďaři v České republice ve 20. a 21. století," pp. 104–109.

with housing and they received wages: from CZK 96 up to CZK 250 for one 8-hour working day depending on the type of work. Complaints of Hungarian labourers against treatment by their employers due to their Hungarian origin, against insufficient nutrition and clothing, etc., were considered by the Czechoslovak authorities more seriously particularly from the beginning of 1948 in order to keep as many Hungarians as workers in the Czech lands as possible. The biggest disappointment on the part of Hungarians was the fact that they were not released after the expiry of one year of employment in Bohemia and sent back to Slovakia, but their employment was extended.

The situation of the Hungarian population, including those Hungarians relocated to work in the Czech lands, significantly changed after February 1948. The Government Resolution of 19 March 1948 endorsed further extension of the stay of Hungarian workers in the Czech lands, which the Ministry of Agriculture supported by assigning parts of land, if possible. On the other hand, Slovak authorities completed the process of confiscation of Hungarian agricultural estates under Regulation No. 104/1945 Zb.n. SNC, and the confiscated property was assigned to its administrators that had managed the individual estates until then.

4.3 OTHER MINORITIES IN CZECHOSLOVAKIA BETWEEN 1945–1948

As we have already suggested, post-war Czechoslovakia was being developed as a nation state of Czechs and Slovaks with a strong Slavic orientation, and as such it was particularly preoccupied with the German and Hungarian minorities. However, there were other ethnic and language groups as well. Attitudes towards such groups varied, often mirroring the relations with the neighbouring countries and a complicated historical development.

Post-war Czechoslovakia had initially a very negative attitude even towards the Polish (Slavic) minority, due to the border dispute surrounding the Teschen (Cieszyn) region. For a long time Poland refused to give up its territorial gains of 1938 and the situation was exacerbated by the disputes surrounding the new Polish-German border which partly collided with the Czechoslovak territorial claims.[723] Until February 1948 these disputes with the neighbouring country and the attitudes towards the Polish minority tended to be misused in political skirmishes. Certain parties even suggested expulsion of the Poles from Czechoslovakia or forced assimilation. However, unlike the German or Hungarian minority the Poles had, at that time, access

723 Karel Kaplan, *Československo v poválečné Evropě* (Prague: Karolinum Press, 2004), pp. 68–98; Siwek, Zahradnik and Szymeczek, *Polská národní menšina v Československu 1945–1954*, p. 25ff.

to their own schools, cultural and common-interest organisations, and they essentially enjoyed equal civil rights.[724]

In 1947 the local Poles were very self-confident in the Teschen (Cieszyn) region, counting on a change of the borders; by contrast, the local Czechs were apprehensive about their future and many of them decided to leave. The Treaty of Friendship and Mutual Assistance between Poland and Czechoslovakia of 10 March 1947 relaxed the tensions to a certain extent. In its appended protocol the contracting parties undertook to protect the Polish and Czech minorities in accordance with the law and the principle of mutuality. This certainly contributed to better national, political, cultural and economic development. Nevertheless, even after the conclusion of the treaty many Poles in the Teschen (Cieszyn) region hoped for a change of the borders. In disputes with Czechoslovak authorities (e.g., the housing or trade licensing offices) the dissatisfied Poles from the Teschen (Cieszyn) region would apply to the Polish Embassy as the arbitrator. The Polish nationalists had contacts in the Katowice radio, and sought to alarm the Teschen (Cieszyn) population by announcements about the annexation of the region to Poland. The relations between Czechoslovakia and Poland fully improved only after the introduction of Communist regime in both countries, as Moscow would not tolerate minority conflicts between the countries of the bloc.[725]

The Ruthenians (Rusyns) and Ukrainians were specifically affected by the historical development. After Sub-Carpathian Ruthenia was annexed by the Soviet Union, only few Ruthenians and Ukrainians remained in Czechoslovakia; moreover, a treaty with the USSR envisaged resettlement in the Soviet Union. Initially, some plans suggested incorporation of eastern Slovakia with Rusyn / Ukrainian population into Soviet Ukraine, or an organised resettlement of the whole minority in the USSR. However, the incorporation plans were resisted even by the minority members, in particular the influential Greek Catholic clergy.[726]

The remaining Ruthenians were probably the most popular minority of all minorities in Czechoslovakia. On 1 March 1945 the Ukrainian National Council of Prjaševščiny (UNRP) was established to represent the minority

724 Stanisław Zahradnik, "Nástin historického vývoje," in *Polská národní menšina na Těšínsku v České republice (1920–1995)*, ed. by Karol D. Kadłubiec (Ostrava: Filozofická fakulta Ostravské univerzity, 1997), p. 28; Jan Šindelka, *Národnostní politika v ČSSR* (Prague: Orbis, 1975), pp. 118–119.

725 See for example Stanisław Zahradnik, "Polský kulturně osvětový svaz – Polski Związek Kulturalno-Oświatowy 1947–1989," *Slezský sborník = Acta Silesiaca* 96, no. 1 (1998): pp. 44–52; Vilém Plaček, "Těšínsko po uzavření československo-polské smlouvy," *Slezský sborník = Acta Silesiaca* 65, no. 1 (1967): pp. 3–20.

726 Ivan Bajcura, *Ukrajinská otázka v ČSSR* (Košice: Vychodoslovenské vydavateľstvo, 1967), pp. 75–78, 89ff.; Šindelka, *Národnostní politika v ČSSR*, pp. 119–121; Michal Barnovský, "K otázke takzvaného ukrajinského buržoázneho nacionalizmu na Slovensku," *Historický časopis* 44, no. 1 (1996): pp. 65–67.

politically. While its status was legally rather unclear and provisional, it pursued ambitious objectives and tried to assume a similar role as the influential Slovak National Council. The Ruthenians / Ukrainians had representatives in all political bodies – the Provisional National Assembly, the Slovak National Council, district councils, etc. Nevertheless, the situation was far from satisfactory because this region had been the most severely affected by the war.

Although certain minorities had been subjected to the Nazi terror (e.g. the Jews), they were treated rather dismissively in the new state. While the inter-war Czechoslovakia recognized the existence of the Jewish (national) minority, after 1945 that was no longer the case.[727] Only about 55,000 Jews survived the Nazi persecution in Czechoslovakia, less than one seventh of the pre-war Jewish population. Immediately after the war the Jews were supported, but that changed later, as evidenced e.g. by the so-called Enrichment Act No. 134/1946 Sb. which significantly increased the inheritance tax, affecting primarily the Jews. After the Jews came back from concentration camps or elsewhere, their property was often never returned to them and anti-Semitism was gaining ground. Property restitution was a lengthy process which favoured municipalities claiming real property in their rebuilding efforts. Until the Communist takeover in February 1948 most property restitutions remained unresolved and after 1948 no larger property was returned.[728]

After the war, anti-Jewish sentiments were particularly widespread in Slovakia where the Jews were vetted over their reliability and accused of their pro-Hungarian attitudes. Such acts were often motivated by the desire to acquire or retain Jewish property. The restitution of Jewish property was widely opposed, and the anti-Semitic propaganda from the war had apparently taken root. Anti-Semitism was particularly strong in eastern Slovakia; however, the worst pogrom occurred in Topoľčany on 24 September 1945, causing injuries to 47 people. The police failed to intervene, the soldiers who had been summoned sided with the crowd, and local authorities later stated that the riot was caused by the Jews trying to enrich themselves. Hence, the state apparatus largely failed, which was a relatively frequent occurrence after the war.[729]

Besides the Jews, the Gypsies (Romanies) were severely affected by the war too. Most Romanies (and the Sinti) who had lived in the Czech lands died during the war, and the Slovak Romanies were badly hit too. The year 1945 was an important milestone for the Czechoslovak Romanies; the original population had been largely eliminated and the Romanies from poor and

---

727 Láníček, *Czechs, Slovaks and the Jews*, chap. 4.
728 Kuklík et al., *Jak odškodnit holocaust?*, pp. 152–194.
729 Ivan Kamenec, "Protižidovský pogrom v Topoľčanoch v septembri 1945," in *Acta Contemporanea* (Prague: Ústav pro soudobé dějiny AV ČR, 1998), pp. 80–94.

war-ravaged Slovakia started to migrate. This process has come to the fore-front of the problems surrounding Romanies in post-war Czechoslovakia, and has been apparent even after the split of Czechoslovakia. The constant migration from poverty-stricken, destitute gypsy villages in eastern Slovakia is often cited as the main cause of friction between Romanies and the rest of the population in Czech lands. The migration was intense; while immediately after the war the number of Romanies in Czech lands was estimated at one thousand, in 1947 the population of Romanies was reported to be 84,438 in Slovakia, and 16,752 in Czech lands.[730]

From the legal point of view, no significant changes were made compared to the First Czechoslovak Republic, and inter-war legislation as well as the laws from the time of the Habsburg Monarchy (which often tended to discriminate against Romanies) continued to be applied. Although Romanies were undoubtedly victims of Nazism, there was no willingness in post-war Czechoslovakia to improve their position and their situation sometimes even deteriorated in comparison with the First Republic. Act No 117/1927 Sb., continued to be applied, providing for the registration of Gypsies in 1947, reintroduction of gypsy ID cards, and the police supervision over their employment. In September 1945 an obligation to work (which was in place during the war) was re-introduced in Czechoslovakia. The situation in Slovakia was even worse. Immediately after the end of the war the authorities tried to regulate the unrestrained movement of Romanies, by seeking to impose a ban on nomadic life. Certain individuals were even placed in temporary labour camps.[731]

---

730 Eva Davidová, *Cesty Romů 1945–1990* (Olomouc: Vydavatelství Univerzity Palackého, 1995), pp. 9–10; Imrich Vašečka, "Migrácia Rómov z ČR a SR – príčiny a potreba intervencií," in *Menšiny a marginalizované skupiny v České republice*, ed. by Tomáš Sirovátka (Brno: Masarykova univerzita, Fakulta sociálních studií, Georgetown, 2002), p. 232; Tomáš Grulich and Tomáš Haišman, "Institucionální zájem o cikánské obyvatelstvo v Československu v letech 1945–1958," *Český lid* 73, no. 2 (1986): pp. 72–73.

731 Davidová, *Cesty Romů 1945–1990*, pp. 10, 13; Nina Pavelčíková, *Romové v českých zemích v letech 1945–1989* (Prague: Úřad dokumentace a vyšetřování zločinů komunismu PČR, 2004), pp. 27–31.

5. CZECHOSLOVAKIA AND ITS MINORITIES DURING THE ERA OF THE COMMUNIST REGIME 1948–1989

5.1 BEGINNINGS OF THE COMMUNIST REGIME 1948–1953

The establishment of the Communist regime in 1948 meant a radical shift in the history of Czechoslovakia which shall be examined rather thoroughly. In Czechoslovakia, the beginning of the Communist regime and integration into the united Soviet bloc was slower and more complicated than in other Eastern European countries. In most of these countries, the enforcement of pro-Soviet regimes was more or less clear since the arrival of Soviet armed forces at the end of World War II, because local (formerly small in numbers) communist parties could lean on the support of the constantly deployed Soviet military. However, in Czechoslovakia, democracy (although limited in some aspects) was re-established in 1945 and there had been long political conflicts about the next orientation of the country. It is necessary to say that the national or rather chauvinistic card was used in post war policies on a regular basis. The Communist party of Czechoslovakia promoted internationalism, and it even supported secessions of regions with minorities in the interwar period. On the contrary, in years 1945–1948 the party bore itself with often open anti-German nationalism, but strict anti-minority policy was also promoted by other permitted parties of the so-called National Front.[732]

In 1946 the Communists won the Parliamentary elections and formed a coalition government headed by Klement Gottwald, Chairman of the Communist Party.[733] After the 1946 elections the Constitutional National Assembly was convened, and its main task was to prepare a new constitution to secure the changes achieved in 1945–1946. At the same time the Czechoslovak Communists intensified their preparations for the seizure of all political power. Czechoslovakia was under the direct influence of the Soviet Union and Stalin's policies. The Czechoslovak Government was, for example, forced, under direct pressure from Stalin, to reject the reconstruction plan launched in June

---

732 See for example René Petráš, *Menšiny v komunistickém Československu* (Prague: Auditorium, 2007), pp. 84–116.

733 Communists won in the Czech lands, where their poll 40 per cent, in Slovakia Democratic party won and the Communists came the second. For the elections and their results see Oskar Krejčí, *History of Elections in Bohemia and Moravia* (New York: Columbia University Press, 1995), table 18a, and 18 b, pp. 196–197.

1947 by the US Secretary of State, George Marshall.[734] The new organization of Communist parties of the emerging Soviet Block, called the Communist Information Bureau,[735] advocated, as early as November 1947, the necessity of a Communist takeover to finish the initial stage of the confrontation with non-Communist parties.[736]

The struggle for power culminated in February 1948, when the governmental crisis led to the change of the whole political system. In the end President Beneš yielded to the Communist pressure and appointed a new government of the so-called "Reborn National Front," led by Klement Gottwald.[737] The situation in Czechoslovakia in 1948 therefore differs if compared with other states of the emerging Soviet Block, as the Communist Party seized power (mis)using the constitutional framework of the democratic Czechoslovakia. The Czechoslovak road to socialism, which was advocated at the beginning, was soon replaced by the Soviet style Stalinism. The regime soon became an open dictatorship characterized by political trials, harsh punishment of political opponents and the Church, the confiscation of property, further nationalization, and the introduction of the Soviet style of collective farms in the countryside. The regime was officially characterized by the Communists themselves as the "dictatorship of the proletariat." This period lasted from 1948 to 1953. In the beginning of the 1950s, political trials were used even against the leading members of the Communist Party.[738]

The most important role in the political trials was vested in the police structures, especially the State Security. Theoretically, the State Security was under the control of the leaders of the Communist Party; however, the most important say in the preparation of political trials at the central level was in the hands of the Soviet security forces.[739] The political trials are regarded as one of the main features of the period of Stalinism. In the USSR the method of publicly exhibited show trials was used as early as in the 1930s, and usually the trials had ideological labels used to a certain extent in the states of the Soviet Bloc after 1948. In Czechoslovakia the most important political trials were connected with the interests of Soviet foreign policy; thus cases of high

734 Josef Korbel, *The Communist Subversion of Czechoslovakia 1938-1948: The failure of Co-existence* (Princeton: Princeton University Press, 1959), pp. 181-183 and Hubert Ripka, *Czechoslovakia Enslaved: The Story of the Communist Coup D'etat* (London: Victor Gollanz, 1950), pp. 56-79.

735 Francesca Gori and Silvio Pons, eds., *The Soviet Union and Europe in the Cold War, 1943-53* (New York: St. Martin's Press, 1996), especially part 2 The Cominform and the Soviet Bloc, pp. 197-221.

736 Korbel, *The Communist Subversion of Czechoslovakia 1938-1948*, p. 186; see also Radomír Luža, "Czechoslovakia between democracy and Communism, 1945-1948," in Mamatey and Luža, *A History of the Czechoslovak Republic 1918-1948*, pp. 409-410.

737 Ripka, *Czechoslovakia Enslaved*, pp. 290-296.

738 Kuklík, *Czech law in historical contexts*, p. 159ff.

739 Meir Cotic, *The Prague Trial: The First Anti-Zionist Show Trial in the Communist Bloc* (New York: Herzel Press, 1987), pp. 20-21.

treason in particular were alleged to have been committed in the interest of the imperialistic Great Powers, Zionism, Holy See, etc.[740]

In the spring of 1950, the Slovak communists Gustav Husák and Clementis were accused of "bourgeois nationalism" and, in the case of Clementis, also of disloyalty to the USSR, as he had criticized the Hitler-Stalin Pact of 1939.[741]Another party conspiracy group was uncovered in Brno, where Regional Party Leader Otto Sling was arrested in October 1950.[742] Since the interrogators and their Soviet advisers became worried that they were not able to construct a sufficiently strong case, they looked for someone from the very top of the Communist leadership. In the end Rudolf Slánský, Secretary General of the Communist Party, was chosen as a suitable candidate for this "monster trial."[743] He was arrested on 24 November 1951, and the preparation for the trial took almost a year. A group of the alleged "anti-state centre" headed by Slánský was formed by the Secret Police and consisted of fourteen high rank communists, eleven of them of Jewish origin.[744] This served the Soviet foreign policy well, because members of the conspiracy centre were accused of Zionism, Trotskyism and cooperation with imperialistic powers.[745]

By a seeming paradox, after the establishment of the CommUnust regime the status of the members of the persecuted minorities, the Germans and the Hungarians, began to improve perceptibly. The anti-German hatred from wartime had abated and the minority question was not openly exploited in political disputes (with the notable exception of the Jewish minority and the above mentioned Slovak question).[746] Later on it even became apparent that the Communist regime was trying to, at least partly, accommodate the minorities, but this effort was complicated and sometimes also inhibited by the surviving chauvinism of the population including persons from the administrative machinery.[747]

The factual overcoming of bilateral interstate conflicts in Central and Eastern Europe played a major role. The question of minorities is always the

---

740 In more details see works by Karel Kaplan. In English especially Karel Kaplan, *Report on the Murder of the General Secretary*, trans. Karel Kovanda (London: I.B. Tauris, 1990), especially p. 14ff.

741 Jiří Pelikán, ed., *The Czechoslovak Political Trials 1950-1954: The Suppressed Report of the Dubček Government's Commission of Inquiry 1968* (Stanford, CA: Stanford University Press, 1971), pp. 87-89.

742 Cotic, *Prague Trial*, pp. 22-23.

743 Edward Táborský, *Communism in Czechoslovakia: 1948-1960* (Princeton, NJ: Princeton University Press, 1961), pp. 95-96.

744 Pelikán, *Czechoslovak Political Trials*, pp. 48-50.

745 Ibid., p. 179ff.

746 See for example René Petráš, "Menšiny v Československu 1945-1989," in *Vývoj práva v Československu v letech 1945-1989: Sborník příspěvků*, ed. by Karel Malý and Ladislav Soukup (Prague: Karolinum Press, 2004), pp. 240-280.

747 René Petráš, "K právům národností - menšin v českých zemích na počátku komunistického režimu," in *Pocta Prof. JUDr. Václavu Pavlíčkovi, CSc. k 70. narozeninám* (Prague: Linde, 2004), p. 140-151.

most dangerous if it is connected to international conflicts, especially if the "mother" states are interested in the issue of minorities living close to the borders. During the interwar period Czechoslovakia witnessed complicated relations with almost all of its neighbours – Germany, Austria and Hungary but also with Poland. After the formation of the quite homogenous Soviet bloc after World War II the situation changed. Moscow had no interest in letting minority disputes complicate the relations between the states of the bloc, so for instance Hungary, which had constantly demanded change of borders and had incited Hungarian minorities since the Peace Treaty of Trianon in 1920, was forced to bring this policy to an end.[748] Out of all the minorities living in Czechoslovakia only the not numerous Jews and Germans had their "mother" state outside the Soviet bloc, even though alongside West Germany there was also East Germany (German Democratic Republic), which finaly became a member of the Soviet bloc as well. Therefore, a number of measures taken by the Czechoslovak Communist regime in favour of the German minority were officially presented as an effort to improve relations with the German Democratic Republic. On the other hand, West Germany was continuously depicted by Communist propaganda as an aggressive, revanchist country. It is necessary to say that the most of the majority population was permanently afraid of German aggression and there was also widespread distrust concerning the loyalty of the Hungarians.

After the establishment of the Communist regime in February 1948, the attitude of Czechoslovakia to previously oppressed groups – Germans and Hungarians, gradually improved. All in all, the question of minorities always stood at the edge of the Communist regime's interest. The share of minorities in the overall population decreased dramatically by the expulsion and relocation of Germans; this naturally contributed to the change of attitude. Furthermore, this undoubtedly weakened or caused the total disappearance of conflicts among states in Central and Eastern Europe, but also the ideology of the Communist regime itself. Communist regimes have been, with some exceptions, officially international, so they refused inequality between nations or chauvinism. Apart from fascism and Nazism, which combine socialist ideas with hard nationalistic rhetoric, the key importance for Communist regimes lies in the theory of class struggle. National disputes were therefore overlooked and nationalists suppressed, which had been quite a successful effort in stable Communist regimes. Unfortunately, during the liberalization of the regimes such as in Hungary in 1956, partly in Czechoslovakia in 1968 and then within the whole former Soviet bloc since its disintegration at the end of the 1980s, the nationalism returned quickly. Altogether it can be stated

---

748   René Petráš, *Cizinci ve vlastní zemi: Menšinové konflikty v moderní Evropě* (Prague: Auditorium, 2012), pp. 186–192.

that communist Czechoslovakia rather overlooked nationalistic problems during the whole era of 1948–1989 and during their outbreak such as in 1968 the representatives of the regime were taken by surprise.[749]

The hasty preparations for new Constitution of the "People's Democracy" led to the enactment of the Constitutional Act of 9 May 1948, officially promulgated on 9 June 1948. The Constitutional Act was formally enacted by the Constituent National Assembly, but was debated mainly by the new political leaders in the Central Committee of the Communist Party and in the bodies of the National Front.[750] The Preamble skilfully used the prevailing anti-German and anti – Hungarian feelings, promulgating Czechoslovakia as a national state of Czechs and Slovaks and as a Slavic state which "had gotten rid of all hostile elements." The May Constitution of 1948, however, did not address the minority question nor did any other legal regulation of minority rights exist. By approximately 1952, the status of nationalities – Hungarians, Poles, and Ukrainians – had already been created and stabilized and, apart from the interwar period, their status was in fact similar. These minorities gained (in terms of totalitarian state) quite adequate cultural and language rights. However, for a long time the position of Ruthenians/Ukrainians was problematic because the Czechoslovak state suppressed their Ruthenian orientation and preferred Ukrainian one. Nothing had changed in the status of Germans as they were not recognised as an official minority, the effects of discriminatory measures from 1945 remained in force, but they at least acquired citizenship rights.[751]

Occasionally, the Communist regime intervened against minority groups (e.g. in the Teschen (Těšín) Silesia or among Ruthenians/Ukrainians) who had emphasized peculiarity of individual nations too openly or promoted establishment of autonomous minority areas. A typical demonstration of these efforts was in the Polish regions the so-called Cieslar Platform and in the Ukrainian regions the functioning of the Ukrainian National Council. [752] Pavel Cieslar, the regional representative of the Czechoslovak Communist Party and the official in Teschen Silesia, claimed that the population of this region, who spoke the Silesian dialect represented a national group which, regardless of the nationality the individuals acknowledged, formed a part of the Poles. In 1952 he asked the regional conference of the Czechoslovak Communist Party for immediate acknowledgment of Polish claims and the formation of a self-governing area. However, this platform was labelled by the Communist Party as "class enemy" and Cieslar was expelled from the

---

749 Petráš, "Menšiny v Československu 1945–1989," pp. 240–280.
750 Kuklík, *Czech law in historical contexts*, pp. 148–149.
751 See for example Jaroslav Kučera, "Die rechtliche und soziale Stellung der Deutschen in der Tschechoslowakei Ende der 40er und Anfang der 50er Jahre" *Bohemia* 33, no. 2 (1992): pp. 322–337.
752 Miloš Hájek and Olga Staňková, *Národnostní otázka v lidově demokratickém Československu* (Prague: Státní nakladatelství politické literatury, 1956), p. 56.

party. As it was admitted by the regime, the complicated situation in Teschen Silesia had led to the formation of "national deviations" within the Communist party – both in favour and against the minority.[753] Similarly, the Ukrainian National Council was considered to be a sort of a parallel to the Slovak National Council, as it laid down claims to gain administrative powers and it promoted the establishment of the Ukrainian autonomous area in Eastern Slovakia. Therefore it was disposed of by the regime.[754]

In the beginning of the 1950s the above mentioned policy of open dictatorship and political trials touched also the minorities, especially Jews, when semi-official anti-Semitism influenced the "monster trial" of Rudolf Slánský. Ukrainian/Ruthenian minority was affected especially by the liquidation of the Greek Byzantine Catholic Church and by the so-called "Ukrainization." This again served the Soviet foreign policy.

5.2 DIFFERENT STATUS AND POSITION OF INDIVIDUAL MINORITIES 1948–1953

The remnant of the German population left in Czechoslovakia was the worst affected minority by the changes of 1945-1948. The German minority was regarded as having been liquidated by the forcible resettlement. Individuals who remained were to assimilate. That gradually began to change since 1948 and already in April and May 1948 first improvement of the status of Germans was brought about.[755] Even though the Central Committee of the National Front confirmed that legal regulations from 1945-1948 period concerning Germans were still in force and applicable, it was emphasized that the Germans should be employed under standard circumstances (e.g. without payroll deductions) and housed in appropriate dwellings. Accroding to circular of the Ministry of Interior dated 18 April 1948 employers had treated the Germans often "in a very hard and asocial manner" and did not respect regulations.[756] The National Front however was not prepared to abrogate other legal regulation affecting Germans because authorities were afraid it would arouse resistance of the Czech public.

Act No. 99/1948 Sb. on National Insurance was enacted on 15 April 1948 and established that all working persons should claim insurance benefits

---

753   Plaček, "Těšínsko po uzavření československo- polské smlouvy," p. 14ff.

754   Bajcura, *Ukrajinská otázka v ČSSR*, pp. 89, 124–125.

755   In detail see René Petráš, "Specifika právního postavení Němců na počátku komunistické éry," in *Německy mluvící obyvatelstvo v Československu po roce 1945*, ed. by Adrian von Arburg, Tomáš Dvořák and David Kovařík (Brno: Matice moravská, 2010), pp. 318–335.

756   Tomáš Staněk, *Německá menšina v českých zemích, 1948–1989* (Prague: Institut pro středoevropskou kulturu a politiku, 1993), pp. 69–71; Kučera, "Die rechtliche und soziale Stellung," p. 324.

disregard the citizenship or nationality – thus with certain restrictions applied also to Germans without Czechoslovak citizenship. The new approach was manifested especially through decree No. 76/1948 Sb. from 13 April 1948, which extended the group of persons eligible to apply for return of Czechoslovak state citizenship. This decree, like many others, applied to Hungarians as well. Germans who were supposed to claim Czechoslovak citizenship were given a certificate by the District National Committee (hereinafter referred to as "DNC"), according to which they were supposed to be considered citizens until their applications would be processed (Section 5). Stabilization of labour law and wage conditions for both Germans and Hungarians were reinforced by Decree of the Ministry of Interior dated 25 May 1948, which invalidated directives implementing the presidential decree No. 71/1945 Sb. on labour duty of persons who have forfeited Czechoslovak citizenship. However, because of the validity of Decree of the Ministry of Interior No. 1/1948 Úř. l. from 24 December 1947, most of the Germans did not reacquire passive and active suffrage.[757]

The effort to integrate Czechoslovak Germans into the society continued in 1949 in an even larger extent. Discriminatory measures in social and civil law sphere were shrinking. Even the Communist Party of Czechoslovakia condemned during its Party Congress in May 1949 nationalism as hostile to official ideology and basically returned to the proletarian internationalism. In spite of these advances, members of German minority were still considerably limited, e.g. in using their language, education in German, etc. Also the situation in social security and labor law was far from ideal. A report from January 1950 identified 29 Acts, directives and instructions in this field, which were still discriminating Germans without Czechoslovak citizenship. Also during the administrative reform of 1949 the allocation of Germans in constituent administrative districts was apparently overlooked in order to prevent their stronger concentration. This general situation had an impact on Germans' lack of interest in claiming the Czechoslovak citizenship and strenghthen their efforts to emigrate.[758] Generally speaking, the proposals for gradual equality for Germans began in the years 1947–1948 and the process was completed basically in the years 1950–1951.[759] Important role was played by the District national committees guided by the Ministry of Interior.[760]It is necessary to say that this development, improving the status of Germans, had often collided with resistance of the Czech population and

---

757 Staněk, *Německá menšina v českých zemích*, pp. 72–74, 77.
758 Ibid., pp. 80–82, 103.
759 The process of equalization of Germans is described for example Jaroslav Kučera, *Odsun nebo vyhnání?* (Prague: H&H, 1992), p. 35.
760 See especially instruction on the Handling of the Persons of German nationality in *Sbírka oběžníků pro KNV vydávaná Ministerstvem vnitra* 2, no. 28 (1950) from March 31, 1950.

inferior bodies of both state and party hierarchy which had in practice slowed it down.

The establishment of diplomatic relations with the German Democratic Republic, which unequivocally stood against any considerations about return of Sudeten Germans, had significant influence. The Czechoslovak government attempted to improve social status of Germans using not Acts of Parliament but directives of the Ministry of the Interior[761] and confidential instructions of the Ministry of Social Welfare. Such methods represent characteristic feature of totalitarian regime. Occasionally even freeze or confiscated property was returned to its previous German owners, yet it was limited and the claimants had to prove, that they were not hostile to the Czechs or Czechoslovak state during the war. Apparently the question of Czechoslovak citizenship still remained to be the key problem because up to the end of 1951, almost 40 000 Germans still had not applied for it. According to the decision of the German Federal Constitutional Court in Karlsruhe from 28 May 1952 most of the German population in Czechoslovakia were still considered German citizens and certificates to support this allegation were sent to Czechoslovakia which caused great outrage in the Prague government.

Act No. 34/1953 Sb. from 24 April 1953 represents a turning point in the German question. It collectively granted Czechoslovak state citizenship to all Germans with permanent residence within the Czechoslovak territory who had not claimed it yet. "Persons of German nationality who forfeited Czechoslovak state citizenship on the basis of the presidential decree No. 33/1945 Sb. and did have permanent residence in the territory of the Czechoslovak Republic became Czechoslovak citizens if they had not acquired citizenship earlier (Section 1)." It is characteristic that the granting of citizenship took place under surveillance and without publicity due to concerns that during rallies of Germans disturbances would occur and many Germans refused to take identity cards anyway.[762] Regardless, the Act indicated that the post-war anti-German policy was to a large extent over. During the process of enacting this Act, it had been emphasized in the National Assembly, that the reason for such a legislation was to employ most of the Germans in Czechoslovakia "in our building efforts" and to strengthten friendship with the German Democratic Republic.

---

761   See for example circular instruction issued by the Ministry of Interior, on January 23 and March 13, 1950 on the administration of return of the Czechoslovak state citizenship to persons of German nationality, Státní okresní archiv Kutná Hora, collection Okresní národní výbor Kutná Hora 1945–1960, box 169, sign. 216.

762   Staněk, *Německá menšina v českých zemích*, p. 96, 104–105, 108–110; Kučera, "Die rechtliche und soziale Stellung, p. 336; Ján Gronský and Jiří Hřebejk, eds., *Dokumenty k ústavnímu vývoji Československa II. (1945–1968)* (Prague: Karolinum Press, 1999), pp. 68–69; Karel Richter, *Češi a Němci v zrcadle dějin*, vol. 2 (Třebíč: Akcent, 1999), p. 282ff.

The most significant Czechoslovak minority after 1945 became the Hungarian one. After the establishment of Communist regimes in Czechoslovakia and Hungary the post war policy was revised and future prospects of this group in Czechoslovakia were taken into account. Measures normalizing legal status of Hungarians were implemented already in 1948: the exchange of population with Hungary was stopped, the land of Hungarian peasants was exempted from confiscation,[763] Hungarians relocated to the Czech borderland were allowed to return, the Hungarian education was restored, civil rights reacquired, Hungarian press and books were published, etc. Hungarians were particularly allowed to claim the Czechoslovak citizenship by Act No. 245/1948 Sb. from 25 October 1948 on State Citizenship of Persons of Hungarian Nationality: "Persons with Hungarian nationality who were Czechoslovak state citizens on 1 November 1938 and do have permanent residence in the territory of the Czechoslovak Republic and are not citizens of any foreign country, do acquire Czechoslovak citizenship on the day this Act comes to force if they take an oath of loyalty to the Czechoslovak Republic" (Section 1 (1)). On 5 March 1949, Csemadok – Czechoslovak Hungarian Workers' Cultural Association was founded. In 1952 it was decided Hungarians should be represented in District National Committees and Regional National Committees, their nationality should no longer prevent them from obtaining leading functions and also bilingualism had been enforced in mixed districts, especially in Southern Slovakia. In 1954 the policy of "reslovakization" was revised and along with other post-war anti-Hungarian measures harshly condemned by the plenary session of the Central Committee of the Communist Party of Czechoslovakia.[764]

Specific development concerning relations of Czechoslovakia to Jews was influenced in particular by changes of the Soviet policy towards Israel. Originally, a positive relation turned very quickly to nearly official anti-Semitism. In 1951, a decision to start a campaign against Zionism was closely connected with the show trial of Rudolf Slánský and others. Speakers at public rallies assaulted Jews for Zionism, used anti-Semitic expressions and some demanded removal of all Jews from public offices. During the Slánský trial itself, strong emphasis was laid on the Jewish origin of most of the accused. Jews, due to their different social structure, were also substantially more affected by the Communist policies after February 1948. From 1948 until the end of 1949 consequently out of 54 000 Jews approximately 30 000 emigrated mostly

---

763 Mojmír Staško, "Právne východiská pozemkovej reformy v kontexte jej vzťahu k maďarskej menšine," *Slezský sborník = Acta Silesiaca* 95, no. 1-2 (1997): pp. 160–166.

764 Šindelka, *Národnostní politika v ČSSR*, pp. 117–118; Imre Molnár, "Kapitoly z poválečných dějin Maďarů vysídlených do Čech," *Střední Evropa* 7, no. 19 (1991): pp. 74–90; Štefan Šutaj, "Slovakia and Hungarian minority between 1945 and 1948," in *Key issues of Slovak and Hungarian History: A view of Slovak Historians* (Prešov: Universum, 2011), p. 227ff.

to Izrael, after that emigration was forbidden. The persecutions reached its peak between 1952-1954, when hundreds of Jews were imprisoned or sent into forced labour camps.[765]

At this time State Security gained praxis in classified actions against the Jewish population, which they used on larger scale in the years of so-called normalization 1970-1989.[766] The action under the code name "Family" in the 1950s tried to uncover family relations of persons of Jewish origin and to check their correspondence (affecting about 30 000 persons). In 1962, the operation ended, labelled as an expression of anti-Semitism and the materials were usually destroyed. During the 1960s these anti-Jewish measures from the turn of the 1940s and the 1950s were criticised surprisingly harshly. According to this criticism the campaign against Zionism often led to displays of distrust and victimization of citizens of Jewish origin and revived anti-Semitism.[767]

Also the Ruthenians/Ukrainians were afflicted by the interferences of the Communist regime.[768] The Ukrainian National Council of the Prešov region was accused of nationalism when it began to consider itself the exclusive political representative of Ukranian minority in Czechoslovakia. Its legalisation was therefore refused just as the suggestions seeking a solution for the status of Ukranian minority in Czechoslovakia. In 1951 the activity of the Ukrainian National Council were put to an end due to the pressure of the state and party organs. Criticism of alleged nationalism was in case of some legal experts leaning against the attempt of the Council to prevent natural assimilation of Ukrainian population.[769]

The biggest problem of Ruthenian/Ukranian minority was traditionally the question of not entirely crystallized national orientation. In the beginning of the 1950s, two major actions took place, which were supposed to strengthen the Ukrainian orientation. In 1950, the Byzantine Catholic Church (affiliated with the Holy See) was harassed on the Soviet initiative and the population was supposed to transfer to Orthodox Christianity (the so-called "Orthodox Action"). Yet the Byzantine Catholic Church was tied to Ruthenian national sentiment and traditions. In 1952 the education was supposed to transfer to Ukrainian language according to resolution of the Central Committee of the Communist Party of Slovakia from 2 June 1952, while the existing education

765 Moshe Yegar, *Československo, sionismus, Izrael* (Prague: Victoria Publishing, 1997), pp. 135–136, 142, 153, 175–176.
766 Oldřich Tůma, "The second consolidation of the communist regime and the descent into collapse (1972–1989)," in *A History of the Czech lands*, ed. by Jaroslav Pánek and Oldřich Tůma (Prague: Karolinum Press, 2009), pp. 576–579
767 Jan Šindelka, *Národnostní otázka a socialismus* (Prague: Svoboda, 1966), pp. 306–307.
768 Bajcura, *Ukrajinská otázka v ČSSR*, pp. 108–134.
769 Šindelka, *Národnostní otázka a socialismus*, p. 303.

was mostly Russian or Ruthenian. Also this iniative led to protests. Those who refused ukrainization were persecuted and part of the minority chose to present themselves from that time on as Slovaks. Both of these actions were, to a certain extent, regarded and criticized as inappropriate already in the time of socialism.[770] Even during the later stages of communist Czechoslovaka the resistance of the Ruthenian population against Ukrainian language expressed itself in the fact that parents preferred Slovak schooling for their children. The matter was solved in the beginning of the 1960s on the basis of resolution submitted by the Central Committee of the Communist Party of Czechoslovakia from 1961 "On the development of the East Slovak region." Thereafter in the area of purely Slovak schools, schools with Ukrainian language and Slovak with some subjects in Ukrainian language also existed.[771]

Establishment of the Communist regime in Czechoslovakia had a significant impact on a minority with specific social structure – Gypsies/Romani (sometimes called also Roma population).[772] The Act No. 117/1927 Sb. aimed against nomadic lifestyle of Gypsies had been used up to 1950, when it was repealed and Gypsies no longer had to succumb to special regime such as nomad identity cards. Until 1950 the Czechoslovak Communist regime had tried to improve especialy the social and material living conditions of this group of population. In "Gypsy camps (hamlets)" in Slovakia, construction of roads and wells began, the electrification was installed and also the problem of previously minimal schooling of children was addressed to reduce illiteracy. The institution responsibile for solving the question in 1950–1957 was the Ministry of Culture, Enlightenment and Information, however the policies were implemented by the national committees under the guidance of the Ministry of Interior.[773] It may be surprising that considerable group of experts believed in national self-awareness of Gypsies, yet later on a decision of directive manner brought the conception of assimilation of Gypsies/Romani with the majority population.[774] The Communist regime was very optimistic in the question of solving the so-called "Gypsy question" and the predictions talked about great successes. It may seem that precisely the egalitarian and at the same time totalitarian state – with many possibilities e.g. in social field – might be able to solve the problem easily but in reality it turned out the other way.

---

770 Šindelka, *Národnostní politika v ČSSR*, pp. 121-123; Ivan Bajcura, *Cesta k internacionálnej jednote* (Bratislava: Pravda, 1983), pp. 159-163.

771 Gabriela Sokolová, et al., *Soudobé tendence vývoje národností v ČSSR* (Prague: Academia, 1987), p. 99.

772 In detail see René Petráš, "Cikánská/romská otázka v Československu na počátku komunistického režimu a návaznost na starší vývoj," *Právněhistorické studie* 38 (2007): pp. 225-247.

773 For their instructions regarding the Gypsy question in 1952 see *Sbírka oběžníků pro KNV vydávaná Ministerstvem vnitra* 4, no. 13 (1952) from March, 5 1952.

774 Davidová, *Cesty Romů 1945-1990*, pp. 13, 191-192.

5.2 1953–1967 (FROM DICTATORSHIP OF PROLETARIAT
TO LIBERAL ERA)

It should be noted that both the doctrine and real policies of the Communist regime in Czechoslovakia changed in accord with changes made both in the Soviet Union (particularly after the death of Stalin) and the whole Soviet bloc, which resulted in a more liberal period in the second half of the 1950s and the 1960s.[775] The regime succeeded in preserving stability even after 1953 and, with excpeion of minor disturbances after monetary reform of 1953, no crisis occurred to compare with the situation in other Central European Soviet satellites (bloody disorders in the German Democratic Republic in 1953, disturbances and political crisis in Poland in 1956 and the almost concurrently suppressed revolution in Hungary). It is necessary to say that this instability in the neighbouring countries with which Czechoslovakia had traditional disputes, especially because of minorities, raised sizeable concerns among Czechs and Slovaks. During the crises in Hungary, border incidents occurred after a part of anti-communist rebels with nationalistic orientation wanted to attack Czechoslovakia because of its Hungarian minority. Destalinization in Czechoslovakia was therefore very circumspect and the Chief of the Communist Party during Stalin era Klement Gottwald remained in his office until his death. After 1956 the Communist Party was forced to review some of the injustices committed during political trials;[776] however, in the beginning, rehabilitation was opened mainly for "purged" members of the Communist Party and only individuals without substantial influence were punished for the crimes from the beginning period of the regime, and not until the 1960s. The majority of political prisoners could apply for parole, and, eventually, amnesty was promulgated in 1960. A more thorough rehabilitation and condemnation of the political trials was demanded by Czechoslovak society especially in the second half of the 1960s as part of the emerging Prague Spring of 1968.[777]

Absurdly, the minority policies rested to a large extent on secret documents which were often unknown to the officials who were to carry out the policy. This led to confusions, unmethodical changes and frequent differences in the minority policy between administrative units (regions and districts). The notion of a "minority" was rejected for being out of line with

---

[775] For theoretical aspects of an attempt to introduce gradually modern aspects of civic society, rule of law and socialist democracy into the socialist society see Vladimír V. Kusin, *The Intellectual origins of the Prague Spring: The Development of reformist ideas in Czechoslovakia 1956-1967* (Cambridge: Cambridge University Press, 1971), esp. chap. 3, "Legal re-thinking," p. 28ff.

[776] It was a part of wider political changes within the Soviet block reflected by the Czechoslovak communists. See interesting analyses in Kusin, *The Intellectual origins of the Prague Spring*, especially pp. 19-22 and 28-30.

[777] Pelikán, *Czechoslovak Political Trials*, p. 148ff.

the tradition of democratic inter-war Czechoslovakia, and the expression "nationality" was used instead (in the sense of national minority): it was not therefore the official minority policy but the nationality question.

The Soviet Union at the end of the 1950s witnessed the optimistic quiver of social development. This was undoubtedly supported by the economic growth, respected position of Moscow in the world, including progress in the politics towards underdeveloped countries but apart from other things some technical successes as exceptionally prestigious (temporary) advance before the USA in astronautics. This brought about considerations of how to swiftly attain unlimited prosperity, i.e. communist phase of society during just two or three decades. Ideas emerged that a classical structures of state would vanish and might be replaced by local government and/or by wider activities of trade unions and other socialist organizations. These visions naturally failed within a few years and contributed to the fall of the Soviet leader Nikita Chruščov.[778] Ideas of an easy achievement of Socialism and later Communism had naturally emerged in Czechoslovakia as well. From the legal point of view it is ridiculous that those ideas were implemented in the Preamble of the new constitution of 1960 as well as in the new name of the country.[779] The Constitution of the Czechoslovak Socialist Republic was enacted by the National Assembly as Constitutional Act No. 100/1960 Sb. on 11 July 1960.[780] The Constitution was heavily influenced by ideology, and the Communist regime openly described its foundation. It was a constitution of the socialist state in accordance with the Soviet pattern of 1936.[781] The Preamble was made in the name of the working people of Czechoslovakia and declared that "Socialism has triumphed in this country under the leadership of the Communist Party of Czechoslovakia." Its aim was to construct even a more advanced socialist society and to lay down the foundations and "to gather strength" for Communism. The Preamble mentioned the friendly alliance and union with the Soviet Union and other countries of its block.[782] The Preamble also depicted

---

778 In detail see René Petráš, "Constitutional development in Czechoslovakia in the 1960s and problems of ethnicity," trans. Renata Hrubá, in Tomášek, *Czech law between europeanization and globalization*, pp. 60-68.

779 Kuklík, *Czech law in historical contexts*, pp. 183-184.

780 For English translation see *Bulletin of Czechoslovak law* 1-2 (1960), p. 19ff. with commentaries and speeches by A. Novotný and Deputy Secretary of the Central Committee of the Communist Party J. Hendrych; and *Constitution of the Czechoslovak Socialist republic*, Prague: Orbis 1960.

781 See commentary in *Bulletin of Czechoslovak law* 1-2 (1960), pp. 28 -32; see also Harold Gordon Skilling, "The Czechoslovak Constitution of 1960 and the Transition to Communism," *The Journal of Politics* 24, no. 1 (1962): especially pp. 142-146.

782 It should be noted that Czechoslovakia was from 1955 loyal member of the Warsaw Pact. See Harold Gordon Skilling, *The Governments of Communist East Europe* (New York: Crowell Comparative Government Series, 1966, pp. 218-219; and A. Ross. Johnson, "The Warsaw Pact: Soviet Military Policy in Eastern Europe," in *Soviet Policy in Eastern Europe*, ed. by Sarah Meiklejohn Terry (New Haven, CT: Yale University Press, 1984), pp. 255-284.

the socialist stage of social development as a possibility to create a harmonic relationship between Czechs and Slovaks.

The socialist system was also defined from the economic point of view. It was based on the exclusion of exploitation of workers, re-emphasized successful changes in ownership structures, including nationalization and collectivization; these along with central planning and labour for the benefit of the society were stipulated as the main features of the socialist economic system. However the beginning of 1960s brought also serious economic problems and the state of economy was one of the sources for calls for more liberal political system. In 1965 the Communist Party approved changes in the economic model. The economic programme proposed by the Czech economist Otto Šik called for both intensive and extensive economic development, emphasizing technological improvements.

During the 1960s the communist system gradually took on a more liberal facade but this was still heavily based on ideology. After the 1960 Socialist Constitution had been enacted the leadership of the Communist Party proclaimed its main political goal in the field of law, namely that new codes would be enacted in order to reflect the socialist character of society.[783] Between 1961–1965 Criminal and Civil Codes, Criminal and Civil Procedure Codes and Labour Code quickly followed. Czechoslovakia was also apparently the only country of the whole Sovier block to enact a complex legal code regulating the functioning of a centrally planned economy – Economic code. Economic relationships (especially those connected with national economy and planning) were removed from the Civil Code and incorporated into a special Economic Code No. 109/1964 Sb., which came into effect on 1 July 1964. It was the result of a long theoretical discussion on the concept of socialist law regulating economic relations between socialist organisations (i.e. state enterprises and other legal entities) in the environment of the planned economy.[784] Meanwhile in other Communist regimes the economy was regulated merely by informal commands or fragmented and often chaotic legal norms.[785]

In the second half of the 1960s a new wave of liberal changes started within the Communist Party and Czechoslovak society. The changes were initiated in response to a call for economic and subsequent political

783   Kuklík, *Czech law in historical contexts*, pp. 190–209.
784   See especially John N. Hazard, Isaac Shapiro and Peter B. Maggs, *The Soviet legal system: Contemporary Documentation and Historical Commentary* (Columbia University, NY: Oceana Publications, 1969), pp. 286–289.
785   In detail see René Petráš, "Snahy Československa oddělit se od právních tradic v první polovině šedesátých let – interdisciplinární aspekty," in *Společnost českých zemí v evropských kontextech: České evropanství ve srovnávacích perspektivách*, ed. by Blanka Soukupová, Róża Godula-Węcławowicz, Miroslav Hroch (Prague: Fakulta humanitních studií Univerzity Karlovy v Praze, 2012), pp. 93–113.

reforms.[786] The Communist Party allowed for liberalization in areas of culture, particularly in film and literature.[787] Czechoslovak cinematography even won two Oscars for the best foreign language movies. The first of them was "A Shop on the High Street" from 1965 (Oscar for the best foreign language movie of 1966) which devoted itself to the sensitive question of anti-Semitism in Slovakia during World War II despite the fact that the Communist regime had not entirely managed the embarrassing anti-Jewish campaign from the beginning of the 1950s yet. From the regime's point of view, a very controversial topic was embodied in the movie "Closely Watched Trains" (1966, Oscar 1967), describing a young railway official's embarrassing love disappointment as the reason for his anti-Nazi resistance. For quite prudish regime this could have meant almost desecration of celebrated resistance. Those rather curious examples of extraordinary success of Czechoslovak movies were supposed to illustrate the peculiar atmosphere in Czechoslovakia before the Prague Spring of 1968.

The regime had a tendency to underrate the national and minority problems. The structures which had dealt with this problem more or less successfully, mostly with the so-called national and Gipsy question, collapsed during realization of radical administrative reform in 1960. The minorities had been quite passive, the biggest Hungarian minority and even after the resettlement still numerous German one were afraid of the revival of harsh post-war interferences and usually did not dare to demand expansion of their rights. The numerous Gypsy/Roma populations lacked (with minor exceptions) elites, so they were not able to oppose social engineering of the Czechoslovak state which wanted them to be involved in modern society. Surprisingly the biggest trouble for the regime caused Poles who were small in numbers but many times showed a tendency to behave just as minorities in interwar Czechoslovakia, confidently enforcing their rights and, in disputes with the state, turning to the Polish diplomats and demanding support of the "mother state."[788]

However, the national and minority question was rather on the edge of interest during this time, unlike in the interwar period. Not even the scientific circles, with a few except were interested in this topic.[789] The nationalistic problem, which radically contributed to the dissociation of the regime in 1968, was not related to minorities, but to the Slovaks. The Constitution of 1960 deserted the theory of the division of powers; on the contrary, it applied the Soviet principle of one uniform centre of powers in the socialist state. The Constitution was centralized, and the Slovak national bodies were again

---

786 For connection between economic, socio-cultural and political reform see for example Galia Golan, *The Czechoslovak Reform Movement* (Cambridge: Cambridge University Press 1973, especially p. 50ff.

787 Ibid., p. 94ff.

788 See for example Petráš, *Menšiny v komunistickém Československu*, pp. 193–285.

789 For more details see Petráš, *Cizinci ve vlastní zemi*, pp. 111–116.

restricted in their powers.[790] The question of federalization was an important part of political discussions during the liberalization of the Communist regime in the second half of the 1960s; it became an important point in the political agenda mainly after Slovak Communists, punished for their national policies in the political ("bourgeois nationalist") trials of the 1950s were rehabilitated.[791]

However the real importance of federalization and of its content was clearly viewed differently by Czech political elites and this fact created yet another problem for future Czech-Slovak relations within common state.[792] During 1960s a notion prevailed in the party and governmental circles, that the minority question had been solved by the establishment of the Communist regime itself and that nobody was really interested in special legal regulation of the status of minorities.[793] It was typical for totalitarian regimes where the minorities did not dare to enforce specific rights for themselves and had to live with what the state had mercifully given them. The Prague Sping of 1968 brought fast and significant revival of the minorities in Czechoslovakia.[794]

Already by the year 1952 a quite unified solution to the status of three nationalities (Hungarian, Polish and Ukrainian) was reached. These minorities had their own national education, they were allowed to use their language in places of their concentration as well as when dealing with offices and also in societal and other public life. In these areas bilingualism existed on marks, signs etc. Distribution of press and books and radio broadcasts in their languages were secured. Members of minorities had representation in administrative bodies, especially on the local and regional level. They were able to develop their culture to which their own cultural societies and associations should have served. However, they were not regarded as political representatives of the national minorities.[795] The legal position of Ruthenians/Ukrainians was problematic to a certain extent because the Czechoslovak state had preferred the Ukrainian orientation for a long time and suppressed the Ruthenian one. A specific question posed the Greek minority which

790 Stanislav Matoušek, "The Slovak National Council," *Bulletin of Czechoslovak law*, no. 1-2 (Prague: Orbis, 1960), p. 93ff.

791 In more details Stanislav Sikora, "Slovakia and the attempt to reform socialism in Czechoslovakia, 1963-1969," in Teich, Kováč and Brown, *Slovakia in History*, pp. 299-314.

792 Carol Skalnik Leff, *National Conflict in Czechoslovakia: The Making and Remaking of a State, 1918-1987* (Princeton, NJ: Princeton University Press, 1988), pp. 123-127.

793 There were some exceptions like in 1960s there were worries in the party and state apparatus that the minority question could be misused by the so-called revanschist propaganda of the Federal Republic of Germany. See for example letter by the Regional Committee of the Communist Party of Czechoslovakia in Ostrava to district national committees, December, 7, 1960, Státní okresní archiv Opava, collection Okresní národní výbor Opava 1954-1960, inventory no. 772.

794 Petráš, "Menšiny v Československu 1945-1989," pp. 240-280.

795 Šindelka, *Národnostní politika v ČSSR*, pp. 123-124; Zahradnik, "Nástin historického vývoje," pp. 29-31.

originated on the Czechoslovak teritory especially by a vast emigration of the Left defeated in Greek civil war by the end of the 1940s. In the 1950s Greeks established their own national organisations in Czechoslovakia.

However, rights of the three nationalities did not apply to other groups – for example to Jews, Gypsies/Roma and not even to numerous Germans. In the case of Germans, the Czechoslovak party and state organs concentrated on the policy of progressive assimilation[796] and particularly German education including primary education was not permitted – only clubs of German language existed. The result was, among others, low education level of German minority and nearly non-existence of German intelligencia. On the official level in the beginning of the 1960s notions that the German minority in fact did not exist anymore sometimes aroused.[797] In case of Czechoslovak Germans there was also a significant decrease in numbers.[798] This discrimination had caused quite sharp critique already during the time of Communist regime.

The Communist regime had especially negative attitude towards the Jewish minority (particularly in the 1950s), Czechoslovakia supported Arabs against Israel in international politics. Due to the Six-Day Arab-Israeli War in 1967, Czechoslovakia severed diplomatic relations with Israel.[799] Yet the majority of Czechoslovak population did not let the regime (or more precisely the Soviet policy imposed on the whole Soviet bloc) to have an affect on it and showed its sympathy with the state of Israel.[800] Neither Jews nor Gypsies/Roma populations were regarded as a recognized nationality according to the theory of that time and were ought to be assimilated.[801] In the interest of fast assimilation it was considered necessary to prevent chauvinism from the side of the majority.

The so-called Gipsy question[802] was supposed to be solved especially by enhancing the cultural level of this population group which was considered to be a process lasting for several decades. The Czechoslovak state organs especially attempted to prevent nomadism through enactment of Act No. 74/1958 Sb. on permanent settlement of nomadic persons. Though it did not mention Gypsies/Roma explicitly (spoke about persons who lead nomadic

---

796 In the case of German minority in the 1960s we talk about forced assimilation and the minority was permanently confined, see Pavol Jacko, "O vývoji a postavení národnostních menšin," *Nová mysl* 23 (1969): p. 1104ff.

797 Staněk, *Německá menšina v českých zemích*, pp. 118, 132–134, 152; Kurt Rabl, "Über die Verfassungsurkunde der ČSSR vom 11. Juli 1960," *Bohemia* 2, no. 1 (1961): p. 537–539.

798 Šárka Hernová, "Němci v ČSR v letech 1950–1980," *Slezský sborník* = *Acta Silesiaca* 85, no. 4 (1987): pp. 267–268.

799 Yegar, *Československo, sionismus, Izrael*, pp. 176–178.

800 See for example Petr Pithart, *Osmašedesátý*, 3rd. ed. (Prague: Rozmluvy, 1990), pp. 112, 175–176.

801 Hájek and Staňková, *Národnostní otázka v lidově demokratickém Československu*, pp. 63–65; Ludvíka Čížkovská, "Politika vlády ČSFR k romské menšině – snaha o vytvoření rámcových podmínek pro rasové a národnostní soužití," *Právník* 131, no. 6 (1992): p. 533.

802 In detail see Petráš, "Cikánská/romská otázka v Československu," pp. 225–247.

way of life), the Act referred mainly to this group or at least to its major part. It was characteristic for this legislative process during Communist regime that the word Gipsy or Roma was not mentioned at all even during long debates on the Act in the National Assembly, whereas on the other hand, a plenty of ideological phrases were used. This group of population undoubtedly irritated the Communist regime also because of its independence on state structures.[803]

On the basis of Act No. 74/1958 Sb. the nomadic way of life of Gypsies and all persons with no permanent residence was brought to an end. The Act was extended by implementing directives of the Ministry of the Interior from 9 December 1958 also to persons leading a half-nomadic way of life, which meant especially Romani who often migrated between Slovakia and the Czech lands but were traditionally settled. The Act involved in its Section 3 strict sanctions as well: "Whoever perseveres in a nomadic way of life even though he was provided with help to permanent settlement will be punished for a criminal offence by imprisonment for 6 months up to 3 years." At the beginning of 1959 the Ministry of the Interior completed a state-wide register and list of persons affected by Act No. 74/1958 Sb. The municipalities, where the Gipsies were staying at the time of the register was taken (beginning of February 1959), had to take charge of them permanently and had to secure them accommodation, employment or places for their children in schools, etc. If any of them wanted to change their residence because of an employment or to get married and move to another place, this change had to be arranged in advance in writings and approved, which did not always happen – so according to E. Davidová "in many cases this resembled a modern and 'well-intentioned' analogy to serfdom."[804]

Social welfare and enlightenment actions enhanced the living standard of Gypsies, yet the attempt to assimilate them into the majority failed. In 1965 the Government Resolution No. 502 of 13 October 1965, on Measures to Resolve the Issues of the Gypsy Population, established the Governmental Committee for the Issues of the Gypsy Population. It was a greatly influential institution which could carry out truly active policy contained in the Principles of the Dispersion and Relocation of the Gypsy Population adopted by it on 18 December. It was supposed to be an exceptional project which the Roma from underdeveloped hamlets in eastern Slovakia were to be relocated to Czech regions. There, they would have helped to solve the problem with reduced workforce and at the same time, their living standard would have improved. The project, however, failed like other projects manipulating the

---

803 René Petráš, "Právo a romské kočování v českých zemích – historický přehled," in *Migrace, tolerance, integrace*, vol. 2 (Opava: Slezské zemské muzeum, Slezský ústav, 2005), pp. 210–219.

804 Davidová, *Cesty Romů 1945–1990*, p. 201.

Roma. The whole transfer was chaotic; regions in eastern Slovakia tried to get rid of the Roma as quickly as possible irrespective of the recommended quotas, whereas Czech regions slowed down the activity and refused to accept them.[805] Voluntary transfer and dispersion in theory was in practice interpreted as a duty of Roma families to move into a determined region regardless of family relationships and other circumstances. In 1967, the relocations culminated; however, practical problems manifested themselves. As early as 1968 the state decided to adopt a new policy, to which the then process of democratisation contributed. The Government Committee for the Issues of the Gypsy Population was abolished by Government Resolution No. 384 of November 1968, and it was the Ministry of Labour and Social Affairs of the Czechoslovak Socialistic Republic which was entrusted with the issue.

In general it is necessary to point out that the policy of the Czechoslovak state towards this minority had changed several times – in some periods it was the practice to recognize them as an independent nation, create standard language and have them form self-governing territorial units.[806] Frequent changes of the governmental policy which had meanwhile deeply interfered with the life of the group (especially after 1958) and whose results could have a positive impact only after decades, had influenced Gypsy/Roma minority very negatively.

In the course of years 1953-1967 certain changes in the status of minorities occurred yet they did not change much about the heart of the matter. In 1956 for instance, the Constitutional Act No. 33/1956 Sb. on Slovak National Bodies was enacted. In accordance with the Article 2 of the Constitutional Act No. 33/1956 Sb., the Slovak National Council was entrusted with the decisions on the matters of national minorities on the Slovak territory. The Slovak National Council was obliged to create "favourable conditions for economic and cultural life of citizens of Hungarian and Ukrainian nationality."

The 1960 Constitution dealt with minorities briefly – it secured rights for Hungarians, Ukrainians and Poles but not for Germans.[807] Its Section 25 stated: "Citizens of Hungarian, Ukrainian and Polish nationality are provided

---

805 Pavelčíková, *Romové v českých zemích v letech 1945-1989*, pp. 89-91; Karel Kaplan, *Kořeny československé reformy 1968*, vol. 3, *Změny ve společnosti*, vol. 4, *Struktura moci* (Brno: Doplněk, 2002), pp. 35-36; Anna Jurová, ed. *Rómska problematika 1945-1967: dokumenty*, vol. 4 (Prague: ÚSD AVČR, 1996), document no. 304, pp. 819-824.

806 See for example Václav Pavlíček, *Ústava a ústavní řád České republiky*, vol. 2 (Prague: Linde, 1995), pp. 196-197.

807 Staněk, *Německá menšina v českých zemích*, pp. 152-153; Marian Posluch, "Die konstitutionelle Entwicklung der Tschechoslowakischen Sozialistischen Republik zwischen 1968 und 1989," in *Normdurchsetzung in osteuropäischen Nachkriegsgesellschaften (1944-1989)*, vol. 4, *Tschechoslowakei (1944-1989)*, ed. by Heinz Mohnhaupt and Hans-Andreas Schönfeldt (Frankfurt am Main: Vittorio Klostermann, 1998), p. 547.

with all possibilities and means of education in their mother tongue and cultural development." The Constitution also formally guaranteed the equality of all citizens without regard to nationality and race.

During the preparation of the Constitution only marginal interest was paid to the question of minorities and its text also stated: "In the spirit of Lenin national policy the new Constitution settles relations of nations and ethnic groups in our country. It proceeds from three main principles: All citizens, without reference to nationality, are equal. Citizens of Hungarian, Polish and Ukrainian nationality enjoy additional rights as ethnic groups. Concurrently the basic principle in force is that the Czechoslovak Socialist Republic is a unified state of two nations – Czechs and Slovaks."[808] In 1960, administrative reform was also enacted, which was to a certain extent disadvantageous for minorities – reorganization caused disintegration of institutional security of the minorities established in the 1950s. New large districts led to a decrease in the minority's proportion on the overall population.[809]

Much of the minority policy of Communist Czechoslovakia was still a closely guarded secret. Until 1968, for example, it was not regulated by law and the government agencies followed secret guidelines from the Communist Party and the Interior Ministry. Members of the minorities, particularly the Jews and the Germans, were permanently under surveillance of the security services.

The legal status of Czechoslovak minorities had until 1968 a number of defects. Two sections of the 1960 Constitution (25 and 74) presented the only legal regulation which led to quite divided practise and frequent arbitrariness of lower bodies. "From time to time some party, state and other bodies were concerned with the problems of nationalities and functioning among them, but their resolutions and directives were not transformed into laws and mostly not even published. Although they were used in praxis, the application of national rights rested with good will of lower instances and individuals who dealt with these problems."[810] Gradually an opinion, that national policy cannot be decentralized to lower bodies and the question must remain in the competence of the centre, prevailed as follows from the practise after the administrative reform of 1960: "The individual districts and regions had oftentimes arbitrarily interpreted the principles of national policy, which

---

808   Based on the speech of MP Hendrych see stenographic protocols of National Assembly of the Czechoslovak Republic 1960–1964, 2ⁿᵈ meeting on July 11, 1960, http://www.psp.cz/eknih/1960ns/stenprot/index.htm.

809   For example In Těšín Silesia, see Zahradnik, "Nástin historického vývoje," p. 30; the national and minority question in the Czech Republic had always been in principle connected to problems of public administration, see for example René Petráš, "Reforma správy a národní otázka na počátku první republiky," *Historický obzor* 13 (2002): 133–137.

810   Šindelka, *Národnostní politika v ČSSR*, p. 125.

resulted in quite different practise of exercising the rights of nationalities."[811] The minorities were not recognized as special minority groups and rights of minority members were strictly confined to language and culture only. The German minority was still not put on the equal footing with Hungarians, Poles and Ukrainians.

5.3 THE PERIOD OF THE PRAGUE SPRING 1968 AND THE CONSTITUTIONAL ACT NO. 144/1968 SB. ON NATIONALITIES

In 1968 in the movement of reforming Communism gained popular support. New political organizations were established, demanding at least "socialism with a human face" and the possibility to form political opposition to the Communist Party and the National Front organizations. The movement to reform the socialist system in Czechoslovakia is usually referred to as the Prague Spring. Changes were proposed to the rigid central planning system and foreign policy. There was also an important discussion on the relations between Czechs and Slovaks.

Particularly President Antonín Novotný advocated the centralized version of Czechoslovak state and repeatedly showed distrust in Slovaks. President's position weakened and finally he was forced to resign. A liberal Slovak communist, Alexander Dubček, was elected the new leader of the Czechoslovak Communist Party. The first proposals to reform the political and economic system were presented in March 1968. One month later, a so-called Action Programme of the Communist Party was adopted. The programme proposed a new model of socialism combining democracy and socialist ideas adjusted to the Czechoslovak environment.[812]

Changes in the Constitution, including real guarantees of civic rights and principles of federation of the Czechoslovak state, were proposed along with forming a state administration independent of the direct political will of the Communist Party.[813] Some civic rights proclaimed by the 1960 constitution regained real content; as a result, many Czechs and Slovaks got their passports and were allowed to travel for the first time in their lives. Several partial reforms touching the constitution and law followed, like the abolishment of preliminary censorship and of the Central Publishing Authority in June

---

811 Jacko, "O vývoji a postavení národnostních menšin," p. 1102.
812 Jaromír Navrátil, ed., *The Prague Spring 1968: A National Security Archive Documents Reader* (Budapest: Central European University Press, 1998), document no. 19, pp. 92–95; see also Zbyněk A.B. Zeman, *Prague Spring: A Report on Czechoslovakia 1968* (London: Penguin Books, 1969), pp. 115–127.
813 Galia Golan, *Reform Rule in Czechoslovakia: The Dubček Era 1968–1969* (Cambridge: Cambridge University Press, 1973), p. 147ff.

1968, proposals to strengthen the role of the Government and Parliament, and a new wave of rehabilitation of victims of the political trials of the 1950s.

The period of the Prague Spring at the end brought in considerable changes to policies regarding minorities. The assumption that minority problems in Czechoslovakia had been solved after WWII and by introduction of socialist system proved unfounded. Minorities themselves, especially the Hungarian and Polish ones, intensified their activities and minority conflicts quickly revived, first and foremost in Southern Slovakia between Hungarians and Slovaks.[814] There were even national disorders in some places.[815] The Hungarian question turned out to be the most pressing. "They protested against the post war policies of reslovakization, deportations and displacement and sought redress. They demanded secondary schools, even a university. They demanded autonomy but many of them were thinking about more."[816] Complications emerged also in Teschen (Těšín) Silesia regarding Polish minority, in Eastern Slovakia concerning Ruthenians/Ukrainians and for the first time since the war also regarding the German minority. Germans, who were considered assimilated by Czech politicians, made themselves heard and demanded especially the formation of their own cultural association. Moreover, for the first time in the history of the Czech lands, Gypsies claimed their minority rights and started to call themselves the Romani (Roma). Leaderships of cultural associations of minorities also for the first time tabled political demands.

New legislation on minorities was discussed together with the preparation of the Constitutional Act on Federalization.[817] First calls for reform among expert, which suggested legislative regulation of the status of nationalities as a whole, occurred already in 1966. Only in 1967 the Czechoslovak state and party organs mentioned also Germans among "nationalities" living in Czechoslovakia.[818] There were discussions about codification of status of nationalities as well as about establishment of social and political representations of minorities. The Action Programme of the Communist Party of Czechoslovakia from 5 April 1968 criticised also the state of the question of minorities ("nationalities"). This important political document also mentioned the German nationality as a special minority group.[819]

---

814 In detail see René Petráš, "Ústavní zakotvení práv národností v Československu v roce 1968 a maďarská otázka," in *Maďarská menšina na Slovensku v procese transformácie po roku 1989: (Historické, politologické a právne súvislosti)* (Prešov: Universum, 2007), pp. 32–39.

815 On conflict between Hungarians and Slovaks see for example Pithart, *Osmašedesátý*, pp. 120–122; Peter Hunčík, "Maďarská menšina ve Slovenské republice," in *Etnické menšiny ve střední Evropě*, ed. by Ivan Gabal (Prague: G plus G, 1999), p. 210.

816 Pithart, *Osmašedesátý*, p. 120.

817 Petráš, "Constitutional development in Czechoslovakia in the 1960s and problems of ethnicity," pp. 60–68.

818 Staněk, *Německá menšina v českých zemích*, pp. 156–157.

819 Ibid., pp. 158–159.

It is necessary however to stress, that politicians and legal experts were far more interested in a solution of the relation between Czechs and Slovaks than in the problem of minorities. The discussions about proposed changes of the Prague Spring together with the problem of minorities were fundamentaly influenced by the tragic end of the reform movement. The Prague Spring was perceived by the communist hardliners in the Soviet Union and within the Soviet block (especially in German Democratic Republic) as a clear danger.[820] They feared for the integrity of the Soviet empire and especially condemned and refused any democratic reforms. In the end the leader of the Soviet Union, Leonid Brežněv, ordered a military intervention. In August 1968 Czechoslovakia was occupied by the armies of the Warsaw Pact, and the Czechoslovak reform communist leaders finally capitulated during negotiations in Moscow, where they signed so-called Moscow Protocol.[821]

Three neighbouring nations, which took part in the intervention, were the countries with which the interwar Czechoslovakia had sharp disputes over minorities, namely Poland, Hungary and to a certain extent also the German Democratic Republic. However representatives of Czechoslovak minorities preserved loyalty to the liberal currents of Czechoslovakia and viewed the participation of their native countries on the aggression as national shame.

The Constitutional Act on the Rights of Nationalities[822] was debated in the National Assembly on 27 October 1968, right after the occupation and all together with the Constitutional Act on Czechoslovak Federation. It was a governmental bill which was introduced by the Minister of Justice Dr. Bohuslav Kučera. He mentioned the close connection with federalization, because more equitable arrangement of the relation between Czechs and Slovaks also required equal regulation of the status of minorities.[823] Minister Kučera stressed also the necessity not only to ensure the equality of citizens before the law, but also to secure respect for differences in legal status of nationalities. Minister of Justice mentioned also international dimension of the problem: "The demand to solve the question of nationalities includes the necessity to respect certain differences dwelling in the fact that not only individual rights of citizens as individuals are confirmed but also rights of a nation as a whole."

Rapporteur on the bill was MP František Garaj, who pointed out some problematic elements. One of them was the right of nations to representation

820 Harold Gordon Skilling, *Czechoslovakia's Interrupted Revolution* (Princeton, NJ: Princeton University Press, 1976), pp. 675–680.

821 For English text of Moscow Protocol of August 26, 1968 see Navrátil, *Prague Spring 1968*, document no. 119, pp. 477–481.

822 For the discussions on its enactment from May 1968 see Národní archiv v Praze (NA), collection Úřad předsednictva vlády ČSSR 1968, 450/1, box 179.

823 National Assembly of the Czechoslovak Republic 1964–1968, stenographic protocols from the 28th assembly held on October 27, 1968, http://www.psp.cz/eknih/1964ns/stenprot/index.htm.

in representative bodies, where it was disputed whether it should be proportional. That was declined as it would complicate the general electoral system. Another problematic topic was the right to education in mother tongue. It was not clear whether it applies to higher school levels as well. Concerns appeared in the public whether constitutional embedding of rights of nationalities is not too far-reaching and it was reminded that minority rights had been misused against the integrity of the Czechoslovak state. According to Garaj in mixed ares (especially in Southern Slovakia) not only minority rights, but full national life of both Slovaks and Czechs must be secured, but without chauvinism. Also deputies of the minorities delivered their opinion on the bill. Hungarian deputy Ladislav (László) Egri emphasized that it is insufficient to proclaim rights of nationalities declaratively by a constitutional act and demanded further legislation by national councils and corresponding administrative reform (aiming at self-government for minority groups). The Czechoslovak Socialist Republic should be a common state not only of Czechs and Slovaks but also of other nationalities living in its territory. Only a minor adjustments were made in the proposal and the bill passed without further discussions.

Constitutional Act No. 144/1968 Sb., on Rights of Nationalities (i.e. minority rights) of 27 October 1968, declared the equality of all Czechoslovak citizens irrespective of their language and nationality. Artcile 1 proclaimed "the Czechoslovak Socialist Republic as a common state of Czech and Slovak nations and nationalities living in its territory."

The Act confirmed existing rights in minority matters and in some cases brought their expansion.[824] Germans were put on equal footings with Polish, Hungarian and Ukrainian (Ruthenian) minorities and all of them were promised special rights in the usage of language, establishment of minority schools, and promotion of their culture.[825] Article 3, Section 1 provided the enumerated minorities with a) right to education in their language, b) right to versatile cultural development, c) right to use their language in official relations in areas populated by the respective nationality, d) right to assemble in national cultural social associations, e) right to press and information published in their language. It was debatable whether rights enumerated by this Act applied to other not individually named groups.[826] Minorities were officially proclaimed a part of the Czechoslovak state, together with the Czech and Slovak nations.

824 René Petráš, "Ústavní zákon č. 144/1968 Sb. z 27.10.1968, o postavení národností," in *Pocta Jánu Gronskému* (Pilsen: Aleš Čeněk, 2008), pp. 86–92.

825 Its text published in Jiří Grospič, ed., *The Constitutional Foundations of the Czechoslovak Federation: The Constitution of the Czechoslovak Socialist Republic, the Constitutional Act Concerning the Czechoslovak Federation, the Constitutional Act Concerning the Status of Ethnic Groups in the Czechoslovak Socialist Republic* (Prague: Orbis, 1973).

826 Pavlíček, *Ústava a ústavní řád České republiky*, vol. 2, p. 196 claims that these applied only to enumerated privileged minorities. Gronský and Hřebejk, *Dokumenty k ústavnímu vývoji Československa II. (1945-1968)*, p. 71 assumes quite a different attitude.

Nationalities were also allowed to establish their own press, theatres and in particular associations. Citizens had the right to freely decide on their nationality and all forms of forcible denationalization were forbidden.

Not only individual civic rights of citizens as members of nationalities, but also collective rights were recognized. The Constitutional Act accepted nationalities as "ethnic groups from the political and constitutional point of view."[827] Artcile 2 promised nationalities its "representative bodies and other elective bodies proportionately to their numerousness." The practical relevance was the appointment of candidates of the National Front for the national committees and Federal Assembly.

Bodies securing rights of nationalities were supposed to be created: both national councils – Czech and Slovak established the Committee for national committees and nationalities, Governments of the Czech and Slovak Republics formed the Governmental Council for Nationalities and special Committees for Minority Affairs were established by Regional National Committees in minority areas.[828]

After the Soviet invasion the minority problem was again frozen, and the special Acts envisaged by Constitutional Act No. 144/1968 Sb. for its implementation were not adopted.[829] Most of the promised rights were guaranteed to the minorities on the local and regional levels only.[830] The Roma (Gypsy) population was not recognized as a minority and was still perceived mainly as a social (and also political) problem, which was for the Communist leadership difficult to address.[831]

5.4 MINORITY QUESTION IN THE YEARS 1970-1989

Within a year after the invasion of 1968 domestic collaborators with the Soviets and the conservative wing within the Communist Party finally prevailed. Gustáv Husák was elected the new leader of the Czechoslovak communists, and a period of stagnation, called "normalization," began.[832] Reform

827 Vladimír Mikule, "Národnostní menšiny v České republice pohledem českého práva," in Gabal, *Etnické menšiny ve střední Evropě*, pp. 57–58.

828 Ján Gronský, ed., *Dokumenty k ústavnímu vývoji Československa III. (1968–1989)* (Prague: Karolinum Press, 2000), p. 73; Hana Frištenská and Andrej Sulitka, *Průvodce právy příslušníků národnostních menšin v České republice* (Prague: Demokratická aliancia Slovákov v ČR, 1995), p. 23.

829 See Josef Kalvoda, "National minorities under Communism: The case of Czechoslovakia," in *Nationalities Papers: Journal of Nationalism and Ethnicity* 16, no. 1 (1988): esp. pp. 9–28.

830 Šindelka, *Národnostní politika v ČSSR*, pp. 126–129; Posluch, "Die konstitutionelle Entwicklung der Tschechoslowakischen Sozialistischen Republik," p. 548.

831 Broader context in Otto Ulč, "Gypsies in Czechoslovakia: a Case of Unfinished Integration," *East European Politics and Societies* 2, no. 2 (1988): p. 306ff.

832 Golan, *Reform Rule in Czechoslovakia*, pp. 264–268.

communists were expelled from the Party, and emigration grew in numbers after 1969.

Some reforms of the Prague Spring were reversed almost immediately after the Soviet invasion; for example, as early as on 13 September 1968 an Act on certain temporary measures in the area of press and other mass-media re-installed the previous censorship and established the Press and Information Bureau. The same day another Act was passed to curtail the freedom of assembly, and the national committees were entrusted with authority to forbid public meetings if they were contrary to the international interests of the Czechoslovak state or were aimed against the socialist order.

After the popular protests in 1969 were crushed and their organizers punished, the rest of the population gradually sank into apathy including the representatives of minorities. Although the social system worked well and the economy grew successfully especially in the 1970s, the period of "normalization" in the 1970s and 1980s was typical of a new wave of persecutions, mainly in the form of censorship, punishment and criminalization of all forms of real and latent opposition. New mechanisms of control over society were introduced combining policies of "stick and carrot."

The largest minority in Czechoslovakia was still the Hungarian one and the Czechoslovak attitude towards neighboring Hungary played an important role. The regime of János Kádár in Hungary rejected traditional Hungarian revisionism symbolized by the critical attitude towards the Trianon Peace Treaty of 1920 but the mere demonstration of quite liberal policies with concurrently successfully developing economy in the "mother" state attracted Hungarians in the South of Slovakia.[833]

The Polish minority was similarly attracted by the developments in Poland. The Polish Communist regime got into a permanent crisis at the beginning of the 1980s and it lasted until the disintegration of the Soviet bloc. Perhaps the USSR itself was willing to accept the fall of the regime and did not want to risk an invasion. The Communist regime in Czechoslovakia had overseen circumspectly activities of the Polish minority during the 1980s and tried hard to prevent contacts with the Polish opposition.[834]

When new Soviet leader Michail Gorbachev proclaimed new policies of the Soviet Communist Party, namely "*perestrojka*" and "*glasnost*"[835], Czechoslovak communists proposed only minor changes in its leadership. There were however attempts to hold talks with West Germany and Israel, which could have led to the improvement of the status of German and Jewish

---

833   Petráš, *Cizinci ve vlastní zemi*, pp. 187–192.
834   Petráš, *Menšiny v komunistickém Československu*, pp. 352–356.
835   For the importance of these policies (together with abandonment of Brežněv doctrine) as preconditions to democratic transformation see Jon Elster, "Constitutionalism in Eastern Europe: An Introduction," *University of Chicago Law Review* 58, no. 2 (1991): p. 453-454.

minorities in Czechoslovakia. However, the fall of the regime came before any real results became visible. At the end of the 1980s in Czechoslovakia, the minorities became partially activated as well as the opposition against the Communist regime. Hungarians were traditionally very dynamic, but quite surprisingly the Gypsies/Roma became active too. The resolving of their demands had been, however, carried out only after the fall of the Communist regime.

The period of 1970-1989 generally brought freezing of minority problems. Even after 1968, politics relating to national minorities was overwhelmed by ideology based upon proclaimed internationalism of minority issues; however, this ideology did not respond to real developments and needs in this area.[836] In case of some minorities (especially Germans) negative demographical development, gradual assimilation and frequently indifference of many members to national life prevailed. The regime of normalization expressed its negative attitude particularly against Jews and just as in the case of Gypsies/Romani, there was an attempt to assimilate them.[837]

The Prague Spring of 1968 and the revival of minorities were criticised during the period of normalization,[838] on the other hand, it was surprisingly admitted that this situation had been to a certain extent caused by a bad position of minorities.[839] Nevertheless, there had been attempts to convince the public that activities of German minority in the Czechoslovak Socialist Republic were influenced by displaced Sudeten Germans – "revanchists."[840] Even more important was the effort to brand liberal movement of the Prague Spring as a Zionist conspiracy.[841] Later on, during the normalization, the Jewish minority was a subject of permanent interest of the State Security (in particular the so-called action Pavouk – Spider). Even Charter 77 was influenced by the Zionist headquarters, according to the Communist propaganda. In the 1980s, the Polish minority invoked considerable worries of the State Security. Its representatives were under the surveillance in order to prevent contacts with Polish Solidarity movement.[842]

A long and relatively stable period of normalization brought only minimal changes to the legal status of minorities in Czechoslovakia. Germans,

---

836 Frištenská and Sulitka, *Průvodce právy příslušníků národnostních menšin*, p. 9.
837 Petráš, "Menšiny v Československu 1945-1989," pp. 240-280.
838 Jacko, "O vývoji a postavení národnostních menšin," p. 1099ff.
839 Jaroslav Chovanec, "Postavenie národností v Československskej socialistickej republike," *Právny obzor* 58 (1975): p. 30; Lubomír Slezák, "Vývoj národnostní struktury obyvatelstva ČSSR za posledních třicet let," in *Socialistickou cestou 1945-75* (Prague: Academia, 1975), p. 98.
840 Staněk, *Německá menšina v českých zemích*, p. 162. Misusing the fear of Germans and anti-Semitism was also common in Poland in 1968, Karel Durman, *Útěk od praporů: Kreml a krize impéria, 1964-1991* (Prague: Karolinum Press, 1998), pp. 81-82.
841 Yegar, *Československo, sionismus, Izrael*, pp. 182-184.
842 Zahradnik, "Nástin historického vývoje," pp. 32-33.

Ukrainians and Hungarians in the Czech lands and Poles in Slovakia were under the pressure of assimilation tendencies. Especially Hungarians and Poles were characterized by considerable identification with their own ethnicity. An important factor contributing to assimilation were mixed marriages. After 1945 a growth in nationally mixed marriages took place. Nationally mixed marriages began to predominate over new marriages of Poles and Germans already in the beginning of the 1950s, and of Ukrainians in the beginning of the 1960's. In the 1980s, virtually all German marriages were mixed, for Poles and Ukrainians the number was approximately 70%, for Hungarians around 25%. Despite all defects in the minority policy of the Communist regime, this indicator is a considerable signal of principally good and equal relations between individual nations in the state. To a certain extent Czechoslovakia and the Soviet bloc as a whole succeeded in breaking down or at least subduing the formerly deep antagonisms among the nations.[843]

Minority policy of the Communist regime had plenty of imperfections. Especially the language question on the local level represented a serious problem. In fact, no uniform approach existed in Czechoslovakia and it was the competence of the Regional national committees to decide on the use of minority languages. Many experts disagreed with this practice and recommended enactment of a legal regulation to regulate the problem on the national level. They also stated that languages of minorities are generally used in administrative bodies only minimally and therefore, particularly in the case of the numerous Hungarians, completely insufficiently.[844]

The structure of educated people was used as a parameter suggesting equal status of nationalities. Especially noticeable was the disproportion between the share of university graduates among Czechs and Slovaks (5,2% and 5,1% in 1980) and among graduates belonging to minorities (Hungarians 2,1% and Germans 1,2%!).[845] The university education in Czechoslovakia had been markedly influenced by the Communist regime, which indicated the success of Slovaks, who had reached almost the same level with Czechs in educational structure. Moreover, the German group had, with the exception of Jewish minority, traditionally (even during the First Czechoslovak Republic) the highest level of literacy and education. This slump to the worst level was officially reasoned by the fact that, strictly speaking, after the displacement only the blue-collar population stayed in the country. However, this only partly explains the development.

843 Sokolová, et al., *Soudobé tendence vývoje národností v ČSSR*, pp. 59–60, 140–141.
844 Bajcura, *Cesta k internacionálnej jednote*, pp. 191–193.
845 Sokolová, et al., *Soudobé tendence vývoje národností v ČSSR*, pp. 48–50; Hernová, "Němci v ČSR v letech 1950–1980," pp. 272–274.

Before the end of the Communist regime, certain pursuits of reforms occurred. The most important legal reform was connected with the draft of a new Constitution of the Czechoslovak Federation, which was discussed by the Communist Party leadership from 1986 until November 1989. The draft was interesting from a constitutional perspective, because it was designed as a single constitutional charter for three entities – the Federation and both Republics.[846] The draft proposed some adjustments by the communist regime in accordance with the Soviet style of *"perestrojka."* For minorities the Act on Nationalities (No. 144/1968 Sb.) was probably supposed to be incorporated into the constitution without major amendments.[847] Apparently, the minority question had not been considered topical by the regime. And yet political changes had kicked in. For example in January 1988 during the visit of German Chancellor Helmut Kohl in Prague, signs of changes in the attitude of Czechoslovakia towards the question of German minority were shown.[848] The positive development in relations with Israel had a similarly favourable influence on the status of the Jewish minority.

The most important minority which was in danger of a complete assimilation was the German group. In the 1970s and 1980s another significant decrease of numbers of Germans in Czechoslovakia took place. However, the official statistics were criticised by the Federal Republic of Germany ("West Germany") as biased. The factors contributing to the decrease were, along with negative demographic structure, also extensive emigration (especially after Czechoslovakia concluded so-called Prague Treaty with the Federal Republic of Germany in 1973)[849] and common minimal national sentiment – many parents simply did not raise their children as Germans. The non-existence of a national education contributed to this trend as well. A directive of the Czech Ministry of Education from 1971 provided an opportunity to ensure education for German children just as for Poles and Slovaks, but only if the number of pupils was sufficient, which was never fulfilled. Therefore, not a single German class existed, only circles of German language were promoted. As a result the knowledge of the native language among children decreased. There was only minimal interest in national life among the young generation of Germans living in Czechoslovakia in general.[850]

---

846 The draft constitutional law was under preparation in the Federal Assembly, see http://www
    .psp.cz/eknih/1986fs/tisky/t0185_00.htm.

847 Gronský, *Dokumenty k ústavnímu vývoji Československa III. (1968–1989)*, pp. 250, 265–266.

848 Staněk, *Německá menšina v českých zemích*, p. 195.

849 See for example Radko Břach, *Smlouva o vzájemných vztazích mezi ČSSR a SRN z roku 1973* (Prague: ÚSD, 1994), pp. 37–39, 58–60.

850 Staněk, *Německá menšina v českých zemích*, pp. 171–175, 185, 192; Hernová, "Němci v ČSR v letech 1950–1980," pp. 267–268.

The year 1968 also witnessed a revival of the Gypsy question. After preparation, which began in March 1968, the Association of Gypsies – Romani was established both in the Czech lands and Slovakia. The attempt was to recognize the status of the nationality of Gypsies living in Czechoslovakia, but it was not successful. The Association of Gypsies/Romani was dissolved under pressure from state and party organs in 1973. And again, the state policy towards this minority changed – particularly in 1970 and 1972. The most important was the Governmental decision No. 231/72 which promoted the concept of social integration. The formerly promoted assimilation was supposed to be abandoned and the differences respected, but the practise often looked otherwise. Legal experts overall did not accept the nationalistic character of this question which they considered to be a social problem with certain ethnic elements. A scientific and especially sociological research was planned but objectively found facts were not made public.[851] Social integration efforts overall failed. Nevertheless, the Gypsy/Romani question was quite different from other minorities; this was admitted in 1989 just as it is today and it requires different methods of solution.[852]

Overall, it is necessary to say that in the 1970s and 1980s the minority question stood on the edge of interest of not only the Communist regime but also of Czechoslovak society and in reality of significant part of minorities themselves. Activaties of the second half of 1980s refers only to individuals and small groups.[853]

---

851   Davidová, *Cesty Romů 1945–1990*, pp. 205–207.

852   Čížkovská, "Politika vlády ČSFR k romské menšině, p. 533; see also Karel Holomek, "Romská menšina v České republice," in Gabal, *Etnické menšiny ve střední Evropě*, pp. 153–171.

853   Petráš, *Menšiny v komunistickém Československu*, pp. 352–365.

6. CZECHOSLOVAKIA IN THE YEARS OF TRANSFORMATION AND DISINTEGRATION IN 1989–1992

6.1 CZECHOSLOVAKIA AND ITS MINORITIES SINCE 1989

Since the mid-1980s, the Communist regime was gradually changing, especially in connection with the so-called period of *"perestrojka."* However, in Czechoslovakia, the liberalization was incomparably more limited than for example in neighbouring Poland and Hungary. This difference incidentally affected minority problems because the cross-border contacts of members of Polish and Hungarian minority had suddenly brought an atmosphere of quite relaxed societies in neighbouring countries. Particularly relations of part of Polish minority to the strong opposition in Poland had caused great concerns.[854] Overall reforms of the Communist regime in Czechoslovakia were predominantly mainly formal or cosmetic and the Communist party was not interested in real changes with the exception of liberalization of economy.

The proposed adjustments of the Communist regime in accordance with the ideas of Soviet *"perestrojka"* were not sufficient to meet the growing appeal for fundamental changes. Partly because of the failure of Prague Spring and partly because of changed internal and international situation majority of the society simply did not want to reform the communist regime. People desired to replace it with a pluralistic democracy and a market economy with a social dimension. Certain revitalization was obvious also among minorities.[855] Poles and Hungarians were inspired by liberalization in their native states. Activists were in many cases harshly persecuted by the state apparatus. In case of German and Jewish minorities, a graduate improvement of relations with the Federal Republic of Germany and Israel played a positive role. The representatives of Gypsies/Romani began to demand respect of their rights. Even though these initiatives were unacceptable from the viewpoint of traditional methods of normalization, the regime was surprisingly helpful. For example it respected the change of terminology from Gypsies into Roma/Romani, promoted by this group since the 1960s.

---

854 Zahradnik, "Nástin historického vývoje," pp. 32–33.
855 Petráš, "Menšiny v Československu 1945–1989," pp. 240–280.

In consequence of the profound changes in the international position of the whole Soviet bloc, the year 1989 brought a domino effect of revolutions within the socialist countries.[856] The Iron Curtain finally disappeared especially after the Czechoslovak "Velvet Revolution" and after the fall of the Berlin Wall. The Velvet Revolution started on 17th November 1989, when students called a demonstration to commemorate the fiftieth anniversary of the Nazi persecution aimed against Czech universities.[857] The peaceful demonstration was stopped by police troops in the centre of Prague, and students were brutally beaten. The events led to the student strike being supported by popular protests which turned into mass demonstrations against the regime. The events of November 1989 soon led to the establishment of organizations of civic opposition against the communist regime[858] and the Communist regime collapsed within a few days without violence. On 28 November 1989 the Communist Party of Czechoslovakia finally agreed in a Czechoslovak version of "Roundtable talks" to give up its monopoly on political power.[859] The so-called Velvet Revolution triumphed.

In 1989 there were no real political and social forces capable of preventing profound political and economic changes.[860] The period of transition from the authoritarian communist regime into a democratic system followed, although not without problems, controversies and discussions on the adequate policies. After the failure of the Prague Spring many Czechoslovaks had been doubtful regarding any possibility of reforming communism. However, there were not many patterns available in the transition period to follow so that political, economic and social changes could be carried out.[861] The transition fundamentally affected also the status of minorities. New Czechoslovak leaders declared their commitment to maintain the democratic legacy of the First Czechoslovak Republic. Therefore some of the changes in the legal system were based on a return to the Central European legal tradition.[862] However this was not possible for the minority rights.

---

856 Timothy Garton Ash, *The Magic Lantern: The Revolution of '89 Witnessed in Warsaw, Budapest, Berlin and Prague* (New York: Random House, 1990).

857 Jiří Suk, "Czechoslovakia's return to democracy (1989-1992)," in Pánek and Tůma, *A History of the Czech lands*, especially pp. 589-591.

858 Suk, "Czechoslovakia's return to democracy," pp. 589-583.

859 Miloš Calda, "Roundtable talks in Czechoslovakia," in *The Roundtable Talks and the Breakdown of Communism*, ed. by Jon Elster (Chicago: University of Chicago Press, 1996), pp. 135-177.

860 Most recently with regard to all strata of Czechoslovak society James Krapfl, *Revolution with a Human Face: Politics, Culture, and Community in Czechoslovakia, 1989-1992* (Ithaca, NY: Cornell University Press, 2013), esp. chap. 1.

861 For analyses of the public opinion on transition schemes see Sharon L. Wolchik, *Czechoslovakia in transition: politics, economics, and society* (London: Pinter, 1991), especially pp. 116-119.

862 It was of course not the case of Czechoslovakia only, although the strategies of individual states varied. See interesting comparisons in Janina Frentzel-Zagórska, *From a One-party State to Democracy: Transition in Eastern Europe* (Amsterdam: Rodopi, 1993), especially pp. 93-97.

Czechoslovakia was especially inspired by the results of Western legal and political thinking achieved after WW II.[863] New democratic foundations were used for a thorough modification of the existing Constitution, symbolized by returning to the democratic principles of the rule of law, human rights, real separation of powers, and free competition among political parties.[864] In March 1990 a series of new laws on freedom of association, freedom of assembly, right of petition, and freedom of press were enacted and were followed on by changes made to the judicial system and state prosecution. The importance of human rights was officially confirmed on 9 January 1991, when Constitutional Act No. 23/1991 Sb., entitled the Charter of Fundamental Rights and Freedoms, was enacted. In its Preamble Czechoslovakia expressly recognized the inviolability of the natural rights of people and the universally shared values of humanity and democracy.[865] This policy was naturally very advantageous also to the minorities. Progressively, an idea refusing the traditional national state gained ground and promoted equality of citizens without regard to nationality.[866]

Another general problem, which has to be mentioned, is an outburst of nationalism in many countries of the disintegrating Soviet bloc. It is a sad tradition that whenever a stiff undemocratic political regime dissolves, the society lets itself be drawn to nationalism or more likely to chauvinism. That can lead to wars with neighbours but also to brutal oppression of minorities. Europe had experienced such outburst of nationalism with the fall of absolutist regimes in 1848 and the same happened in some countries of the Soviet bloc at the turn of the 1980s and 1990s.[867]

However, the worst conflict arose in Yugoslavia, a socialist state independent from Moscow. Disintegration of the state in 1988 (converted into federation in 1945) began as a secession of more developed parts, Slovenia and Croatia, from the rest of the state which was hit by an economic and political crisis. Nevertheless, the situation developed rapidly into bloody wars in Croatia, later on also in Bosnia or Kosovo. These wars in former Yugoslavia were a major impulse for revival of international interest in minority protection. The Council of Europe, an organization of mainly European democratic countries, engaged in this question intensively in the beginning of the 1990s. It is very important to remark that unlike the European Union or NATO, into

---

863   For wider philosophical context of this approach see especially Jiří Přibáň, *Legal Symbolism: On Law, Time and European Identity* (Burlington, VT: Ashgate Publishing, 2007), especially p. 159ff.

864   Rett R. Ludwikowski, *Constitution-making in the Region of Former Soviet Dominance* (Durham, NC: Duke University Press, 1996), pp. 164–165.

865   Text in English: Constitutional acts of Czech and Slovak Federal Republic and acts concerning the civil rights and freedoms adopted by the Federal Assembly of the Czech and Slovak Federal Republic. Federal Assembly and Czechoslovak Academy of Sciences, Prague 1992.

866   Petráš, *Cizinci ve vlastní zemi*, pp. 114–117.

867   Petráš, *Menšiny v komunistickém Československu*, pp. 377–392.

which the socialistic countries entered only after many years since the fall of the Communist regime, entering into the Council of Europe was swift. Thanks to that, former socialist countries, including Czechoslovakia and its successor states, became involved in preparation and enforcing of key international documents such as the Framework Convention for the Protection of National Minorities, which established a new standard of their legal status.[868]

After the fall of the regime in Czechoslovakia itself, the minority problem remained on the edge of interest of the society, which was mostly interested in its political and social transformation and in economic reform. There was one important issue representing a certain failure in the first two years of transformation. Czech and Slovak political representatives did not succeed in finding a suitable bilateral model for the coexistence of the Czech and Slovak nations within one common state.[869] Initial discussions spiralled around a name for the federation acceptable for both sides, around a new division of competences and around the concept of "authentic federation" advocated by Václav Havel as a contrast to "socialist" formal one.[870] By the end of 1990 a compromise was reached on the power sharing of the competences of federal bodies.[871] In fact discussions on the name of the state resembled historical controversies between Czechs and Slovaks and showed the depth of the crisis of the common Czechoslovak state. Under the new Constitutional Act of April 1990 Czechoslovakia was quickly renamed as the "Czech and Slovak Federal Republic."

The noticeable enhancement of nationalism in Slovakia led to great concerns that the revival of national feeling of Slovaks may provoke minorities too and the numerous Hungarians above all. The Hungarian minority comprised approximately one tenth of Slovak population, and posed the most numerous minority in Czechoslovakia by far already since the displacement of Germans. At the same time, Budapest had traditionally supported its minorities and even promoted restoration of the Great Hungarian state. During the functioning of the Soviet bloc, the irredentism, supported by the Hungarian state, was unacceptable. Yet, after the collapse of the USSR, Hungary came with more active support for Hungarian minorities living abroad. Such policy could lead to conflicts mainly with Romania and Czechoslovakia or

---

868 Monika Forejtová, *Mezinárodněprávní ochrana menšin* (Pilsen: Západočeská univerzita, 2002), p. 82.

869 In more details see Eric Stein, *Czecho-Slovakia: Ethnic Conflict, Constitutional Fissure, Negotiated Breakup* (Ann Arbor: The University of Michigan Press, 1997); see also Sharon L. Wolchik, "The politics of transition and the break-up of Czechoslovakia," in *The end of Czechoslovakia*, ed. by Jiří Musil (Budapest: Central European University Press, 1995), pp. 225–241.

870 In more details Jan Rychlík, "The Possibilities for Czech-Slovak Compromise, 1989–1992," in *Irreconcilable Differences? Explaining Czechoslovakia's Dissolution*, ed. by Michael Kraus and Allison Stanger (Lanham, MD: Rowman & Littlefield, 2000), especially pp. 50–54.

871 Ibid., p. 54.

since 1993 independent Slovakia. In case of Southern Slovakia, at least two exceptionally dangerous aspects were combined – Hungarian irredentism and simultaneously Slovak nationalism, which was just creating its own statehood. Perhaps a little surprisingly the development was milder than anyone expected. There had been certain disputes between Czechoslovakia or Slovakia and Hungary indeed, but their extent was limited and most importantly, the Hungarian minority in Southern Slovakia remained quite calm.[872]

A majority of the society in Czechoslovakia and later in the Czech Republic and Slovakia as well as in Hungary supported the idea of becoming a candidate for accession to the European Communities (later the European Union) and NATO, which undoubtedly contributed to a peaceful development. Politicians of both countries were very well aware of the fact that national conflicts could spoil these efforts. In Hungary, parliamentary elections in May 1994 might be viewed as the turning point since the public was fed up with the formerly excessive government's interest in Hungarian minorities abroad.[873] In Slovakia, the development was more complicated, especially at the time of Vladimir Mečiar's government, but Slovak politicians have since 1993 realised that apart from Czechoslovakia, independent Slovakia is only half the size of Hungary, while the Hungarian minority is numerous and lives concentrated close to the borders, so any radical anti-minority policy would not pay off for Bratislava.

Perhaps the biggest problem concerning Hungarian minority in the beginning of the 1990s, was the dispute over Gabčíkovo-Nagymaros, dam with hydroelectric power plant aimed to produce electricity and regulate the Danube. Extensive works affected the region with the very numerous Hungarian minority. Works on the project of the dam began already in the 1970s and inter alia was supposed to prevent repeated catastrophic flooding and improve navigability of the river. Preparation and building of the dam was under way already in the time of the Soviet bloc, just like the cooperation between Czechoslovakia and Hungary based on bilateral treaty. Extensive building works on creating this enormous water dam were executed on the territory of both states. Economic protests strengthened at the end of the 1980s and in the course of 1989 Budapest unilaterally disrupted the construction, even though it had been finished by 90%. After 1989 changes a part of Slovaks viewed unilateral suspension of the construction by Budapest as a demonstration of Hungarian chauvinism or even anti-Slovak action. Similarly, appeasement of some Czech politicians and their criticism of the project were regarded as literally betrayal of Slovak interests. From the representatives of

---

872 Péter Morvay, "Menšiny v Maďarsku a maďarská menšinová politika od roku 1918 do současnosti," in Gabal, *Etnické menšiny ve střední Evropě*, pp. 194–195.

873 Petráš, *Cizinci ve vlastní zemi*, pp. 193–194.

Hungarian minority some radical statements were made, according to which the construction aimed to terminate compact settlement of Hungarians in Czechoslovakia. The problem also showed the deep crises of the Czechoslovak federation and the clash of competences between Czechoslovak federal organs and Slovakia, which had a growing tendency to act independently. In 1991 Czechoslovakia decided to continue the construction only in Slovak territory, regardless of planned construction in the Hungarian territory. A key move, which was diverting most of the flow to Slovakia on 23 October 1992, was in fact already Slovak initiative. It is necessary to remark, that after elections in June 1992 Czechoslovakia began to head towards disintegration and Slovakia conducted some steps in fact independently even before the official break up of the Czechoslovak state on 1 January 1993. Even after getting the dam into provisional operation in October 1992 many disputes between Slovakia and Hungary occurred, but the situation calmed down gradually. Great concerns of the ecologists about building of such a gigantic work did not come true. In the end, Hungarian minority in Slovakia was affected by the works only minimally and the nationalistic aspect of the disputes lost, to considerable extent, its strenghth. The argument over Gabčíkovo-Nagymaros overall presents a remarkable example of a conflict into which a minority aspect was involved. In this particular case, problems of economic, ecological and even political (disintegration of regimes promoting gigantic work), nationalistic (revival of Hungarian-Slovak hatred), constitutional (disputable competences of bodies in the time of Czechoslovak disintegration) and minority character were interconnected.

6.2 PARTICULARITIES OF INDIVIDUAL MINORITIES IN CZECHOSLOVAKIA

The potentially most dangerous Hungarian problem fortunately has not led to open or violent conflicts. However, it was not the only minority problem of Czechoslovakia. In the Czech lands, the minority question remained basically on the edge of interest, with the exception of peculiar "discussions about the so-called Beneš's decrees," a conflict over the evaluation of wartime and post-war Czech-German relations. Both Czech and Slovak societies were mostly concerned with the problems of Gypsies/Romani yet it was never a classic minority problem but rather a social issue. The "majority" Czech and Slovak society especially perceived their different social and cultural level connected to a specific way of life. Even though Gypsies/Romani obtained the right to acknowledge their own nationality, in principle during census in 1991, only a small part of them actually did so. The attempts to arouse some kind of Romani national renaissance failed. The key aspect was naturally the fact that Gypsies/Romani cannot rely on support of any native state, so traditionally the most dangerous aspect of minority question never existed in their case. In spite of extraordinary activities of the Communist regime in social sphere, the differences between Gypsy/Romani population and Czech and Slovaks lingered especially in the 1950s and 1960s.[874] Gypsies/Romani in the Czech lands were mostly immigrants from Slovakia after 1945 or their descendants and in the main lived on the edge of society.[875] Gypsy hamlets in Central and Eastern Slovakia had literally catastrophic living and cultural standard, resembling underdeveloped countries of the third world. During the so-called normalization in 1970-1989, the regime resigned all penetrative steps in politics and primarily maintained stability, involving also the status of Gypsies/Romani.

Economic transformation of 1990s negatively affected the Gypsy/Romani population. Apparently the key problem was high proportion of unemployment. In the time of an ineffective centrally planned economy of the socialist state the need of unqualified workers was sizeable and that is what an overwhelming part of the Gypsies/Romani were. Tolerance of the employers towards low working morale was vanishing quickly and Gypsies/Romani in general have never had a reputation as reliable workers. In later years, already during existence of the independent Czech Republic and Slovakia, such a situation formed in the labour market that underqualified work in the Czech Republic was massively carried out by foreigners, typically from Ukraine, which squeezed the Gypsy/Romani labour forces. In Slovakia, the unemployment was several times higher in the long term, which affected again mostly the Gypsies/Romani. A certain problem in the question of their unemployment was in fact the generous social system, which secured higher incomes for families with many children than what the qualified workers earned. To Gypsies/Romani, legal employment became often financially disadvantageous. It is also not possible to overlook the fact, that the working duty that functioned since World War II was abolished. Along with already mentioned unemployment it is necessary to mention the gradual creation of a housing market, which resulted in the extrusion of Gypsies from areas with valued real estates.

The Gypsies/Romani represent quite the numerous minority in the Czech Republic (approximately 2% of population) and particularly in Slovakia (perhaps even 10% of population). Under new democratic circumstances an opportunity arose to organize this group and, with the assistance of their own political parties or associations, to promote their demands. It was, however, characteristic for Romani parties to be extraordinarily crumbled and to have

---

874 Petráš, "Cikánská/romská otázka v Československu," pp. 225-247.
875 Petráš, "Právo a romské kočování v českých zemích," pp. 210-219.

limited effectiveness. Economic problems of their associations were nothing uncommon. Improving status of Gypsies/Romani was then promoted more effectively by their proponents from the ranks of majority society, some of whom had literally and enthusiastically endorsed a multicultural society. The interest of international and European organisations and array of western states in the situations of Gypsies/Romani also played an important role. The Czech Republic and, with the exception of the short era of Vladimir Mečiar, also Slovakia quickly became countries with high democratic standards, yet the status and actual treatment of Gypsies/Romani was often criticised from abroad.

The largest minority, if this term can be used for the era of Czechoslovakia at all, were for many decades the Slovaks in the Czech lands. Although a considerable number of Slovaks came to the Czech lands already at the time of inter-war Czechoslovakia, the main period of this numerically heavy migration started no sooner than after 1945; at the beginning it was particularly connected with populating originally German regions, later with industrialisation (Ostrava region), and with strengthening the participation of Slovaks in authorities in Prague.[876] That migration was of crucial importance from a statistical perspective despite the fact that it was intra-state migration then; however, the actual importance of this specific immigration should not be overestimated. Even though a minority that has remained the most numerous to this day was created quite quickly [the number of Slovaks in the Czech lands (in thousands): 1930-44, 1950-258, 1961-276, 1970-321, 1980-359, 1989-419],[877] there has never been a real immigration or minority issue. The existence of this group has always been marginalised by both authorities and citizens, who in fact did not, and often still do not, perceive it as a minority group. Even though this group was numerous, its assimilation proceeded very quickly and not only because of the minimal language difference between the Czech and Slovak languages. Pursuant to census, numerousness of this group was the highest in 1980 when 359 000 Slovaks lived in the Czech lands. However, census in 1991 registered only 315 000 Slovaks in the situation when the immigration of Slovaks to the Czech lands still continued. In the first census in the independent Czech Republic in 2001 only 193 000 people registered as Slovak nationals.[878] A key element was the prevalence of mixed marriages when approximately 70% of Slovaks lived in mixed Czech-Slovak families and more than 60% of children from these families had embraced Czech

---

876 For details see Petráš, *Menšiny v komunistickém Československu*, pp. 109–112, 232–234, 360–361.

877 *Federální statistický úřad: Historická statistická ročenka ČSSR* (Prague: Státní nakladatelství technické literatury, 1985), p. 429; *Statistická ročenka České a Slovenské federativní republiky 1990* (Prague: Státní nakladatelství technické literatury, 1990), p. 100.

878 Oľga Šrajerová, "Slovenská menšina v České republike," in *Menšiny a právo v České republice*, ed. by René Petráš, Helena Petrův and Harald Christian Scheu (Prague: Auditorium, 2009), p. 193.

nationality. Relations of Slovaks with Czechs as well as the relations between two successor states have been trouble-free, social status and cultural level corresponded to the majority society or transcended them slightly, for example in terms of educational structure. An interest in national life is limited in the case of a major part of this minority, which manifests itself mainly through parents being uninterested in sending children to minority schools, which vanished in 2001.[879] Slovaks in the Czech Republic are a perfectly problem-free minority and the relationship of the Czech environment to them is great. Even those who use their mother tongue in public life or at work do not encounter legal problems or any opposition in their surroundings.

In connection with the very large but quickly assimilating Slovak minority in the Czech lands, it is necessary to mention Czechs living in Slovakia as well. This group had been small in numbers since World War II, it did not present a problem and its existence was only known due to census statistics. Strong Slovak nationalism from the beginning of the 1990s raised certain concerns because the experiences of anti-Czech tempers from 1938/1939 period and World War II were alarming. During the interwar years in Czechoslovakia many Czechs moved to Slovakia where they worked mostly as state officials or teachers, which lead to creation of quite a numerous minority. However, this minority became the target of considerable pressure from its surroundings and Slovak bodies at the time of disintegration of the interwar period in Czechoslovakia and was partly forced to return to the Czech lands. Concerns about any repetition of this situation in the 1990s proved unfounded and a Czech minority still exists in Slovakia without any problems.

Aside from a large Hungarian minority, specific Gypsy/Romani groups, whose prevailing part does not acknowledge their own nationality and not numerous Czech minority, also Ruthenians and Ukrainians do live in Slovakia. The identity of these two groups has always been very controversial. During the interwar period Czechoslovakia did not assume an unambiguous attitude toward national identity. It viewed them as a specific part of Russians or individual Ruthenian nationality and in practice tolerated the use of Ruthenian dialects. Nevertheless, in 1952 the Communist regime began to promote expressly Ukrainian orientation, while Ruthenianship was suppressed. The so-called ukrainianization and its real impact have been up to now a surprisingly complicated theme. Only after temporary liberalization in 1968 was it admissible again to use both terms Ukrainian and Ruthenian but in census both groups were considered as one.

The census in March 1991 provided for free choice of Ruthenian or Ukrainian nationality. During the census, people usually filled out the forms

---

879 Andrej Sulitka, "Národnostní menšiny v České republice po roce 1989 a národnostněmenšinová politika," in Petráš, Petrův and Scheu, *Menšiny a právo v České republice*, pp. 171–172.

independently, so the bodies could not influence the content, as it is common for such questions. 17 000 people registered as Ruthenians and 14 000 as Ukrainians. However the fact that it came to a division of one community with common origin, language and history posed a problem. The dividing line ran even within the families.[880] Discussions about national identity continued in following years. The contradiction was whether local people are a specific nation or Ukrainians who are one of the largest nations in Europe. The results of census indicate that opinions of the people were quite balanced. The whole problem was of course influenced by the fact that Ukraine achieved independence at the end of 1991 and this brought an end to a certain identification of Ukrainian orientation with the interests of the USSR. However, up to the present time, there has been a striking difference between pro-western nationalistic regions in the West and pro-Russian or even Russificated districts in the East and South of the independent Ukraine. Admittedly, the relevance of Ruthenian or Ukrainian question has been marginal in Slovakia.

The only "classic" minority, hence a group with their own clear-cut language and national sentiment in the Czech lands, have been after the relocation of Germans the Poles in the Teschen (Těšín) Silesia. Yet the group is small in numbers and represents only a few thousands of the people. As the formerly stable Soviet bloc disintegrated, concerns about revival of national conflicts arose, including a dispute between Poland and Czechoslovakia over the Teschen (Těšín) Silesia. In the Czech lands the existence of Polish minority had been overlooked and some local problems, such as occasional vandalism of Czech hooligans on Polish signs caused only minimal response in the public. The interest in Polish minority in the Teschen (Těšín) Silesia was far greater in Poland, but Warsaw assessed the Czech minority policy rather positively and had no interest in complicating their foreign policy because of Teschen.

In the Czech Republic itself, Poles presented the only group, who actively demanded their rights. That was clear from local committees for national minorities, which were supposed to be established within the framework of local self-government, but in reality functioned only in the Teschen Silesia, due to lack of interest of other minorities. Poles had at their own disposal not only elementary but also secondary minority schools. Polish culture had considerable state support; overall the helpfulness of the state and the money provided were substantial, given the small numerousness of the Polish minority group.

An interesting development arose in relation to small Jewish minority. Determination of this group is traditionally tricky because the religious

---

880 Jana Plichtová, ed., *Minority v politike: Kultúrne a jazykové práva* (Bratislava: Česko-slovenský výbor Európskej kultúrnej nadácie, 1992), p. 251. (Conclusions of working group for Ruthenian and Ukrainian minorities – Robert Magosci, Ľudovít Haraksim).

foundation keeps losing its importance in modern society and only part of the group acknowledges their own nation. After World War II, a deep decline of religious life caused yet another complication. Many emigrants who considered themselves Jewish were surprised that local Jewish communities in western countries refuse to respect their Jewish identity. After 1989 an exceptional revival of this community in Czechoslovakia followed. Even though this group was numbering only in the thousands after the holocaust and extensive emigration during the communist era, the society's interest in Jewish culture was immense. In the Czech lands it became popular to reconstruct synagogues or Jewish cemeteries. On the other hand, in Slovakia there was a partial revival of anti-Semitism, which was strong at the time of independent pro-Nazi state in 1939-1945. Czechoslovakia and later on the Czech Republic became reliable supporters of Israel in Europe, while many western democracies were quite critical toward Israeli politics. The independent Jewish community in Czechoslovakia was going through a complicated development connected with searching for their own identity. There were very active groups within the community but they were quite often strongly set against each other. Definition of the Jewish community belonged to some of the most significant problems because in most of the countries the definition is understood religiously but the religiosity had fallen exceptionally in particular in the Czech lands. Mostly such persons had endorsed membership in Jewish community, whose families were afflicted by the holocaust without regard to religion. Some Jewish communities began to be orthodox oriented and such approach was hardly acceptable to them.[881]

From the legal point of view, the Jewish minority was reflected also by the restitution laws, but restitutions became quite a complicated problem. As early as 1990 Czechoslovakia had started with the restitution of property, i.e. returning property to its former private owners.[882] Restitution was regarded as both a just solution and another manner of privatization.[883] Initially, it was decided to return only property nationalized or confiscated after the Communist coup, i.e. after 25th February 1948. First of restitutions laws, Act No. 403/1990 Sb. dealt with remedies to "certain property injustices," especially when property had been nationalized without compensation or when privately owned apartment houses and other properties were expropriated under by national committees. According to this Act also aliens could claim restitution or compensation provided that their claims have not been

---

881 Blanka Soukupová, "Židovská menšina v českých zemích v současnosti (1989-2005)," in Petráš, Petrův and Scheu, *Menšiny a právo v České republice*, pp. 210-228.

882 Anders Fogelklou and Fredrik Sterzel, eds., *Consolidating legal reform in Central and Eastern Europe: An Anthology* (Uppsala: Iustus Forlag, 2003), p. 56ff.

883 Vojtěch Cepl, "A note on the Restitution of Property in Post-Communist Czechoslovakia," *Journal of Communist Studies* 7, no. 3 (1991): 367-375.

previously settled by bilateral international treaties (lump sum agreements) concluded by Czechoslovakia until 1989.[884]

There was also limited restitution of Church property including the Jewish religious communities, with a major portion to be decided later. In 1991 the most important of restitutions law, Act No. 87/1991 Sb. on out-of-court rehabilitation was enacted. It brought some important changes to the original concept of restitution. Only Czechoslovak citizens with permanent residence in the country, who lost their personal property between February 1948 and 1990 (or their heirs) were eligible to get their property back. Special Act, with similar conditions, was enacted for the restitution of land. This in fact meant that the restitution of some portions of the property of Jews and the restitution of the property of Sudeten Germans were excluded.

When it was not possible to return the property itself to the original owners or their heirs, compensation was paid. The rest of state property was privatized in a way called "the big privatization," organized mainly as a so-called "coupon" privatization.[885]

Only after the so-called Washington Conference on Holocaust Era Assets,[886] the Czech Republic enacted special Act No. 212/2000 Sb. on alleviation of some property injuries caused by the holocaust. The whole problem of the restitutions of Jewish property in successor states of Czechoslovakia was exceptionally complicated by the fact that discussions about compensating the Jews for the persecutions and injustices caused to them during World War II became world-wide in the mid-1990s and one of the most important impulsions were claims against Switzerland to deal with bank account of the holocaust victims which lay dormant as well as against German and Austrian firms using slave labor.[887]

According to V. Houžvička "the new Czechoslovak Republic was aware of the fundamental importance of relations with Germany in the throes of reunification."[888] The positive approach of Czechoslovak representatives towards Germany, especially Václav Havel or Jiří Dientsbier, was formed during the discussions of the dissident group Charter 77 in the 1980s. Especially

---

884 See Kuklík, "Interference with proprietary rights between 1945 and 1948."
885 For the legal aspects see Anna Gelpern, "The laws and politics of reprivatization in East-Central Europe: A Comparison," *University of Pennsylvania journal of international business law* 14, no. 3 (Fall 1993): pp. 317–322; and Mahulena Hošková, "The evolving regime of the new property law in the Czech and Slovak Federal Republic," *American University Journal of International Law and Policy* 7, no. 3 (1991–92): pp. 611–612.
886 *Proceedings of the Washington Conference on Holocaust-Era Assets, November 30 – December 3, 1998*, ed. by James D. Bindenagel (Washington, DC: US Gov. Print. Off., 1999).
887 Michael J. Bazyler, "The Holocaust restitution Movement in Comparative Perspective," *Berkeley Journal of International Law* 20, no. 11 (2002); see also Kuklík et al., *Jak odškodnit holocaust?*, pp. 24–50.
888 Houžvička, *Czechs and Germans 1848-2004*, p. 395-396.

Václav Havel was prepared to apologize to the Germans, who were transferred after the WWII.[889] Stormy public debate followed, in which especially the Czech general public voiced deeply emotional opinions, whereas especially the representatives of the Sudeten Germans in the Federal Republic of Germany (The Sudentendeutsche Landsmannschaft) interpreted Havel's words as an admission of Czechoslovak quilt in the legal sense of the word.[890] The debates until the Treaty on good Neighbourhood and Friendly Cooperation was signed on 27 February 1992 concentrated mainly on the property questions and the Czechoslovak legislation symbolized by the so called Beneš's decrees was criticized from the German side, while the Czechoslovak side claimed the war losses and unpaid reparations.

The influence of united Germany aroused in 1990s concerns not only of Czech public[891] but also of European politicians. Original concerns about Germany misusing its dominance did not come true; on the contrary Germany became an engine of deepening European integration. German relations to its Eastern neighbours, historically complicated by the displacement of Germans after World War II, were usually correct. Germany also reacted very cautiously to provocations from both Poland and the Czech Republic, when some politicians tried to play the German card, especially in Poland in 2005 during the so-called Merkelgate.[892]

The German minority in neither the Czech lands nor Slovakia was not substationaly activated by the changes of 1990s. Assumptions of many researchers, who contended that after the fall of Communism many more Germans would acknowledge their nationality, did not come true. In the Czech Republic, the German question was more complicated than in Slovakia, where small German minority (called Carpathian Germans) was treated more favorable. The relationship towards the German question was closely connected with the discussions about presidential, or pejoratively Beneš's decrees. This discussion in fact dealt with the whole Czech-German relations during the time of Munich 1938, the Protectorate, Second World War and the forcible transfer of most of the German populations. Of the minorities that counted more than three million people (in a state whose population stood originally at 14 million) just under 200,000 remained. The Czechoslovak government in 1945 regarded the Germans as the main threat to the state and aimed to liquidate the minorities by forcible resettlement. The decrees were used mainly as a legal basis for confiscation of property, forfeit of the state citizenship and punishment of war criminals. The remainders of the German

889 Ibid.
890 Ibid., p. 397.
891 Ibid., for the reasons for "fears of Germany" see especially p. 438ff.
892 Petráš, *Cizinci ve vlastní zemi*, pp. 161–163.

minority survived in very difficult conditions as restrictions on civil liberties and unpaid forced labour dating from the post-war period were only abolished in stages.

Among expelled Germans and their descendants, they talked the so-called right for mother country from the very beginning and the restitution requirements were raised.[893] Even though the population of the formerly German borderland of the Czech lands feared returning the mostly real property acquired from Germans during time of the firm Soviet bloc, such concerns were completely illusive. Theorizations of German lawyers, who thought that affiliation of Czech borderland to Czechoslovakia might still be illegal, were rather absurd.[894] Yet the change of regime had brought new conditions under which a strong and powerful Germany, and possibly Austria as well, could promote some restitutions or indemnification of displaced Germans. Furthermore, in Czechoslovakia extensive restitutions of property were prepared and adopted in 1991, which was seen as a part of economic transformation. As a turning point, the date from when the property was ought to be returned, was chosen to be 25 February 1948, so the extensive restitutions applied only to the Communist regime confiscations (with the exception of limited restitution of Jewish property). Therefore restitution acquirers were returned also the property, which they had obtained often from displaced Germans, especially in the years 1946-1947.

Naturally, this problem outlasted the disintegration of Czechoslovakia and the Czech Republic had to deal with it as well. Moreover, from the perspective of public interest the problem became more intense because the concerns of the population did not concentrate on complicated Czech-Slovak relationship. It is also necessary to note that apart from excited reception of European idea and development of human rights, symbolised especially by President Václav Havel and simultaneous neoliberal advocacy of a market economy and incorporation into world markets, enforced particularly by Václav Klaus, anti-European and nationalistic tendencies were taking shape in Czech society and they sometimes played the anti-German card. However there were some anti Czech and anti Polish tendencies voiced by the

---

893 See for example Otto Kimminich, *Das Recht auf die Heimat*, 3rd ed. (Bonn: Kulturstiftung der Deutschen Vertriebenen, 1989), pp. 115-117; Houžvička, *Czechs and Germans 1848-2004*, pp. 351-354.

894 See for example Theodor Veiter, *Nationalitätenkonflikt und Volksgruppenrecht im ausgehenden 20. Jahrhundert* (Munich: Bayerische Landeszentrale für Politische Bildungsarbeit, 1984), pp. 72-74; Peter Schneider, "Die völkerrechtliche Bedeutung und Beurteilung der Artikel IX und XIII des Potsdamer Protokolls," in *Das Recht auf die Heimat*, ed. by Kurt Rabl (Munich: Lerche, 1960), p. 73; Herbert Czaja, "Schutzpflicht von Verfassungs wegen und menschenrechtliche Pflichten für Deutsche unter fremder Herrschaft," in *Menschenrechte und Selbstbestimmung unter Berücksichtigung der Ostdeutschen* (Bonn: Kulturstiftung d. Dt. Vertriebenen, 1980), pp. 54-69.

Sudetendeutsche Landsmannschaft on the German side as well.[895] Discussions became most intense when the Czech Republic was making preparations for membership in the European Union. Such concerns prevailed, that Sudeten Germans would harshly promote some form of indemnification or, in the opposite case, would induce Germany or Austria to veto accession of the Czech Republic to the European Union. It is necessary to add, that these tendencies were indeed present during confirmation of the Czech membership in the EU and the Beneš's decrees as well as the Czech system of restitutions were in 2002 reviewed by leading German and European legal experts including prof. Ch.Tomuschat, prof. J. Frowein, prof. U. Bergnitz and the Rt. Hon. Lord Kingsland, QC in their expert opinions, which dissmised most of the Sudeten German legal claims against the postwar Czechoslovak legislation.[896]

In the Czech Republic itself the historical discussions about displacement were far more complicated and touched also the overall attitude to the Czechoslovak history. Complicated historical and legal disputes concerning displacement of Germans have been under way in the Czech Republic and Poland partly up until the present time and in a remarkable way fit in worldwide tendencies to re-examine past and seek apologies for historical wrongdoings.[897]

After the year 1989 also "new minorities" whose importance has been increasing came into existence in the Czech lands, e.g. Ukrainian and Vietnamese minorities and some other smaller groups,[898] despite the fact that immigration used to be and still is often perceived as marginal.[899] As for the Vietnamese, the situation is specific, as the arrival of immigrants at the end of the 20th century was the continuation of certain bonds from the time of the communist regime. On the whole, considering Communist Czechoslovakia and the entire Socialistic bloc, we can see that there was a minimum number of persons interested in migrating; therefore, immigration policy whatsoever was not in fact necessary. Also the number of foreigners living here was minimal, thus, no thorough regulation of the issue whatsoever was needed until the change of conditions in the 1990s. However, commencing in the 1960s and 1970s roughly, a phenomenon typical of developed western countries occurred, that is the arrival of foreign workers, though in a moderate

---

895 Houžvička, *Czechs and Germans 1848-2004*, pp. 471-476.

896 Ibid., pp. 324-325.

897 Dan Diner and Gotthard Wunberg, eds., *Restitution and Memory: Material Restoration in Europe* (New York: Berghahn books, 2007), esp. pp. 9-15.

898 For details see René Petráš, "Migrace a právní postavení přistěhovalců v českém právu z historické perspektivy," in *Migrace a kulturní konflikty*, ed. by Harald Christian Scheu (Prague: Auditorium, 2011), pp. 114-141; and René Petráš, "The Creation and Legal Status of the Slovak, Roma and Vietnamese Minorities in the Czech Republic," *Acta Humana* 4 (2015): pp. 39-46.

899 *Cizinci v České Republice = Foreigners in the Czech Republic 2006* (Prague: Český statistický úřad, 2006).

measure. It first concerned Polish, and also later those persons were almost entirely from the countries that were members of the Council for Mutual Economic Assistance (Comecon – RVHP). Unfortunately, it was the politics that made themselves felt strongly there, where instead of the needs of the Czechoslovak economy it was the political interests, i.e. the support of pro-Soviet regimes, such as Vietnam, Cuba, Mongolia, and Angola, that played a leading role.

Employing Vietnamese citizens developed mainly on the basis of an agreement of 1980, whereas the highest number of workers, namely 27,100, was in Czechoslovakia in 1983. Like in the cases of other developing countries supported by Moscow, and therefore by Prague as well, the inflow of workers was preceded by vocational training of apprentices and trainees under the agreements from 1974 and 1979. However, the number of foreign workers was always limited. Based on intergovernmental agreements there were only 23,113 workers from Vietnam, 3,790 from Poland, 274 from Mongolia, 142 from Angola, and 101 from Cuba working in the territory of the Czech Republic at the end of the year 1990. The communist regime made effort to separate those foreign workers from the domestic population. They were not supposed to immigrate and settle permanently with families, but only to seek the temporary employment of individuals who often stayed in special quarters. After the fall of the regime, it was decided as early as in 1990 (Resolution of the Government No. 274) that this co-operation, which was often considered a hindrance to a new pro-western policy, be quickly terminated. The number of persons working here on the basis of those intergovernmental agreements was decreasing rapidly; to illustrate, there were only 1,110 workers from Vietnam, 210 from Poland, and 10 from Angola in the spring of 1993.

In the years 1989–1992, hence during re-establishing Czechoslovak democracy, the minority problems occurred more often in Slovakia than in the Czech lands. However, they always stood in shadow of the main problem of Czechoslovakia at that time, which was the gradual disintegration of the state. It is necessary to point out that disintegration of Czechoslovakia was conditioned primarily by revived national aspirations of Slovaks, which elicited rather surprised reactions in the Czech lands. The situation was similar with the major minority problem, the question of Hungarians in Southern Slovakia.[900]

The disputes on the division of competences and mutual relations between the Czech and Slovak Republics were followed with different views on the speed of political and economic reforms; for example, a possibility to

---

900 Vladimír Paukovič, "Vybrané aspekty etnického spolužitia po roku 1989," in Plichtová, *Minority v politike: Kultúrne a jazykové práva*, pp. 130–132.

prepare a new constitutional basis of the Federation in the form of a "state agreement" was discussed.[901]

After parliamentary elections in June 1992 it became evident that the victorious political representations in both parts of the Federation lost any determination to maintain the common state. The inevitable outcome was the "Velvet Divorce."[902] Moreover, the Slovak National Council adopted a Declaration on Slovak Sovereignty on 17th July 1992, and the Slovak Constitution on 1 September 1992.[903] This resulted in the organized and orderly split of the common state, when especially the federal organs lost.[904] The Federal Assembly adopted a series of laws on the dissolution of the Federation and on the split of federal property. The Czech and Slovak Republics concluded a series of international treaties. On 16th December 1992 the Czech National Council adopted the Constitution of the Czech Republic (Constitutional Act No. 1/1993 Sb.), together with the Constitutional Act governing measures to be taken in relation to the dissolution of the Czechoslovak Federation.[905] An independent Czech Republic and the Slovak Republic came into existence on 1st January 1993.[906]

6.2 LEGAL REGULATION OF MINORITY STATUS IN CZECHOSLOVAKIA AFTER 1989

The discussion on minority rights was connected with the preparations for the Charter of Fundamental Rights and Freedoms, which was adopted at the beginning of 1991. It is necessary to add in here that it is still in force in the Czech Republic; in Slovakia the text of the Charter was adopted into the Constitution without major amendments.[907]

---

901 E. Stein, *Czecho-Slovakia: Ethnic Conflict, Constitutional Fissure, Negotiated Breakup*, pp. 105–108; see also Václav Žák, "The velvet divorce, institutional foundations," in *The end of Czechoslovakia*, ed. by Jiří Musil (Budapest: Central European University Press, 1995), pp. 245 –267.

902 See Žák, "The velvet divorce," pp. 262–264.

903 For its text in English see Ludwikowski, *Constitution-making*, pp. 578–604; for its analyses see E. Stein, *Czecho-Slovakia: Ethnic Conflict, Constitutional Fissure, Negotiated Breakup*, pp. 273–281.

904 "New Czech, Slovak Leaders Accelerate Separation," special report, *East European constitutional Review* (Summer 1992): p. 9; and David Franklin, "Divorce Proceedings Continue between Czechs and Slovaks"; "Federal Bodies Lose Relevance," special report, *East European constitutional Review* (Summer 1992), pp. 14–15.

905 For its text in English see Ludwikowski, *Constitution-making*, pp. 374–386; see also Constitution of the Czech Republic, http://www.usoud.cz/en/legal-basis/.

906 In more details Kuklík, *Czech law in historical contexts*, pp. 224–226.

907 In detail see René Petráš, "Problematická koncepce práv menšin v Listině základních práv a svobod," in *Ochrana práv a svobod v proměnách práva na počátku 21. století: v českém, evropském a mezinárodním kontextu* (Prague: Auditorium, 2011), pp. 155–162.

The rights of national minorities were incorporated into the Charter of Fundamental Rights and Freedoms, in comparison with the Constitutional Act No. 144/1968 Sb, in a rather abbreviated version. Although there is a separate Chapter on the Rights of National and Ethnical Minorities in the Charter, it is the shortest chapter of all and consists only of two Sections. However, it is not possible to overrate the importance of the Constitutional Act No. 144/1968 Sb. Because, as the sociological surveys prove, it was surprisingly unknown among the minorities and many had no idea it existed. However it had at least symbolic significance to the minorities, because it presented a special legal regulation of their status. Such overlooking of the minority question was typical for the Czech lands, but in Slovakia tendencies emerged to limit the minority rights, triggered by the fear of potential Hungarian irredentism. Nevertheless, the Hungarian question in Slovakia did not get complicated very much in following years. Even in the independent Czech Republic, the position of minorities remained entirely on the edge of society's interest, with the exception of specific Gipsy question. Two Sections of the Charter of Fundamental Rights and Freedoms remained the basis of legal status, yet they anticipated enactment of further implementing laws. A curiosity was that this special law was passed in the Czech Republic only on 10 July 2001 as Act No. 273/2001 Sb. on rights of members of national minorities.[908]

To evaluate the legal status of minorities in Czechoslovakia and its successor states objectively, it is necessary to keep in mind that the standard of minority rights began to evolve significantly in the 1990's. From a broader perspective, the interest in minorities began to appear on the international level mainly during the interwar period, in particular in the 1920s, in connection with international legal protection of minorities within the League of Nations and again from the 1990s, when the key role was played by the Council of Europe initiatives. The interwar system of minority protection was seemingly worldwide while the Council of Europe is "only" a regional organisation but the actual difference is not so substantial. International obligations to protect minorities were imposed, save for exceptions, only upon European countries. Especially the disintegration of the Soviet bloc, the bloody conflicts in the former Yugoslavia and democratization of Eastern Europe posed a major impulse for reviving the problem of international legal protection of minorities.[909]

After World War II the minority question had a rather problematic reputation due to its misuse by Hitler. The attempts to revive any kind of

---

908 In detail see René Petráš, ed., *Aktuální problémy právního postavení menšin v České republice: Sborník příspěvků z odborného semináře Menšiny a právo v České republice* (Prague: Úřad vlády, 2010).

909 Forejtová, *Mezinárodněprávní ochrana menšin*, p. 82.

international legal protection of minorities system were therefore unsuccessful for a long time. The Council of Europe, established in 1949, focused on the protection of human rights in democratic part of Europe.[910] Its interest in minorities had been minimal for a long time because the member states resisted such activities.[911] The reason for this was that in Western Europe in fact relatively few minorities lived in period 1948-1989. Some states even proceeded from the conception of unrecognizing national minorities, because awarding any specific rights would be understood as inconsistent with the principle of equality of all before under the law. France was traditionally a symbol of this concept. Certain discussions about minority protection arose within the Council of Europe particularly in the late 1950s, yet without any notable consequences.[912]

An essential element, emerging progressively since the 1960s in particular, was the so-called rights revolution, hence the slowly expanding protection of individuals' rights, which considerably improved conditions for example of people living on the edge of society, such as notable humanization of the prison system. Though this process applied to national minorities only marginally for a long time, it created mechanisms applicable to enforcement of rights of these groups. A typical long-term phenomenon is strengthening of the judicial power, which does not hesitate to interpret legal norms in favour of individuals' position. A symbol of these changes was the remarkable success of the European Court of Human Rights in Strasbourg. The Court embarked, during the 1970s, upon the development of a progressive European jurisprudence.[913] To mention other aspects, it was development of non-governmental organisations, which do not hesitate to take up hard fight for rights of groups, which used to stand on the edge of society. The most striking example is gradual but in a way surprisingly rapid change of position of homosexuals from a criminal offence into a life style about which many celebrities nearly boast.

The fall of the Communist regime represented an exceptional impulse for national minorities' rights protection development. An important role was played by the Council of Europe and its European Court of Human Rights, which in the post-Cold War era went from being the guarantor of human

910 Scheu, *Standard ochrany národnostních menšin v rámci Rady Evropy.*

911 Dieter Blumenwitz and Gilbert Gornig, eds., *Minderheiten – und Volksgruppenrechte in Theorie und Praxis* (Bonn: Kulturstiftung der Deutschen Vertriebenen, 1993), p. 29ff; Felix Ermacora, *Nationalitätenkonflikt und Volksgruppenrecht* (Munich: Bayerische Landeszentrale für Politische Bildungsarbeit, 1978), p. 107ff.

912 Harald Christian Scheu, "Začátky ochrany národnostních menšin v Radě Evropy," in Petráš, Petrův and Scheu, *Menšiny a právo v České republice*, pp. 285-288.

913 See for example Jonas Christoffersen and Mikael Rask Madsen, eds., *The European Court of Human Rights between Law and Politics* (Oxford: Oxford University Press, 2013), esp. Introduction by editors and chapter 2 by Ed Bates, p. 2ff.

rights solely in Western Europe to becoming increasingly involved in the transition to democracy and the rule of law in Eastern Europe. Also the Conference on Security and Cooperation in Europe was active; on the contrary European Communities, at the time of their transformation into the EU, hardly showed any interest in minorities.[914] Altogether, in the 1990s Europe remarkably elaborate mechanisms for national minorities' protection were created, with no equivalent in other world regions. A particular impulse for development of the protection of minorities posed mainly national conflicts in the disintegrating Soviet Union and Yugoslavia. While, apart from its older bloody traditions, Europe presented a notable continent of peace since World War II, now it had to deal with extensive number of horrifyingly brutal conflicts, precipitated mostly by nationalism. Therefore creation of any mechanisms to protect minorities was regarded as a very pressing task. From the legal point of view, in the beginning of these discussions in 1990, it was taken into consideration to create supplementary protocol to pivotal Covenant sanctioned by the Council of Europe, hence the European Convention on Human Rights from 1950. However, it emerged that a specific character of minorities' rights required a specific solution. In 1992, the European Charter for Regional or Minority Languages was finished and opened for signature on 5 November, yet it has a specific character and development, because its preparation began already in the 1980s. Its specific conception in particular is only partly applicable to protection of minorities.[915]

The most significant initiatives within the Council of Europe took place in 1993. An expert committee on national minorities' protection (CAHMIN) was established after extensive negotiations in November 1993. Its purpose was to prepare a special international treaty. This so-called Framework Convention for the Protection of National Minorities was opened for signature to the member states on 1 February 1995. Even though acceptance of the Framework Convention by the member states was rather slow, a key turning point had been set. The Framework Convention originated new standard of protection of national minorities and also quite complicated system of supervision under its abidance in the states that accepted it. Further development of international protection of minorities on the European regional level is in detail complicated and cannot be examined in here.

---

914 Paul Widmer, "Europäische Bemühungen zur Lösung von Minderheitenfragen," *Europa Archiv* 48, no. 9 (1993): p. 266, 271; Ivo Pospíšil, "Pojetí menšin v evropském právu," in *Reprezentace zájmů menšin v EU*, ed. by Roman Chytilek and Miroslav Mareš (Brno: Centrum pro studium demokracie a kultury, 2006), p. 25, 34; Jan Jařab, "Menšinová politika Evropské unie," in *Reprezentace zájmů menšin v EU*, ed. by Roman Chytilek and Miroslav Mareš (Brno: Centrum pro studium demokracie a kultury, 2006), pp. 8-13.

915 Harald Christan Scheu, "Vývoj ochrany menšin v Radě Evropy po roce 1989," in Petráš, Petrův and Scheu, *Menšiny a právo v České republice*, pp. 289-294.

Nevertheless, it is necessary to remind that the key steps took place right at the time of quick Czechoslovak democratization and disintegration. It is also convenient to mention the date, on which one of the two most important conventions of the Council of Europe, the European Charter for Regional or Minority Languages, was opened for signature. It was on 5 November 1992, right at the time of the final disintegration of the Czechoslovak Federation. The interest of Czech and Slovak public was logically devoted to interstate problems then. During this period, the European integration made one of its most significant steps, establishment of the EU on the basis of the Maastricht Treaty from 7 February 1992, which came into force on 1 November 1993. Czechoslovakia and its successor states had aspired to enter European structures practically since the revolution in November 1989. However, it is obvious that both European integration evolving into the EU and the Council of Europe were going through substantial changes touching the minorities, right at the time of disintegration of Czechoslovakia.

CONCLUSION

The national minority question played an important part in the history of Czechoslovakia especially during the interwar period covering the era of the so-called First Republic from 1918-1938, but also during World War II and in the immediate years following it. The situation in Czechoslovakia and after all, the development before establishment of a state on this territory, received a considerable response in the world. Not once was it an inspiration for solution of national and minority problems. The minority question had certain importance also after the displacement of Germans following WWII, when the number of members of minorities decreased several times from more than 4 million – mainly Germans – to less than one million (mostly Hungarians) in a state with 14 million inhabitants. Apparently, legal regulation had always played a key role for minority status. Regulation has gone through a series of complicated changes; as a result there are approximately ten completely different systems of minority legislation within Czechoslovakia, which is what this publication aims to deal with. While there is plenty of professional literature on the general historical aspects of the status of minorities, the legal aspects are not so well examined. The authors of this book deal with the issues of ethnic and language minorities in Czechoslovakia from a long term perspective; this book, intended primarily for foreign readers, will not be their last contribution to the research of this complicated issue. Unfortunately, the minority question is becoming activated again in the recent years in Europe and thorough knowledge of older problems and concepts of solutions may facilitate examination of current problems as well.

BIBLIOGRAPHY

Primary Sources

Archives
Allgemeines Verwaltungsarchiv Wien
Collection Ministerium des Innern, Präsidiale 3-1848-1918
Collection Ministerrats-Präsidium
Archiv Ministerstva zahraničních věcí (AMZV) [The Archives of the Foreign Ministry], Prague
Collections
- II. sekce - Společnost národů [2nd section League of Nations]
- Mírová konference v Paříži a reparace 1918-1938 [The Peace Conference in Paris and Reparation 1918-1938]
- Pařížský archiv [Paris Records Collection]
- Telegramy odeslané [Telegrams sent] 1941-1945
- Londýnský archiv důvěrný [London archives - confidential]
Archiv Národního muzea v Praze (ANM) [The Archives of the National Musem in Prague]
- collection J. Kapras
- collection E. Sobota
- collection E. Beneš
- collection I. Dérer
Archiv Poslanecké sněmovny Parlamentu ČR (APS) [The Archives of the Parliament of the Czech Republic in Prague]
- Revoluční národní shromáždění 1918-1920 [Revolutionary National Assembly]
Archiv Ústavu T. G. Masaryka [Archive of the T. G. Masaryk Institute - AÚTGM], Prague
- Edvard Beneš (EB) II Collection
Архив внешней политики Российской Федерации [Archive of Foreign Policy of the Russian Federation], Moscow
- Collection 06 (Secretariat of V. M. Molotov)
Archivio storico diplomatico, Rome
Collection Affari politici 1931-1945
Hoover Institution Archives (HIA), Stanford, CA
- Poland, Ministerstwo Spraw Zagranicznych (P-MSZ)
- Táborský Collection
- Feierabend Collection
Institut Polski i Muzeum im. Gen. Sikorskiego (IPMS), London, fund Ambasada Londyn
Law Library of Congress, Washington D.C. (materials related to the Mid European Law Project)
Národní archiv v Praze (NA) [The National Archives in Prague]
Collections
- Ministerstvo vnitra - stará registratura (MV) [Ministry of the Interior - old registry]
- Předsednictvo ministerské rady [Administrative Board of the Ministerial Council]
- Fond Úřad předsednictva vlády 1952 [Administrative Board of the Ministerial Council 1952]
- Fond Úřad předsednictva vlády ČSSR 1968 [Administrative Board of the Ministerial Council 1968] - 450/1

Moravský zemský archiv v Brně
Collections
- Fond Krajský národní výbor v Brně III, 1955–1959
[Regional National Committee Brno]
- Fond Krajský národní výbor v Jihlavě 1949–1960
[Regional National Committee Jihlava]
Royal Institute of International Affairs Archives (RIIAA), London
School of Slavonic and East European Studies, University College London
- K. Lisický Collection
- R. W. Seton Watson Collection
Státní okresní archiv Kutná Hora
- Fond Okresní národní výbor Kutná Hora 1945–1960
[District National Committee Kutná Hora 1945–1960 Collection]
Státní okresní archiv Opava
- Fond Okresní národní výbor Opava 1954–1960
[District National Committee Opava 1954–1960 Collection]
The National Archives (TNA), London
Collections
- Cabinet (CAB)
- Dominion Office (DO)
- Foreign Office (FO), 371
- FO 404, Confidential Prints
- German Foreign Ministry (GFM). Copies of captured records of the German, Italians and Japanese Governments
- Treasury
- FO 1049, Control Commission for Germany (British Element), Political Division
- FO 1079 European Advisory Commission: Minutes and Papers
Vojenský ústřední archiv – Vojenský historický archiv [Central Military Archives – Historical Military Archives – VÚA-VHA], Prague
Collections
- Štáb pro vybudování branné moci
- Hlavní velitelství [Headquarters]

Edition of Documents
Bán, András. *Pax Britannica: Wartime Foreign Office Documents Regarding Plans for a Postbellum East Central Europe*. Boulder, CO: Social Science Monographs; Highland Lakes, NJ: Atlantic Research and Publications, 1997.
Bernatzik, Edmund. *Die österreichischen Verfassungsgesetze mit Erläuterungen*. Vienna: Manz, 1911.
Buriánek, František, Rudolf Mertlík, Jan Pilař, and Josef Strnadel, eds. *The 17th November: Almanac about the Resistance of Czechoslovak Students in the years 1939–1945*. Prague: Central Union of Czechoslovak Students, 1945
Cesta ke květnu [Road to May]. Vol. 1. Edited by Miloš Klimeš. Prague: Nakl. Československé akademie věd, 1965.
Cizinci v České Republice = Foreigners in the Czech Republic 2006. Prague: Český statistický úřad, 2006.
Constitution of the Czechoslovak Republic. Introduction by Jiří Hoetzel and V. Joachim. Prague: Orbis, 1920.
Constitution of the Czechoslovak Republic. 2nd ed. Prague: Czechoslovak Ministry of Education, 1948.
Constitution of the Czechoslovak Socialist republic. Prague: Orbis, 1960.
Constitutional acts of Czech and Slovak Federal Republic and acts concerning the civil rights and freedoms adopted by the Federal Assembly of the Czech and Slovak Federal Republic. Prague: Federal Assembly and Czechoslovak Academy of Sciences, 1992.
The Constitutional Foundations of the Czechoslovak Federation. Prague: Orbis, 1978.

Československá zahraniční politika v roce 1938. Edited by Jindřich Dejmek. Dokumenty československé zahraniční politiky. Vol. 2. Prague: Ústav mezinárodních vztahů, 2001.

Československá zahraniční politika v roce 1942. Vol. 1, (1. 1. – 31. 7. 1942) [Czechoslovak Foreign Policy in 1942]. Edited by Jan Němeček, Jan Kuklík, Helena Nováčková, and Ivan Šťovíček. Dokumenty československé zahraniční politiky B/3/1. Prague: Ústav mezinárodních vztahů, Historický ústav AV ČR, 2011.

Československá zahraniční politika v roce 1942. Vol. 2, (1. 8. –31. 12. 1942) [Czechoslovak Foreign Policy in 1942]. Edited by Jan Němeček, Jan Kuklík, Blanka Jedličková, and Daniela Němečková. Dokumenty československé zahraniční politiky B/3/2. Prague: Ústav mezinárodních vztahů, Historický ústav AV ČR, 2015.

Český národ soudí K.H. Franka [Czech nation puts K.H. Frank on trial]. Edited by Karel Kajiček. Prague: Ministerstvo informací, 1946.

Deák, Ladislav, ed. Viedenská arbitráž. 2. november 1938: Dokumenty [Vienna Arbitration. November, 2 1938: Documents]. 3 vols. Martin: Matica slovenská 2002, 2003, 2005.

Declaration of independence of the Czechoslovak nation by its Provisional Government. [New York]: [Printed for the Czechoslovak Arts Club by the Marchbanks Press], 1918.

Deset let československé zahraniční politiky: činnost Ministerstva zahraničních věcí. Prague: nákladem ministerstva zahraničních věcí, 1928.

Documents on British Foreign Policy. 3rd series. Vol. 2. London: H.M.S.O., 1949.

Documents on British Policy Overseas: The Conference of Potsdam July–August 1945. Series 1. Vol.1. London H.M.S.O., 1984.

Documents on Polish-Soviet Relations 1939-1945. 2 vols. London: Heinemann, 1961-67.

Dodd, Walter F., ed. Modern Constitutions: A Collection of the Fundamental Laws of Twenty-two of the Most Important Countries of the World, With Historical and Bibliographical Notes. Chicago: The University of Chicago Press, 1909.

Foreign Relations of the United States [FRUS]. Diplomatic Papers: The Conference of Berlin (Potsdam Conference), 1945. Vol. 2. Washington, DC: U.S. G.P.O., 1960.

Foreign relations of the United States [FRUS]. 1946, Paris Peace Conference: Documents. Vol. 4. Washington, DC: US Gov. Print. Off., 1970.

Gronský, Ján, and Jiří Hřebejk, eds. Dokumenty k ústavnímu vývoji Československa I. (1918–1945) [Documents on constitutional development of Czechoslovakia (1918-1945)]. Prague: Karolinum Press, 1997.

Gronský, Ján, and Jiří Hřebejk, eds. Dokumenty k ústavnímu vývoji Československa II. (1945–1968) [Documents on constitutional development of Czechoslovakia (1945-1968)]. Prague: Karolinum Press, 1999.

Gronský, Ján, ed. Dokumenty k ústavnímu vývoji Československa III. (1968–1989) [Documents on constitutional development of Czechoslovakia (1968-1989)]. Prague: Karolinum Press, 2000.

Grospič, Jiří, ed. The Constitutional Foundations of the Czechoslovak Federation: The Constitution of the Czechoslovak Socialist Republic, the Constitutional Act Concerning the Czechoslovak Federation, the Constitutional Act Concerning the Status of Ethnic Groups in the Czechoslovak Socialist Republic. Prague: Orbis, 1973.

Haider, Barbara, ed. Die Protokolle des Verfassungsausschusses des Reichsrates vom Jahre 1867. Fontes rerum Austriacarum. Österreichische Geschichtsquellen. Abt. 2. Diplomataria et Acta 88. Vienna: Verlag der Österreichischen Akademie der Wissenschaften, 1997.

Harna, Josef, and Jaroslav Šebek. Státní politika vůči německé menšině v období konsolidace politické moci v Československu v letech 1918-1920 [State Policy towards the German Minorityin the period of consolidation of political power in Czechoslovakia 1918-1920]. Prague: Historický ústav AV ČR, 2002.

Federální statistický úřad: Historická statistická ročenka ČSSR [The Federal Statistical Office: Historical Statistical Yearbook of Czechoslovakia]. Prague: Státní nakladatelství technické literatury, 1985.

Král, Václav, ed. Die Deutschen in der Tschechoslowakei 1933-1947. Prague: Nakladatelství Československé akademie věd, 1964.

Lippóczy, Piotr, and Tadeusz Walichnowski. *Przesiedlenie ludności niemieckiej z Polski po II wojnie światowej w świetle dokumentów* [The Resettlement of Germans from Poland after WWII in the Light of Documents]. Warsaw: Państwowe Wydawnictwo Naukowe, 1982.

Łukomski, Grzegorz. *Kresy zachodnie i wschodnie w pracach Rządu Rzeczypospolitej Polskiej na Uchodźstwie 1939-1945: Wybór źródeł* [The Western and Eastern Borderlands in Activities of the Polish Government in Exile 1939-1945: Anthology of Documents]. Warsaw: Oficyna Wydawnicza Adiutor, 2006.

Malá, Irena, ed. *Z protokolů schůzí 5. československé vlády (Benešovy) 1921-1922* [From the Minutes of the Meetings of the Fifth Czechoslovak (Beneš) Government 1921-1922]. Prague: Státní ústřední archiv v Praze, 1989.

Navrátil, Jaromír, ed. *The Prague Spring 1968: A National Security Archive Documents Reader*. Budapest: Central European University Press, 1998.

Němeček, Jan, Helena Nováčková, Ivan Šťovíček, and Miroslav Tejchman, eds. *Československo-sovětské vztahy v diplomatických jednáních 1939-1945: Dokumenty* [Czechoslovak-Soviet relations in the diplomatic negotiations 1939-1945: Docments]. 2 vols. Prague: Státní ústřední archiv v Praze, 1998-1999.

Od uznání československé prozatímní vlády do vyhlášení válečného stavu Německu 1940-1941 [From the recognition of the Czechoslovak Provisional Government until the declaration of war on Germany 1940-1941]. Edited by Jan Němeček, Jan Kuklík, Helena Nováčková, and Ivan Šťovíček. Dokumenty československé zahraniční politiky B/2/1. Prague: Ústav mezinárodních vztahů, Historický ústav AV ČR, 2006.

Od uznání československé prozatímní vlády do vyhlášení válečného stavu Německu 1940-1941 [From the recognition of the Czechoslovak Provisional Government until the declaration of war on Germany 1940-1941]. Edited by Jan Němeček, Jan Kuklík, Helena Nováčková, and Ivan Šťovíček. Dokumenty československé zahraniční politiky B/2/2. Prague: Ústav mezinárodních vztahů, Historický ústav AV ČR, 2009.

Odsun: Die Vertreibung der Sudetendeutschen; Dokumentation zu Ursachen, Plannung und Realisierung einer "ethnischen Säuberung" in der Mitte Europas 1848/49-1945/46. Edited by Kurt Heißig, and Roland J Hoffmann. Munich: Sudetendeutsches Archiv, 2010.

Simmonds, William, ed. *The Constitutions of the Communist World*. The Hague: Nijhoff, 1980.

Proceedings of the Washington Conference on Holocaust-Era Assets, November 30 - December 3, 1998. Edited by James D. Bindenagel. Washington, DC: US Gov. Print. Off., 1999.

Protokoły posiedzeń Rady Ministrów Rzeczypospolitej Polskiej [Minutes of the Meetings of the Council of Ministers of the Polish Republic]. Edited by Wojciech Rojek, and Andrzej Suchcitz. Vol. 5. Cracow: Secesja, 2001.

Reports of International Arbitral Awards. Vol. 28. United Nations Publications. [U.S.A.]: United Nations - Nations Unies, 2007.

Romsics, Ignác, ed. *Wartime American Plans for a New Hungary: Documents from the U.S. Department of State, 1942-1944*. Boulder, CO: Social Science Monographs; Highland Lakes, NJ: Atlantic Research and Publications, 1992.

Rychlík, Jan, Thomas D. Marzik, and Miroslav Bielik, eds. *R.W. Seton-Watson and His Relations with the Czechs and Slovaks: Documents 1906-1951*. Vol. 1. Prague: Ústav T.G. Masaryka; Martin: Matica slovenská, 1995.

Sbírka nálezů Nejvyššího správního soudu ve věcech administrativních: nálezy z roku . . . [Collection of decisions of the Supreme Adminsitrative Court administrative series: decisions from year . . .]. Edited by Josef Václav Bohuslav. 16 vols. Prague: Právnické vydavatelství (V. Tomsa), 1920-1934.

Sbírka oběžníků pro KNV vydávaná Ministerstvem vnitra [Collection of Instructions for Regional National Committees Issued by the Ministry of Interior]. 2-4 (1950-1952)

Sborník zahraniční politiky. Vol. 2. Prague: Ministerstvo Zahraničních věcí, 1921.

Sprawa polska w czasie drugiej wojny światowej na arenie międzynarodowej: Zbiór dokumentów [The Polish Issue during WWII in the International Arena: Collection of Documents]. Edited by Stefania Stanisławska. Warsaw: PWN, 1965.

Statistická ročenka České a Slovenské federativní republiky 1990 [Statistical Yearbook of the Czech and Slovak Federative Republic]. Prague: Státní nakladatelství technické literatury, 1990.

Těsnopisecké zprávy o schůzích Národního shromáždění Československého [Shorthand Reports on the Meetings of the Czechoslovak National Assembly]. 4 vols. Prague: [Tiskem "Politiky"], 1919–1920.

Tisky k těsnopiseckým zprávám o schůzích Národního shromáždění československého [Printed texts to shorthand reports on the meetings of the Czechoslovak National Assembly]. Vol. 9 and 10, *Rok 1919–1920*. Prague: [Tiskárna Poslanecké sněmovny], 1920.

Treaties and Other International Agreements of the United States of America 1776–1949. Edited by Charles I. Bevans. Vol. 3. Washington, DC: Department of State Publication, 1969.

Vondrová, Jitka, ed. Češi a sudetoněmecká otázka, 1939–1945: *Dokumenty* [Czechs and the Sudeten German Question, 1939–1945: Documents]. Prague: Ústav mezinárodních vztahů, 1994.

W stronę Odry i Bałtyku. Wybór dokumentów (1795–1950) [Towards the Oder and the Baltic Sea. Anthology of Documents (1795–1950)]. Edited by Wojciech Wrzesiński. Vol. 3. Wroclaw: Oficyna Wydawnicza Volumen, 1990.

Zápisy ze schůzí československé vlády v Londýně [Record from the meetings of the Czechoslovak Government in London]. Edited by Jan Němeček Ivan Šťovíček, Helena Nováčková, Jan Kuklík, and Jan Bílek. Vols. 1–4/2. Prague: Právnická fakulta UK – Historický ústav AV ČR – Masarykův ústav a Archiv AV ČR, 2010–2015.

Selected Secondary Sources

Adler, Franz. *Grundriß des tschechoslowakischen Verfassungsrechtes*. Reichenberg: Stiepel, 1930.

Agnew, Hugh. *The Czechs and the Lands of the Bohemian Crown*. Stanford, CA: Hoover Institution Press, 2004.

Ash, Timothy Garton. *The Magic Lantern: The Revolution of '89 Witnessed in Warsaw, Budapest, Berlin and Prague*. New York: Random House, 1990.

Azcárate, Pablo de. *League of Nations and National Minorities: An Experiment*. Translated from Spanish by Eileen E. Brooke. Washington, DC: Carnegie Endowment for International Peace, 1945.

Bajcura, Ivan. *Cesta k internacionálnej jednote* [Journey to international unity]. Bratislava: Pravda, 1983.

———. *Ukrajinská otázka v ČSSR* [The Ukrainian Issue in CSSR]. Košice: Vychodoslovenské vydavateľstvo, 1967.

Bamberger-Stemmann, Sabine. *Der Europäische Nationalitätenkongreß 1925 bis 1938: Nationale Minderheiten zwischen Lobbyistentum und Großmachtinteressen*. Marburg: Herder-Institut, 2000.

Bán, András. *Hungarian-British Diplomacy, 1938–1941: The Attempt to Maintain Relations*. London: Routledge, 2004.

Barnovský, Michal. "K otázke takzvaného ukrajinského buržoázneho nacionalizmu na Slovensku" [Notes on the so-called Ukrainian Bourgeois Nationalism in Slovakia]. *Historický časopis* 44, no. 1 (1996): 64–82.

Baxa, Bohumil. *Zákon o zřízení župním a jeho nedostatky* [The Act on the Establishment of Regions and its Shortcomings]. Prague: Státovědecká společnost, 1922.

Bazyler, Michael J. "The Holocaust restitution Movement in Comparative Perspective." *Berkeley Journal of International Law* 20, no. 11 (2002): 11–44.

Bělehrádek, František. "Zákony o školství národním a jejich změny" [Acts on National Education and Their Modifications]. *Česká Revue* 14 (1921): 23–28, 63–66, 115–124.

Beňa, Jozef. *Vývoj slovenského právneho poriadku* [Development of the Slovak legal order]. Banská Bystrica: Iris, 2001.

Benda, Jan. *Útěky a vyhánění z pohraničí českých zemí 1938–1939* [Escapes and expulsions from the borderland of Czech lands 1938–1939]. Prague: Karolinum Press, 2012.

Beneš, Edvard. *The Fall and Rise of a Nation: Czechoslovakia 1938–1941*. Edited by Milan Hauner. Boulder, CO: East European Monographs, 2004.

————. *Memoirs of Dr. Eduard Beneš: From Munich to New War and New Victory*. London: Houghton Mifflin, 1954.

Beneš, Václav. "Czechoslovak democracy and its problems, 1918–1920." In Mamatey, and Luža, *A History of the Czechoslovak Republic 1918–1948*, 39–98.

Beneš, Zdeněk, and Václav Kural, eds. *Facing History: The Evolution of Czech-German Relations in the Czech Provinces, 1848–1948*. Prague: Gallery, 2002.

Bernatzik, Edmund. *Über nationale Matriken: Inaugurationsrede gehalten von Edmund Bernatzik*. Vienna: Manz, 1910.

Blumenwitz, Dieter, and Gilbert Gornig, eds. *Minderheiten – und Volksgruppenrechte in Theorie und Praxis*. Bonn: Kulturstiftung der Deutschen Vertriebenen, 1993.

Boháč, Antonín. *Národnostní mapa republiky československé* [Ethnic Map of the Czechoslovak Republic]. Prague: Národpisná spol. českoslovanská, 1926.

Bosl, Karl, ed. *Aktuelle Forschungsprobleme um die Erste Tschechoslowakische Republik*. Munich: Oldenbourg Verlag, 1969.

Boyer, Christoph. "Přidělování státních zakázek v ČSR ve 30. letech – prostředek likvidace sudetoněmeckého hospodářství?" [Granting Public Procurement Contracts in the CSR in the 1930s – a Means of Liquidation of Sudeten German Economy?]. In *Ztroskotání spolužití* [The Failure of Co-existence], edited by Jörg K. Hoensch, and Dušan Kováč, 118–181. Prague: Ministerstvo zahraničních věcí České republiky, 1993.

Břach, Radko. *Smlouva o vzájemných vztazích mezi ČSSR a SRN z roku 1973* [Treaty on mutual relations between the CSR and FRG of 1973]. Prague: ÚSD, 1994.

Brandes, Detlef. "A müncheni diktátum egy megkésett cseh alternatívája" [A Delayed Czech alternative to the Diktat of Munich]. *Történelmi szemle* 38, no. 2–3 (1996): 219–228.

————. *Germanizovat a vysídlit: Nacistická národnostní politika v českých zemích* [Germanize and resettle: Nazi National Policy in the Czech Lands]. Prague: Prostor, 2015.

————, Holm Sundhaussen, and Stefan Troebst, eds. *Lexikon der Vertreibung. Deportation, Zwangsaussiedlung und ethnische Säuberung im Europa des 20. Jahrhunderts*. Vienna: Böhlau, 2010.

————. *Die Sudetendeutschen im Krisenjahr 1938*. Munich: Oldenbourg, 2008.

————. *Der Weg zur Vertreibung 1938–1945: Pläne und Entscheidungen zum „Transfer" der Deutschen aus der Tschechoslowakei und aus Polen*. Munich: Oldenbourg, 2001.

Braun, Karl. "Der 4. März 1919: Zur Herausbildung sudetendeutscher Identität." *Bohemia* 37, no. 2 (1996): 353–380.

Brian Simpson, Alfred W. *Human Rights and the End of Empire: Britain and the Genesis of the European Convention*. Oxford: Oxford University Press, 2004.

Broklová, Eva. "Švýcarský vzor pro Československo na Pařížské mírové konferenci" [Swiss Model for Czechoslovakia at the Peace Conference of Paris]. *Český časopis historický* 92, no. 2 (1994): 257–267.

Brown, David Martin. *Dealing with Democrats: The British Foreign Office's relations with the Czechoslovak émigrés in Great Britain, 1939–1945*. Frankfurt am Main: Peter Lang, 2006.

Brügel, Johann Wolfgang. *Czechoslovakia before Munich: The German minority problem and British appeasement policy*. Cambridge: Cambridge University Press, 1973.

————. "The Germans in pre-war Czechoslovakia." In Mamatey, and Luža, *A History of the Czechoslovak Republic 1918–1948*, 167–187.

————. "Noch einmal: Zur Frage der Deutschenvertreibung aus der Tschechoslowakei." *Bohemia* 4, no. 1 (1963): 393–403.

————. "The Recognition of the Czechoslovak Government in London." *Kosmas: Journal of Czechoslovak and Central European Studies* 2, no. 1 (1984): xxx.

————. *Tschechen und Deutsche 1918–1938*. Munich: Nymphenburger Verlagshandlung, 1967.

Bryant, Chad. *Prague in Black: Nazi Rule and Czech Nationalism*. Cambridge, MA: Harvard University Press, 2007.

Bubeník, Jaroslav, and Jiří Křesťan. "Zjišťování národnosti jako problém statistický a politický" [Determination of Nationality as a Statistical and Political Problem]. *Paginae historiae* 3 (1995): 119–140.

Bubeník Jaroslav, and Jiří Křesťan. "Národnost a sčítání lidu: k historickým souvislostem polemiky mezi Antonínem Boháčem a Emanuelem Rádlem" [Nationality and Census: Historical Circumstances of Polemics between Antonín Boháč and Emanuel Rádl]. *Historická demografie* 19 (1995): 119-134.

Burger, Hannelore. *Sprachenrecht und Sprachgerechtigkeit im österreichischen Unterrichtswesen 1867-1918.* Vienna: VÖAW, 1995.

Burian, Michal. *Assassination: Operation Anthropoid 1941-1942.* 2nd ed. Prague: Ministry of Defence of the Czech Republic, 2011.

Burian, Peter. "The State Language Problem in Old Austria (1848-1918)." *Austrian History Yearbook* 6-7 (1970-1971): 81-103.

Bystrický, Valerián. "Slovakia from the Munich Conference to the declaration of independence." In Teich, Kováč, and Brown, *Slovakia in History,* 157-175.

Calda, Miloš. "Roundtable talks in Czechoslovakia." In *The Roundtable Talks and the Breakdown of Communism,* edited by Jon Elster, 135-177. Chicago: University of Chicago Press, 1996.

Čelovský, Bořivoj. *Mnichovská dohoda 1938* [Munich Agreement 1938]. Ostrava: Tilia, 1999.

Cepl, Vojtěch. "A note on the Restitution of Property in Post-Communist Czechoslovakia." *Journal of Communist Studies* 7, no. 3 (1991): 367-375.

Černý, Bohumil, Jan Křen, Václav Kural, and Milan Otáhal, eds. *Češi, Němci, odsun* [The Czechs, the Germans, the Expulsion]. Prague: Academia, 1990.

César, Jaroslav and Bohumil Černý. *Politika německých buržoazních stran v Československu v letech 1918-1938* [The Policy of German Bourgeois Parties in Czechoslovakia in 1918-1938]. Vol. 1. Prague: ČSAV, 1962.

Chenoweth, Erica, and Adria Lawrence, eds. *Rethinking Violence: States and Non-state Actors in Conflict.* Cambridge, MA: MIT Press, 2010.

Chmelař, Josef. "Československá zahraniční politika v roce 1936" [Czechoslovak Foreign Policy in 1936]. *Zahraniční politika* 15 (1936): 726-734.

Chovanec, Jaroslav. "Postavenie národností v Československej socialistickej republike" [Position of nationalities in the Czechoslovak Socialist Republic]. *Právny obzor* 58 (1975): 27-39.

Christoffersen, Jonas, and Mikael Rask Madsen, eds. *The European Court of Human Rights between Law and Politics.* Oxford: Oxford University Press, 2013.

Chytilek, Roman, and Miroslav Mareš, eds. *Reprezentace zájmů menšin v EU* [Representation of minority interests in EU]. Brno: Centrum pro studium demokracie a kultury, 2006.

Čížkovská, Ludvíka. "Politika vlády ČSFR k romské menšině - snaha o vytvoření rámcových podmínek pro rasové a národnostní soužití" [Policy of the ČSFR government in relation to Gipsy minority - an attempt to create general conditions for racial and national coexistence]. *Právník* 131, no. 6 (1992): 532-533.

Clark, Bruce. *Twice a Stranger: How Mass Expulsion Forged Modern Greece and Turkey.* London: Granta Books, 2007.

Claude, Inis L. *National Minorities: An International Problem.* Cambridge, MA: Harvard University Press, 1955.

Cohen, Gary B. *The Politics of Ethnic Survival: Germans in Prague, 1861-1914.* 2nd ed. West Lafayette, IN: Purdue University Press, 2006.

Cohen, Robin. *The Cambridge Survey of World Migration.* Cambridge: Cambridge University Press, 1995.

Connor, Ian. *Refugees and Expellees in post-war Germany.* Manchester: Manchester University Press, 2007.

Cordell, Karl and Stefan Wolff. *Ethnic Conflict: Causes, Consequences, and Responses.* Cambridge: Polity, 2009.

Cornwall, Mark. "'A leap into ice-cold water': the manoeuvres of the Henlein movement in Czechoslovakia, 1933-1938." In Evans and Cornwall, *Czechoslovakia in a Nationalist and Fascist Europe 1918-1948,* 123-142.

————. "The Rise and Fall of a 'Special Relationship'? Britain and Czechoslovakia 1930-1948." In *What difference did the war make?*, edited by Brian Brivati and Harriet Jones, 130-150. Leicester: Leicester University Press, 1993.

Cotic, Meir. *The Prague Trial: The First Anti-Zionist Show Trial in the Communist Bloc.* New York: Herzel Press, 1987.

Crampton, Richard. *Eastern Europe in the Twenties Century - and after.* 2nd ed. London: Routledge, 1997.

Crowhurst, Patrick. *Hitler and Czechoslovakia in World War II: Domination and Retaliation.* London: I.B. Tauris, 2013.

Cumper, Peter, and Steven Charles Wheatley, eds. *Minority Rights in the 'New' Europe.* The Hague: Martinus Nijhoff Publishers, 1999.

Czaja, Herbert. "Schutzpflicht von Verfassungs wegen und menschenrechtliche Pflichten für Deutsche unter fremder Herrschaft." In *Menschenrechte und Selbstbestimmung unter Berücksichtigung der Ostdeutschen.* Bonn: Kulturstiftung d. Dt. Vertriebenen, 1980.

Dann, Otto, Miroslav Hroch, and Johannes Koll, eds. *Patriotismus und Nationsbildung am Ende des Heiligen Römischen Reiches.* Cologne: SH-Verlag, 2003.

Davidová, Eva. *Cesty Romů 1945-1990* [The roads of Gypsies 1945-1990]. Olomouc: Vydavatelství Univerzity Palackého, 1995.

Dejmek, Jindřich. "Britská diplomacie, Československo a Sudetoněmecká strana" [British Diplomacy, Czechoslovakia and the Sudeten German Party]. *Moderní dějiny* 9 (2001): 161-236.

————. *Historik v čele diplomacie: Kamil Krofta* [A Historian Leading Diplomacy: Kamil Krofta]. Prague: Karolinum Press, 1998.

Deset let československé zahraniční politiky: činnost Ministerstva zahraničních věcí [Ten Years of Czechoslovak International Policy]. Prague: Nákladem Ministerstva zahraničních věcí, 1928.

Dewitz-Krebs, Goswin von. *Das verbotene Parteiverbot: ein theoretischer Beitrag.* Vol. 3/1. Göttingen: Dewitz-Krebs, 2003.

Deyl, Zdeněk. *Sociální vývoj Československa 1918-1938* [The Social Development of Czechoslovakia 1918-1938]. Prague: Academia, 1985.

Dick Howard, Arthur E., ed. *Constitution Making in Eastern Europe.* Washington, DC: Woodrow Wilson Center Press, 1993.

Diner, Dan, and Gotthard Wunberg, eds. *Restitution and Memory: Material Restoration in Europe.* New York: Berghahn books, 2007.

Douglas, Ray M. *Orderly and Humane: The Expulsion of the Germans after the Second World War.* New Haven, CT: Yale University Press, 2012.

Durman, Karel. *Útěk od praporů: Kreml a krize impéria, 1964-1991* [Escape from battalions: Kremlin and a crisis of an empire, 1964-1991]. Prague: Karolinum Press, 1998.

Dyk, Viktor. *O národní stát 1925-1928* [Fight for a National State 1925-1928]. Prague: Neubert, 1937.

Eberhardt, Piotr. *Ethnic groups and population changes in 20th century East Central Europe: History, Data and Analysis.* London: M. E. Sharp, 2003.

Elster, Jon. "Constitutionalism in Eastern Europe: An Introduction." *The University of Chicago Law Review* 58, no. 2 (1991): 447-482.

Epstein, Leo. *Der nationale Minderheitenschutz als internationales Rechtproblem.* Berlin: Engelmann, 1922.

————. *Das Sprachenrecht der Tschechoslowakischen Republik.* Reichenberg: Gebrüder Stiepel, 1927.

————. *Studien-Ausgabe der Verfassungsgesetze der Tschechoslowakischen Republik.* Reichenberg: Gebrüder Stiepel, 1923.

Ermacora, Felix. *Nationalitätenkonflikt und Volksgruppenrecht.* Munich: Bayerische Landeszentrale für Politische Bildungsarbeit, 1978.

Eubank, Keith. "Munich." In Mamatey, and Luža, *A History of the Czechoslovak Republic 1918-1948,* 239-252.

Evans, Robert J.W, and Mark Cornwall, eds. *Czechoslovakia in a Nationalist and Fascist Europe 1918–1948*. Oxford: Oxford University Press, 2007.

———. *The Making of the Habsburg Monarchy 1550–1700: An Interpretation*. Oxford: Clarendon Press, 1979.

Fogelklou, Anders, and Fredrik Sterzel, eds. *Consolidating legal reform in Central and Eastern Europe: An Anthology*. Uppsala: Iustus Forlag, 2003.

Forejtová, Monika. *Mezinárodněprávní ochrana menšin* [International protection of minorities]. Pilsen: Západočeská univerzita, 2002.

Frank, Matthew. *Expelling the Germans: British opinion and the post 1945 population transfer in context*. Oxford: Oxford University Press, 2008.

Franklin, David. "Divorce Proceedings Continue between Czechs and Slovaks"; "Federal Bodies Lose Relevance." Special report, *East European constitutional Review* 2 (1992): xxx

Frentzel-Zagórska, Janina. *From a One-party State to Democracy: Transition in Eastern Europe*. Amsterdam: Rodopi, 1993.

Friedländer, Saul. *The years of extermination: Nazi Germany and the Jews, 1939–1945*. New York: Harper Collins Publishers, 2007.

Frind, Wenzel. *Das sprachliche und sprachlich-nationale Recht*. Vienna: Manz, 1899.

Frištenská, Hana, and Andrej Sulitka. *Průvodce právy příslušníků národnostních menšin v České republice* [Guidebook to the rights of members of national minorities in the Czech Republic]. Prague: Demokratická aliancia Slovákov v ČR, 1995.

Frommer, Benjamin. *National Cleansing: Retribution against Nazi Collaborators in Postwar Czechoslovakia*. Cambridge: Cambridge University Press, 2005.

Gabal, Ivan, ed. *Etnické menšiny ve střední Evropě* [Ethnical minorities in Central Europe]. Prague: G plus G, 1999.

Galandauer, Jan. *Vznik Československé republiky 1918* [The Birth of the Czechoslovak Republic 1918]. Prague: Svoboda, 1988.

Gawrecki, Dan. "Polská menšina v Československu 1918–1938" [The Polish Minority in Czechoslovakia 1918–1938]. In Valenta, Voráček and Harna, *Československo 1918–1938*, 620–628.

Gelpern, Anna. "The laws and politics of reprivatization in East-Central Europe: A Comparison." *University of Pennsylvania journal of international business law* 14, no. 3 (Fall 1993): 315–372.

Golan, Galia. *The Czechoslovak reform movement*. Cambridge: Cambridge University Press, 1973.

———. *Reform Rule in Czechoslovakia: The Dubček Era 1968–1969*. Cambridge: Cambridge University Press, 1973.

Gori, Francesca, and Silvio Pons, eds. *The Soviet Union and Europe in the Cold War, 1943–53*. New York: St. Martin's Press, 1996.

Grant Duff, Shiela. *A German Protectorate: The Czechs under Nazi Rule*. London: Macmillan, 1942.

Grňa, Josef. *Sedm roků na domácí frontě* [Seven years at the national front]. Brno: Blok, 1968.

Grulich, Tomáš, and Tomáš Haišman. "Institucionální zájem o cikánské obyvatelstvo v Československu v letech 1945–1958" [Institutionalised Interest in Gypsy Population in Czechoslovakia in 1945–1958]. *Český lid* 73, no. 2 (1986): 72–85.

Gruner, Wolf. *Jewish Forced Labor Under the Nazis: Economic Needs and Racial Aims, 1938–1944*. Translated by Kathleen M. Dell'Orto. New York: Cambridge University Press, 2006.

Gsovski, Vladimir, and Kazimierz Grzybowski, eds. *Government Law and Courts in the Soviet Union and Eastern Europe*. 2 vols. New York: Atlantic Books; F.A. Praeger, 1959.

Gütermann, Christoph. *Das Minderheitenschutzverfahren des Völkerbundes*. Berlin: Duncker & Humblot, 1979.

Hahn, Fred. "Bylo Československo 1918–1938 národní nebo národnostní stát?" [Was Czechoslovakia in 1918–1938 a National or Nationalities' State?]. *Střední Evropa* 10 (1994): 25–35.

Hahnová, Eva. *Dlouhé stíny předsudků: Německé a anglické stereotypy o Češích v dějinách 20. století* [Long shadows of prejudice: German and English stereotypes about Czechs in the 20th century history]. Prague: Academia, 2015.

————. *Sudetoněmecký problém: Obtížné loučení s minulostí* [The Sudetengerman Problem: Difficult departure from history]. Prague: Prago Media, 1996.

Hájek, Miloš, and Olga Staňková. *Národnostní otázka v lidově demokratickém Československu* [Nationality question in People's Czechoslovakia]. Prague: Státní nakladatelství politické literatury, 1956.

Hartmann, Antonín. *Předpisy jazykového práva* [Language Law Regulations]. Prague: Československý Kompas, 1925.

Hassinger, Hugo. *Die Tschechoslowakei: Ein geographisches, politisches und wirtschaftliches Handbuch*. Vienna: Rikola Verlag, 1925.

Hazard, John N., Isaac Shapiro, and Peter B. Maggs. *The Soviet legal system: Contemporary Documentation and Historical Commentary*. Columbia University, NY: Oceana Publications, 1969.

Hernová, Šárka. "Němci v ČSR v letech 1950–1980" [Germans in Czechoslovakia in 1950–1980]. *Slezský sborník = Acta Silesiaca* 85, no. 4 (1987): 264–275.

Hlavačka, Milan. "Samospráva Království Českého jako předstupeň státní samostatnosti?" [Self-governance of the Kingdom of Bohemia as an Initial Stage of the State Independence?]. In *Vývoj české ústavnosti v letech 1618–1918*. [Development of the Czech Constitutionality in 1618–1918], edited by Karel Malý and Ladislav Soukup, 600–622. Prague: Karolinum Press, 2006.

Hobsbawm, Eric J. *Nations and Nationalism since 1780: Programme, Myth, Reality*. 2nd ed. Cambridge: Cambridge University Press, 2012.

Hobza, Antonín. "Publikace a platnost mírových smluv v čsl. republice" [The Publication and Validity of the Peace Treaties in the Czechoslovak Republic]. *Právník* 62 (1923): 11–22.

————. Úvod do mezinárodního práva mírového [An Introduction to International Peace Law]. Vol. 1. Prague: printed by author, 1933.

Hoensch, Jörg K. *Geschichte der Tschechoslowakischen Republik 1918–1965*. Stuttgart: Kohlhammer, 1966.

Hoetzel, Jiří. *Nová organisace politické správy* [New Organisation of Political Administration]. Prague: Spolek československých právníků Všehrd, [1927].

Holomek, Karel. "Romská menšina v České republice" [Romany minority in the Czech Republic]. In Gabal, *Etnické menšiny ve střední Evropě*, 153–171.

Horáček, Cyril. *Jazykové právo československé republiky* [Language Law of the Czechoslovak Republic]. Prague: Knihovna sborníku věd právních a státních, 1928.

————. "Nová judikatura nejvyššího správního soudu z oboru jazykového práva" [New Case Law of the Supreme Administrative Court in the Area of Language Law]. *Právník* 69, no. 8 (1930): 241–252.

Hošková, Mahulena. "The evolving regime of the new property law in the Czech and Slovak Federal Republic." *The American University Journal of International Law and Policy* 7, no. 3 (1991–92): 605–616.

Houser, Jaroslav, and Valentin Urfus. "Politická správa na Slovensku za buržoasní předmnichovské republiky" [Political Administration in Slovakia during the Bourgeois Pre-Munich Republic]. *Historický časopis* 9 no. 2 (1961): 275–284.

Houžvička, Václav. *Czechs and Germans 1848–2004: The Sudeten Question and the Transformation of Central Europe*. Prague: Karolinum Press, 2015.

Hroch, Miroslav. *Na prahu národní existence* [On the Threshold of the National Existence]. Prague: Mladá fronta, 1999.

————. *V národním zájmu* [In the Name of the Nation]. Knižnice Dějin a současnosti 9. Prague: Nakladatelství Lidové noviny, 1999.

Hronský, Marián. *The Struggle for Slovakia and the Treaty of Trianon 1918–1920*. Bratislava: Veda, 2001.

Hudson, Manley O. "The Protection of Minorities and Natives in Transferred Territories." In *What Really Happened at Paris*, edited by Edward M. House and Charles Seymour, 204–230. New York: Charles Scribner's Sons, 1921.

Hunčík, Peter. "Maďarská menšina ve Slovenské republice" [Hungarian minority in the Slovak Republic]. In Gabal, *Etnické menšiny ve střední Evropě*, 204-218.

Jacko, Pavol. "O vývoji a postavení národnostních menšin" [About the development and status of national minorities]. *Nová mysl* 23 (1969): 1099-1107.

Jaksch, Wenzel. *Europe's Road to Potsdam*. Translated and edited by Kurt Glaser. New York: Praeger, 1964.

Janák, Jan. *Vývoj správy v českých zemích v epoše kapitalismu* [Development of Administration in the Czech Lands in the Era of Capitalism]. 2nd ed. Vol. 2. Prague: SPN, 1971.

Jančík, Drahomír, Eduard Kubů, and Jiří Šouša. *Arisierungsgewinnler: Die Rolle der deutschen Banken bei der „Arisierung" und Konfiskation jüdischer Vermögen im Protektorat Böhmen und Mähren 1939-1945*. Wiesbaden: Harrassowitz, 2011.

Jařab, Jan. "Menšinová politika Evropské unie" [Minority Politics of the EU] In Chytilek and Mareš, *Reprezentace zájmů menšin v EU*, 8-19.

Jarolim, Johann. "Die Reform des Minderheitenschutzes von Dr. Heinrich Rauchberg, Professor an der Deutschen Universität in Prag." *Juristen-Zeitung für das Gebiet der Tschechoslowakischen Republik* 12 (1931): 38-39.

Jaszi, Oscar. *The Dissolution of the Habsburg Monarchy*. Chicago: The University of Chicago Press, 1929.

Jesser, Franz. *Volkstumskampf und Ausgleich im Herzen Europas*. Nuremberg: H. Preussler, 1983.

Johnson, A. Ross. "The Warsaw Pact: Soviet Military Policy in Eastern Europe." In *Soviet Policy in Eastern Europe*, edited by Sarah Meiklejohn Terry, 255-284. New Haven, CT: Yale University Press, 1984.

Jurová, Anna, ed. *Rómska problematika 1945-1967: dokumenty* [The Roma Issue 1945-1967: Documents]. Vol. 4. Prague: ÚSD AVČR, 1996.

Kahánek, Ferdinand. *Stát, země a župy.* [The State, Province and Regions]. Prague: Melantrich, 1926.

Kaľavský, Michal. "Postavenie národných menšín na Slovensku v rokoch 1918-1938" [The Status of National Minorities in Slovakia between 1918 and 1938]. *Slovenský národopis* 39 (1991): 143-156.

Kallab, Jaroslav. "Otázka ochrany menšin jako problém mezinárodního práva" [The Question of the Protection of Minorities as a Problem of International Law]. In *Problém ochrany menšin* [The Problem of the Protection of Minorities], edited by Alois Hajn, 25-26. Prague: Orbis, 1923.

Kalousek, Vratislav. "Přehled zákonodárné činnosti ministerstva vnitra v prvém tříletí" [The Overview of the Legislative Activity of the Ministry of the Interior in the First Three Years]. *Věstník ministerstva vnitra republiky Československé* 3 (1921): 409-414.

Kalvoda, Josef. "National minorities under Communism: The case of Czechoslovakia." *Nationalities Papers: The Journal of Nationalism and Ethnicity* 16, no. 1 (1988): 1-21.

Kamenec, Ivan. "Protižidovský pogrom v Topoľčanoch v septembri 1945" [The Anti-Jewish Pogrom in Topoľčany in September 1945]. In *Acta Contemporanea*, 80-94. Prague: Ústav pro soudobé dějiny AV ČR, 1998.

Kann, Robert A. *A History of the Habsburg Empire 1526-1918*. Berkeley: University of California Press, 1974.

———. *The Multinational Empire: Nationalism and National reform in the Habsburg Monarchy 1848-1918*. Vol. 2. New York: Columbia University Press, 1950.

Kaplan, Karel. *Československo v poválečné Evropě* [Czechoslovakia in Post-War Europe]. Prague: Karolinum Press, 2004.

———. *Kořeny československé reformy 1968* [Roots of Czechoslovak Reform 1968]. Vol. 3, *Změny ve společnosti* [Changes in the Society]. Vol. 4, *Struktura moci* [Structure of Power]. Brno: Doplněk, 2002.

———. *Pravda o Československu 1945-1948* [The Truth about Czechoslovakia 1945-1948]. Prague: Panorama, 1990.

———. *Report on the Murder of the General Secretary*. Translated by Karel Kovanda. London: I.B. Tauris, 1990.

Kapras, Jan. *Přehled vývoje české jazykové otázky* [Overview of the Development of the Czech Language Issue]. Prague: R. Brož, 1910.

Kárník, Zdeněk. *České země v éře první republiky* [The Czech Lands in the Period of the First Republic]. 3 vols. Prague: Libri, 2000, 2002, 2003.

Kazbunda, Karel. *Otázka česko-německá v předvečer velké války* [The Czech-German Issue on the Eve of the Great War]. Prague: Karolinum Press, 1995.

Kelsen, Hans. *The Communist Theory of Law*. New York: F.A. Praeger, 1955.

Kimminich, Otto. *Das Recht auf die Heimat*. 3rd ed. Bonn: Kulturstiftung der Deutschen Vertriebenen, 1989.

Klapka, Otakar. *Samospráva a zřízení župní* [Self-government and the Establishment of Regions]. Prague: Nakladatelství Parlament, 1923.

Klepetař, Harry. *Seit 1918: eine Geschichte der Tschechoslowakischen Republik*. M.-Ostrau: Julius Kittls Nachfolger, 1937.

———. *Der Sprachenkampf in den Sudetenländern*. Prague: Ed. Strache, 1930.

Klimek, Antonín. *Velké dějiny zemí Koruny české* [Comprehensive History of the Lands of the Bohemian Crown]. Vol. 13. Prague: Paseka, 2000.

———. *Velké dějiny zemí Koruny české* [Comprehensive History of the Lands of the Bohemian Crown]. Vol. 14. Prague: Paseka, 2002.

King, Jeremy. *Budweisers into Czechs and Germans*. Princeton: Princeton University Press, 2002.

Kochavi, Arieh J. *Prelude to Nuremberg: Allied War Crimes Policy and the Question of Punishment*. Chapel Hill: University of North Carolina Press, 1998.

Kocích, Milan. "Poznámky k právní úpravě školské, osvětové a spolkové činnosti národnostních menšin v buržoasní ČSR" [Notes on Legal Regulation Concerning the Activities Relating to Schooling, Education, and Associations of National Minorities in the Bourgeois CSR]. In *Sborník prací z dějin státu a práva*, 155–171. Prague: Univerzita Karlova, 1979.

Kocsis, Karoly, and Eszter Kocsis-Hodosi. *Ethnic Geography of the Hungarian Minorities in the Carpathian Basin*. Budapest: Hungarian Academy of Sciences, 1998.

Komjathy, Anthony Tihamer, and Rebecca Stockwell. *German Minorities and the Third Reich: Ethnic Germans of East Central Europe Between the Wars*. New York: Holmes & Meier, 1980

Korbel, Josef. *The Communist Subversion of Czechoslovakia 1938–1948: The failure of Co-existence*. Princeton: Princeton University Press, 1959.

Korčák, Jaromír. *Geopolitické základy Československa* [Geopolitical Foundations of Czechoslovakia]. Prague: Orbis, 1938.

Kořalka, Jiří. *Češi v habsburské říši a v Evropě 1815–1914* [The Czechs in the Habsburg Empire and in Europe 1815–1914]. Prague: Argo, 1996.

Kovařík, David. "'Brněnský pochod smrti 1945': Mýty a skutečnost" [Death March of Germans from Brno in 1945. Myths and Reality]. In *Konec soužití Čechů a Němců v Československu: Sborník k 60. výročí ukončení II. světové války* [The End of co-habitance of Czechs and Germans in Czechoslovakia: The Anthology to commemorate 60th anniversary of the end of WWII], edited by Hynek Fajmon and Kateřina Hloušková, 63–79. Brno: Centrum pro studium demokracie a kultury, 2005.

———. "Mezi mlýnskými kameny: Němečtí antifašisté v Československu v roce 1945" [German antifascist in Czechoslovakia in 1945]. *Dějiny a současnost* 29, no. 4 (2007): 41–43.

Kovtun, George J. *The Czechoslovak Declaration of Independence: A History of the Document*. Washington, DC: Library of Congress, 1985.

Kovtun, Jiří. *Masarykův triumf* [Masaryk's Triumph]. Prague: Odeon, 1991.

———. *Slovo má poslanec Masaryk* [Deputy Masaryk has the floor]. Prague: Československý spisovatel, 1991.

Krajčovičová, Natália. "Slovakia in Czechoslovakia, 1918–1938." In Teich, Kováč, and Brown, *Slovakia in History*, 137–157.

Krapfl, James. *Revolution with a Human Face: Politics, Culture, and Community in Czechoslovakia, 1989–1992*. Ithaca, NY: Cornell University Press, 2013.

Kraus, Michael, and Allison Stanger, eds. *Irreconcilable Differences? Explaining Czechoslovakia's Dissolution.* Lanham, MD: Rowman & Littlefield, 2000.

Krejčí, Jaroslav. *Czechoslovakia at the Crossroads of European History.* London: I.B. Tauris, 1990.

Krejčí, Oskar. *History of Elections in Bohemia and Moravia.* New York: Columbia University Press, 1995.

Krčmář, Jan. *The Prague Universities: Compiled according to the sources and records.* Prague: Orbis, 1934.

Křen, Jan. *Konfliktní společenství* [Dissentious Community]. Prague: Academia, 1990.

———, Dušan Kováč, and Hans Lemberg, eds. *V rozdelenej Európe: Češi, Slováci, Nemci a ich štáty v rokoch 1948-1989* [In a divided Europe: Czechs, Slovaks, Germans and their states in 1948-1989]. Bratislava: Academic Electronic Press, 1998.

Kučera, Jaroslav. "Koncepce národního státu Čechů a Slováků a jeho realita v životě první republiky" [The Conception of the National State of Czechs and Slovaks and its Reality in the Life of the First Republic]. In Valenta, Voráček and Harna, *Československo 1918-1938*, 602-610.

———. *Minderheit im Nationalstaat: Die Sprachenfrage in den tschechisch-deutschen Beziehungen 1918-1938.* Munich: R. Oldenbourg Verlag, 1999.

———. *Odsun nebo vyhnání?* [Displacement or expulsion?]. Prague: H&H, 1992.

———. "Die rechtliche und soziale Stellung der Deutschen in der Tschechoslowakei Ende der 40er und Anfang der 50er Jahre" *Bohemia* 33, no. 2 (1992): 322-337.

Kuklík, Jan. *Czech law in historical contexts.* Prague: Karolinum Press, 2015.

———. "Interference with proprietary rights between 1945 and 1948 and their reflection in so-called 'indemnity agreements' and in privatization and 'restitution' legislation after 1989." Translated by Renata Hrubá. In Tomášek, *Czech law between europeanization and globalization,* 29-40.

———. "Hungarian Population in the Czech Lands Between 1945 and 1949." *Acta Humana* 4 (2015): 27-38.

———. *Mýty a realita takzvaných Benešových dekretů: Dekrety prezidenta republiky 1940-1945* [Myth and reality of the so-called Beneš's decrees]. Prague: Linde, 2002.

———. "Transfer or expulsion? The fate of the German minority in post-war Czechoslovakia from the Czechoslovak law point of view." In *War die „Vertreibung" Unrecht? Die Umsiedlungsbeschlüsse des Potsdamer Abkommens und ihre Umsetzung in ihrem völkerrechtlichen und historischen Kontext,* edited by Christoph Koch, 121-151. Frankfurt am Main: Peter Lang, 2015.

———, Helena Hofmannová, Katarína Kukanová, René Petráš, and Pavel Šturma. *Jak odškodnit holocaust? Problematika vyvlastnění židovského majetku, jeho restituce a odškodnění* [How to compensate the Holocaust: The expropriation of Jewish Property and its compensation]. Prague: Karolinum Press, 2015.

———, Jan Němeček, and Jaroslav Šebek. *Dlouhé stíny Mnichova: Mnichovská dohoda očima signatářů a její dopady na Československo* [Lasting shadows of Munich]. Prague: Auditorium, 2011.

———, and Jan Němeček. *Frontiers, Minorities, Transfers, Expulsions: British diplomacy towards Czechoslovakia and Poland during WWII.* Vol. 1. Prague: Faculty of Law, Charles University Institute of History CAS, 2015.

———, and Jan Němeček. "Memorandum by Hans Kelsen on the Breaking up of Czecho-Slovakia." In *Das internationale Wirken Hans Kelsen,* edited by Clemens Jabloner, Thomas Olechowski, and Klaus Zeleny. Schriftenreihe des Hans Kelsen-Instituts 38, 107-119. Vienna: Manz Verlag, 2016.

———, and Jan Němeček. *Od národního státu ke státu národností? Národnostní statut a snahy o řešení menšinové otázky v Československu v roce 1938* [From a National State to the State of Nationalities? Statute of nationalities and attempts to resolve the nationality questions in Czechoslovakia in 1938]. Prague: Karolinum Press, 2013.

———, and Jan Němeček. *Osvobozené Československo očima britské diplomacie* [Liberated Czechoslovakia as seen by the British diplomacy]. Prague: Karolinum Press, 2011.

————, and Jan Němeček. "Repudiation of the Munich Agreement during the Second World War as seen from Czechoslovak Perspective." In *The disintegration of Czechoslovakia in the end of 1930s: Policy in the Central Europe*, edited by Emil Voráček, 97–122. Prague: Institute of History, 2009.

Kural, Václav. Češi, Němci a mnichovská křižovatka [The Czechs and Germans at the Munich Crossroads]. Prague: Karolinum Press, 2002.

————. "Jazykový problém a jazykové právo v ČSR 1918–1938 z hlediska česko-německého" [The Language Issue and Language Law in ČSR 1918–1938 from the Czech-German Perspective]. *Slezský sborník = Acta Silesiaca* 89, no. 1 (1991): 32–38.

————. *Konflikt místo společenství?* [A Conflict Instead of a Community?]. Prague: R Press, 1993.

————. "Lidský potenciál sudetských Němců a vznik Československa" [Human Potential of the Sudeten Germans and the Foundation of Czechoslovakia]. *Slezský sborník = Acta Silesiaca* 89, no. 2 (1991): 94–109.

————. *Vlastenci proti okupaci: Ústřední vedení odboje domácího 1940–1943* [Patriots against occupation; Central leadership of national resistance]. Prague: Karolinum Press, 1997.

Kusin, Vladimir V. *The Intellectual origins of the Prague Spring: The Development of reformist ideas in Czechoslovakia 1956–1967*. Cambridge: Cambridge University Press, 1971.

Kutnar, František. *Obrozenské vlastenectví a nacionalismus* [Revivalist Patriotism and Nationalism]. Prague: Karolinum Press, 2003.

Kyogoku, Toshiaki. "Národní agitace a obecní školství na Moravě na přelomu 19. a 20. století: Boj o české dítě" [National Agitation and Compulsory Schooling in Moravia at the turn of 19th and 20th Century: The Fight for a Czech Child]. In *Místo národních jazyků ve výchově, školství a vědě v habsburské monarchii 1867–1918* [The Role of National Languages in Upbringing, Education and Science in the Habsburg Monarchy in 1867–1918], 563–578. Prague: Výzkumné centrum pro dějiny vědy, 2003.

Kvaček, Robert. *První světová válka a česká otázka* [World War I and the Czech Issue]. Prague: Triton, 2003.

Lacina, Vlastislav. *Formování československé ekonomiky 1918–1923* [The Shaping of the Czechoslovak Economy 1918–1923]. Prague: Academia, 1990.

————. *Velká hospodářská krize v Československu 1929–1934* [The Great Economic Crisis in Czechoslovakia 1929–1934]. Prague: Academia, 1984.

Ladas, Stehpen P. *The Exchange of Minorities: Bulgaria, Greece and Turkey.* New York: Macmillan, 1932.

Láníček, Jan. *Czechs, Slovaks and the Jews, 1938–48: Beyond Idealisation and Condemnation.* Basingstoke: Palgrave Macmillan, 2013.

Laponce, Jean A. *The Protection of Minorities.* Berkeley: University of California Press, 1960.

Laštovka, Karel. "K otázce postupu při provádění zákona o župních a okresních úřadech" [To the Issue of the Approach When Implementing the Act on Regional and District Authorities]. *Věstník ministerstva vnitra republiky Československé* 2 (1920): 285–289.

————. *Zákon župní* [The Act on Regions]. Bratislava: Právnická Jednota, 1925.

Lemberg, Hans. *Porozumění: Češi, Němci, východní Evropa, 1848–1948* [Comity: Czechs, Germans, Eastern Europe, 1848–1948]. Prague: Lidové noviny, 2000.

Lettrich. Jozef. *History of Modern Slovakia.* New York: F. Prager, 1955.

Lipscher, Ladislav. *Verfassung und politische Verwaltung in der Tschechoslowakei 1918–1939.* Vienna: Oldenbourg, 1979.

Loebl, Eugene. *Sentenced and Tried: The Stalinist Purges in Czechoslovakia.* London: Elek Books, 1969.

Ludwikowski, Rett R. *Constitution-making in the Region of Former Soviet Dominance.* Durham, NC: Duke University Press, 1996.

Lukacs, John. *The Great Powers and Eastern Europe.* New York: American Book Company, 1953.

Luschka, Felix von. "Im Parlament der Ersten Tschechoslowakischen Republik: Erinnerungen eines sudetendeutschen Abgeordneten 1920–1938." *Bohemia* 4 (1963): 228–274.

Luža, Radomír. "The Czech resistance movement." In Mamatey, and Luža, *A History of the Czechoslovak Republic 1918-1948*, 343-361.

———. "Czechoslovakia between democracy and communism 1945-1948." In Mamatey, and Luža, *A History of the Czechoslovak Republic 1918-1948*, xxx.

———. *The Transfer of the Sudeten Germans: A Study of Czech-German Relations, 1933-1962*. London: Routledge, 1964.

Macartney, Carlile A. *The Habsburg Empire, 1790-1918*. London: Weidenfeld & Nicolson, 1968.

———. *National States and National Minorities*. Oxford: Oxford University Press, 1934.

Machačová, Jana, and Jiří Matějček. *Nástin sociálního vývoje českých zemí 1781-1914* [Outline of Social Development in the Czech Lands 1781-1914]. Opava: Slezské zemské muzeum, 2002.

Magocsi, Paul Robert. "Utváření národní identity: Podkarpatská Rus (1848-1948)" [Shaping the National Identity: Sub-Carpathian Ruthenia (1848-1948)]. Part 2. *Střední Evropa* 15, no. 92/93 (1999): 114-129.

Malíř, Jiří. "Národnostní klíč z roku 1914 v zemských hospodářských a finančních záležitostech - cesta k 'druhému moravskému paktu'?" [The Ethno-national Key from 1914 in Provincial Economic and Financial Matters - a Path to 'the Second Moravian Pact'?]. In *Milý Bore-: profesoru Ctiboru Nečasovi k jeho sedmdesátým narozeninám věnují přátelé, kolegové a žáci*, edited by Tomáš Dvořák, Radomír Vlček, and Libor Vykoupil, 137-145. Brno: Historický ústav AV ČR; Historický ústav FF MU; Matice moravská, 2003.

Malloy, Tove H., and Francesco Palermo, eds. *Minority Accommodation through Territorial and Non-Territorial Autonomy*. Oxford: Oxford University Press, 2015.

Malý, Karel. "Sprache - Recht und Staat in der tschechischen Vergangenheit." In *Sprache - Recht - Geschichte*, edited by Joern Eckert, and Hans Hattenhauer, 257-281. Heidelberg: C.F. Müller, 1991.

———. "Vznik ČSR a problematika státního občanství" [The Foundation of the Czechoslovak Republic and the Issue of Citizenship]. *Právník* 127, no. 10 (1988): 908-912.

Mamatey, Victor S., and Radomír Luža, eds. *A History of the Czechoslovak Republic 1918-1948*. Princeton, NJ: Princeton University Press, 1973.

Mark, Eduard. *Revolution by Degrees: Stalin's National-Front Strategy for Europe, 1941-1947*. Working Paper No. 31. Washington, DC: Woodrow Wilson International Centre for Scholars, 2001.

Marrus, Michael, and Anna Bramwell, eds. *Refugees in the Age of Total War*. London: Routledge, 1988.

Marrus, Michael. *The Unwanted: European Refugees in the Twenties Century*. Oxford: Oxford University Press, 1985.

Martuliak, Pavol. "Kolonizačná akcia pri I. pozemkovej reforme na Slovensku" [Colonisation During the 1st Land Reform in Slovakia]. In *Československá pozemková reforma 1919-1935 a její mezinárodní souvislosti* [The Czechoslovak Land Reform 1919-1935 and the International Context], 81-85. Uherské Hradiště: Slovácké museum, 1994.

Matelski, Dariusz. *Niemcy w Polsce w XX wieku* [Germans in Poland in the 20th Century]. Warsaw: PWN, 1999.

Matoušek, Stanislav. "The Slovak National Council." Bulletin of Czechoslovak law no. 1-2. Prague: Orbis, 1960: 93-95.

Maurer-Horn, Susanne. "Die Landesregierung für Deutschböhmen und das Selbstbestimmungsrecht 1918-1919." *Bohemia* 38, no.1 (1997): 37-55.

Michal, Jan M. "Postwar economic development." In Mamatey, and Luža, *A History of the Czechoslovak Republic 1918-1948*, 428-460.

Mikule, Vladimír. "Die Dekrete des Praesidenten der Republik zur Stellung der Deutschen und ihre heutige rechtliche Bedeutung." In *Die Deutschen und Magyaren in den Dekreten des Präsidenten der Republik*, edited by Karel Jech, 186-212. Brno: Doplněk, 2003.

———. "Národnostní menšiny v České republice pohledem českého práva" [National minorities in the Czech Republic from the viewpoint of Czech law]. In Gabal, *Etnické menšiny ve střední Evropě*, 50-70.

Miller, David Hunter. *My Diary at the Conference of Peace*. XIII. [New York]: [Printed for the author by the Appeal printing Company], 1924.

Milotová, Jaroslava, Eduard Kubů, Drahomír Jančík, Jan Kuklík, and Jiří Šouša. *The Jewish Gold and Other Precious Metals, Precious Stones, and Objects Made of Such Materials - Situation in the Czech Lands in the Years 1939 to 1945*. Prague: Sefer, 2011.

Molnár, Imre. "Kapitoly z poválečných dějin Maďarů vysídlených do Čech" [Chapters from post-war history of Hungarians resettled to Bohemia]. *Střední Evropa* 7, no. 19 (1991): 74–90.

Moravcová, Dagmar. *Československo, Německo a evropská hnutí 1929–1932* [Czechoslovakia, Germany and European Movements 1929–1932]. Prague: Institut pro středoevropskou kulturu a politiku, 2001.

Morvay, Péter. "Menšiny v Maďarsku a maďarská menšinová politika od roku 1918 do současnosti" [Minorities in Hungary and Hungarian minority policy from 1918 until today]. In Gabal, *Etnické menšiny ve střední Evropě*, 186–203.

Mosný, Peter. *Podkarpatská Rus: Nerealizovaná autonómia* [Sub-Carpathian Ruthenia: Non-realized Authonomy]. Bratislava: Slovak Academic Press, 2001.

———. "Postavenie národnostných menšín v právnom poriadku predmníchovského Československa" [The Status of National Minorities in the Legal Order of Pre-Munich Czechoslovakia]. *Acta Iuridica Cassoviensia* 15 (1990): 15–30.

———. "Poznámky k jazykovému právu v Československu 1918–1938" [Notes on Language Law in Czechoslovakia 1918–1938]. In Plichtová, *Minority v politike*, 110–114.

Mrázek, Josef. "Ochrana menšin z hlediska mezinárodního práva" [The Protection of Minorities from the Perspective of International Law]. *Právník* 132, no. 6 (1993): 478–497.

Musil, Jiří, ed. *The End of Czechoslovakia*. Budapest: Central European University Press, 1995.

Naimark, Norman M. *Fires of Hatred: Ethnic Cleansing in Twentieth-century Europe*. Cambridge, MA: Harvard University Press, 2002.

Nebeský, Jaroslav: "Polská menšina na československém Těšínsku" [The Polish Minority in the Cieszyn Region of Czechoslovakia]. *Zahraniční politika* 15 (1936): 95–111, 196–205.

Němeček, Jan. *Od spojenectví k roztržce* [From the Alliance to the Rift]. Prague: Academia, 2003.

"New Czech, Slovak Leaders Accelerate Separation." Special report, *East European constitutional Review* (Summer 1992): 10.

Nosková, Helena. "Maďaři v České republice ve 20. a 21. století" [Hungarians in the Czech Republic in 20th and 21st Century]. In *Kdo jsem a kam patřím? Identita národnostních menšin a etnických komunit na území České republiky* [Who am I and where do I belong? Identity of national minorities and ethnic communities in the CR], edited by Dana Bittnerová and Mirjam Moravcová, 99–116. Prague: Sofis, 2005.

Novák, Otto. *Henleinovci proti Československu* [The Sudeten German Party against Czechoslovakia]. Prague: Naše vojsko, 1987.

Olivová, Věra. *Československé dějiny 1914–1939* [Czechoslovak History 1914–1939]. Vol. 1. Prague: Karolinum Press, 1993.

Opočenský, Jan. *The Collapse of the Austro-Hungarian Monarchy and the Rise of the Czechoslovak State*. Prague: Orbis, 1928.

———. *Vznik národních států v říjnu 1918* [Formation of National States in October 1918]. Prague: Orbis, 1927.

Osuský, Štefan. "Ochrana menšín" [Protection of Minorities]. *Prúdy* 4 (1922): 10–22.

Pánek, Jaroslav, and Oldřich Tůma. *A History of the Czech lands*. Prague: Karolinum Press, 2009.

Parker, Robert A. C. *Chamberlain and Appeasement: British Policy and the Coming of the Second World War*. London: Macmillan, 1993.

Paukovič, Vladimír. "Vybrané aspekty etnického spolužitia po roku 1989" [Selected aspects of ethnical coexistence after 1989]. In Plichtová, *Minority v politike*, 130–132.

Pavelčíková, Nina. *Romové v českých zemích v letech 1945–1989* [Romanies in Czech Lands in 1945–1989]. Prague: Úřad dokumentace a vyšetřování zločinů komunismu PČR, 2004.

Pavlíček, Václav. "K ústavním aspektům práv menšin po vzniku Československa" [On Constitutional Aspects of Minority Rights after the Foundation of Czechoslovakia]. In Valenta, Voráček and Harna, Československo 1918–1938, 594–601.

———. O české státnosti: Úvahy a polemiky 1: Český stát a Němci [On the Czech Statehood: Reflections and Debates 1: Czech State and Germans]. Prague: Karolinum Press, 2002.

———. Ústava a ústavní řád České republiky [Constitution and constitutional order of the Czech Republic]. Vol 2. Prague: Linde, 1995.

Pelikán, Jiří, ed. The Czechoslovak Political Trials 1950–1954: The Suppressed Report of the Dubček Government's Commission of Inquiry 1968. Stanford, CA: Stanford University Press, 1971.

Perek, Václav. "Jazyková otázka v advokátní komoře pražské" [The Language Issue in the Bar Association in Prague]. Právník 69 (1930): 182–185.

Perman, Dagmar. The Shaping of the Czechoslovak State: Diplomatic History of the Boundaries of Czechoslovakia, 1914–1920. Leiden: E.J. Brill, 1962.

Peroutka, Ferdinand. Budování státu [The Building of a State]. 3rd ed. Vols. 1–3. Prague: Academia – NLN, 1991.

Peška, Zdeněk. Československá ústava a zákony s ní souvislé [The Czechoslovak Constitution and Related Laws]. 2 vols. Prague: Československý kompas, 1935.

———. Kulturní samospráva národních menšin [Cultural Self-governance of National Minorities]. Prague: Orbis, 1933.

———. Národní menšiny a Československo [National Minorities and Czechoslovakia]. Bratislava: Právnická fakulta University Komenského, 1932.

———. "Otázka národnostních menšin na Pařížské mírové konferenci" [The Issue of National Minorities at Paris Peace Conference]. Zahraniční politika 9 (1930): 212–227.

Petráš, René, ed. Aktuální problémy právního postavení menšin v České republice: Sborník příspěvků z odborného semináře Menšiny a právo v České republice [Topical problems of legal status of minorities in the Czech Republic: Anthology of contributions from specialized lecture Minorities and law in the Czech Republic]. Prague: Úřad vlády, 2010.

———. "Cikánská/romská otázka v Československu na počátku komunistického režimu a návaznost na starší vývoj" [Gipsy/Romany question in the beginning of the Communist regime and succession to former development]. Právněhistorické studie 38 (2007): 225–247.

———. Cizinci ve vlastní zemi: Menšinové konflikty v moderní Evropě [Foreigners in their own country: Minority Conflicts in Modern Europe]. Prague: Auditorium, 2012.

———. "Constitutional development in Czechoslovakia in the 1960s and problems of ethnicity." Translated by Renata Hrubá. In Tomášek, Czech law between europeanization and globalization, 60–68.

———. "The Creation and Legal Status of the Slovak, Roma and Vietnamese Minorities in the Czech Republic." Acta Humana 4 (2015): 39–46.

———. "Der international-rechtliche Schutz von Minderheiten in der Zwischenkriegsära und seine Bedeutung für die Deutschen in der Tschechoslowakei (vor allem im Gebiet der Vysočina)." In Tschechen und Deutsche in der Vysočina. Havlíčkův Brod: Muzeum Vysočiny, 2014.

———. "K právům národností – menšin v českých zemích na počátku komunistického režimu." In Pocta Prof. JUDr. Václavu Pavlíčkovi, Csc. k 70. narozeninám [To the rights of nationalities – minorities in the Czech Lands in the beginning of Communist regime, available. In Honour of Prof. Václav Pavlíček for his 70th birthday]. Prague: Linde, 2004.

———. "Menšiny v Československu 1945–1989." In Vývoj práva v Československu v letech 1945–1989: Sborník příspěvků. Edited by Karel Malý and Ladislav Soukup. Prague: Karolinum Press, 2004.

———. Menšiny v komunistickém Československu [Minorities in communist Czechoslovakia]. Prague: Auditorium, 2007.

———. Menšiny v meziválečném Československu [Minorities in interwar Czechoslovakia]: Právní postavení národnostních menšin v první Československé republice a jejich mezinárodněprávní ochrana. Prague: Karolinum Press, 2009.

———. "Migrace a právní postavení přistěhovalců v českém právu z historické perspektivy"

[Migration and the Legal Status of Immigrants in Czech Law from the Historical Perspective]. In *Migrace a kulturní konflikty* [Migration and Cultural Conflicts], edited by Harald Christian Scheu, 114–141. Prague: Auditorium, 2011.

———. "Minderheiten in der Zwischenkriegs-Tschechoslowakei – ihre rechtliche und faktische Stellung." *Historica / Historical Sciences in the Czech Republic* 10 (2003): 197–228.

———. "Právo a romské kočování v českých zemích – historický přehled." In *Migrace, tolerance, integrace* [Law and Romany nomadism in Czech Lands – historical overview. In Migration, tolerance, integration]. Vol. 2, 210–219. Opava: Slezské zemské muzeum, Slezský ústav, 2005.

———. "Problematická koncepce práv menšin v Listině základních práv a svobod" [Problematical conception of rights of minorities in the Charter of Fundamental Rights and Freedoms]. In *Ochrana práv a svobod v proměnách práva na počátku 21. století: v českém, evropském a mezinárodním kontextu* [Protection of rights and freedoms in transformations of law in the beginning of the 21st century: in Czech, European and international context], 155–162. Prague: Auditorium, 2011.

———. "Reforma správy a národní otázka na počátku první republiky" [Reform of public administration and national question in the beginning of the First Czechoslovak Republic]. *Historický obzor* 13 (2002): 133–137.

———. "The Revolutionary National Assembly in Czechoslovakia 1918–1920: Contentious Issues." In *Hohes Haus! 150 Jahre moderner Parlamentarismus in Österreich, Böhmen, der Tschechoslowakei und der Republik Tschechien im mitteleuropäischen Kontext*. Vienna: Verlag der Österreichischen Akademie der Wissenschaften, 2015.

———. "Snahy Československa oddělit se od právních tradic v první polovině šedesátých let – interdisciplinární aspekty" [The attempts of Czechoslovakia to sever from legal traditions in the first half of the 1960's]. In *Společnost českých zemí v evropských kontextech: České evropanství ve srovnávacích perspektivách* [Society of Czech Lands in European contexts], edited by Blanka Soukupová, Róża Godula-Węcławowicz, Miroslav Hroch, 93–113. Prague: Fakulta humanitních studií Univerzity Karlovy v Praze, 2012.

———. "Specifika právního postavení Němců na počátku komunistické éry" [Particularities of legal status of Germans in the beginning of communist era]. In *Německy mluvící obyvatelstvo v Československu po roce 1945* [German speaking population in Czechoslovakia after 1945], edited by Adrian von Arburg, Tomáš Dvořák and David Kovařík, 318–335. Brno: Matice moravská, 2010.

———. "Ústavní zákon č. 144/1968 Sb. z 27.10.1968, o postavení národností." In *Pocta Jánu Gronskému* [Constitutional Act No. 144/1968 Sb. from 27 October 1968 on the status of nationalities. On Honour of Ján Gronský]. Pilsen: Aleš Čeněk, 2008.

———. "Ústavní zakotvení práv národností v Československu v roce 1968 a maďarská otázka" [Constitutional embedding of rights of nationalities in Czechoslovakia in 1968 and the Hungarian question]. In *Maďarská menšina na Slovensku v procese transformácie po roku 1989: (Historické, politologické a právne súvislosti)* [Hungarian minority in Slovakia in the process of transformation]. Prešov: Universum, 2007.

———, Helena Petrův, and Harald Christian Scheu. *Menšiny a právo v České republice* [Minorities and law in the Czech Republic]. Prague: Auditorium, 2009.

Pithart, Petr. *Osmašedesátý* [The year 1968]. 3rd ed. Prague: Rozmluvy, 1990.

Plaček, Vilém. "Těšínsko po uzavření československo- polské smlouvy" [Těšín Silesia after completion of Czechoslovak-Polish contract]. *Slezský sborník = Acta Silesiaca* 65, no. 1 (1967): 1–19.

Plichtová, Jana, ed. *Minority v politike: Kultúrne a jazykové práva* [Minorities in politics: Cultural and Language Rights]. Bratislava: Česko-slovenský výbor Európskej kultúrnej nadácie, 1992.

Polian, Pavel. *Against Their Will: The History and Geography of Forced Migrations in the USSR*. Budapest: Central European University Press, 2004.

Polonsky, Antony. *The Great Powers and the Polish question, 1941–45: A documentary study in Cold War Origins*. London: London School of Economics, 1976.

Popély, Árpád. "Case studies 1944–1948: Czechoslovakia." In *Minority Hungarian Communities in the Twentieth Century*, edited by Nándor Bárdi, Csilla Fedinec, and László Szarka, translated by Brian McLean, 299–304. Boulder, CO: Social Science Monogaphs; Highland Lakes, NJ: Atlantic Research and Publications, 2011.

Posluch, Marian. "Die konstitutionelle Entwicklung der Tschechoslowakischen Sozialistischen Republik zwischen 1968 und 1989." In *Normdurchsetzung in osteuropäischen Nachkriegsgesellschaften (1944–1989)*. Vol. 4, *Tschechoslowakei (1944–1989)*, edited by Heinz Mohnhaupt and Hans-Andreas Schönfeldt, 537–553. Frankfurt am Main: Vittorio Klostermann, 1998.

Pospíšil, Ivo. "Pojetí menšin v evropském právu" [Minorities conception in the European law]. In Chytilek and Mareš, *Reprezentace zájmů menšin v EU*, 20–37.

Pošvář, Jaroslav. "Správní delikty podle zákona o obraně státu" [Administrative Delicts under the Defence of the State Act]. *Právník* 75 (1936): 421–424.

Praźmowska, Anita. *Britain and Poland 1939–1943: The Betrayed Ally*. Cambridge: Cambridge University Press, 1995.

Preece, Jennifer Jackson. *National Minorities and the European Nation-States System*. Oxford: Clarendon Press; New York: Oxford University Press, 1998.

Prinz, Friedrich. "Benešův mýtus se rozpadá" [Beneš's Myth Falling into Pieces]. *Střední Evropa* 8, no. 24 (1992): 41–54.

———, ed. *Deutsche Geschichte im Osten Europas: Böhmen und Mähren*. Berlin: Siedler, 2002.

Přibáň, Jiří. *Legal Symbolism: On Law, Time and European Identity*. Burlington, VT: Ashgate Publishing, 2007.

Prochazka, Theodor. "The second republic, 1938–1939." In Mamatey, and Luža, *A History of the Czechoslovak Republic 1918–1948*, 235–270.

———. *The Second Republic: The disintegration of post-Munich Czechoslovakia, October 1938–March 1939*. Boulder, CO: East European Monographs, 1981.

Prokop, Ladislav. "Čtyři léta jazykového nařízení" [Four Years of a Language Decree]. *Národnostní obzor* 1 (1930–1931): 33–34.

Průcha, Václav, Jana Geršlová, Alena Hadrabová, Lenka Kalinová, František Vencovský, and Zdislav Šulc. *Hospodářské a sociální dějiny Československa 1918–1992*. Vol. 2. [Economic and social history of Czechoslovakia 1918–1992]. Brno: Doplněk, 2009.

Purgat, Juraj. *Od Trianonu po Košice* [From Trianon to Košice]. Bratislava: Epocha, 1970.

Rabl, Kurt. "Über die Verfassungsurkunde der ČSSR vom 11. Juli 1960." *Bohemia* 2, no. 1 (1961): 511–544.

Rabinowicz, Aaron. "The Jewish Minority: Legal Position." In *The Jews of Czechoslovakia; Historical Studies and Surveys*. Vol. 1. Philadelphia: Jewish Publication Society of America; New York: Society for the History of Czechoslovak Jews, 1968.

Raschhofer, Hermann. *Die Sudetenfrage*. Munich: Isar Verlag, 1953.

Raška, Francis Dostál. *The Czechoslovak Exile Government in London and the Sudeten German Issue*. Prague: Karolinum Press, 2002.

Rauchberg, Heinrich. *Der nationale Besitzstand in Böhmen*. 3 vols. Leipzig: Duncker & Humblot, 1905.

Reich, Andreas. "Das tschechoslowakische Bildungswesen vor dem Hintergrund des Deutsch-Tschechischen Nationalitätenproblems." *Bohemia* 36, no. 1 (1995): 19–38.

Rechcígl, Miloslav, ed. *Czechoslovakia Past and Present: Political, international, social, and economic aspects*. Vol. 1. The Hague: Mouton, 1968.

Renner, Karl. *Das Selbstbestimmungsrecht der Nationen in besonderer Anwendung auf Oesterreich*. Leipzig: F. Deuticke, 1918.

Richter, Karel. *Češi a Němci v zrcadle dějin* [Czechs and Germans in the Mirror of History]. Vol. 2. Třebíč: Akcent, 1999.

Říha, Jan. *Organisace politické správy v republice Československé* [Organisation of Political Administration in the Republic of Czechoslovakia]. Prague: Československý Kompas, 1928.

Ripka, Hubert. *Czechoslovakia Enslaved: The Story of the Communist Coup D'etat*. London: Victor Gollanz, 1950.

Robbins, Keith. "Britain and Munich reconsidered: a personal historical journey." In Evans and Cornwall, *Czechoslovakia in a Nationalist and Fascist Europe 1918-1948*, 231-240.

Robinson, Jacob, Oscar Karbach, Max M. Laserson, Nehemiah Robinson, and Marc V. Vishniak. *Were the minority treaties a failure?* New York: Institute of Jewish Affairs, 1943.

Roszkowski, Wojciech. *Land Reforms in East Central Europe After World War One.* Warsaw: Institute of Political Studies, Polish Academy of Sciences, 1995.

Rothkirchen, Livia. *The Jews of Bohemia and Moravia: Facing the Holocaust.* Lincoln: University of Nebraska Press; Jerusalem: Yad Vashem, 2005.

Rupnow, Dirk, "'Zur Förderung und beschleunigten Regelung der Auswanderung . . .' Die Zentrallstelle für jüdische Auswanderung in Wien." In *Ausgeschlossen und entrechtet, Raub und Rückgabe: Oesterreich von 1938 bis heute,* edited by Verena Pawlowsky and Harald Wendelin, 13-30. Vienna: Mandelbaum, 2006.

Rutowska, Maria, Zbigniew Mazur, and Hubert Orłowski. "History and Memory: mass expulsions and transfers 1939-1945-1949." *Biuletyn Instytutu Zachodnego* 21 (2009): 4-28.

Rychlík, Jan. "The Possibilities for Czech-Slovak Compromise, 1989-1992." In *Irreconcilable Differences? Explaining Czechoslovakia's Dissolution,* edited by Michael Kraus and Allison Stanger, 49-65. Lanham, MD: Rowman & Littlefield, 2000.

———. "Teorie a praxe jednotného československého národa a československého jazyka v 1. republice" [The Theory and Practice of the Unitary Czechoslovak Nation and Language in the First Republic]. In *Masarykova idea československé státnosti ve světle kritiky dějin* [Masaryk's Idea of the Czechoslovak Statehood in the Context of the Criticism of History], 69-77. Prague: Ústav T. G. Masaryka, 1993.

Sadílek, Petr, and Tamás Csémy. *Maďaři v České republice 1918-1992* [The Hungarians in the Czech Republic 1918-1992]. Prague: Svaz Maďarů žijících v českých zemích, 1993.

Sander, Fritz. *Die Gleichheit vor dem Gesetze und die nationalen Minderheiten.* Prague: [Lese- u. Redehalle d. dt. Studenten], 1937.

———. "Der Machnik-Erlaß und die Verfassungsurkunde." *Prager Juristische Zeitschrift* 16, November 1, 1936.

———. "Spionagegesetz und Rechtsstaat." *Prager Juristische Zeitschrift* 16, November 1, 1936.

———. "Verfassungsrechtliche Bemerkungen zum Staatsverteidigungsgesetze." *Juristen-Zeitung für das Gebiet der Tschechoslowakischen Republik* 17 (1936): 109-113.

———. "Weitere verfassungsrechtliche Bemerkungen zum Staatsverteidigungsgesetze." *Juristenzeitung für das Gebiet der Tschechoslowakischen Republik* 17 (1936): 137-140.

Schambeck, Herbert, ed. *Österreichs Parlamentarismus: Werden und System.* Berlin: Duncker & Humblot, 1986.

Schechtman, Joseph B. *Postwar Populations Transfers in Europe 1945-1955.* Philadelphia: University of Pennsylvania Press, 1962.

Schelle, Karel. "Příprava zákona o organizaci politické správy z roku 1927" [The Preparation of the Act on the Organisation of Political Administration of 1927]. In *Pocta prof. JUDr. Karlu Malému, DrSc., k 65. narozeninám* [Hommage to Prof. JUDr. Karel Malý, DrSc. on his 65th Birthday]. Edited by Ladislav Soukup. Prague: Karolinum Press, 1995.

———. *Vývoj správy v předválečném Československu* [Development of Administration in Pre-war Czechoslovakia]. Vol. 1. Brno: Masarykova univerzita, 1991.

Scheu, Harald Christan. *Standard ochrany národnostních menšin v rámci Rady Evropy* [The Standard of Protection of National Minorities within the Council of Europe]. Práce posluchačů Právnické fakulty UK 8. Prague: Univerzita Karlova, 1997.

———. "Vývoj ochrany menšin v Radě Evropy po roce 1989" [Minorities protection development in the Council of Europe after 1989]. In Petráš, Petrův, and Scheu, *Menšiny a právo v České republice,* 289-296.

———. "Začátky ochrany národnostních menšin v Radě Evropy" [Rudiments of national minorities protection within the Council of Europe]. In Petráš, Petrův, and Scheu, *Menšiny a právo v České republice,* 285-289.

Scheuermann, Martin. *Minderheitenschutz contra Konfliktverhütung?* Marburg: Verlag Herder-Institute, 2000.

Schneider, Peter. "Die völkerrechtliche Bedeutung und Beurteilung der Artikel IX und XIII des Potsdamer Protokolls." In *Das Recht auf die Heimat*, edited by Kurt Rabl. 70–89. Munich: Lerche, 1960.

Schranil, Rudolf. *Gutachten zur tschechoslowakischen Verwaltungsreform.* Prague: Kommissionsverlag der "Prager Juristischen Zeitschrift", 1927.

Scruton Roger. The Reform of Law in Eastern Europe. *Tilburg Foreign Law Review* 1, no. 1 (1991): 7–14.

Seibt, Ferdinand. *Německo a Češi* [Germany and the Czechs]. Prague: Academia, 1996.

Semotanová, Eva, Zlatica Zudová-Lešková, Tomáš Janata, Pavel Seemann, et al. *Frontiers, massacres and replacement of populations in cartographic representation: Case studies (15th–20th centuries).* Prague: Institute of History, 2015.

Serapionova, Jelena. "Národnostní práva podle ústavy Československé republiky roku 1920" [Nationality Rights under the Constitution of the Czechoslovak Republic of 1920]. In *Kroměřížský sněm 1848–1849 a tradice parlamentarismu ve střední Evropě: sborník příspěvků ze stejnojmenné mezinárodní konference konané v rámci oslav 150. výročí říšského sněmu v Kroměříži 14.–16. září 1998 = Der Reichstag von Kremsier 1848–1849 und die Tradition des Parlamentarismus in Mitteleuropa: Sammelband mit Beiträgen der gleichnamigen inaternationalen Konferenz veranstaltet im Rahmen der Feierlichkeiten anläßlich des 150. Jahrestages des Reichstages von Kremsier, 14.–16. September* [Kremsier Assembly 1848–1849 and Parliamentary Tradition in Central Europe], 77–83. Kroměříž: KATOS, 1998.

Seton-Watson, Robert W. *A History of the Czechs and Slovaks.* London: Hutchinson, 1943.

———. *The New Slovakia.* Prague: F. Borový, 1924.

Sharp, Samuel L. Nationalization of key industries in eastern Europe. Washington, DC: Foundation for Foreign Affairs, 1946

Shaw, Martin. *What is Genocide?* New York: John Wiley & Sons, 2013.

Sikora, Stanislav. "Slovakia and the attempt to reform socialism in Czechoslovakia, 1963-1969." In Teich, Kováč, and Brown, *Slovakia in History*, 299–315.

Siwek, Tadeusz, Stanisław Zahradnik, and Józef Szymeczek. *Polská národní menšina v Československu 1945–1954* [Polish National Minority in Czechoslovakia 1945–1954]. Prague: Ústav pro soudobé dějiny AV ČR, 2001.

Skalnik Leff, Carol. *National Conflict in Czechoslovakia: The Making and Remaking of a State, 1918–1987.* Princeton, NJ: Princeton University Press, 1988.

———. *National Conflict in Czechoslovakia: Nation versus State.* Boulder, CO: Westview Press, 1997.

Skilling, Harold Gordon. "The Czechoslovak Constitution of 1960 and the Transition to Communism." *The Journal of Politics* 24, no. 1 (1962): 142–166.

———. "The Czechoslovak Constitutional System: The Soviet impact." *Political Science Quarterly* 67, no.2 (1952): 198–224.

———. *Czechoslovakia 1918–88: Seventy Years from Independence.* Oxford: St. Antony's College, 1991.

———. *Czechoslovakia's Interrupted Revolution.* Princeton, NJ: Princeton University Press, 1976.

———. *The Governments of Communist East Europe.* New York: Crowell Comparative Government Series, 1966.

Slapnicka, Helmut. "Recht und Verfassung der Tschechoslowakei 1918–1938." In *Aktuelle Forschungsprobleme um die Erste Tschechoslowakische Republik.* Edited by Karl Bosl. Munich: Oldenbourg 1969.

Slezák, Lubomír. "Vývoj národnostní struktury obyvatelstva ČSSR za posledních třicet let" [Development of national structure of Czechoslovak population in the last thirty years]. In *Socialistickou cestou 1945-75.* 85–100. Prague: Academia, 1975.

Slovník veřejného práva československého [Dictionary of Czechoslovak Public Law]. Vol. 2. Brno: Polygrafia - Rudolf M. Rohrer, 1932.

Smetana, Vít. *In the shadow of Munich: British Policy towards Czechoslovakia from the Endorsement to the Renunciation of the Munich Agreement (1938-1942)*. Prague: Karolinum Press, 2008.

Sobota, Emil. "Čtvrt století Perkova zákona" [25 Years of Lex Perek]. *Národnostní obzor* 2 (1931-1932): 88-99.

———. "K pojmu národnostního práva" [On the Concept of Nationalities Law]. *Národnostní obzor* 4 (1933-1934): 222-224.

———. *Národnostní autonomie v Československu?* [Autonony of Nationalities in Czechoslovakia?]. Prague: Orbis, 1938.

———. *Národnostní právo československé* [Czechoslovak Nationalities Law]. Brno: Barvič a Novotný, 1927.

———. *Republika národní či národnostní?* [Republic of Nations or Nationalities?]. Prague: Čin, 1929.

———. *Výklad našeho jazykového práva* [The Interpretation of Our Language Law]. Prague: Ústřední dělnické knihk. a naklad. Ant. Svěcený, 1926.

———. *Zákonodárné návrhy Sudetoněmecké strany s hlediska demokracie* [Legislative Drafts by the Sudeten Democratic Party from the Point of View of Democracy]. Prague: Jan Laichter, 1938.

Sokolová, Gabriela et al. *Soudobé tendence vývoje národností v ČSSR* [Contemporary tendencies in development of nationalities in Czechoslovakia]. Prague: Academia, 1987.

Šolle, Zdeněk, ed. *Vzájemná neoficiální korespondence T.G.Masaryka s Eduardem Benešem z doby pařížských mírových jednání (říjen 1918 - prosinec 1919)* [The Unofficial Correspondence between T.G. Masaryk and Eduard Beneš during Paris Peace Negotiations (October 1918 - December 1919)]. Vol. 2. Prague: Archiv Akademie věd ČR, 1994.

Soukupová, Blanka. "Židovská menšina v českých zemích v současnosti (1989-2005)" [Jewish minority nowadays in the Czech Lands]. In Petráš, Petrův, and Scheu, *Menšiny a právo v České republice*, 210-228.

Spiliopoulou Åkermark, Athanasia. *Justifications of Minority Protection in International Law*. London: Kluwer Law International, 1996.

Šrajerová, Oľga. "Slovenská menšina v České republike" [Slovak minority in the Czech Republic]. In Petráš, Petrův, and Scheu, *Menšiny a právo v České republice*, 189-197.

Staško, Mojmír. "Právne východiská pozemkovej reformy v kontexte jej vzťahu k maďarskej menšine" [Legal foundations of land reform in context of its relation to Hungarian minority]. *Slezský sborník = Acta Silesiaca* 95, no. 1-2 (1997): 160-166.

Staněk, Tomáš. *Německá menšina v českých zemích, 1948-1989* [German minority in the Czech Lands 1945-1989]. Prague: Institut pro středoevropskou kulturu a politiku, 1993.

———. *Odsun Němců z Československa, 1945-1947* [Transfer of Germans from Czechoslovakia 1945-1947]. Prague: Academia; Naše vojsko, 1991.

———. *Poválečné „excesy" v českých zemích v roce 1945 a jejich vyšetřování* [Post-war 'riots' in Czech lands and their investigations]. Sešity Ústavu pro soudobé dějiny AV ČR 41. Prague: Ústav pro soudobé dějiny AV ČR, 2005.

———, and Adrian von Arburg. "Organizované divoké odsuny? Úloha ústředních orgánů při provádění 'evakuace' německého obyvatelstva (květen až září 1945)" [Organized wild expulsions? The Role of Central Authorities in organizing of 'evacuation' of German inhabitans (May-Sep 1945)]. *Soudobé dějiny* 13, no. 3-4 (2006): 321-376.

Stein, Eric. *Czecho-Slovakia: Ethnic Conflict, Constitutional Fissure, Negotiated Breakup*. Ann Arbor: The University of Michigan Press, 1997.

Stein, Felix. "Zur Frage der Sprachenrechte der Reichsdeutschen und Österreicher in der Tschechoslowakischen Republik." *Juristen-Zeitung für das Gebiet der Tschechoslowakischen Republik* 9 (1928): 158-160.

Steiner, Robert. "Der strafrechtliche Gehalt des Staatsverteidigungsgesetzes." *Juristenzeitung für das Gebiet der Tschechoslowakischen Republik* 17 (1936): 161-165, 169-173 and 18 (1937): 15-19, 36-48, 81-91.

Stone, Julius. *International guarantees of minority rights: Procedure of the Council of the League of nations in theory and practice*. London: Oxford University Press, 1932.

Stone, Norman, and Eduard Strouhal, eds. *Czechoslovakia: Crossroads and Crises 1918-1988*. New York: St. Martin's Press, 1989.

Szarka, László. "Národnostní statut a rozpory mezi Benešem a Hodžou 1935-1940" [Nationality Status and Discordances between Beneš and Hodža 1935-1940]. *Střední Evropa* 8, no. 26 (1992): 50-53.

Šebek, Jaroslav. "Masaryk, Beneš, Hrad a Němci 1935-38" [Masaryk, Beneš, the Castle and the Germans 1935-1938]. In *T.G.Masaryk a vztahy Čechů a Němců (1882-1937)* [T.G.Masaryk and the Relationship Between the Czechs and Germans (1882-1937)]. Prague: Masarykova společnost v Praze, 1997.

Šindelka, Jan. *Národnostní otázka a socialismus* [National question and socialism]. Prague: Svoboda, 1966.

———. *Národnostní politika v ČSSR.* [National politics in Czechoslovakia]. Prague: Orbis, 1975.

Sudetendeutsche Beschwerde an den Völkerbund über den Erlaß des Ministeriums für nationale Verteidigung der Tschechoslowakischen Republik betreffend die Vergabe staatlicher Lieferungen. Karlsbad: Karl H. Frank, 1936.

Suk, Jiří. "Czechoslovakia's return to democracy (1989-1992)." In Pánek and Tůma, *A History of the Czech lands*, 587-616.

Sulitka, Andrej. "Národnostní menšiny v České republice po roce 1989 a národnostněmenšinová politika" [National Minorities in the Czech Republic after 1989 and National Minorities Policy]. In Petráš, Petrův, and Scheu, *Menšiny a právo v České republice*, 148-185.

Šutaj, Štefan. *"Akcia Juh" – odsun Madarov zo Slovenska do Čiech v roku 1949* ["Action South" – the transfer of Hungarians from Slovakia to Bohemia in 1949]. Prague: Ústav pro soudobé dějiny AV ČR, 1993.

———. *Maďarská menšina na Slovensku v procesoch transformácie po roku 1989: Identita a politika: Teoretická a empirická analáza dát zo sociologicko-sociálnopsychologického a historického výskumu* [Hungarian Minority in Slovakia in Transformation Processes after 1989: Identity and Politics: Theoretical and Empirical Data Analysis of Social-Sociopsychological and Historical Research]. Prešov: Universum, 2006.

———. *Reslovakizácia : Zmena národnosti časti obyvateľstva Slovenska po II. svetovej vojne* [Reslovakization: Change of Nationality of Some Slovak Citizens after World War II]. Košice: Spoločenskovedný ústav SAV, 1991.

———. "Slovakia and Hungarian minority between 1945 and 1948." In *Key issues of Slovak and Hungarian History: A view of Slovak Historians*, 227-243. Prešov: Universum, 2011.

———, Marián Gajdoš, Anna Jurová, and Milan Olejník. "Ethnic minorities and their culture in Slovakia in the context of historical development of the twentieth century." In *Slovak contributions to the 19th International Congress of Historical Sciences*, edited by Dušan Kováč, 135-149. Bratislava: Veda, 2000.

Švorc, Peter. "Zápas o Podkarpatskú Rus v 20. rokoch 20. storočia na pôde Spoločnosti národov" [The Struggle for Sub-Carpathian Ruthenia in the 1920s in the League of Nations]. In *Evropa mezi Německem a Ruskem* [Europe between Germany and Russia], 267-284. Prague: Historický ústav AV ČR, 2000.

Táborský, Edward. *Communism in Czechoslovakia: 1948-1960*. Princeton, NJ: Princeton University Press, 1961.

———. *The Czechoslovak Cause: An Account of the Problems of International Law in Relation to Czechoslovakia*. London: H.F. & G. Witherby, 1944.

———. *Czechoslovak Democracy at Work*. London: Allen & Unwin, 1944.

———. "Politics in exile, 1939-1945." In Mamatey, and Luža, *A History of the Czechoslovak Republic 1918-1948*, 322-342.

Tapié, Victor Lucien. *The Rise and Fall of the Habsburg Monarchy*. London: Praeger Publisher, 1971.

Taylor, Alan John P. *The Habsburg Monarchy 1809-1918: A History of Austrian Empire and Austria-Hungary*. London: Hamish Hamilton, 1948.

Tebinka, Jacek. *Polityka brytyjska wobec problemu granicy polsko-radzieckiej 1939-1945* [British Policy towards the Problem of Polish-Soviet Frontiers]. Warsaw: Wydawn. Neriton; Instytut Historii PAN, 1998.

Teich, Mikuláš, ed. *Bohemia in History*. Cambridge: Cambridge University Press, 1998.

———, Dušan Kováč, and Martin D. Brown, eds. *Slovakia in History*. Cambridge: Cambridge University Press, 2011.

Teichová, Alice. *The Czechoslovak Economy 1918-1980*. London: Routledge, 1988.

———. "The Protectorate of Bohemia and Moravia (1939-1945): The economic dimension." In Teich, *Bohemia in History*, 267-305.

Temperley, Harold William Vazeille. *A History of the Peace Conference of Paris*. Vol. 5. London: Frowde, 1921.

Textor, Lucy Elizabeth. *Land Reform in Czechoslovakia*. London: Allen & Unwin, 1923.

Ther, Philipp. "A Century of Forced Migration. The Origins and Consequences of 'Ethnic Cleansing'." In *Redrawing Nations: Ethnic Cleansing in East-Central Europe, 1944-1948*, edited by Philipp Ther and Ana Siljak, 43-72. Lanham, MD: Rowman & Littlefield Publishers, 2011.

———. *The Dark Side of Nation-States: Ethnic Cleansing in Modern Europe*. Translated from the German by Charlotte Kreutzmüller. New York: Bergham, 2013.

Tomášek, Michal, ed. *Czech law between europeanization and globalization: New phenomena in law at the beginning of 21st century*. Prague: Karolinum Press, 2010.

Tůma, Oldřich. "The second consolidation of the communist regime and the descent into collapse (1972-1989)." In Pánek and Tůma, *A History of the Czech lands*, 569-580.

Two years of German oppression in Czechoslovakia. [London]: Czechoslovak Ministry of Foreign Affairs, Department of Information, 1941

Ulč, Otto. "Gypsies in Czechoslovakia: a Case of Unfinished Integration." *East European Politics and Societies* 2, no. 2 (1988): 306-332.

———. *The Judge in a Communist State: A View from Within*. Columbus: Ohio University Press 1972.

Urban, Otto. "Czech society 1848-1918." In Teich, *Bohemia in History*, 198-214.

Valenta, Jaroslav. "Legenda o 'rebelech, s nimiž se nevyjednává'" [The legend of 'rebels with whom talks are not held']. *Moderní dějiny* 2 (1994): 197-214.

———, Emil Voráček, and Josef Harna, eds. *Československo 1918-1938: osudy demokracie ve střední Evropě*. Sborník z mezinárodní vědecké konference. Vol. 2. Prague: Historický ústav AV ČR, 1999.

Varinský, Vladimír. "Nútené práce na Slovensku v rokoch 1945-1948" [Forced labour in Slovakia in 1945-1948]. *Soudobé dějiny* 1, no. 6 (1994): 724-736.

Vašečka, Imrich. "Migrácia Rómov z ČR a SR - príčiny a potreba intervencií" [The Migration of Romanies from the Czech Republic and Slovakia - the Causes and the Need for Intervention]. In *Menšiny a marginalizované skupiny v České republice* [The Minorities and Marginalised Groups in the Czech Republic], edited by Tomáš Sirovátka, 227-244. Brno: Masarykova univerzita, Fakulta sociálních studií, Georgetown, 2002.

Veiter, Theodor. *Nationalitätenkonflikt und Volksgruppenrecht im ausgehenden 20. Jahrhundert*. Munich: Bayerische Landeszentrale für Politische Bildungsarbeit, 1984.

Vojáček, Ladislav. "K právní úpravě postavení politických stran v I. ČSR" [On the Legal Regulation of the Status of Political Parties in the First CSR]. In *Aktuální otázky českého a československého konstitucionalismu: Sborník příspěvků z vědecké konference věnované prof. JUDr. Bohumilu Baxovi* [The Topical Questions of the Czech and Czechoslovak Constitutionalism], 287-295. Brno: Masarykova univerzita, 1993.

Vorel, Jaroslav. *Zákon o obraně státu* [The Defence of the State Act]. Prague: Čin, 1936.

Vyšný, Paul. *The Runciman Mission to Czechoslovakia: Prelude to Munich*. Basingstoke: Palgrave Macmillan, 2003

Wandruszka, Adam. *The House of Habsburg: Six hundred years of a European dynasty*. Westport, CT: Greenwood Press, 1975.

————, and Peter Urbanitsch, eds. *Die Habsburgermonarchie 1848-1918: Verwaltung und Rechtswesen.* 2nd ed. Vol. 2. Vienna: Verlag der Österreichischen Akademie der Wissenschaften, 2003.

Wandycz, Piotr Stefan. *Czechoslovak-Polish Confederation and the Great Powers 1940-1943.* Bloomington: Indiana University, 1958.

Weinfurter, Arnošt. "Slovo k 'jazykové otázce' v České advokátní komoře" [A Note on the 'Language Issue' in the Czech Bar Association]. *Právník* 70 (1931): 323-326.

Weyr, František. *Československé právo správní* [Czechoslovak Administrative Law]. Brno: Nákladem Čes. akadem. spolku Právník, 1922.

————. *Soustava československého práva státního* [The System of the Czechoslovak State Law]. 2nd ed. Prague: Fr. Borový, 1924.

Wheeler-Bennett, John W. *Munich: Prologue to tragedy.* 2nd ed. New York: Duell, Sloan & Pearce, 1963.

Widmer, Paul. "Europäische Bemühungen zur Lösung von Minderheitenfragen." *Europa Archiv* 48, no. 9 (1993): 265-276.

Wiewóra, Boleslaw. *The Polish German Frontier in the light of International law.* Poznań: Instytut Zachodni, 1964.

Winters, Stanley, Robert B. Pynsent, and Harry Hanak, eds. *T. G. Masaryk (1850-1937).* 3 vols. London: St. Martin's Press, 1989-1990.

Wiskemann, Elizabeth. *Czechs and Germans: A Study of the Struggle in the Historic Provinces of Bohemia and Moravia.* London: Oxford University Press, 1938.

————. *Germany's Eastern Neighbours: Problems relating to the Oder-Neisse line and the Czech frontier regions.* London: Oxford University Press, 1956.

Wolchik, Sharon L. *Czechoslovakia in transition: politics, economics, and society.* London: Pinter, 1991.

————. "The politics of transition and the break-up of Czechoslovakia." In Musil, *The end of Czechoslovakia,* 225-244.

Yapou, Eliezer. "Autonomie, která se neuskutečnila: plány na autonomii Sudet z roku 1938" [Autonomy That Didn't Come True: Plans for the Autonomy of Sudeten in 1938]. *Střední Evropa* 7, no. 20 (1991): 42-59.

Yegar, Moshe. *Československo, sionismus, Izrael* [Czechoslovakia, Zionism, Israel]. Prague: Victoria Publishing, 1997.

Young, Robert J. *France and the origins of the Second World War.* London: Macmillan, 1996.

Žáček, Václav. *Češi a Poláci v minulosti* [The Czechs and the Poles in the Past]. Vol. 2. Prague: Academia, 1967.

Zahradnik, Stanisław. "Nástin historického vývoje" [An Outline of Historical Development]. In *Polská národní menšina na Těšínsku v České republice (1920-1995)* [The Polish National Minority in the Cieszyn Region in the Czech Republic (1920-1995)], edited by Karol D. Kadłubiec, 32-34. Ostrava: Filozofická fakulta Ostravské univerzity, 1997.

————. "Polský kulturně osvětový svaz – Polski Związek Kulturalno-Oświatowy 1947-1989" [Polish Cultural and Educational Union 1947-1989]. *Slezský sborník = Acta Silesiaca* 96, no. 1 (1998): 44-52.

Žák, Václav. "The velvet divorce, institutional foundations." In Musil, *The end of Czechoslovakia,* 245-267.

Zayas, Alfred M. de: *Nemesis in Potsdam: The Anglo-Americans and the Expulsion of the Germans: Background, Execution, Consequences.* London: Routledge & Kegan Paul, 1977.

Zelenka, Josef. "Terror" [The Terror]. Part 2. *Právník* 60, no. 11 (1921): 334-347.

Zeman, Zbyněk A.B. *The Break-Up of the Habsburg Empire 1914-1918. A Study in National and Social Revolution.* New York: Octagon Books, 1977.

————. *The Making and Breaking of Communist Europe.* Oxford: Blackwell, 1991.

————. *Prague Spring: A Report on Czechoslovakia 1968.* London: Penguin Books, 1969.

Zimmerman, Volker. "Pachatelé a přihlížející: Pronásledování židů v Sudetské župě" [Culprits and watchers: Persecutions of Jews in the Sudetenland]. In *Terezínské studie a dokumenty,* edited by Miroslav Kárný and Eva Lorencová, 129-148. Prague: Academia, 1999.

Zinner, Paul E. *Communist Strategy and Tactics in Czechoslovakia, 1918-1948.* New York: Praeger, 1963.